# BORDER WARS

# OF

## TEXAS

Ross' Fight with Comanche Chief Big Foot

# Border Wars of Texas

Being an Authentic and Popular Account, in Chronological Order, of the Long and Bitter Conflict waged Between Savage Indian Tribes and the Pioneer Settlers of Texas.

## Wresting of a Fair Land From Savage Rule
## A Red Record of Fierce Strife

Profusely Illustrated with Spirited Battle Scenes by Special Artists. Rare Portraits of Famous Rangers, Indian Fighters and Pioneers, Maps, Etc.

By

## JAMES T. DeSHIELDS
*Member Texas Historical Association*

Author of "Frontier Sketches," "Texas Border Tales," "Cynthia Ann Parker, the Story of Her Capture," "Life of Jack Hays," "Stephen Fuller Austin," "Sam Houston and Texas," "Siege of the Alamo," Etc.

MATT BRADLEY
*Revising Editor*

STATE HOUSE PRESS
Austin, Texas
1993

originally published in 1912

*Library of Congress Cataloging-in-Publication Data*

DeShields, James T., 1861-1948.
Border wars of Texas / by James T. DeShields
p. cm.
Includes index
ISBN 0-938349-98-8 (cloth : acid free paper)
ISBN 0-938349-99-6 (limited : acid free paper)
1. Texas—History—To 1846. 2. Indians of North
America—Texas—Wars. 3. Frontier and pioneer
life—Texas. I. Title.

F389.D47 1993
976.4—dc20                        93-15163

Printed in the United States of America

*dustjacket and cover design by David Timmons*

STATE HOUSE PRESS
P.O. Box 15247
Austin, Texas 78761

DEDICATED

to

The Sons and Daughters of Those Noble Pioneer
Fathers and Mothers

Who, boldly entering the savage-infested wilderness, battled so
bravely for supremacy; and which finally obtaining, made possible all the glorious blessings that have followed. Dangers and
hardships they endured, the inestimable heritage bequeathed,
we now enjoy. All honor to the pioneers of Texas, than whom
there were none more courageous and indomitable.

THE AUTHOR

# Notes to the New Edition

Of whatever value or importance this history may be to present or future times, the events which it relates are, and always will be, the beginning of Texas history. The Indians will always appear in the opening chapters. . . .                    *James T. DeShields*

In his original foreword to *Border Wars of Texas*, James T. DeShields disclosed that the "borders" about which he was writing were the disputed territories between the encroaching Anglo settlements and the frontier domains which the Indians believed were theirs. This volume covers the early years of the battles between the advancing Anglo-American pioneers and the retreating Indians from 1819 to the close of the Republic era in 1846—DeShields had in mind but never completed a second volume to cover the wars in the latter half of the nineteenth century. By the time he published *Border Wars of Texas* in 1912, DeShields had already gained a literary reputation as a Texas frontier historian with many published articles and two published works: *Frontier Sketches* (1883) and *Cynthia Ann Parker* (1886). He was also well known as an art collector and patron of Texas artists who shared his view of Texas history—Louis Eyth, Henry Arthur McArdle and Robert Onderdonk all of whom, like DeShields, portrayed Texas history as inevitably victorious.

Born in Louisiana in 1861, DeShields moved with his family to Texas at the end of the Civil War and grew up in Bell County where many frontier conditions still prevailed. He attended Salado College and Baylor University, and early began his extensive collection of manuscripts, books and paintings of Texas history. His numerous acquaintances and interviews with living frontiersmen gave him access to primary source material which served him well in his writings. When he became familiar with the work of Galveston portraitist Louis Eyth (1838-ca. 1889), DeShields commissioned him to illustrate several of his books. Although the locations of many of Eyth's paintings are unknown—they may have been destroyed in a 1918 fire in DeShields' home—his major painting "Battle at Plum Creek" is preserved within the pages of *Border Wars of Texas*.

In his introduction to *Painting Texas History to 1900*, Sam DeShong Ratcliffe wrote that DeShields' writings "had the feel and texture of campfire tales that exalted the exploits of what had been and, to a certain extent, still was a warlike culture." Dorman H. Winfrey of the Texas State Library wrote in 1976, "DeShields' *Border Wars of Texas* is time-tested; it remains a major source of Indian and pioneer history. . . . the book has proved to be of undiminished value and a new generation will now find it of interest."

When DeShields died at age eighty-seven in 1948, the Dallas *Morning News* wrote of the "Border Historian":

> Texas owes much to James Thomas DeShields. . . .
> Much of the state's historical and legendary lore might have escaped public notice if he had not gathered it and set it down in print. His books and articles have given thousands of Texans a better understanding and appreciation of their state's colorful and heroic past. Today they are valuable sources for a new generation of writers. . . . [whose] work has been made easier by pioneer writers like James DeShields.

Although this new edition of *Border Wars of Texas* has been retypeset for clarity and readability, only the obviously typographical errors in the original edition have been corrected.

ERIK MASON, EDITOR
STATE HOUSE PRESS

James T. DeShields, Author

Matt Bradley, Editor

# Foreword

The present volume is the progressed efforts of the author's long cherished design to prepare a popular and reliable narrative of border warfare and Texas frontier history, no satisfactory account in connected form having ever before appeared; indeed it is the first serious attempt in that direction, and the author's purpose will have been accomplished if it should prove of value and be handed down to posterity with increasing interest to each generation, which is but natural as we recede further and further from that dark era of fearful strife so long waged between the red men and their white conquerors.

Let the reader remember that this work has been put forth and executed through great labor and painstaking research for data, and a judicious sifting of the wheat from the chaff, that the story might conform to truth, and thus possess a positive value, a mine of historical wealth which will prove the most wholesome of mental pabulum; though the story be told with lack of facileness; with more regard for exactness of statement than ornateness of style or grandiloquence.

The complete story in all its thrilling details will never be told, from the lack of reliable data and because of the vastness of such an undertaking—as so fittingly expressed by the versatile J.H. Beadle, as he crossed Red River into Texas on his tour of the "Western Wilds":

"Here we enter the land of border romance. Hence to the Rio Grande southwest, and to the Rocky Ridge west and northwest, every grove, canyon and valley has been the scene of some romantic and daring incident; but should I attempt to repeat all that are told here, the world itself, to borrow a simile from Scripture, would not contain the books that should be written."

Very properly the narrative opens with the arrival of the

first American settlers within the game preserves of the native and ferocious Caranchua tribe—the present volume chronicling the bitter strife down through the colonial and revolutionary periods, and closing with the last days of the Texas republic; a second volume covering the era of statehood and ending with the last conflict between red and white men on Texas soil, in comparatively recent years.

Along this line our State's history has been sadly deficient, and tradition only has preserved much of deep interest for the pen of the faithful historian. The present work, however, does not aspire to the dignity of a State's history, but rather as an urn in which are gathered the fragments, sifted, and shorn of fiction; and which may serve the conscientious and capable historian to weave a more complete chronicle of a matchless and incomparable history.

For more than a third of a century the writer has utilized his spare moments in the gathering of materials for this work; narratives of Indian hostilities to the early settlers and subsequently against the frontier settlers; verifying reports of engagements by interviews with many of the actors and eye witnesses of the actions and events related, and by untiring and voluminous correspondence with others and with those best informed on the early history of settlements and affairs of the frontier; of course carefully consulting all published histories, and especially files of our early newspapers—the most profitable source of all—no efforts having been spared in any direction to attain a completeness of facts, and hence I may confidently say that no other history has been written that has been so carefully collated from original sources of information upon the subject to which it relates, and I might, perhaps, also say that none will ever be. The early settlers are not only passing away, but have passed. The recollections of the few who remain can add but little, either of narrative or correction, to the defective record as a whole, of Indian hostilities.

Historians have often regretted that the reader can be but imperfectly introduced to the private and domestic life of the people. The dignity of councils, the parade of camps and armies, prevent the historian from attempting the "short and simple annals of the poor." The history of Indian hostilities, in some measure incidentally supplies this defect, affording a glimpse of the people as they were, vivid and faithful as a photograph. I can say that the impartial truth of history has been strictly adhered to in the pages now before the reader.

Of whatever value or importance this history may be to present or future times, the events which it relates are, and always will be, the beginning of Texas history. The Indians will always appear in the opening chapters, and their wild, uncouth figures will be defined on the horizon to which attention will be first directed, while their opposers and final conquerors, the equally courageous and dauntless pioneers and border troopers will stride boldly forth in the great pageant and mingle freely in every page of the fiery and blood-reeking border history.

The scenes here recounted, the deeds of prowess, acts of heroism, tales of adventure, cruel sufferings and harrowing events portrayed, will never again be enacted; there are no more frontiers to be defended, the day and usefulness of the pioneer is past; the Indian, as a foe, is forever gone; there will never be more border wars.

JAMES T. DeSHIELDS
San Marcos, Texas, October, 1912

# Editor's Note

In presenting this volume of Texas Border History to the public, the editor does so with positive faith and confidence in the author's ability, courage and strict adherence to the truth. As a Texas historian his works are accepted as authority by the best educators of the land; while his unflinching regard for authenticated facts, in the face of popular but fictitious traditions, is unquestioned. His selection, over many competitors, by the Alamo Heroes' Monument Association, to write the "Story of the Siege of the Alamo", shows the undoubted merit of his writings on notable Texas events, and gives added weight to this work.

While the labor of the editor has been stupendous and long continued, he feels that the results attained more than compensates the arduous toil.

He sends forth this volume with much confidence that it will fill a long felt want in Texas history.

MATT BRADLEY, Tioga, Texas
November, 1912

# CONTENTS

# ILLUSTRATIONS

# BORDER WARS OF TEXAS

T he history of that period in which the Spaniards occupied Texas—1690 to the Mexican revolution in 1820—and not inappropriately called "The Mission Era," has much to do with the native and migrated tribes who had occupied the country from earliest times. But no systematic account of the Indian troubles of this period has ever been attempted; and indeed the materials for such a narrative are yet to be searched out and translated from the documents and archives of that time. Enough, however, is known to warrant the assertion that the bold Apaches and Comanches in their perennial raids and depredations were the dread and scourge of the western frontier under both Spanish and Mexican rule.

Being in fact the rightful owners of the country, to which a native tribe gave name,* by priority of occupation at least, these brave and warlike tribes held all intruders as vassals to their powerful confederacy. The following statement by historian

---

* From an old tradition we learn, and are inclined to believe, that "Texas" is an Indian name, derived from the word "Tehas," and signified, paradise; and applied to the country in the gorgeous beauty of its virgin existence, was certainly an appropriate name.

Kennedy will serve to illustrate the conditions in that section
during the time referred to:

"In the destruction of the Missions, the Comanches were
the principal agents. Encouraged by the passive submission of
the Mexicans of mixed blood, they carried their insolence so far
as to ride into Bexar, and alight in the public square, leaving
their horses to be caught and pastured by the obsequious
soldiers of the garrison, on pain of chastisement. To raise a
contribution, they would enter the town with a drove of Mexican horses, stolen by themselves, and under pretense of having
rescued the caballado from hostile Indians, would exact a reward for their honesty! They openly carried off herds of cattle
and horses from the settlements east of the Rio Grande, sparing
the lives of the herdsmen, not from motives of humanity, but
because they deemed it impolitic to kill those who were so
useful in raising horses and mules for the benefit of the Comanches."

Thus we see the lordly Comanches were more than a match
for the Spaniards and Mexicans, and after more than a century
of untiring effort to conciliate and christianize these Indians,
and to people the territory of Texas, Mexico* was willing to give

* "The leading object of the Mexican Government in allowing the colonization of Texas," says Newell, "was undoubtedly the protection of her
frontiers from the hostile invasion of the Indians. The Comanches and
other tribes had waged a constant and ruinous warfare against the Spanish
settlements at Bexar and Goliad, on the western limits of Texas and
extended their ravages also beyond the Rio Grande. Mexico, even under
the government of old Spain, had been unable to subdue or restrain them,
and she would have had to abandon Texas altogether, if not other parts
of her territory, had she not found a people, willing, for the sake of a small
portion of her soil, to go in and subdue them." (History of the Texas
revolution, pages 14-15)—"and yet," adds Yoakum, "the colonists have
been charged with ingratitude. Wherein? They were invited to a desert.
They came, and found it inhabited by Indians and those of such audacity,
that even in San Antonio, where the Mexicans mostly lived, they compelled the citizens and soldiers in the place to hold their horses while they
paraded about the town; these savages the colonists had to subdue at their
own expense and on their own account. Mexico gave them nothing—the
lands only were valuable because they made them so. They were determined to keep it free, not only from Indian cruelty, but Mexican tyranny."
(Texas, Vol. 1, Pages 245-246.)

up in despair. But a new era dawned in the history of Texas, henceforward the red men must deal with a more formidable intruder—that invincible vanguard of western civilization—the American pioneer.

## FIRST FIGHT.*

The first conflict between Anglo-Americans and Texas Indians occurred on Galveston Island late in the fall of 1819, antedating more than a year the arrival of Moses Austin at San Antonio de Bexar, seeking permission to establish a colony in the province of Texas.

At that time the patriotic but unfortunate General James Long, venturing a second expedition into Texas, was fortified with fifty-odd of his followers at Bolivar Point, opposite the east end of Galveston Island. A French sloop, freighted with Mexican supplies, wines, etc., and bound for Cassano, stranded near the present city of Galveston. The Caranchua Indians, to the number of 200 warriors, were encamped in the immediate vicinity, and at once attacked and butchered all on board the luckless craft, destroying the cargo, and indulging in a drunken carousal and war dance.

Long determined to avenge this outrage, and after nightfall, with thirty men, crossed over in small boats to the island; and while the orgies were at their height, made a vigorous attack upon the unsuspecting and jubilant savages. Quickly rallying from their surprise and confusion, the Indians secured their weapons, and yelling furiously, met their assailants with

---

* Prior to this engagement, in 1818, while Galveston Island was occupied by Jean LaFitte, the celebrated pirate chief, some of his men kidnapped a young Caranchua squaw. Through revenge, the Indians crossed over to the island and discovering a party of the pirates out hunting, ambushed and killed four of them; whereupon LaFitte, with 200 men and two small pieces of artillery attacked some 300 of the tribe then encamped at a place since locally known as the "Three Trees," and after a desperate fight, in which some thirty warriors were slain and a much larger number wounded, forced them to disperse to the mainland. None of LaFitte's men were killed, but a number were badly wounded with arrows.

determined courage. Superior in numbers, they were a full match for the whites. A desperate hand to hand fight of doubtful issue, now ensued; but Long effected a timely retreat to his boats, leaving thirty-two Indians killed, and many wounded; three of his own men were killed and two (George Early and another) badly, besides several slightly, wounded. Two Indian boys were taken prisoners and retained by the whites, one being accidently killed some time afterwards.

In 1821, after LaFitte was forced to abandon his "little kingdom" by the United States naval authorities, a Dr. Parnell, with a party of about twenty men, visited the island to search for supposed buried treasures. Encountering about 100 Caranchuas at their favorite camp, the "Three Trees," the Americans again attacked and defeated the Indians, who left the island, forever, it is said, carrying off several dead and wounded, and leaving one of their children prisoner. The only casualty to the whites was the slight wounding of Dr. Parnell— an arrow pinning his cap to the skin of his head, which he failed to notice till after the fight.

"It was these attacks," suggests historian Yoakum, "that made the Caranchuas so hostile to Austin's colonists in after years."

## AUSTIN'S INFANT COLONY.

A new era had dawned in the history of Texas. The fair land was not destined to remain an unsettled and savage infested land—civilization was rapidly advancing to the Southwest, the American pioneer was coming as the courier and advance guard. Austin and his first colonists had boldly entered the wilderness, and were determined to maintain a foothold, though they did so under difficulties, and suffering great privations. The first settlers arrived on the Brazos River during the last days of December, 1821, and the dawn of New Year's day, 1822, marks the date of the first permanent Anglo-American settlement in Texas.

Austin's colony soon attracted the attention of home-seek-

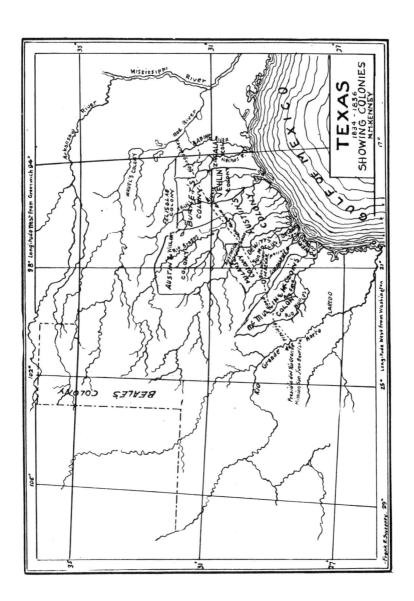

TEXAS
1834 - 1836
SHOWING COLONIES
M.H.KENNEY

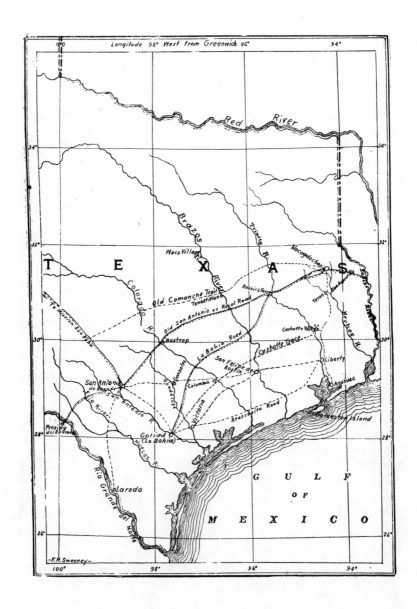

ers throughout the whole Southwest, and other settlers continued to arrive overland and by water. In June, 1822, the schooner, "Only Son," with upward of ninety emigrants (among them Horatio Chrisman, who became the noted surveyor and Indian fighter of Austin's Colony) and supplies for the new colony, anchored in Matagorda Bay. A few days later another vessel, from New Orleans, entered the mouth of the Colorado. Among the passengers aboard the vessel, from New Orleans, was Samuel M. Williams, afterwards the famous secretary of Austin's Colony. The passengers from both vessels were landed on the west bank of the Colorado, at a point three miles above its mouth, where they went into camp and erected temporary storage for their goods. Before leaving for the interior, a treaty of friendship was formed with the Indians, and four young men were left to guard their property, while six of their number, including Helm and Clare, were dispatched to La Bahia for means of transportation. On returning with Mexican carts, they found the camp had been attacked, guards murdered, and the supplies all destroyed or carried away by the faithless and fiendish savages. This was a most serious loss to the emigrants, and caused them much suffering for lack of provisions, and other necessities.

The sad news reaching the settlement, a party of colonists were soon collected, armed, and in pursuit. Locating the camp of the enemy, the settlers made a surprise attack, recovering a remnant of their supplies, and routing the Indians with some loss.

Thus hostilities commenced, and, with brief intervals, was carried on for years, resulting in the loss of many valuable lives and the final extermination of this once powerful and formidable coast tribe. With savage stealth, the Indians often lay in ambush till the men would leave their cabins, when, without warning, they would rush upon the unprotected and helpless women and children, who pleaded for mercy in vain. On one occasion, only one child out of a large family, was found alive, but it was mortally wounded by an ugly arrow.* The whites

* Mrs. Helm's "Scrap of Early Texas History," Page 36.

may not have been so wantonly cruel and bloodthirsty; they were equally stubborn and determined. The conflict was inevitable, irresistible—one of expulsion and extermination. Scores of tragedies were enacted between the emigrants in Austin's Colony and the Aborigines during the first years of its feeble existence—the particulars of which, alas! were never recorded. Such reliable notes as we have been able to gather, mostly from the "Kuykendall Reminiscences," will be given in the order of their occurrence.

## SKULL CREEK ENCOUNTERS.

During the spring of 1823 a severe drought prevailed, and but a scant crop of corn was made that season in the colony. In the summer three young men were ascending the Colorado River with a canoe load of corn, which they had raised on the cane lands below the settlements.* Near the mouth of Skull Creek, a few miles from the present town of Columbus, in Colorado county, they were waylaid and fired upon by the Indians, Loy and Alley being killed. John C. Clark, however, with seven severe wounds, swam to the opposite shore, and, by secreting himself in a dense thicket, escaped, and recovered—to live many years and accumulate immense wealth. He died in 1861.

Later, the same day, and near the same place, Robert Brotherton, a young man recently from St. Louis county, Missouri, unexpectedly rode among the same party of Indians, thinking they were friendly Tonkawas. Losing his gun in the struggle to free himself, he put spurs to his horse and escaped with a painful arrow wound in the back.

Reaching the settlement, Brotherton gave the alarm. "When this news was received," says Kuykendall, "about a dozen of the settlers led by my uncle, Robert Kuykendall, went

---

* The manner in which the land was prepared was simple. The cane was burned off and holes made in the ground with handspikes, where the corn was planted. The land being very rich, a good yield was obtained in this manner. "Dewees Letter from Texas," Page 39.

in pursuit of the Indians. The Tonkawas were at that time camped near his house, and the settlers thought it prudent to take their chief (Carita) with them to insure the good behavior of his people during the absence of the party, whose families would be unprotected until their return.

"Upon arriving near the mouth of Skull Creek, the party halted in order to spy out the Indians, and some time after dark, they heard them in a thicket pounding briar root. Locating the enemy, the settlers dismounted, secured their horses, and awaited the coming day." By the morning twilight they were enabled to find a small path which led into the thicket and to the camp of the Indians, "and as silently as possible," says one of the party, "we crawled into a thicket about ten steps behind the camp. Placing ourselves about four or five steps apart, in a sort of semi-circle, and completely cutting off their retreat from the swamps." As the first Indian arose, the signal for action was given. The surprise was complete. The settlers rushed on the camp and delivered a deadly fire. Nine or ten warriors were killed on the spot; ten more were slain in their wild attempt to retreat; two escaped badly wounded. The encampment was destroyed, and the settlers returned home without further incident. This was a severe blow to the Caranchuas, and it caused them to leave the settlement for a time and to use more stealth and precaution in their depredations.

During the fall and winter of 1823-24 Austin's colony was in a very feeble condition. The empresario Austin, recounting the trials and privations of his colonists at this early period, says, "They were totally destitute of bread and salt; coffee, sugar, etc., were remembered and hoped for at some future day. There was no other dependence for subsistence but the wild game, such as buffalo, bear, deer, turkeys and wild horses, (mustangs). The Indians rendered it quite dangerous ranging the country for buffalo; bear were very poor and scarce, owing to failure in mast, and poor venison, it is well known, is the least nutritious of all the meat kind. The mustang horses, however, were fat and very abundant, and it is estimated that at least one hundred of these were eaten the two first years.

"The Caranchua Indians were very hostile on the coast; the Wacos and Tehuacanies were equally so in the interior, and committed constant depredations. Parties of Tonkawas, Lipans, Beedies and others were intermingled with the settlers; they were beggarly and insolent, and were only restrained the first two years by presents, forbearance and policy; there was not force enough to awe them. One imprudent step with these Indians would have destroyed the settlement, and the settlers deserve as much for their forbearance during the years 1822 and 1823, as for their fortitude.

"In 1824, the strength of the settlement justified a change of policy, and a party of Tonkawas were tried and whipped in the presence of their chiefs for horse stealing."

Thus the empresario Austin himself has given us a brief, but vivid picture of what must have been the difficulties, privations and dangers which had to be borne and overcome during the first years of his colony. Austin himself was absent from his colony for several months, being very unexpectedly called to the city of Mexico, to secure ratification of his colonization contract by the new, revolutionary formed, government of Iturbide. The Indians were more or less troublesome and threatening; provisions were scarce, "store bought," clothing was an almost unknown luxury, and many privations, as well as real sufferings, were experienced. To give the reader a better knowledge of the deplorable conditions and gloomy prospects existing in the infant colony at that period, we extract briefly from letters and narratives of some of the early settlers:

Colorado River, Coahuila, and Texas
December 1, 1823

Dear Friend: Since I last wrote, our sufferings have been very great for want of provisions. On account of dry weather our crops were very poor, and are now entirely spent. The game has left this section of the country, and we are now very much pressed for food. There have been a great many new settlers come on this fall, and those who have not been accustomed to hunting in the woods for support, are obliged to suffer. Were it not for a few boys who have no families, their wives and children would suffer much more than they now do; in fact, I fear some of them would starve. Those of us who have no families of our own reside with some of the families of the settlement. We remain here, notwithstanding the scarcity of provisions, to assist in protecting the settlement. We are obliged to go out in the morning, a party of us, to hunt food, leaving a part of the men at home to guard the settlement from Indians, who are very hostile to us. Indeed, we dare not go out and hunt except in companies, as we are obliged to keep on a lookout, lest the savages fall upon us; and one cannot hunt and watch too. Game is now so scarce that we often hunt all day for a deer or a turkey, and return at night empty handed. It would make your heart sick to see the poor little half naked children, who have nothing to eat during the day, watch for the return of the hunters at night. As soon as they catch the first glimpse of us they eagerly run to meet us, and learn if we have been successful in our hunt. If the hunters return with a deer or turkey, the children are almost wild with delight; while on the other hand, they suddenly stop in their course, their countenances fall, the deep bitter tears well up in their eyes and roll down their pale cheeks.

'Tis truly heart-rending to see us return home after a hard days hunt without any game, knowing, as we do, that the women and children are entirely without food, and can have nothing until we find it in our hunt. No one can know our sufferings, or even imagine our feelings, unless they have been in similar situations. And to render our situation the more dreadful, our sufferings the more acute, we are often obliged to get the women of the different settlements together, and make a kind of fort to protect them from the merciless savages. It is surprising to see how bravely the delicate females bear up under their sufferings, without a murmur or complaint. 'Tis only by their looks they show their feelings. When we seem the least discouraged, they cheer us with kind words and looks, and strive to appear cheerful and happy. They do more when we are worried out with toil and fatigue—they take our guns in their hands and assist us in standing guard.

"Our prospects for the winter look very gloomy. If the Indians attack us, I scarcely know what we shall do; but I hope for the best, and trust that we shall be provided for in some way. Were it not for the Tonkawa Indians, a small tribe who are friendly to us and supply us with dressed deerskins, we should be almost entirely destitute of clothing. Once in a great while we are able to obtain a small piece of unbleached domestic, or a bit of calico, at the exorbitant price of seventy-five cents a yard, from some one passing through the country; but this is very seldom. The common dress of men and children is made of buckskin, and even the women are often forced to wear the same.

Your affectionate friend,<br>W.B. Dewees."

Captain Jesse Burnam in his "Reminiscences," after telling of his enfeebled condition from sickness, and that "we got out of bread" and had no food for two days, says:

"At last I heard one of my children say, 'I am so hungry.' I was too feeble to hunt, but I got up and began to fix my gun slowly. I didn't feel as though I could walk, but I started on my first hunt. I had not gone far when I saw two deer, a fawn and its mother. I shot the fawn first, knowing the doe would not run far, then I shot and killed her. 'O ho,' I said, 'two deer in one day, and my first hunt!' I took the fawn to camp to my hungry children and took William, my oldest boy, and a horse after the doe. My wife had dressed a skin and made William a shirt, but it lacked one sleeve, so she dressed the fawn skin that day and made the other sleeve.

"We were still out of bread, and it had been nine months since we had seen any. A man from lower down the country came up and told me he had corn that he had planted with a stick—there were no plows or hoes in the colony. I gave him a horse for twenty bushels and went twenty-six miles after it with two horses, and brought eight bushels back. I walked and led my horse. I had prepared a mortar* before I left home to beat it in, and a sieve made of deer skin stretched over a hoop and with holes punched in it. We would have to be very saving, of course, and were allowed only one piece of bread around.

"About this time my oldest daughter's dress wore out before we could get any cotton to spin, and she wore a dress of dressed buckskin. I had pants and a hunting shirt made of deerskin. My wife colored the skin brown and fringed the hunting shirt, and it was considered the nicest suit in the colony."

Horatio Chrisman, the famous surveyor and early Indian fighter of Austin's colony, says: "All these emigrants suffered for want of provisions. We had about eight acres of corn which if not worked immediately, was certain to be lost. I could not stop the plow to hunt. I took no sustenance save a few stinted drinks of buttermilk until after I finished plowing over the eight acres. My plow animal was an old, slow, blind mule." A few weeks afterward, Mr. Chrisman learned that James Whitesides—whose residence was on the east side of the Brazos—had gone to the United States on business, and that his family, consisting of his wife and two little boys, had little or nothing to eat but lettuce. Sending out his excellent hunter, Martin Varner, he secured a very large buck, which he threw across his horse and carried to Mrs. Whitesides, a distance of twenty miles. "Aunt Betsey," says Chrisman, "never forgot this favor."

The lot of these first pioneers was indeed a hard and rugged one, but in common, and they were ever ready to assist and protect each other at their own discomfort, and often at the risk of their lives.

* Many of the first emigrants to Austin's Colony had not even a hand mill, and for a long time their only means of manufacturing meal was by pounding the corn with a wooden pestle in a mortar made in a log or stump. The first saw and grist mill propelled by water, was erected on Mill Creek, by the Cummings family. It went into operation in the year 1826. One or two horse mills had been erected a short time before.—Kuykendall's Reminiscences.

During the summer Capt. Chrisman was without a shirt, and wore a buckskin hunting shirt instead. Toward autumn he learned that Col. Jared Groce had some goods. He therefore visited the colonel to replenish his wardrobe. He bought a few yards of course brown "Holland," from which he had a Mrs. Byrd to make him two shirts—"the best I ever wore, as they lasted three years." But we are digressing.

## HORSE THIEVES.

Another sort of annoyance to the struggling colonists, and one that for a while threatened to be more serious than Indian troubles, was a clan of Mexican and American robbers and horse thieves that infested the colony about this time—some of them erstwhile denizens of the "Neutral Grounds," where they held undisputed sway and found a safe retreat. Others, "men who had fled from justice in the United States, and come to the colony with the hope of committing their depredations with greater impunity."—Yoakum's Texas, Vol. l, page 228.

"During the same summer," (1823), says Kuykendall in his Reminiscences, "A Frenchman and two Mexicans, all residents of Louisiana, returning from the Rio Grande with a small cavalcade, passed through our neighborhood and crossed the Brazos at the La Bahia road. As they passed by the residence of Martin Varner, (near the present town of Independence), they stole his most valuable horse. Our Alcalde, Joseph H. Bell, ordered me to raise a few men and pursue the thieves. The men who went with me were Martin Varner, Samuel Kennedy, James Nelson, Oliver Jones and George Robinson. About midnight of the day we started, we arrived at the creek much swollen by a recent rain. Dark as it was, we swam this stream, and about an hour before day, on the waters of the Trinity, we came upon the camp; and at daylight captured the thieves, and recovered Varner's and ten or eleven other horses. The culprits were tried by the local authorities and sentenced to receive thirty-nine lashes, which sentence was duly executed; after which the Frenchman was released, it appearing that he was only accessory to the theft. The principal was now carried before Alcalde Bell for further proceedings; again whipped, and released on the east side of the Brazos, with orders to depart the Colony."*

Colonel Austin, as civil and military commandant, now adopted more drastic measures, determined to rid his colony of the scourge. An opportunity soon offered to carry out his plan. "A still greater outrage" continues Kuykendall, "was perpetrated this summer by another party of Mexicans from the border of Louisiana. They were enroute to the Rio Grande, and finding a small party of Mexicans on Skull Creek, with a cavalcade which they were driving east, the Louisianans camped with them. The ensuing night they fell upon their Rio Grande brethren, and after murdering two or three and dispersing the rest, took possession of the cavallada. Carrasco, the owner of the horses, though wounded, escaped to the settlement on the Colorado; whereupon uncle Robert Kuykendall with a few men, started in pursuit of the thieves. It was soon discovered they had separated into two parties (having divided the horses), one of which had crossed the Colorado a short distance below the La Bahia road, and the other many miles above it. The latter party, after crossing the river, fell into and followed the San Antonio road and escaped to Louisiana, but the former was pursued and overtaken on the west bank of the Brazos, at the Cooshatte crossing. Two of them were killed and their heads stuck on poles at the roadside. The horses were also taken and restored to their owner. After this example, the 'border ruffians' ceased their depredations within the bounds of Austin's Colony."

However, the Tonkawas, ever professing friendship for the whites, could not restrain their propensity for stealing, and committed numerous petty depredations.

"Toward the latter part of this summer," says Kuykendall, "a party of Tonkawas stole a horse from my father and several

---

* "At first" says Yoakum, "they were pursued, the property reclaimed, and the robbers whipped and turned loose, but this only seemed to exasperate and cause them to add murder to robbery, in order to prevent detection."

from Mr. Wheat. Father, Thomas Boatwright, my brother
Barzillai and myself, pursued the thieves. At the infant town of
San Felipe, then containing but two or three log cabins, we were
joined by Austin and a few others, who went with us to Fort
Bend, where we were joined by a few more men, making our
force thirty strong. On approaching the Tonkawa camp, Carita,
the chief, met the party, professing regrets that five of his young
men had stolen the horses; that the animals would be restored
and the thieves punished. Delivering the horses, the old chief
pointed out the five men who had committed the theft, each of
whom was sentenced to receive fifty lashes, and have one half
of his head shaved. The sentence was fully carried out on four,
one being excused for sickness, Chief Carita inflicting one half,
and Capt. Kuykendall the other half of the lashes."

At this time there were two divisions of this tribe; the other
encampment being on the Colorado under Chief Sandia. The
combined number of warriors "did not much exceed one hundred—it certainly did not reach one hundred and fifty."*

With the return of spring, favorable seasons and a fair yield
of crops, came new life and renewed hopes for the struggling
colonists. "New comers" were locating at different points, and
a more prosperous and peaceful condition prevailed in the
Colony. But the settlers were not long left undisturbed. The
Caranchuas soon renewed hostilities. In June of this year, a
party of Caranchuas halted near the camp of Capt. Robert
Kuykendall, on Peach Creek, a few miles below Eagle Lake,
killing some of his stock and shooting at his little ten year old
son, who escaped and rode for assistance. Kuykendall, with his
wife and smaller children secreted themselves in a thicket. Capt.
Ingram and a dozen neighbors soon came to their relief. The
settlers followed the trail of the retreating Indians, which
wound for several miles through a dense cane brake. When the
pursuers arrived at the Colorado River, they espied the Indians
on the opposite bank, where they were drying meat. "Spurring
their horses to a gallop, they plunged into the river in the face

* Kuykendall's Reminiscences.

of the enemy, who saluted them with a swarm of arrows, and fled to the adjacent cane brake. In the camp Alexander Jackson stooped to pick up a buffalo robe, when a 'cloth yard' arrow was driven through his elbow. At the moment, a companion, John V. Clark, saw the Indian who had shot Jackson, in the cane brake, with his bow raised to shoot again. Clark quickly aimed and fired, the Indian falling dead, the rifle ball cutting his wrist in two, and penetrating his breast. The Indians being secure in their cane brake retreat, the settlers deemed it prudent to give up further pursuit."

## THE FAMOUS CANOE FIGHT.

About this time Capt. White, an old trader who lived at La Bahia, and owned a small boat, had an adventure with the Caranchuas. Embarking at Port Lavaca his vessel, loaded with salt to exchange for corn, he steered up the Colorado to what is called "Old Landing," two miles from its mouth, where he landed, leaving his boat in charge of two or three Mexicans, and went up to the settlement in search of corn. A party of Caranchuas were encamped near the landing, and professing friendship for White and his Mexican companion, requested him to visit them on his return, as they wished to trade for corn. Going up Peach Creek to the Kincheloe settlement, White found corn in exchange for his salt—the corn to be delivered to his boat, and the salt received there. Meantime the settlers were informed of the situation, and a runner sent sixty miles above for Capt. Jesse Burnam, who hastily collected a company of twenty-five and marched on the Indians. We quote Burnam's own account: "White was to inform the Indians of his return, by making a camp fire. He gave the signal just at daylight. I left twelve of my men at the boat, for fear the Indians might come from a different direction, while I took the other half and went down the river, to the Indians' landing place. About half an hour by sun, the Indians came rowing up the river, very slowly and cautiously, as though they expected danger. The river banks were low, but with sufficient brush to conceal us. Just as they were landing, I fired on them, my signal shot killing one Indian, and in less than five minutes we had killed eight. The other two swam off with the canoe, which they kept between them and us, but finally one of them, raising his head to guide the canoe, received a mortal shot. I returned home without the loss of a man."*

## DISASTROUS FIGHT IN THE CANE BRAKE.

Through favorable reports sent out by Austin, his colony continued to increase in population—giving a semblance of strength that would better enable him to cope with the Indians. The land office was opened, surveyors appointed, and we are informed, about two hundred and fifty titles were issued to the original "300" settlers during this year.** While the colonists busied themselves selecting locations, surveying lands, and making improvements, tidings came that a small party of emigrants, enroute from the mouth of the Brazos, had been attacked and murdered by the exasperated Caranchuas. Colonel Austin, to retaliate, and prevent a repetition of such outrages, in September, commissioned Capt. Randal Jones, with a company of twenty-three men, to proceed down the Brazos in canoes, reconnoiter the coast as far as Matagorda Bay, and, if found, show no mercy to the party that massacred the emigrants, as well as any other hostiles. Landing at a favorable position, scouts were sent out to reconnoiter. We quote from Jones' Journal: "Convinced that the Indians were secretly preparing for an attack, two of the scouts were dispatched up the river for reinforcements. At Bailey's store, on the Brazos, they were joined by eight or ten colonists already collected to watch the maneuverings of about a dozen Indians who had visited that place for ammunition. At daybreak the following morning, an attack was made, a few Indians were killed, and their discomfited companions

* Reminiscences of Capt. Jesse Burnam, in Texas Historical Quarterly—Vol. 5, pages 17 and 18.
**247 was the exact number of titles issued in 1824.

Long's Fight on Galveston Island

The Canoe Fight

Fate of the Bee Tree Hunters

routed."

In the meantime, directed by the loud wailing for their fallen comrades at Bailey's, Capt. Jones ascertained that some thirty Indians were encamped on the west bank of a small, sluggish tributary of the San Bernard—since called Jones Creek. Approaching under cover of night, within sixty yards of the encampment, the company halted, quickly prepared for action, and "when it was light enough to see their sights" made a furious attack. Although greatly surprised, the Indians quickly hid themselves in the reeds and tall marsh grass, where they fought with great desperation and advantage. Exposed to the deadly balls and arrows of the Indians, the whites finally retreated, with a loss of three of their number, Spencer, Bailey and Singer. The Indians, too, suffered severely, their dead being estimated at fifteen. A proportionate number were wounded on either side.

John Henry Brown says, "It was a clear repulse of the whites, whose leader, Capt. Jones, was an experienced soldier of approved courage. Such a result was lamentable at that period in the colony's existence."

The whites returned home, and the Indians retreated westward across the San Bernard. Greatly incensed, and somewhat emboldened, the Caranchuas now became more hostile and troublesome."*

## AUSTIN LEADS EXPEDITION AGAINST CARANCHUAS.

As the confines of Austin's colony were extending in every direction, many outrages were perpetrated on the more venturesome and exposed settlers. Col. Austin, now deeming his forces sufficiently strong, determined to chastise and expel the thieving and murderous Caranchuas from his colony. Accord-

---

* During this year, Capt. Chrisman, while out surveying with small parties of "land locators," had several skirmishes and numerous adventures with the Caranchuas on the San Bernard River and Gulf Prairie.

ingly, in July, he headed an expedition of forty or fifty armed men from San Felipe. Crossing the Colorado near Eagle Lake, and proceeding down the west side of the river to "Jennings Camp;" thence to the Lavaca below the mouth of the Nabadad; most of the route being through the prairie country. Pioneers were detailed to open roads through the dense thickets and cane brakes, bordering streams they crossed. But the Indians had warning of this expedition and fled from the colony—west, toward the San Antonio River.

Returning to the capital for fresh supplies and reinforcements, Austin determined to pursue and deal these Indians a telling blow while they were united in their retreat.

This second expedition, of some ninety men, thirty of whom were negroes, the slaves of Col. Jared E. Groce, mounted, armed and commanded by him, left San Felipe in August; passing the Colorado at the Atascocito crossing, and following the Atascocito road to the Guadalupe River near the present town of Victoria;* thence marching in the direction of La Bahia, expecting to strike the Indians west of the San Antonio River, on either Espirita Santo or Aransas Bays. "But on the Mana-huilla Creek, a few miles east of that town," says John Henry Brown, "he was met by the priest, Alcalde and citizens, who appeared as mediators for the Indians. The Caranchuas, aforetime nominally belonging to the Mission of La Bahia as converted Indians, now seeing danger approaching, professed penitence, and appealed to the priest and Alcalde to avert their threatened destruction. The result was a conference and quasi-treaty, in which the Indians solemnly pledged themselves to never again come east of the San Antonio or Guadalupe Rivers. The colonists thereupon returned home."

For a time these Indians remained quiet, the good priest exerted himself in their behalf, and hopes were entertained that he would succeed in bringing them under the benignant influence of Christian civilization. But "to the manner born" the

---

* 'At that time there was not a single habitation on the Guadalupe River from its head to its mouth'—Kuykendall Reminiscences

Caranchuas could not long restrain their murderous and thieving propensities; the treaty was soon broken, and for more than twenty years they continued to commit many petty, and some serious depredations. "In fact," says Kuykendall, "some of the greatest atrocities ever committed by these Indians in Austin's Colony, were perpetrated after this treaty was made.*

In the winter of this year, the families of Flowers and Cavanaugh were murdered by the Caranchuas. Capt. Buckner, with a company, pursued the Indians to their camp on the bay about three miles east of the present town of Matagorda, where at day break he made a surprise attack, killing some thirty, and completely routing them. This was the greatest loss these Indians ever sustained in any one fight with the colonists. Sometime during the year 1832, Capt. John Ingram led a party of nineteen men in an attack on an encampment of Caranchuas on Live Oak Creek, within the present limits of Matagorda County. The party fired on the Indians at the dawn of day, killing four or five and dispersing the remainder.

"Near the mouth of the Guadalupe, in 1834," says John Henry Brown, "they were only deterred from attacking the party of Major James Kerr, surveying lands for De Leon's Colony, by a ruse practiced upon them by him; and during that year they were whipped in a fight near Laguna Verde, or Green Lake, now in Calhoun County, by a party of Mexican and American settlers commanded by the brave Capt. Placido Venibides." "In the year 1834 or 1835," says Kuykendall, "the Tonkawas, instigated by the Mexicans of Victoria, treacherously assassinated fifteen or twenty of the Caranchuas. The Tonkawas went to the camp of the Caranchuas, taking with them a small boy, who secretly cut the bow strings of the Caranchuas, when the Tonkawas fell upon them and murdered all but two or three."

In the Spring of 1836, the Caranchuas still counted twenty-five or thirty warriors. When the army of invasion reached our frontier, they joined it, and fought against us at the Mission of

* In the year 1826, Capt. Aylett C. Buckner, defeated a party of Caranchuas below Elliott's Crossing.

Refugio in March, 1836. They had previously offered to fight for the Americans, but their offer was either rejected or neglected.

About 1840 they were encamped on the Guadalupe River, below Victoria, near the junction of the San Antonio, and on account of some depredations committed by them, were attacked by the Mexican and American settlers of that vicinity, and many killed. "They fled to the southwest, along the coast," says Kenney, "and their brief history hastens to its catastrophe."

In 1843 they were camped about fifty miles southwest of Corpus Christi, where they were found by a Mexican ranging company under Capt. Rafael Aldrete, who had known them from his childhood as cannibal savages. He at once attacked and almost annihilated them, very few escaping. Their last notable, hostile act was the murder of Capt. John Kemper at his home on the Guadalupe, Victoria County, in November, 1845. Mrs. Kemper, with her two little children, and her mother, after the Indians had attempted to burn them with the dwelling house, escaped in the stormy night, and crept to the house of Alonzo Bass, situated twelve miles distant, on the Calito.

"The last that was seen of these Indian" says Kenney, "was in 1847, when a remnant of some eight or ten Caranchuas crossed the Rio Grande at its mouth, begging their way into Mexico and oblivion." "In the year 1855," adds Kuykendall, "the once formidable tribe of Caranchuas had dwindled to six or eight individuals, who were residing near San Fernando, State of Tamaulipas, Mexico."

# CHAPTER II.

As we have seen, the principal and most ferocious tribe with which Austin's colonists came in contact, on their arrival and for the first few years, were the Caranchuas. But it was not long before the Wacos, Tehuacanies and allied tribes, were depredating.

In the Spring of 1824, a party of Wacos went down the Brazos as far as the Kuykendall settlement, where they stole thirteen head of valuable horses, and escaped with their booty, having been pursued some forty miles to the head of Cummings Creek where the trail was lost. Following this successful raid, the Wacos again visited the settlements, and stole all the horses of Mr. John Cummings. "We followed the thieves as far as the Yegua, about fifty miles," says Kuykendall, "where we lost the trail in consequence of the great number of wild horses and buffalo which then ranged through that section of country." Many other depredations were committed by these Indians about this period, but details are too meager for record.*

* In consequence of repeated thefts committed by the Wacos and Tehuacanies, Col. Austin, in July, 1824, sent Capt. Aylett C. Buckner, with Judge Duke, James Baird, Thomas H. Borden, Selkirk, Jones and McCloskey, on a mission to treat with these tribes. They took with them some goods to barter with the Indians for horses. They crossed the Brazos at the San Antonio road and proceeded up the river on the east side to the Tehuacanie village, crossing over to the Waco village, the site of the present city of Waco. They were well received by the Indians, who had recently returned . from their summer buffalo hunt, and were feasting on buffalo meat, green corn and beans. They had also pumpkins and melons. They dwelt in comfortable lodges, conical in shape, the frames of which were of cedar poles or slats, thatched with grass. The largest of these lodges (their council

In the Spring of 1826, Austin resolved to make a campaign against the Wacos and Tehuacanies, whose depredations had now become frequent. Rendezvousing on the Brazos at the crossing of the San Antonio road, about the middle of May, a force of about one hundred and ninety men was soon collected and organized, Col. Austin in command, with Aylett C. Buckner, Horatio Chrisman, Bartlett Sims, William Hall and Ross Alley, captains of companies.

The first days march brought the expedition to the Little Brazos, where they left all provisions, save rations for three days, and a forced march was ordered against the Indians.

On arriving in the vicinity of the Indian encampment, scouts were sent to reconnoiter, and found it deserted. "Appearances" says Kuykendall, "indicated that the Tehuacanie village had been deserted about two weeks. The Waco village was on the west side of the river a little farther up. We could not reach it, as the river was much swollen, but ascertained that it, too, was uninhabited. The Indians were doubtless gone on a buffalo hunt. Their patches of corn were in silk and tassel. There was an abundance of beans, of which we picked a mess or two, but nothing was destroyed."

Thus disappointed and their rations being entirely exhausted, the expedition returned to their supply depot—and to the Brazos, where it was disbanded.

---

## EARLY TRIALS OF DeWITT'S COLONISTS.

Early as 1822, while Austin's colony was yet in its infancy,

house) was fifty-nine paces in circumference. The Wacos and Tehuacanies spoke the same language, and were essentially the same people. Judge Duke estimated the two tribes would number between 200 and 300 warriors. They had a great number of horses and mules—a small plug of tobacco being the price of a horse, and a plug and a half that of a mule. They smoked the pipe of peace with the embassy, and pledged themselves to peace and amity with the colonists. The embassy remained with the Indians between two and three weeks, and returned home by the same route they went out."—Kuykendall's Reminiscences.

several American gentlemen, among them Green DeWitt of Missouri, appeared in the city of Mexico, seeking empresario contracts. Owing to the unsettled political conditions of the country at that period, DeWitt's petition to settle four hundred families in the province of Texas, was not approved till after the promulgation and enactment of the first general colonization law of Coahuila and Texas, March 24, 1825.

Anticipating the success of his application, which was duly granted April 15, 1825, DeWitt had pre-arranged with Major James Kerr, late of Missouri, but then of Austin's Colony, as agent and surveyor for the colony.

In August of this year, Major Kerr, (having recently buried his wife and two children on the Brazos), with his negro servant and six men, viz. Erasmus ("Deaf") Smith, Basil Durbin, Gerron Hinds, John Wightman, James Musick and ____ Strickland, leaving San Felipe de Austin reached a spot on Kerr's Creek (near the present town of Gonzales), where they halted, speedily erected cabins and laid off a site for the capital of the future colony, which was named Gonzales, in honor of Don Rafael Gonzales, the first Governor of Coahuila and Texas. The location was most favorable, but the town itself was of slow growth and for a while of uncertain existence, as will be seen. "The survey of lands for future colonists, was prosecuted as rapidly as possible," says Brown, "and a few weeks later, Francis Berry and family settled near the creek. Of this family were also John and Betsey Oliver, grown children of Mrs. Berry by a former husband.

About the first of October, DeWitt arrived from Saltillo, and remained in the colony three or four weeks before proceeding on his way to Missouri. During the year, a number of prospectors visited the country, and after selecting locations left, to return later. Thus these few brave settlers at old Gonzales in 1825-6, were truly pioneers, the advance guards of American civilization on that then remote and greatly exposed frontier, their nearest neighbors being DeLeon and half a dozen Mexicans, at the infant settlements of Guadalupe Victoria, sixty miles southward; and with no roads in any direction, save their own freshly made trail sixty-five miles east to the Colorado. But the lot of these isolated settlers was not intolerable, and would have speedily improved but for an unexpected calamity. Parties of Indians, professing friendship, frequently called, passing to and fro; and demonstrating no signs of hostility, the colonists apprehended no danger. "Thus matters stood," says historian Brown, "when the first day of July, 1826, arrived. There was a celebration of the fourth of July at Beason's, at the Atascocito crossing of the Colorado, a few miles below the present town of Columbus. Major Kerr had gone on a buffalo hunt. It was agreed that Basil Durbin, John and Betsey Oliver, and Jack the servant boy of Kerr, should go on horseback to the Colorado celebration. They started on Sunday, July 2, and encamped for the night on Thorne's Branch, fourteen miles east, having no apprehension of danger at the time. The little party however, were doomed to disappointment, for about midnight, while soundly sleeping on their blankets, they were suddenly aroused by the firing of guns and the yells of the Indians. Durbin was shot in the shoulder by a musket ball and badly wounded, but escaped with his companions into a thicket near by, the horses and other effects being left in the possession of the enemy. From loss of blood and intense pain, Durbin repeatedly swooned, but was restored by the efforts of his companions and enabled to walk, by noon on the following day, back to Major Kerr's cabin, where the party was astonished to find John Wightman lying dead and scalped in the passage way between the rooms, and the house robbed of everything, including important papers and three compasses, and that an unsuccessful attempt had been made to burn it. They hurried to Berry's cabin and found it closed, and on the door, written with charcoal, 'Gone to Burnham's on the Colorado.'

"When Durbin and his companions left on the previous day, Strickland, Musick and Major Kerr's negroes (Shade, Anise and their four or five children), went to Berry's to spend the afternoon, leaving Wightman alone at the cabins. Returning later in the day, they found Wightman as described, yet warm in his own blood. Hurrying back to Berry's with the tidings, the

1. Col. Green De Witt, 2. Jas. A. Sylvester,
3. Joel W. Robinson and 4. Alex S. Thompson

1. General Walter P. Lane, 2. Elisha Anglin,
3. Hayden Edwards and 4. Sterling C. Robertson

entire party started for the Colorado, where they safely arrived, and were a few days later joined by Deaf Smith and Hinds. Durbin's wounds had already rendered him very weak, but his only alternative was to reach the same place on foot, or perish by the way. The weather was warm, and there was imminent danger of gangrene making its appearance in his wound, to prevent which, it was kept poulticed with mud and oak juice. Leaning on Betsey Oliver's arm, he arrived at Burnham's on the afternoon of the sixth, three days and a half after starting from the place."

Durbin's wound soon healed, the musket ball remaining in his shoulder till death, and he lived to participate in a number of other adventures. Seven years later he received six rifle balls in his person at one time, and, as if he bore a charmed life, survived, carrying seven balls in his body till his death in 1858.

Thus was DeWitt's colony, like Austin's at the mouth of the Colorado, christened with blood, and thus for the moment ended the first efforts to found a settlement within its limits.

Following these events, Major Kerr and a few companions moved to a point on the west bank of the Lavaca, now in Jackson County, where block-houses were built, and a nucleus formed for the revival of the enterprise. The place, only temporarily occupied for defensive and rallying purposes, was subsequently known as the "Old Station." Major Kerr established his permanent home on the east bank of the Lavaca, near the station.

On the 12th of December, 1826, Major Kerr, under the authority invested in him as surveyor-general, commissioned Byrd Lockhart as deputy-surveyor of the colony—a judicious selection—and the survey of land, despite danger from hostile Indians, proceeded with all reasonable dispatch, and emigrants continued to arrive and locate near the station on the Lavaca.

DeWitt, with his family, arrived at the "Old Station" in October, 1827, and during the succeeding winter, with his own and a number of other families, repaired to Gonzales and its vicinity, and then, with the opening of the year 1828, began the permanent settlement of the region destined to become the

Lexington of Texas in the revolution of 1825-36.*

As early as May, 1824, the Mexican Congress had passed an act temporarily combining the provinces of Coahuila and Texas into a State, with a provisional legislature, (Don Rafael Gonzales being elected governor), and in March, 1825, as we have seen, the newly formed government promulgated a general State colonization law.

The fame and success of Austin and his colony, together with the more liberal provisions of the new colonization act, induced a number of persons to seek empresario privileges. Among those who secured grants and fulfilled or attempted to carry out, their contracts, were Robert Leftwich, of Nashville, Tennessee, (permission April 15th, 1825, to settle 900 families in what was afterwards known as Robertson's Colony); Hayden Edwards, a Kentuckian, then resident of Louisiana, (concession April 18th, 1825, to settle 800 families in the Nacogdoches

---

* The venerable pioneer, Noah Smithwick, who visited DeWitt's Colony in the summer of 1828, in a letter to the author from his last home at Santa Anna, California, a few months before his death (Oct. 21, 1899) gives the following pen picture of colonial life at that period: "The colonists, (DeWitt's) consisting of a dozen families, were living, if such existence could be called living, huddled together for security against the Indians. The rude log cabins, windowless and floorless, have been so often described as the abode of the pioneer, as to require no description here; suffice it to say that save as a partial protection against rain and sun, they were absolutely devoid of comfort . . . Col. DeWitt, my host, had bread, though some of the families were without. Flour was $10.00 a barrel. But few people had money to buy anything more than coffee and tobacco. Money was as scarce as bread. Game was plentiful the year round, so there was no need of starving. Men talked hopeful about the future; children reveled in the novelty of the present, and the women bore their part with heroic endurance. Deprived of friends and former comforts, they had not even the solace of constant employment. The spinning wheel and loom had been left behind—there was as yet no use for them—there was nothing to spin. There was no house to keep in order; the meager fare was so simple as to require little time for its preparation. There was no poultry, no dairy, no garden, no books or papers—and had there been, many of them could not read; no schools, no churches—nothing to break the dull monotony of their lives save an occasional attack from Indians, the howl of some wild animal, or the stampede of a herd of buffalo or mustangs. The men at least had the excitement of killing game and hunting bee trees, roping mustangs, hunting buffalo, locating lands and watching for hostile Indians."

district of east Texas); and Don Martin de Leon, a native Mexican, but then and since 1805, residing in the province of Texas, (concession of October 6th, 1825, to settle forty one Mexican families, south of DeWitt's colony, and between the Lavaca and Guadalupe Rivers). A number of other concessions were made about this period to parties who failed of success, notably to Ben R. Milam, the famous "hero of San Antonio," to settle 200 families north of the old San Antonio road, and between the Colorado and Guadalupe Rivers. But brave Milam was a soldier, rather than civilian, and sacrificed his life in a more glorious cause—on the altar of liberty, falling in the moment of victory. Thus the spirit of colonization was infused throughout the whole southwest and a constant tide of immigration was flowing into Texas, giving to the country some assurance of permanent prosperity and stability.

## EDWARDS' COLONY AND THE FREDONIAN WAR.

But in the midst of the general prosperity, a dark cloud arose in the east, which for a time, threatened the destruction of the province. We refer to the Fredonian revolt in Edwards' Colony. Hayden Edwards had wealth and enterprise, and intended to fill his contract in good faith; but his location proved exceedingly unfortunate. For a long time a roving and migratory class of motley people, had occupied the country about Nacogdoches, "heroes of the Neutral Ground," men who, committing an offense, either in Mexican or American territory, here sought an asylum. Here, too, an antagonism had arisen between the Anglo-Americans and the Mexicans, created, perhaps, by the ill-fated filibustering expeditions of Nolan, Magee and Long.

Edwards' contract required him not only to respect, but to give preference to Mexican claimants. As soon as one of the new emigrants had made a selection and commenced an improvement, some Mexican would appear and set up a claim for his land. The alcalde was appealed to; but he, being elected by Mexican votes, invariably decided in favor of his constituents. At an election for a new alcalde, a majority of the votes cast were for Chaplin, a son-in-law of Edwards; but Norris, who although an American, was in the interest of the Mexicans, was counted in, and by order of the political chief, invested with the office. Thus supported by the military, the tyranny of the alcalde soon became intolerable. Foote, the historian, and an intimate friend of Edwards, gives the following picture of that turbulent period:

"Nacogdoches now became a scene of wild uproar and confusion; acts of lawless and cruel violence marked the history of every day, and indeed of every hour; bands of Regulators, as they were called, pervaded the whole country, under the ostensible sanction of the alcalde, and ready to execute any mandate to which he might give utterance. Private families were often driven from their habitations, to make way for the piratical minions of the alcalde, who sighed for the comforts which the honest assiduity of the colonists had assembled about their domiciles, and which they were too lazy and luxurious to acquire, except by violence exercised upon their peaceful owners. Respectable colonists were dragged from their beds at midnight by an armed mob, and hurried before the alcalde, in order to undergo a secret inquisition relative to acts that they had never so much as thought of committing; even the passing traveler was not free from molestation and outrage, but was compelled to pay tribute for the privilege of transit through the country, under penalty of forfeiting whatever merchandise or other property that was found in his possession."

It was not to be expected that free born and liberty loving Americans would tamely submit to such acts of injustice and tyrannical oppression.

During the summer of 1826, Hayden Edwards visited the United States to bring more colonists, leaving his brother, Benjamin Edwards, in charge of the colony. In the absence of the empresario, serious charges were preferred against him to Governor Blanco. On July 21st, Benjamin Edwards addressed empresario Austin a long letter in which he recounted his grievances and asked for advice. In due course of time Austin gave Edwards a reply, in which he said: "The subject has caused me great unhappiness, but I had decided not to interfere with it in any way. It is a dangerous one to touch, and particularly to write about. You wish me to advise you. I scarcely know what course will be best. The uncertainty as to the precise nature of the charges against you, renders it difficult, nay impossible, to name a regular defense. I think, however, I would write directly to the governor of the State. Give him a full statement of facts, and a very minute history of the acts of your principal enemies and their opponents, and their manner of doing business in every particular, both in regard to your brother as well as all others."

Accordingly, Benjamin Edwards directed a long, and, unfortunately, somewhat dictatorial message to his excellency, Governor Don Victor Blanco, vindicating his brother's course, and remonstrating very emphatically against such treatment; to which that irate functionary, on the 20th day of October, replied: "That by the virtue of the supreme authority with which he was invested, he had decreed the annulment of the contract of Hayden Edwards; and further more, ordered the expulsion from the colony, of both the Edwards brothers." Hayden Edwards returned just as the news of this high-handed and arbitrary act reached the colony. He had spent several thousand dollars in bringing colonists to the country, and naturally became very indignant, resolving upon resistance and revenge *vi et armis.*

At this juncture two celebrated half-breed Indian chiefs Richard Fields and John Dunn Hunter, appeared in the arena, with grievances of their own, in behalf of their people the Cherokees. Governor Trespalacios had promised to secure them titles to the land they occupied, but the Mexican Government was slow in the excitement of the moment, and chafing for revenge the colonists entered into a league, offensive and defensive with the Indians.

This compact was formally signed on December 20, 1826, by Hayden Edwards and Harmon B. Mayo, on the part of the

Americans, and Richard Fields and John Dunn Hunter, on the part of the Indians. The allied parties at once proceeded to organize a legislative council. Martin Parmer, better known as the "Ring-Tailed Panther" was elected president.

In this alliance it was stipulated that the whites were to have the territory below the old San Antonio road and for a short distance above; the remainder of the province, westward to the Rio Grande, was given to the Indians. Slavery, which had been prohibited in Mexico, was to be established in both territories.

Denominating themselves "Fredonians," the injured insurgents raised the standard of revolt, and boldly declared their independence. The flag of Independent Fredonia was unfurled to the breeze, and, "doubtless" says the historian of this ill-planned and hopeless revolt, "Old Norther, himself, who so often swept over the prairies of Texas, stood aghast at the chilling exhibition."

One of the first acts of the executive council created at Nacogodoches, was to depose the alcalde, Norris, and appoint another. While these troubles were brewing, Peter E. Bean, a survivor of Nolan's expedition, and whose life history reads like a romance, was stationed at Fort Teran, as Indian agent. Learning of these troubles, Bean, with a small company of cavalry, marched upon Nacogdoches for the purpose of quelling the disturbance and to restore Mexican authority. Bean did not seem to apprehend that he would have much difficulty. He, however, found the disturbance more serious than anticipated, and on learning that the Fredonians, about two hundred strong, were occupying the old stone fort, prudently decided to wait for a reinforcement from San Antonio. In the meantime, he succeeded in detaching most of the Indians from the league. Fields and Hunter, however, were faithful to the last, and were barbarously assassinated by the very tribes for whose welfare they had labored long and patiently. The assassin's first shot not proving immediately fatal, poor Hunter implored the murderer to spare his life, exclaiming, "it is hard thus to die by the hands of my professed friends." The appeal was in vain. Another shot closed the career of this strange and extraordinary man.

News of the revolt reaching Bexar, Governor Saucedo dispatched Col. Matio Ahumada, with two hundred soldiers to suppress the insurrectionists. The part which Austin took in this affair has excited a good deal of comment and some severe criticism. Historian Foote, who was a warm friend of the Edwards', conveys the idea that Austin was greatly perplexed and hesitated long whether he would join the Fredonian movement or make war against it. Such was not the fact. On the contrary, he advised the leaders of this revolt that their cause was one of consummate folly, and that they were rushing upon certain destruction. Indeed, as an honorable and true citizen of his adopted country, he could not have done otherwise. In such a controversy, neutrality was impossible, and instead of hesitating a moment, Austin, on the 22nd day of January, 1827, issued the following address:

To the Inhabitants of the Colony:

The persons* who were sent on from this colony by the political chief and military commandant, to offer peace to the Nacogdoches madmen, have returned without having effected anything. The olive branch of peace which was held out to them has been insultingly refused, and that party has denounced massacre and dissolution on this colony. They are trying to excite all the northern Indians to murder and plunder, and it appears as though they have no other object than to ruin and plunder this country. They openly threaten us with Indian massacre and the plunder of our property. To arms, then, my friends and fellow-citizens, and hasten to the standard of our country. The first hundred men will march on the 26th.

---

* Austin sent a delegation of citizens—Abner Kuykendall, Judge Ellis, Francis W. Johnson, and James Cummings—from his colony, accompanied by James Kerr from DeWitt's colony, to confer and fraternally remonstrate with the Fredonians, and endeavor to dissuade them from rash measures. The delegation failed to accomplish the object desired.

Necessary orders for mustering and other purposes will be issued to the commanding officers. Union and Mexico!

S. F. Austin
San Felipe de Austin,
22nd. January, 1827

The news of Colonel Ahumada's approach completely demoralized the Fredonians. They miscalculated their strength. No help reached them from the settlement of Pecan Point, on Red River, nor from Ayish Bayou. But they were still more chagrined at the course of Austin's colony, and hastily retreated across the Sabine, leaving a few of their partisans, who were captured by the Mexicans. And now it was that Austin exerted his influence to good purpose; instead of putting them to death, according to the custom, they were, at his earnest solicitation, pardoned and set at liberty. This magnanimous conduct called forth a letter from Edwards, in which he returned grateful thanks to Ahumada for his humanity.

And thus the unfortunate rebellion passed away and was numbered with the things that were.

# CHAPTER III.

**D**efeated in almost every engagement, and melting away before the unerring rifles of Austin's colonists, the formidable coast tribe—the Caranchuas—had been forced to retreat and sue for peace. DeWitt's Colony, surviving the serious misfortunes which befell it in the Summer of 1826, was rapidly taking on new life and energy.

The Fredonian mutiny did not seriously affect or retard the growth of Austin's Colony, and with its quelling a period of comparative peace and prosperity prevailed. But this state of quiet was not of long duration. The Wacos and Tehuacanies who had been more or less troublesome all along, now became openly hostile and were depredating on the settlers of the Brazos and Colorado, to an alarming extent. "Indeed" says Yoakum, "the grant of Milam, laying between the Guadalupe and Colorado Rivers, and north of the Bexar road, could not well be settled because of hostile Indians."

In the winter of 1828-9, a party of these Indians entered Fayette county, camping—so the bluffs would protect them from the chilling winds—in the bed of Ross Creek; where they might have remained undisturbed had they not killed a worthy Mexican resident of the neighborhood. Whereupon a party consisting of James Tomlinson, J. J. Ross, A. A. Anderson, John Vryer and others, attacked and routed the murderous intruders, killing eight of them outright, and severely wounding seven more, who managed to escape, but perished soon, it was supposed, as only one of this unfortunate party was known to have reached his tribe."*

"When the Indians were attacked," says J. J. Ross, who furnished the above facts, "some were lying down, some parching corn, and others were engaged in a scalp dance. An attempt was made to burn the bodies of the dead Indians, but with poor success—only crisping their skins. Their bleaching bones long remained on the battle ground."

About this time one Thomas Thompson opened a small farm near the present town of Bastrop, and occasionally visited it to cultivate and take care of his crops. On going there in July, 1829, he found the Indians in possession. Returning below for assistance he was joined by ten men with whom he approached the Indian camp at night. At daylight they killed four of the savages and routed the others.

Of course these affairs were unfortunate and served to increase hostilities—Yoakum says they opened the war. At any rate, "numerous cases of murder and theft had occurred, and it became necessary to apply a remedy"—which empresario Stephen Austin promptly did.

---

## THE WAR OPENS AGAINST THE WILD TRIBES.

Captain Abner Kuykendall:

The Indians have robbed a large drove of horses from a traveler who stopped at Ratcliff's on the Lavaca. They were pursued two days by a few men and overtaken between the Colorado and Brazos, below the San Antonio road. There was one white man—supposed to be an American—and fifteen Indians. It is highly important that the trail should be followed so as to ascertain what Indians and white man or men have become so base as to commit this depredation; and to punish them—also recover the horses.

A party of volunteers is ready at Beason's to follow the

* Statement of Mr. Pennington, an Indian trader, then among this tribe.

robbers, and a number will go from here. It is their wish and
also mine, that you take the command; and I hope and expect
that you will undertake the expedition if your health will permit.

I hereby authorize you in the name of the Government, and
of the civil authorities, whom I have consulted, to take the
command of said party of volunteers, and to pursue and kill
said robbers, be they Indians or whites, and to recover the stolen
horses, and do such other acts as in your judgment be deemed
necessary, equitable and proper, to punish the robbers and
afford security to our exposed and scattered settlements, by
making a severe and striking example which will have the effect
to prevent the repetition of similar outrages by the lawless
bands who are moving through these unsettled wilds.

You will, however, be cautious of offending innocent persons, as you will be responsible for any wanton cruelty committed by your men while acting by your orders, on the innocent.
You will keep a journal of your proceedings and report same to
me on your return.

Town of Austin, August 23, 1829.
Stephen F. Austin, Col. of Ma.

This order was received by Capt. Kuykendall the evening
of the same day it was written, and in obedience thereto, with
his two sons, William and Barzillai, he left on the ensuing
morning for the Colorado, where he arrived the same day and
was joined by eight men—"most of whom were old frontiersmen"—to-wit: Norman Woods, John F. Berry, Elijah Ingram,
John Williams, Thomas Thompson, Seaborn Jones, ____ Hazlitt,
and one not remembered.

## FIERCE FIGHT NEAR THE OLD CABIN.

"We now counted eleven," says Kuykendall, whose narrative we follow, "and resolved to pursue the Indians without
losing further time to increase our force. We forded the Colo-

rado at the crossing of the La Bahia road and proceeded eight or nine miles up the river, when about noon, we discovered people moving about an old cabin. As we knew the inhabitants of this neighborhood had, some time previously, been driven from their homes by the Indians, this circumstance excited some surprise, and Hazlitt and another man were dispatched on foot towards the cabin to ascertain the character of its visitors. The rest of us sat in our saddles, concealed by a point of woods.

"In order to approach near the house, Hazlitt and his companion had to pass through a cornfield. They had not proceeded far in the field when an Indian shot an arrow at Hazlitt, and raising a war whoop, fled to the cabin. As he ran straight between the rows of corn, Hazlitt shot him in the back. The instant we heard the alarm we galloped forward and saw five Indians on foot, running up the river, trying to reach a thicket on its bank, two or three hundred yards above the cabin. Spurring our horses to their best speed, we intercepted them a short distance below the thicket. As we dismounted, each man dropped the coil of his tethering rope from the pommel of his saddle and charged the Indians on foot. They were now compelled to fight us in the open prairie or leap down the precipitous bank of the river. They chose the latter alternative. Norman Woods shot one as he was in the act of leaping off the bluff. The remaining four threw away their arrows and plunged into the Colorado. As they swam toward the opposite shore, we plied them with two or three rounds of rifle balls, and sank two midway the river. The remaining two reached the opposite shore with mortal wounds from which we could distinctly see the blood flowing. One of them uttered a few words in a very loud voice and almost instantly afterward our ears were assailed with terrific yells from the thicket above us, accompanied by a flight of arrows and discharge of fire arms. Turning toward our unexpected assailants, we saw several of them running toward our horses. We also ran in the same direction, and all the Indians, except two, returned to the thicket. These two Indians succeeded in reaching our horses, of which each selected and mounted one and drove all the rest save two, before them—yelling and firing off their guns to frighten the horses and urge them to greater speed. The two men whose horses were left, mounted them and pursued the Indians, the rest of us following as fast as possible on foot. After trailing nearly a mile and a half we discovered our horses standing in a grove. Suspecting a ruse, we approached them with caution, but found no enemy.

"Having now recovered all our horses but two (those of Thompson and Williams), we returned to the scene of action. Every Indian had disappeared. The one shot by Woods was still alive, sitting under the bank. Deeming it an act of mercy to put an end to his suffering, Woods shot him in the head.

"After collecting the arms of the defeated Indians, consisting of bows and arrows and one or two shot guns, we went into the field to look for the Indian shot by Hazlitt. We did not find him, but picked up his belt which had been cut in two by the rifle ball. This satisfied us that he had received a mortal wound. His body was afterwards found outside the field. The remains of the two who reached the opposite side of the river were also found afterwards—making six killed. Not one of our party was hurt, though Berry, after the engagement, fainted from the effect of heat and over-exertion.

"There were at least forty or fifty of these Indians—Wacos and Tawacanies. They were well provided with ropes and bridles, and had doubtless come on a stealing expedition. The survivors left the Colorado without committing any depredations.

"As we were reduced to but nine mounted men, two of whose horses were already broken down, we were constrained to forego the pursuit of the thieves who had stolen the cavallada, and returned home. That evening we traveled about five miles on our return, and slept at a spring about three miles above the present town of La Grange."

## THE SAN SABA EXPEDITION.

Immediately after arriving home and reporting to Col. Austin, Capt. Kuykendall received the following order:

"You will call a muster of your company and endeavor to raise volunteers to go against the Indians. If you cannot get volunteers enough to make one fourth the number of men composing your company, you will raise them by draft. You will rendezvous at this place with at least one fourth the men composing your company, on the 12th of September next, armed and equipped as the law directs, with provisions for a campaign of forty days. By order of S. F. Austin.

Oliver Jones, Adjt."

Capt. Abner Kuykendall.

Similar orders were issued to Bartlett Simms and other captains of the militia in the colony. "About the same time, but without concert," says John Henry Brown, "a company of thirty-nine men of DeWitt's Colony, under Capt. Henry S. Brown, left Gonzales on a mission against the depredating hostiles, supposed to be in the mountains."

The contingents of the different companies from Austin's Colony, rendezvoused on the east side of the Colorado about twelve miles below the present town of La Grange, where, between the 15th and 20th of September, the required force of one hundred men was collected and organized, under the command of Abner Kuykendall.

Striking the San Gabriel, the expedition marched up that stream—scouring the country between the Brazos and Colorado—and across the country to a point near the head of what is now known as the Salt Fork of the Lampasas, and some thirty miles from the mouth of the San Saba; where it halted and sent out spies to locate the encampment of the Indians.

Returning on the second morning, the spies reported a large encampment on the west bank of the Colorado, two or three miles below the mouth of the San Saba, and "that they were engaged in a dance, as they could distinctly hear the sound of a sort of castinet which the Indians used on such occasions."

It was evident the Indians were not aware of the approaching forces, and planning a night march, Kuykendall determined, if possible, to make a surprise attack at daylight the following morning. At sundown the command was in motion and on the march. We quote from Kuykendall: "Night soon closed around us. There was no moon but the sky was cloudless and starry. Our route lay over a prairie, studded with low hills, and in some places very rocky. Hour after hour the long double files of horsemen followed the guide. There was no confusion in our ranks, rarely was a word spoken, yet our march was far from being noiseless. The hard, metamorphic limestone rang like metal beneath the tread of our horses, and ever and anon we invaded the domain of a community of rattlesnakes, of which we were promptly notified by rapid vibrations of their rattles. Our guide conducted us toward nearly every point of the compass, and at length, long after midnight, declared he was bewildered and could conduct us no further until daylight. All now suspected the fidelity of our guide—a Mexican who had once lived with the Wacos and Tawacanies. Perhaps he was actuated by cowardice, perhaps by revived affection for his quandom friends; but whatever his motives, it is highly probable that but for his conduct the expedition would have been completely successful."

Still anxious to effect a surprise attack, Kuykendall concealed his force in a dense cedar-brake to await another night, meanwhile sending out six of his men, Wm. Dever, Amos Gates, Sebe Jones, Jeff Prayor and one other, with a Chickasaw Indian, named John, on foot to explore a route to the Colorado River and locate a crossing.

They had proceeded about one and one half miles, when they were discovered by twenty-five mounted Indians, who charged upon them, yelling like demons. It was a hard race and a miraculous escape for the spies, who by making repeated stands and runs, succeeded in reaching their companions and giving the alarm. "Meantime" says Kuykendall, "the loud cries of the Indians had been heard at our camp and the whole command was hastening to the rescue. When William Dever perceived that succor was close at hand he shot, and it was believed, mortally wounded one of the Indians. At this moment our whole force came up, and the Indians fled at full speed. Following in rapid pursuit, the village was soon discovered in a bend of the river, almost concealed by a low wooded hill—the valley around being almost literally covered with mounted Indians—men, women and children, flying to the yellow cedarbrakes in the adjacent hills."

The Texans dashed across the river, and into the village, but most of the Indians had fled and but few shots were fired, one by Nestor Clay, killing an Indian, a Tehuacanie chief.

Detachments were sent in pursuit but the Indians had escaped to their mountain fastnesses; only a few women and children were overtaken, who were of course unmolested.

The Indians lost their entire camp equipage, including a considerable amount of corn, blankets, robes, brass kettles, etc., and a large number of horses, all of which was secured by the victors.

"We encamped upon the ground evacuated by the Indians," says Kuykendall. "Their conical, buffalo skin covered lodges were still standing, and within them we found their entire store of winter provisions, namely, several hundred bushels of corn and beans, and a quantity of dried buffalo meat. Many buffalo robes were also found and on the fires were still boiling, several kettles of corn and beans—all of which property was consigned to the flames, or otherwise destroyed. The site of this encampment was very beautiful and had apparently often been temporarily occupied by the Indians; but there were no traces of agricultural operations. Early the ensuing morning, Captain Henry Brown, with a company of thirty men from Gonzales rode into camp."

"He had discovered the camp," says John Henry Brown, "secreted his men, put out concealed watches, and, like Kuykendall, expected to attack at dawn the following morning. He had passed through the mountains on the east side of the Guadalupe, across the Piedernales and Llano, to the head of the San Saba. He encountered two small bands. In the first he killed three Indians. Near the Enchanted Rock, he surprised the second band. Five or six Indians fell, the remainder escaped into the dense brush. Both appeared to be only hunting parties of warriors. It was on this trip that Captain Brown, with his men, became the first discoverers of the Enchanted Rock. He had followed the San Saba down to its mouth, and a little below discovered the Indian encampment. Neither Brown nor Kuykendall knew of the other being in that section until after the attack upon, and routing of the Indians."

\* \* \* \* \*

Such bold expeditions by such sagacious leaders went far toward keeping the Indians in check, but it was impossible to effectively protect the long line of exposed frontier, and bands of hostile marauders were constantly scooping down, and slipping in, stealing, killing, and then quickly retreating, back to their mountain homes.

## EARLY BORDER CHIEFS.

The commanders of these early expeditions boldly penetrating so far into the Indian country, as they did, deserve at least further brief notice.

ABNER KUYKENDALL was one of the very early settlers in Austin's Colony, having emigrated from Arkansas Territory, and camped on the west side of the Brazos River, at the La Bahia road crossing, on Nov. 26, 1821.

About the first of January, 1822, he settled more permanently on New Year's Creek, some ten miles west of the Brazos, and about four miles south of the present town of Independence.

Kuykendall brought several head of cattle and a few hogs to the colony. He was extensively known and highly esteemed by his fellow colonists as a brave and worthy gentleman. He was early appointed Captain of Militia and served in most of the campaigns and expeditions against Indians during the colonial period.

The following letter gives briefly the facts of the tragic and deplorable fate of this early pioneer and venerable patriarch of Austin's Colony:

1117 Bell Ave., Houston, Texas

James T. DeShields, Esq,
Farmersville, Texas.
My Dear Sir:
Yours of Dec. 6th received and contents noted. In reply will say Capt. Abner Kuykendall was killed in 1834 at San Felipe, by a man named Clayton, who was hung for the crime—his being the second of the only two legal executions for murder in Austin's Colony. Kuykendall was stabbed in the neck with a knife which broke off, and he died of lockjaw.

Clayton was a Mississippian. He was raised by an aunt living near Natchez. He killed a cousin in Mississippi in 1832 or 1833, and ran away to Texas. His aunt heard of his last trouble and came to San Felipe in 1834, but when she found how he had killed Kuykendall, she returned home without seeing him. Mrs. Clayton stayed at my father's house while here.

I knew Joe Kuykendall, a brother—was a prisoner with him in 1836, and knew him many years after, until his death in Fort Bend county. He came to Texas in 1822. Hoping the information may profit you,

Yours truly,
J.R. Fenn

Capt. Kuykendall's place of nativity and date of birth are unknown—his wife was a daughter of Owen Shanon, and a sister of John and Jacob Shanon. Two of her nephews, Matthew and Jacob, may yet survive.

HENRY STEPHENSON BROWN was born in Madison county, Kentucky, March 8, 1793, and in December, 1824, in company with his brother, John, afterwards known as "Waco" Brown, landed at the mouth of the Brazos with a large stock of goods for the Mexican and Indian trade. Engaged in this hazardous business at that period, it is but natural that they should encounter many dangers and participate in numerous thrilling adventures, the details of which would fill a volume. We make brief extracts from the biographies of these brave and worthy pioneers, and early defenders of infant Texas: "In 1825 Capt. Brown sent his brother with a large cargo of goods to trade with the Comanches in the upper county. James Musick, Thomas Jamison and Andrew Scott went with him. They succeeded in reaching Clear Fork of the Brazos River, without being molested and found the Indians very friendly, and anxious to trade. And soon they were wending their way homeward with eleven hundred horses and mules, and as many buffalo robes as they could manage, on their pack mules. The Indians assisted them a day or two on their way, and on the fourth night they camped on the Brazos, about where the present town of Meridian stands. All retired congratulating themselves upon the success of their expedition, and what was their surprise, when midnight yells, and the firing of guns disturbed their quiet slumbers. All sprang to their feet. Mr. Brown, being a cripple from white swelling, fell over one of his companions. All thinking that he was dead, fled into the bottom. Brown secreted himself in some brush nearby, where he remained until daylight, naturally thinking that his companions would do likewise. But to his dismay, he found himself all alone, lame, and weak, without food; yet with a brave resolution he started, limping homeward. After traveling for three days, with blistered feet and aching heart, and almost famishing, he was suddenly surrounded by a band of Waco Indians. Most of them seemed anxious to kill him but some pleaded for his life, which was spared on account of his lameness. He was then mounted and carried to their principal village, where the present city of Waco is located. His companions, supposing that he fell dead, traveled all the first night, and concealed themselves in thickets during the day. In this manner they traveled until they reached the settlements, where they reported the death of Brown and their great loss of property.

"Simultaneously with this expedition, was Capt. Brown's first trip to Mexico, but fortunately with much better success, as he returned in a few months with a large number of horses and mules for the Louisiana and Mississippi trade, and a consider-able amount of Mexican coin. On reaching San Felipe, he heard of the sad fate of his brother, but had a presentiment that he still lived, and resolved upon his rescue. In a short time after his arrival, he started with forty-one volunteers in search of his brother. On arriving at the Waco village, he found them hostile, and attacked them. After some resistance, and killing several of their number, they fled, and nine of them were shot while crossing the river. Heavy rains prevented further pursuit, and in fact gave much difficulty in returning home, owing to the boggy condition of the country through which they passed, now embracing the counties of Milam, Burleson and Lee.

"While halting on the Medina River, he was attacked by twelve Tehuacana Indians who had followed, and intended robbing him. In the fight he killed several, and the others fled.

"Resuming his vocation, Captain Brown made a second trip into Mexico, and returned in the fall of 1826 with several hundred horses.

"While halting at San Felipe, a man was discovered ap-proaching rapidly from the west. He seemed to be an Indian riding on horseback. Dashing up, he suddenly reined his horse, dismounted and sprang toward Capt. Brown, exclaiming, 'Brother Henry, don't you know me?' He was the lost and mourned brother. Briefly he explained his eighteen months' captivity; how he had tried every means of escape until he had succeeded while with a company of seventeen on Cummings Creek, now in Fayette County—the band having come down to rob and kill the settlers. Now was the opportunity—with his own well armed party and a few volunteers, about 20 in all, Capt. Brown rode all night and at daylight the following morn-ing, surprised the Indians killing all except one who escaped to carry tidings of the fate of his comrades to his people on the Brazos."

With varying success Capt. Brown continued his business as a trader, making frequent trips to and from Mexico. The sequel to one of his return trips is thus given by his son and biographer—John Henry Brown—"In the month of December,

1828, Capt. Brown was returning from a trading expedition to Mexico, having as the proceeds of his venture, about 500 horses and a considerable amount of silver in rawhide wrappers. He had with him nine Mexican ranchers, a faithful Cherokee Indian, named Luke, and two or three Americans. At night on the road between San Antonio and Gonzales, his animals were stampeded and driven off by a party of hostile Indians, leaving a portion of his men on foot. He repaired to Gonzales and increased his force to twenty nine men. With these he moved leisurely up the country through the mountains, and finally crossed the Colorado a little above the mouth of Pecan Bayou, into the present territory of Brown County, hoping to surprise an Indian village, and recover his own or an equal number of horses and mules.

"He suddenly came upon an encampment almost destitute of horses, and scarcely any women or children. Quite a fight ensued, the defiant Indians, killing one of Brown's Mexicans, besides wounding several of his men slightly. But several Indians falling, the balance suddenly fled into the creek bottom.

"Capt. Brown, still anxious to find the object of his search, traveled westerly till night, and encamped. During the night some of the guard discovered a camp fire apparently about two miles distant. As day dawned the party mounted, and moving cautiously, struck the village just as it was light enough to see. Six of the Mexicans, under prior instructions, stampeded the Indians' horses. The other twenty three men covered the rear, and prepared for battle. Forty or fifty mounted Indians made pursuit and heavy skirmishing ensued, until four or five warriors had been tumbled from their horses. They drew off until reenforced by about as many more who, however, made no attack, but traveled parallel with the retreating party, occasionally showing themselves, till the sun went down. But all this time the horses had been pushed in a gallop, and rendered too tired to be easily stampeded at night—the forlorn hope of the enemy."

Thus the retreat continued by day and night, till the party arrived at Gonzales in January, 1829, with the booty—some 500 head of horses—which were equally divided among the captors.

Capt. Brown died at Columbia, Texas, July 26, 1834, and rests from his toils within a few feet of Josiah H. Bell, and the once noted Capt. Bird Lockhart.

---

## MURDER OF ELIJAH ROARK.

Among other early and worthy colonists on the Brazos was Elijah Roark, a native of North Carolina, who removed with his family "in a large wagon drawn by six mules" and settled on Oyster Creek, in 1824.

Frugal and industrious, his efforts were soon rewarded with crop yields and an increasing stock of cattle, hogs, etc. At that time San Antonio, some 230 miles distant, with but two small settlements en route—at the crossing of the Colorado, and at Gonzales—was the nearest and in fact, the only market in Texas. About the 10th of December, 1829, Mr. Roark, with one man and his little son, Leo, left on his annual market trip with about 100 fat hogs and a wagon load of butter, cheese, bacon, lard, soap, candles and various other things, which they expected to exchange for dry goods, coffee, sugar, salt and other family supplies.

Traveling slow to avoid fatigue of the porkers, the little party reached the "Forty Mile Water Hole"—that distance short of San Antonio—where they camped for the night of Dec. 24, little thinking of the fate that was so soon to befall them. After supper and a pleasant converse on former Yule-tide pleasures, the usual preparations were made for the night—intending an early morning start. We give the sad sequel as told by Leo Roark himself: "One man was to keep guard while the other two slept. Father kept the first watch, and the other man the second. I went on guard about two o'clock, putting on my shoes and hat. The weather had been very warm, but while I was sitting by the camp fire, the wind began to blow from the north. It was getting cold, so I put on my coat, took my gun and knife, and walked a short distance. There was a large log near the road about 100 yards from the camp. Father told me I must walk past the log and turn back. I got to the log and was afraid to pass it. I thought I would go back and wake Father. The mules were staked near, and they were so restless I knew there was something wrong. Before I got back the Indians surrounded the camp. I shot at them and this woke the men. They did not get on their feet before they were murdered. I tried to catch a mule that was tied to a stake, but could not get near the mule. I laid down my gun and tried to cut the rope, but could not as the Indians were so near I had to run. I lost my hat, knife and gun. I was west of the camp and knew the way to San Antonio. Leaving the road, I ran into the mesquite thickets and did not look back nor stop to rest till daylight. Being very thirsty I could find no water, but ate mesquite beans. I traveled all day and late in the evening found water. Here I rested a few moments, but was afraid to lay down as I was so tired and sleepy. With much effort I continued my journey and arrived in San Antonio late in the night. The Mexicans were celebrating Christmas. Next day I got assistance and returned to bury my father. Arriving at the camp it was a horrible sight, both men stripped and scalped, the wagon burned, the mules carried off, and everything taken or destroyed.

"After burying the dead, we built a log pen over the graves to prevent the wolves from digging them up—the burning of the wagon scared the wolves away, or they would have devoured the bodies."

It was three months before Leo returned home—with a company of Mexican soldiers on their way to Nacogdoches. The family did not hear of the death of Mr. Roark and companion till then. The news was a great shock, and a source of sorrow to all the neighborhood.

Brown's narrative of this affair—History of Texas, Vol. l, pp. 159-61—while supplying some important details, is difficult to reconcile with the above absolutely reliable account, and is evidently erroneous. Leo Roark's statement, which we have followed, was copied from the journal of Dr. Pleasant W. Rose, as written therein under date of January, 1834. Dr. Rose's daughter, Mrs. Dilue Harris, in her reminiscences, based on this journal, says: "Mrs. Roark was a widow four years, and had a large family, two grown sons, twin daughters, one daughter grown, two little children, a boy named Andrew, and a girl born several months after the death of the father. I lived by the Roarks three years, and went to school with the two brothers, Jackson and Leo. Mrs. Roark could not talk about the death of her husband, but her son, Leo, often spoke about it; remembering the horrible scene he passed through during that eventful Christmas."

Brown's narrative cannot be correct. He says Robert Spears and Andrew Cox were killed, and that David McCormick escaped and rode with Leo to San Antonio. Beason was from the Colorado, and was killed by Indians—perhaps about the same time Roark was murdered. McCormick was probably in San Antonio when Leo arrived there. At that time it was almost impossible to get correct news. It would be months before events happening near San Antonio would be heard at Brazoria.

Beason's father settled where the town of Columbia now stands. The place was called Beason's Ferry. Santa Anna with his forces crossed the Colorado at Beason's in 1836.

Of the brave boy, Leo, it may be said he lived to participate in several Indian fights, and other stirring events of our history; the affair at Anahuac in 1832; the battles around San Antonio in 1835, and in the battle of San Jacinto. He married a Miss Pevyhouse, and reared a large and respectable family. In 1893, sixty three years after the awful tragedy of that eventful Christmas night, this venerable pioneer died in Ellis County, Texas, full of years and of honors.

# CHAPTER IV.

he year 1830 marks the beginning of an important era in the political history of Texas. Heretofore, during the first years of colonial existence, the American settlers had been left undisturbed save by the hostile tribes of Indians who had constantly harassed them on all sides, as we have seen. But much vigilance had been exercised by Austin and other empresarios in repelling and punishing the savages; and now that the population of the several colonies and settlements were rapidly increasing, they were better able to cope with the common foe.

But now it was that another and most serious drawback to the colonies occurred. Ever jealous of their grasping neighbors on the north, and presumably fearing a too rapid increase in the American population of coveted Texas, on April the 6th of this year, the Mexican Government, now dictated by the arrogant, unprincipled and liberty hating military chieftain, President Anastasia Bustamente, issued the famous and infamous decree—the eleventh article of which virtually prohibited further immigration into Texas from the United States.

As might have been expected, this act spread gloom over the colonists, many of whom, coming in advance, had been industriously occupied in making preparations for the arrival, and, to some degree, the comfort of others—in many instances the wife and children; and coming thus without previous notice or intimation, there was no time to turn back or to warn those who were on the eve of moving, (having perhaps, sacrificed home and property), of the fate that awaited them on their arrival at the border line—garrisoned with Mexican troops to prevent their further progress.

To humiliate and further annoy the colonists, more than a thousand soldiers were sent to the province, and distributed at such points as their services might be needed. The greater portion of these soldiers, it is said, were discharged convicts and enlisted vagabonds, who were to be supported by the money collected from duties and by colonial taxation. Piedras, as ranking officer, with 320 men, was stationed at Nacogdoches, to prevent further emigration from the United States; and this, too, at the time when Robertson's Colony was settling and many families were enroute; Bradburn, with a force of 150 at Anahuac; Ugarteches, 120 at Velasco; Col. Bean, with a force at Fort Teran on the Neches, as Indian agent to the central government—besides the forces at San Antonio and Goliad.

Bradburn was the first to manifest a direct hostile spirit. Says Thomas Jefferson Chambers: "he introduced martial law for the citizens; he took from them their property without their consent and without consideration; he had many of them arrested and imprisoned in the fort of Anahuac; and his troops, who were guilty of robbing and stealing, were by him protected from punishment." But it is not our purpose to enter into a discussion or review of the transpiring and approaching events of our political history at this period, interesting and important as the subject may be, and reference is made thus far somewhat incidentally.

Fortunately for the colonists, while occupied with their internal affairs, the Indians at this date appear to have been less troublesome—overawed for the time perhaps, by the expeditions of Kuykendall and Brown, the previous year. Then, too, the Cherokees, Wacos and Tehuacanas had become involved in a serious strife among themselves.

The trouble encountered by one of these bands, enroute to their people in Texas, and while temporarily halting on Red River in the winter of 1828-29, is graphically narrated by John Henry Brown, in the only reliable account of this affair—written and published more than half a century ago: "They had not been at this place very long before their village was discovered by a party of Wacos, on a robbing expedition from the Brazos; and these freebooters, true to their instincts from time immemorial, lay concealed till the silent midnight hour, and then, stealthily entering the herds of the sleeping Cherokees, stampeded their horses, driving off a large number. To follow them was labor in vain—but to quietly forget the deed was not the maxim among the red sons of Tennessee.

## RED WARRIORS IN DEADLY STRIFE.

"A council was held and the matter discussed. After the opinions of the warriors had been given, the principal war chief rose, and in substance said: 'My brothers. The wild men of the far off Brazos have come into our camp while the Cherokees slept. They have stolen our most useful property. Without horses we are poor, and cannot make corn. The Cherokees will hasten to plant their corn for this spring, and while that is springing from the ground, and growing under the Great Spirit, and shall be waving around our women and children, we will leave some old men and women to watch it, and the Cherokee braves will spring upon the cunning Wacos of the Brazos as they sprang upon us.'

"The corn was planted, and in the month of May, 1829, a war party of fifty-five, well armed, left the village on foot in search of the Wacos. At this time the principal village of the Wacos, was on the bluff where the beautiful city of Waco now greets the eye on the west bank of the Brazos. One band of the Tehuacana (Ta-wak-a-na) Indians, who have always been more or less connected with the Wacos, were living on the east bank of the river, three miles below. Both bands had erected rude fortifications, by scooping up the earth in various places and throwing up a circular embankment three or four feet high, the remains of which still are to be seen. The principal work of this kind at the Waco village occupied a natural sink in the surface.

"The Cherokees struck the Brazos above the village some forty miles, and traveled downwards until they discovered signs of the proximity, and then secreted themselves in the cedar brake till night. The greater portion of the night was spent in examining the position, through experienced scouts. Having made the necessary observations, the scouts reported near daylight, when the war chief admonished them of what they had come for—revenge! Waco scalps! horses! and led them forth from their hiding place, under the bank of the river, to a point about four hundred yards from the wigwams of the slumbering Wacos. Here they halted till the rays of light, on that lovely May morning, began to gild the eastern horizon. The time for action had come. Moving with the noiseless, elastic step peculiar to the sons of the forest, the Cherokees approached the camp. But a solitary Waco was aroused, and was collecting the remains of his fire of the previous night, preparatory to his morning repast. His Indian ear caught the sounds of footsteps on the brush, a glance of his lynx eye revealed the approaching foe. A single shrill yell from him, which echoed far and near through the Brazos forest, brought every Waco to his feet. The terrible Cherokee war-whoop was their morning greeting, accompanied by a shower of leaden rain. But though surprised, the Wacos out numbered their assailants many times, their women and children must be protected or sacrificed, their ancient home, where the bones of their fathers had been buried for ages, was assailed by unknown intruders. The chief rallied the warriors, and made a stand, the fight became general, and as the sun arose majestically over the towering trees of the east, he beheld the red men of Tennessee and the red men of Texas in deadly strife. But the bows and arrows of the Wacos could not compete with the unerring rifles of the Cherokees. The Wacos were falling rapidly, while the Cherokees were unharmed.

"After half an hour's strife, amid yells and mutual imprecations, the Wacos signalled a retreat, and they fell back in confusion, taking refuge in the fortified sinkhole. Here, though hemmed in, they were quite secure, having a great advantage. Indeed they could kill every Cherokee who might peradventure, risk his person too near the brink.

"The Cherokees had already killed many, and now held a council, to consider what they should do. It was proposed by

The Cherokee's Revenge for His Slain Boy

1. Wm. A. A. "Big Foot" Wallace,  2. Samuel M. Williams,
3. "Ran" Foster, The Hunter and
4. Moses Austin, Father of Stephen F. Austin

one brave that they should strip to a state of nature, march into the sink-hole in a body, fire their pieces, then drop them, and with tomahawks alone endeavor to kill every man, woman and child among the Wacos. A half breed named Smith, who was in favor of this desperate measure, as an incentive to his comrades, stripped himself, fastened a dozen horsebells (which he had picked up in camp) around his waist, and commenced galloping and yelling around the sink-hole, now and then jumping on the embankment and then cursing the Wacos lustily. The arrows were hurled at him by the score, but he fell not.

"Just as the Cherokee council was coming to a close, at about an hour after sunrise, they heard a noise like distant thunder on the opposite side of the river, and delayed a few moments to discover its cause. Very soon they discovered a large body of mounted Indians rising the river banks a little below them. What could it mean? they murmured one to another. The story is soon told. A messenger had rushed from the Wacos in the outset, for the Tehuacana village, begging help, and now two hundred Tehuacana warriors, mounted and ready for the fray, were at hand. The whole aspect of the day was changed in a moment. To conquer this combined force was impossible—to escape themselves would require prudence. The Tehuacanas, in coming up, cut off a Cherokee boy, twelve years old, killed and scalped him, and placed his scalp, and held it up defiantly to the view of the Cherokees. The boy was an only child, and his father beheld this scene. The brave man's eye glared with fury. Without a word he threw from his body every piece of his apparel, seized a knife in one hand, a tomahawk in the other. 'What will you?' demanded the chief. 'Die with my brave boy. Die slaying the wild men who have plucked the last rose from my bosom!' The chief interceded and told him it was madness; the Cherokee listened not; with rapid strides he rushed among the Tehuacanas, upon certain death; but ere death had seized its victim, he had killed several and died shouting defiance in their midst.

"The Tehuacanas occupied the post oaks just below the Cherokees, and kept up a lusty shouting, but ventured not within rifle shot. The latter seeing that on an open field they could not resist such numbers—having taken fifty-five Waco scalps, (equal to their own number) and having lost two men and the boy—now fell back into the cedar brake and remained there till night. They were convinced that their safety depended upon a cautious retreat, for if surrounded on the prairie, they would be annihilated. When night came on they crossed the river, traveling down the sand bank a mile or two, as if they were going down the country, thence, turning up the stream, waded up the edge of the water some six or seven miles, (the river being low and remarkably even), and thus eluded pursuit. In due time they reached their Red River villages, without the thousand horses they anticipated, but with fifty-five Waco scalps—glory enough in their estimation. The entire band was now speedily collected and amid much rejoicing and with great noise, it is said, indulged in one of the grandest war dances ever witnessed in Texas."

---

## THE CHEROKEE AND TEHUACANA FIGHT.

"The Cherokees, it seems, did not forget the Tehuacanas, but held them to strict account—determined to take revenge on them for their interference in the engagement with the Wacos— as the sequel will show. To this end it appears, early in the summer of 1830, they armed and equipped one hundred and twenty of their bravest and best fighters, who marched upon one of the principal villages of the enemy.

"The Tehuacanas, like the Wacos, had several principal villages, favorite resorts, from some peculiarity, as fine springs of water, abundance of buffalo, etc. One of them, and perhaps their most esteemed locality, was at the southern point of the hills of the same name, now in the upper edge of Limestone County. Around these springs there is a large amount of loose limestone on the surface, as well as in the hills, and the whole surrounding country is one of rare beauty and loveliness.

"The Tehuacanas had erected several small enclosures of these loose stones, about three feet high, leaving occasional spaces some two feet square, resembling the mouths of furnaces. Over the tops they threw poles and spread buffalo hides, and when attacked, their women, old men and children, would seek refuge in the same, and lying flat on the ground, would send their arrows and bullets through these apertures whenever an enemy came in range. From the attacks of small arms, such a protection, however primitive, was generally quite effective.

"This party of Cherokees, having been informed of the locality of this place, and the value set upon it by the Tehuacanas, and knowing that it was a considerable distance from the Wacos, determined to seek it out and there wreak vengeance upon those who had by their own act called forth feelings of hostility. Guided by an Indian who had explored the country as a trapper, they reached the place in due season. When discovered, the Tehuacanas were engaged at a play of ball around the little fort. The Cherokees stripped for action at once, while the ball players, promptly ceased that amusement, rushed their women and children into the retreats, and prepared for defense. They had quite a large village, and outnumbered the Cherokees in fighting men.

"A random fight commenced, the Cherokees using the surrounding trees as protection, and taking the matter as a business transaction, made their advances from tree to tree with prudence. Their aim, with the 'rest' against the trees, told with effect, and one by one, notwithstanding their hideous yells and capering to and fro, the Tehuacanas were biting the dust.

"The moment one was wounded, unless a very brave fellow, he would crawl into the hiding place among the women and children, unless, perchance, on his way, a Cherokee ball brought him to the ground.

"The fight continued this way an hour or more, when, upon a signal, the whole body retired within the breastworks. At this time the Cherokees, elated by what they supposed to be a victory, charged upon the open holes, ringing their victorious war-whoop most furiously. But they were soon convinced that though concealed, the besieged were not powerless, for here they received a shower of arrows and balls from the hidden enemy which tumbled several of their braves alongside of those they killed on the other side. Yet, excited as they had become, they were not easily convinced that prudence in that case was the better part of valor. On the contrary, they maintained the unequal contest for some time, until one of their old men advised a talk.

"They withdrew a short distance and held a consultation. Their leaders said they had come there for revenge and they would not relinquish their design so long as a Cherokee brave was left to fight—that to go back to their people and report a defeat, would disgrace them—they would die on the field rather than bear such tidings. 'Where there's a will, there's a way' is a trite old adage, and at this juncture of affairs, it was verified by the Cherokees. The old man who had advised the 'talk,' now made a suggestion, which was seconded by all. He proposed that a party should be sent off a short distance to cut dry grass and bring a load; that men, loaded with this material, should cautiously approach each hole in the breastworks, from the sides, using the grass as a shield on the way; that the door holes should be stopped up with it, (with new supplies constantly arriving), and set on fire, by which very simple process the inmates would be suffocated or compelled to throw off the hides and leap out, breathless and more or less blinded through the smoke, while the Cherokees, stationed around in circles, would have an easy time in butchering their astonished red brethren. This was a rich idea and delighted with the anticipated fun on their part, and misery among their enemies, the Cherokees speedily made all their arrangements and disposed of their fighting men to the best advantage. The grass was placed in the required position, and at the same moment, set on fire. For a moment or two no response was heard from within; but very soon the smoke was seen escaping through the rocks and from under the skins, proving that each little refuge was full of the strangulating exhalation. To endure such a torture long, was beyond human power; and in a little while a doleful howl issued forth, followed by a significant upheaving of the buffalo-skin roofs, and a rush of the gasping victims, blinded by smoke, leaping over the walls, they knew not where. To render the picture more appalling, the exulting Cherokees set up a terrible yelling, and dealt death to the doomed creatures with their guns, tomahawks and scalping knives until all were slain, or had made their escape from the dreadful sacrifice by headlong flight. Quite a number of squaws and children, and perhaps a few men, had been unable to rise, and died from suffocation inside the works."

And thus ended this tragic scene in the course of our Indian warfare. Comparatively few of the Tehuacanas escaped. The surviving women and children were preserved prisoners, and a considerable number of horses, blankets, skins, and indeed the entire camp equipage, fell into the hands of the victors, who returned to their people on Red River in triumph, displaying not only their booty, but a large number of the greatest of all Indian symbols of glory, scalps.

While no serious troubles from Indians appear to have been committed during this and the succeeding year or two, the isolated and extreme border settlers suffered from occasional thieving forays of the Wacos and Tehuacanas.

In November, a party of eleven Wacos entered the settlements some twenty miles west of San Felipe. They were on foot, and well supplied with ropes and bridles. A party consisting of Adam Lawrence, Thomas Stevens, Abner Kuykendall, Charles Gates, B. Kuykendall, George Robinson, William Cooper and five others, were soon collected to intercept the Indians. Discovering them camped near the house of John Stevens, on Caney Creek, the settlers made a surprise attack at dawn.

"Favored by a gully and a dense fog, we approached within thirty feet of the Indians (part of whom had not yet risen), before they perceived us, at which moment we delivered our fire." As the Indians fled one of them shot William Cooper through the heart, killing him instantly. This caused considerable confusion and delay on the part of the settlers. "Late in the morning," says Kuykendall, "the trail of the Indians was followed as far as the bottom of Caney Creek, five or six hundred yards, some red strips marked their course across the prairie and two or three conical shaped pieces of rotten wood, with which these Indians are generally provided, to plug their wounds, were picked up on the trail, saturated with blood." The carcass of one of these Indians was found in the bottom, and from the Mexicans at Tenoxtitlan, some two weeks later, it was learned that seven of them died from their wounds before reaching their homes.

1831—Despite the prohibitory decree of the previous year and the forebodings of political troubles, the American population of Texas continued to increase—numbering about twenty thousand. The most part of these prohibited emigrants came, however, under the general provisions of the law, on their own account, halting east of the Trinity, where they fixed homes.

Having designated their lands, these settlers were anxious for legal possession, and, to that end, "in 1831 the Governor of the State had commissioned Don Francisco Madero as commissioner to issue titles to the settlers on and near the region of Liberty." Justly exercising the authority of his position, and most gratifying to the people of that section, Madero created the municipality of Liberty, appointing Hugh B. Johnson as Alcalde.

But for this, the Commissioner was arrested and imprisoned, the Alcalde removed and the municipality of "Libertad" dissolved—a new Ayuntamiento being set up by the despotic and obdurate military satrap, Bradburn, with its seat at Anahuac under his immediate surveillance. Thus far, this suffices to show the general trend of the events transpiring in, and most affecting, the colonies.

Fortunate for the otherwise vexed colonists, no serious depredations by Indians appear to have been committed at this time. However, the year 1831, says Yoakum, did not pass away without being witness to a battle, which, considering the number engaged and its results, was the hardest contested field in Texas.

One of the early and unique pioneer characters of Texas, was Caiaphas K. Ham, born in the year 1803. He was an intimate friend and associate of the Bowies in Louisiana, and came to Texas in 1830, residing with Colonel James Bowie and his beau-

tiful Spanish wife—the daughter of Vice Governor Vera-
mendi—at the Mission of San Jose, on the San Antonio River
some four miles below the city.

Soon after his arrival in Texas, Mr. Ham decided to join the
Comanche Indians for the purpose of buying horses for the
Louisiana market. At that time, 1830, this tribe was at peace with
the Texans. "Being in San Antonio frequently," says Ham's
narrative, "on almost every occasion I saw parties of Comanche
Indians who came in to trade. My desire was to know something
of them and the country they wandered over. Colonel Bowie at
first opposed the scheme, but finding I was determined, he
assisted me in getting things in good shape. A Comanche chief
named Incorroy, came in. An interpreter was employed and a
treaty made. I was adopted into the chief's family, with an
assurance that I could return to the whites whenever I chose. A
supply of powder, balls, butcher knives and brass rings, was
laid in." The object in adverting to this freak will be seen farther
on, when it will be discovered that this trading expedition had
an important bearing upon an affair affecting Colonel Bowie.

"We left San Antonio," continues Ham's narrative, "and
started for the chief's camp. I had no care on my mind; in the
morning I saddled one horse and packed another—the latter
being turned over to the care of my Indian mama.

"About this time a party of Wacos were encamped near us.
They wanted to trade, and had good horses. Incorroy instructed
me how to trade—I gave one pint of powder, eight balls, one
plug of tobacco, one butcher knife, and two brass rings, for a
horse."

After some five months, Ham received a message from
Colonel Bowie advising him to return to San Antonio at once,
as the Mexican Government was preparing to make war upon
the Indian tribes; and that if found among the Comanches he
would be killed with them. During his stay with the Indians,
Ham had gained their friendship completely, and had himself
become attached to his red friends. When he left the chief,
twenty-five warriors escorted him to San Antonio. Mr. Ham
was convinced that the real motive for his recall from the

Indians was an intention on the part of the Bowies to revisit the celebrated silver mine near San Saba, which had been discovered, and partially examined by Bowie, it appears, some time previous to 1831.

The shaft was about eight feet deep, the bottom was reached by means of steps cut in a live oak log. Bowie used his tomahawk in getting possession of some of the ore; which he carried to New Orleans, had it assayed, and it "panned out" rich. He soon returned to San Antonio and quietly set about organizing a select little party to revisit and examine the mine. Mr. Ham was one of the party selected.

These facts are deemed permissible in this connection as shedding some light on the thrilling episode to follow.

## BOWIE'S FAMOUS INDIAN FIGHT.

Perhaps the celebrated engagement known as "Bowie's Indian Fight" is without a parallel on this continent; certainly a more skillful and heroic defense against such fearful odds was never made on Texas soil.

Organized, equipped and led by the Bowie brothers, the little exploring party consisting of Rezin P. and James Bowie, David Buchanan, Robert Armstrong, Jesse Wallace, Matthew Doyle, Thomas McCaslin, C. K. Ham, James Coryell, (for whom Coryell county was named), and two servant boys, Charles, a negro, and Gonzales, a Mexican, set out from San Antonio on November 2, 1831, to locate and re-open the long abandoned and lost silver mines of Almagres, SOMEWHERE, in the vicinity of the old San Saba Mission. The secret of the location of this celebrated and rich silver mine was well guarded by the Indians, who wished to prevent another influx of miners and adventurers into their hunting grounds—a condition that brought about the fate of the San Saba Mission, when its inmates, the miners, and people there congregated, were suddenly fell upon and all massacred by the incensed Indians in 1758.

The little party traveled out and met with no adventure of note until the 19th, when they were overtaken by a party of friendly Comanches, who informed Bowie that a large body of hostile Indians were on his trail swearing that they would take the scalp of every white man in the party. The hostile Indians were the Tehuacanas, Wacos and Caddos, numbering 164 well armed braves. They were too strong for Bowie to risk a fight, and even when the Comanche chief offered to join Bowie with his band of sixteen men, the odds were so fearful that Bowie declined the generous offer and pressed forward with the intention of reaching the old fort on the San Saba before night. But the Texans soon struck a rocky road, and their horses' feet were so worn and sore that they were compelled to stop for the night in a small grove of live oaks. This grove was in an open prairie, interspersed with rocks and clumps of trees. Near it, on the west, was a stream of water, and on the north, a thicket of small trees about ten feet high. Into this thicket, and through prickly pears, the Texans cut a road, in order that they might be prepared for defense in case of an attack by the Indians. They then posted sentries and hobbled their horses, but they were not molested until the next morning, when they discovered Indians on their trail before they could get ready to depart for the fort. One of the Indians was some distance in advance of his comrades. He was on foot with his head to the ground, following the trail of the Texans. Bowie and his men flew to arms. The red men gave a loud warwhoop and began their preparations for an attack. While some of the bucks on horseback were reconnoitering the ground, the Texans decided, on account of the fearful odds, against them—164 to 11—to avoid, if possible, a fight so unequal and desperate. It was agreed that Rezin Bowie should go out and parley with the Indians and try to make terms of peace. He went, accompanied by David Buchanan. They walked to within forty yards of the enemy's line and invited the Indians to send out their chief, so that they could have a talk with him. The Indians who had been addressed in their own tongue replied with a "How do! How do!" followed by a volley of rifle shots, one of which wounded Buchanan in the leg. Bowie replied with the contents of his double barreled shot gun, and pistol, then taking his wounded comrade on his back, started for the camp.

The Indians fired another volley, and Buchanan was wounded twice more, but not mortally. The savages then pursued with tomahawks and were close upon Bowie and his unfortunate companion, when the Texans charged them with rifles, killing four and putting the others to flight. Bowie and his men then returned to their positions and for five minutes all was quiet.

Then there came fierce yells from a hill red with Indians, and so near that the Texans could hear the voice of the chief as he urged his men to charge. "Who is loaded?" cried the Texas leader. "I am," answered Cephas Ham. "Then shoot that chief," said Bowie, and Ham fired, breaking the leg of the Indian and killing his pony. As the wounded chief went hopping around his horse, four of the Texans, who had reloaded, fired, and he fell. Several of his men, who advanced to bear his body away, were killed, and the whole band fell back beyond the hill. But they soon covered the hill again, bringing up their women, and there was rapid firing on both sides. Another chief, advancing on horseback and urging his men forward, was killed by James Bowie. Meanwhile a number of the Indians succeeded in getting under the creek bank in the rear of the Texans. They opened fire at forty yards distance and Matthew Doyle was shot through the breast, and Thomas McCaslin, running forward to avenge him, was shot through the body. The firing then became general from all quarters and the Texans, finding themselves too much exposed, retreated to the thicket, where they were in point blank range of the riflemen under the creek bank and soon dislodged them.

In the thicket the Texans were not only well screened, but had a clear view of the Indians on the prairie. They baffled the savages in their shots, by moving six or eight feet the moment they fired, for the only mark for the red men was the smoke of the Texans' guns, and they would immediately put a shower of balls on the spot where they saw the smoke.

After the fight had continued in this way for two hours, the Indians saw that they could not dislodge the Texans with bullets, and they resorted to fire. By this they expected to route the little party and secure an opportunity of carrying off their dead and wounded under cover of the smoke, for the rifles of the rangers had brought down several at every round. They set fire to the dry grass to the windward of the thicket. The flames soared high and rushed forward with great fury. The Texans cleared away the grass around their wounded comrades and made whatever barriers they could against the flames by piling up rock and bushes to make a flimsy breastwork. Meanwhile the Indians, who had succeeded in carrying off their dead and wounded under cover of the smoke, returned again to the attack. The wind suddenly shifted to the north and the red men quick to see the advantage it gave them, seized their chance and again set fire to the grass. The flames went roaring ten feet high toward the thicket, while the shouts and yells of the savages rent the air.

This was the critical moment in the fight. The sparks began to fly so fast that no man could open his powder horn without danger of being blown to pieces. In case the Indians should make a charge under cover of the smoke, which was expected, they could give only one effectual fire and then rely on their knives. Besides, there was great danger from the flames, but as they came to the edge of the cleared space around the wounded, those stalwart men smothered them with buffalo hides, bear skins and blankets.

The savages did not charge, but the fire left so little of the thicket that the Texans took refuge in the ring they had made around the wounded, and began raising their breastworks higher with earth and loose rocks. The Indians, who succeeded in removing their dead and wounded from the field under cover of the smoke, seeing the Texans were still alive and dangerous, became discouraged, and as night approached, retired from the field.

The Texans strengthened their breastworks and filled their vessels and skins with water and awaited the attack which they expected the following morning. All night they heard the savages wailing over their dead and at day light they shot a chief who was mortally wounded, which was according to the custom of their tribe. They did not renew the attack the next

morning, but went to a cave about a mile away for shelter and
to bury their dead. Two of the rangers ventured out of the little
fort and went to the place where the Indians had spent the night.
There they counted forty-eight bloody places on the ground
where the dead and wounded Indians had been laid as they
were brought from the battlefield.

According to the best authorities, it is estimated that the
Indians had eighty odd killed and wounded. The Indians themselves admitted they had 52 killed, and half as many wounded.
The Texans lost one killed and had three wounded. The little
party remained in their rudely fortified camp for eight days
after the fight, attending their wounded, and watching for an
opportunity to slip away and elude pursuit. The homeward
journey consumed ten days. The manner of their reception is
thus pathetically told by one of the number—Mr. Ham.

"The Comanches, believing it impossible for eleven men to
defend themselves successfully against the fearful odds of fifteen to one, went into San Antonio and reported the almost
certain death of Bowie and his party. It was the general opinion
that the explorers had been massacred. Stephen Bowie had
arrived in Texas and accepted the report as true. He was raising
a company to avenge the sanguinary murder of his two brothers. The shades of night had fallen on the city. Sad hearts were
bewailing the fate of the adventurous Americans. A party of
men, mostly on foot, weary and soiled by travel, entered the
streets of the Queen City of the West. Some of the men were
recognized. A shout went up; it was repeated, it spread from
street to street, from house to house. Stout men quivered with
excitement, tears of joy dimmed bright eyes. Fearless men
rushed forward to grasp in friendship and admiration, the
hands of citizens who had proved themselves heroes in a contest
demanding courage, prudence, endurance and all the noble
qualities adorning the soldier and the patriot. 'Bowie's party
have returned! They have won a glorious victory!' was the cry.
House to house was illuminated. The people in their heart of
hearts decreed them a triumph. And well they deserved it. The
pages of history record but few such achievements. It stands

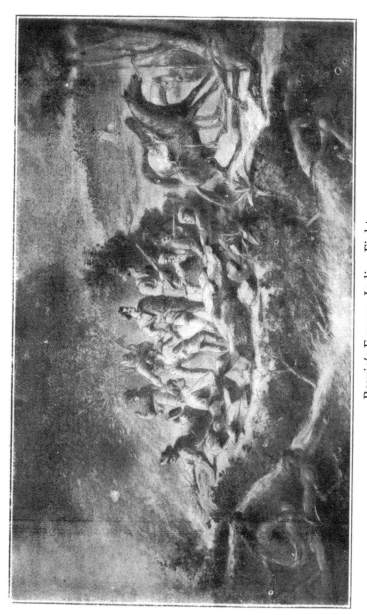

Bowie's Famous Indian Fight

almost alone upon the scenic walls of Fame's grand temple. The valorous men who braved their breasts to the assaults of a savage enemy in overwhelming numbers, who fought without fear and without hope, and rolled back the tide of barbaric aggression,* should be remembered and honored as long as civilization endures and gratitude has a place in the human heart." (Unpublished memoirs of Col. John S. Ford.)

Ere Long, nothing daunting the brave Bowies, they determined to again seek, and yet possess, the coveted treasure; and to this end, we are told, they organized and equipped a second, and more formidable expedition, of some thirty men, which was well nigh starting when the Texas war for independence opened; and, true to their patriotic promptings, the Bowie brothers were among the first to heed the call to arms. They hastened to Gonzales, led at Concepcion, and were among the first to respond to the cry, "Who will follow old Ben Milam into San Antonio?" Three months later James Bowie fell in the Alamo, bequeathing his name and heroism to all succeeding generations of Texans; while Rezin P. Bowie, mourning the untimely fate of his brother, and leader in all matters, of an adventurous nature at least, retired to his home and estate in Louisiana, where he led a profitable and exemplary, but less hazardous, life, till his death in New Orleans, January 17, 1841.

And thus tragically closed the history of this famous, but, perhaps, forever lost, Almagres—since ever called the "Bowie Mine," because Bowie was the only American who ever knew the secret of its location. "His expedition began," says one, "under the rainbow of promise, but closed under the cloud of appalling disaster."

Since that time, eighty years ago, many other adventurous and enterprising parties have sought in vain to locate this mine. The treasure is yet hidden, and will likely remain a mystery.

The following letter will throw some light on the character of the Bowies, and is here appropriately inserted:

* The citizens of Bexar in a memorial to the general engagement, stated that within ten years—1822 to 1832—ninety seven citizens, besides soldiers killed in battles, had been murdered by hostile Indians.

New Orleans, La. May 3, 1889

Mr. Jas. T. DeShields,

Dear Sir:

I am, as you have been informed, connected with the Bowies, being the grand-daughter of Col. Rezin P., and grand niece of Col. James Bowie; and as such I thank you for your kind intentions in regard to them. Some "penny-a-liners" more fit to write for five cent, blood and thunder, sensational publications, than for history, have seen fit to describe them as pirates, border ruffians and characters of such ilk, simply because Grand-father originated the knife bearing his name; and that for use only as a hunting knife. The Bowies were men of honor, and gentlemen, possessing both intelligence and handsome physiques. They loved adventure and excitement of a legitimate nature; they never sought quarrels, for they were peaceful and amiable, but fear had no home in their souls; and combined with a just idea of their own rights, was the courage to defend them.

Not only were they heroes, but the sons of a hero, for their father, Rezin Bowie, Sr., was one of Gen. Marion's men, and their mother was of sterling worth. She met her husband in Georgia, during the Revolution, when with the spirit of a patriot, she was nursing back to life the defenders of her country.

I handed your letter to my brother, (Major John S. Moore, 167 Gravier St.) and would advise you to address him personally, he is often in receipt of such requests as yours.

My mother is living, and with my brother, she is the only living child of my grand-father. Uncle James left no children, his wife and two babies died previously to his death at the Alamo.

We have excellent portraits of Grandpa and Uncle James. Thanking you once more, I remain,

Respectfully yours,
Mrs. Eugine Soniet de Fosset.

# CHAPTER V.

hile memorable in the history of Texas as the year in which the colonists first took up arms in defense of their liberties and vested rights against Mexican military usurpation and despotism, the records show but few incidents of Indian warfare in 1832.*

Yoakum, however, tells us that "the Indians along the Texan frontier were generally mischievous—in fact there was scarcely a month that passed, but some murder or robbery was perpetrated by them." So we see that the year 1832 was not an exception. Hence it was some consolation to the Texans that, during this year, the different tribes had a good deal of fighting among themselves, especially a great battle between the Comanches and Shawnees, in which the former were badly defeated.

---

* But this year did not pass away without much apprehension of serious troubles with Indians. "This was a year of suffering for Texas; for no sooner had they been relieved from the contest with the Mexicans, than they were still more alarmed by the ravages of the Indians, who were making continued depredations upon the frontiers. Their fears were not without foundation; for the powerful bodies of Indians in their vicinity were truly formidable." Against these savages their own moral and physical resources constituted about the sole means of defense, for at that time there were less than seventy Mexican soldiers in Texas, and these were sustained by the citizens of Bexar. And too, the calamities of the settlers were still further increased by the appearance of the dreaded cholera, which had been long traveling westward, desolating hamlets, towns and cities, in its well marked course; and which reached Texas in the fall of this year, raging with fearful violence and claiming as its victims, many of the valuable and useful citizens of the struggling colonies.

## SHAWNEES OUTWIT COMANCHES.

In 1832 a party of five hundred Comanches came into San Antonio. At that time a party of Shawnees, twenty-five in number, were encamped in the hills, about thirty-five miles north of the town. A Comanche Indian attempted to carry off one of the Shawnee women, who was in the town. She fled to her own people, gave them information of what occurred, and they prepared an ambush for their enemies at a point where they expected them to encamp. The Comanches came as anticipated, and took off their packs. Just at this time, the Shawnees opened fire on them; and though they rallied often, so deadly was the effect and so secure the position of the attacking party, that the Comanches at last fled, leaving one hundred and seventy-five dead on the field. The discomfitted party returned to San Antonio, and the Mexican authorities sent out a force to assist them; but the Shawnees had made good their retreat, and thus far escaped the wrath of the exasperated Comanches.*

It will be remembered that at this period, and perhaps during the next few years, the Comanches were on friendly terms with the Americans.** We have seen that a large delega-

* Telegraph and Texas Register, Aug. 14, 1839
**Although the Comanches frequently raided the Mexican settlements along the Rio Grande, killing rancheros and capturing women and children, during the first years of the nineteenth century, they were all along friendly to the American settlers, and no serious hostilities can be charged to this tribe previous to about 1834-35. Ample evidence can be produced that these Indians maintained their friendship for the Americans till provoked to hostility. David G. Burnet, afterward prominent in the political affairs of Texas, lived with the Comanches from 1817 to 1819, and gives them a good reputation. Likewise, Gen. S.F. Austin had ample demonstrations of their honorable intentions and friendly feelings toward the American settlers. And it may be remembered that late as 1831, the people of Gonzales gave a barbecue dinner to about one hundred Comanches—the ladies of that then village assisting in serving the repast and entertaining their swarthy visitors; who after regaling themselves, mounted their horses and departed, with mutual expressions of good will. But this is in marked contrast with all that soon follows concerning the Comanches and their attitude toward the whites. Once provoked to hostility, they commenced a most cruel, and bloody warfare—waged with relentless severity

tion of this tribe met Sam Houston, as Indian agent of the United States, in friendly council at San Antonio during the last days of this year or the first of 1833. "During 1833 and 1834," says Kenney, "their name does not appear in the hostilities ascribed to known tribes, but Indian hostilities in general, would blacken many pages."

## BATTLE OF VELASCO.

Recurring to political affairs, and further noticing the war-like commotions of the Americans and Mexicans, in the colonies, during this year, it will be seen that Bradburn, the Mexican commandant at Anahuac, in violation of civil law, arrested and imprisoned, seventeen colonists, including Wm. B. Travis, Samuel T. Allen and Patrick C. Jack. The settlers flew to arms, hastened to Anahuac and demanded their release. This was promised in return for the surrender of twenty of Bradburn's soldiers who had been captured. The soldiers were delivered, the settlers meanwhile retiring to Turtle Bayou, where they held a mass meeting June 13, at which they passed resolutions denouncing Bustamente, and pledging support to the Mexican Constitution of 1824, and the "patriot Gen. Santa Anna." The commissioners sent to receive the Texan prisoners were denied admission to the fort and were fired on. It was recognized that nothing further could be done without cannon and reinforcements. John Austin, in command of a detail of men, was sent to Brazoria for both.

During his absence, Col. Piedras, commander at Nacogdoches and Bradburn's military superior, arrived at Anahuac, set Travis and his companions at liberty, and removed Bradburn

for nearly half a century against the settlements in Texas. Whether true or not, it is said the Comanches were first provoked to enmity by a company of French traders from New Orleans, enroute to Santa Fe, and who gave poisoned bread to a begging party of Comanches. The fatal results following greatly incensed the Indians, who thereupon determined on revenge, and declared war upon the whites in general.

from office. Not knowing what was transpiring at Anahuac, John Austin, with one hundred and twelve men and a schooner, carrying cannon, started from Brazoria. When they reached Velasco the Mexican officer, Ugartechea, in command at that post, refused to permit the schooner to pass. Thereupon was fought the battle of Velasco, the first collision between the colonists and Mexican soldiery in which blood was shed in regular warfare, much more of an actual conflict than the battle of San Jacinto, four years later, and one of the most brilliant actions ever fought within the limits of the United States—equal in point of success to the exploit of Dick Dowling and his men at Sabine Pass during the war between the States, and inferior only to the defense of the Alamo by Travis and his comrades in 1836.

False rumors of occurrences in Texas reaching Mexico, where Santa Anna was engaged in a struggle with the tyrant Bustamente for the supremacy, Santa Anna immediately despatched to Texas, Gen. Jose Antonio Mexia, with four hundred infantry and five armed vessels to learn what the intentions of the Texans were. Stephen F. Austin, while at Victoria, the capital of Tamaulipas, learned of this expedition and hastened to Matamoras, where he joined Mexia and proceeded with him to the mouth of the Brazos. Mexia visited Brazoria, San Felipe and other places, and was thoroughly convinced that the Texans were loyal to the Republic and genuine supporters of the liberal cause. A banquet was given in his honor, at which speeches were made glowing with patriotic enthusiasm and toasts were drunk to Santa Anna. He then returned to Mexico, taking with him most of the troops stationed in the coast country and at San Antonio. Shortly thereafter James W. Bullock and three hundred men demanded that Piedras declare for Santa Anna. Piedras refused. A brisk fight ensued, with the result that Piedras retired with his forces, or rather retreated from his post at Nacogdoches during the night, to the Angelina River, where he was overtaken by a detachment of colonists, under James Bowie to whom he surrendered—his soldiers at once shouting, "Long live Santa Anna!"

These remarks make permissible, extracts from a recently discovered and highly interesting letter, penned by the empresario, Alex. S. Thompson, colleague and partner with Sterling C. Robertson of the famous "Nashville Company," afterwards known as "Robertson's Colony."

The organization of this company was fully perfected in 1830, and the following year Thompson came out to the colony bringing his family. Nashville subsequently became the capital of Milam County for several years, and a son, W. D. Thompson, was the first county clerk in 1837. The ruins of his home may yet be seen on the site of this old town. Another son, "Mac" Thompson, was one of the seventeen unfortunate Meir prisoners who drew the black beans, and were shot. Alex S. Thompson lived many years in Burleson county, where he died in 1863, aged seventy-eight years. But to the letter:

Texas, Austin Colony, Aug. 5, 1832

My Dear Son:

I suppose you have seen in the public prints something of our commotions, and no doubt felt anxious for us. A few weeks ago the clouds of war hung thick over us, but now are all dispersed, and more prosperous times are approaching than ever have been seen in this country.

Our commotions in this colony arose from Colonel Bradburn having taken four or five Americans of the district in which he lived, and put them in confinement.

The alcalde of said district went to him and demanded them, wishing to have them tried by the civil authorities. He refused, but at length agreed that the Ayuntemento might try them, which they did, and set them at liberty.

A short time afterwards, Bradburn had them again in confinement. This irritated the people of this colony, and a good many of them volunteered and went down to Bradburn and demanded the prisoners. He required time to deliberate, which they granted, but it is said he sent off for help, and then refused, after forfeiting his honor. Our men then sent on for all the cannon that was in the colony, which they got and put on board a vessel at Brazoria, but the Colonel that commanded at the mouth of the Brazos, would not let them pass. They then attacked the fort and after a fight of eight hours the fort surrendered, having fired ninety rounds of artillery and 4,000 musket shots. Our vessel discharged 116 rounds of cannon. I have not learned how many rifle balls, but such bold militia I have never heard of before.

They stood in the open prairie and fought without cover, and even marched up in thirty-two paces of the mouth of the cannon and shot the Spaniards as fast as they approached to fire. It is said there were 150 in the fort and 190 of our men. They killed six of our men and we killed thirty four and wounded, I think about forty.

About that time Colonel Piedras, who commanded at Nacogdoches, went to our army on the Trinity and treated with them and went down to Bradburn and arrested him, and delivered all the prisoners to them, which they passed over to the civil power.

The men thus attained their object, and returned home peaceably, first showing the military that the constitution should be adhered to and the civil power rule.

Soon after this, Colonel Austin, who was in the interior, came on with a colonel in Santa Anna's service and was joined by the whole colony. They sent on expresses to the different garrisons, which had already consented to join them

Austin says as soon as the legislature meets, the State will declare in favor of Santa Anna.

I do not suppose they will have any more fighting here. It is now past a doubt that Santa Anna will gain his point. General Teran has killed himself, and I have understood nearly all his army that were not killed have joined Santa Anna, who now holds all the ports of entry, and commands all the revenue. He has men and money plenty, while the other side is destitute of money, and their men are continually deserting them and joining Santa Anna.

Santa Anna is said to be a true republican, and determined not to lay down his arms without republicanism prevails. He has declared himself in favor of religious toleration and free emigration, which are two things very desirable for this country, and so soon as that takes place, our country will begin to flourish. We shall then have the right kind of people to settle our rich prairies, and bottom lands, and those of us who have ventured and suffered so much will then be repaid for all our toils and troubles.

Alex S. Thompson

## AD LAWRENCE'S FAMOUS LEAP.

In the summer of 1832 occurred an adventure, that as told by the hero in his own homespun phrase, affords the mind's eye a glimpse of the Texas of old, and its inhabitants of renown. The hero in question was Adam or "Ad" Lawrence, a gift of Tennessee to Texas, I believe, and who first settled near the headwaters of the Trinity River about 1829.

Certainly no man could have been by nature better adapted to the profession he had chosen. Though modest in manner, simple and unaffected in language, and of kind and gentle disposition, he was athletic in body, undaunted in spirit, and inured to hardships. He was especially fitted to risk the dangers of frontier life.

About 1838 or 1839 Lawrence settled on the south side of Brushy Creek, about four miles west from what was known as the "Hole in the Rock," in Williamson county, and where he died in 1880, at the ripe age of ninety years. A nephew, G. W. Lawrence, may still reside in the vicinity. Ad Lawrence is said to have been the first white man who crossed Brushy Creek at the place since known as "Lawrence's Crossing." He was not only a brave and daring Indian fighter, but one of the most expert mustang ropers that ever threw a lariat in Texas. On the occasion referred to, Lawrence and three companions went out "mustanging." Far out into the broad prairie a herd of about one hundred mustangs was sighted, feeding on the tall, luxuriant grass. As they cautiously approached, the horses showed no signs of flight. Coming nearer, the hunters prudently halted, being much surprised that the animals exhibited no signs of alarm. An instant later and the anomaly was explained in rather a surprising manner. Says Ad: "The long grass of the prairie suddenly became alive with Indians. There was one to each pony, and they all mounted at a jump and made for us at full speed, coiling their lariats as they rode. There was no time for swapping horses, so we all turned tail and made a straight shoot for the nearest settlement on the Trinity, about ten miles off. Our animals were all fine, but the nag I rode was a black mare, a little ahead of anything in the country for speed and bottom. We rather left them the first three miles, but then their ponies began to show themselves. I tell you, you've no idea how much an Indian can get out of those mustangs. Instead of being a weight to them, they seem to help them along, and they kept up such a fearful yelling, 'pears like you might have heard them to Red River. We noticed that they divided, one half striking off to the left, and we soon found out the reason, for we quickly came to the bank of a deep gully or ravine, which had to be headed; it couldn't be crossed. They knew every inch of the ground, and one party made straight for the head of the ravine, while the balance struck in below to cut us off in that direction. 'Twas no use talking—we had to ride about a quarter of a mile to the left, right in their very faces, and head that branch. My nag was still tolerably fresh; the others were beginning to blow right smartly. I rode just fast enough to keep in the lead. I didn't care particularly about getting off without knowing what became of my companions. Just as I came to the head of the hollow, the Indians were within about a hundred yards, and yelling awfully.

"They thought they had us sure. I gave my mare the rein and just touched her with my spur, and turned the corner with about fifty arrows whizzing about my ears. One stuck in my buckskin jacket, and one in my mare's neck. You may believe she didn't go any slower for that—for a while I thought she cleared about twenty feet at a jump. Soon as I got headed right again, I looked around to see what had become of the others. One look showed me. They were all down. About half of the redskins had stopped to finish them, and the balance were

coming for me like red hot lightning. I felt kinder dizzy-like for
a minute, and then straightened up and determined to get away
if I could. I hadn't much fear, if I didn't have to head another
branch. I could see the timber of Trinity three miles away, and
I gave my mare her own head. She had been powerful badly
scared, and had been working too hard, and she was puffing a
good deal.

"I managed to pull out the arrow which was sticking in her
neck. Then I worked off my heavy buckskin coat, which was
flopping about with the arrow sticking in it, catching a good deal
of wind, and threw it away. I kept on about a mile further
without gaining or losing much. Then I made up my mind to
stop and let my nag blow a little, because I knew if I didn't she
couldn't hold up much longer. So I pulled up, and alighted and
looked around. Seemed as if the whole country was alive with
Indians. About forty in a bunch a few yards behind, and one not
a hundred yards off. I loosened my saddle girth so she could
breathe good, took my bridle in my left hand, and pulled my
butcher knife with my right. It was the only weapon I had; I had
dropped my rifle when I got dizzy. The Indian was game. He
never stopped until he got within ten feet of me. Then he
throwed away his bow, jumped off, and came at me with a long
knife like mine. There wasnt time for a long fight. I had made
my calculations, and he was too sure he had me. He ran full
against my knife and I left him laying there. I heard an awful
howl from the others, and I pulled off my heavy boots, tightened
my girth, and mounted. A few minutes more and I struck the
timber of the Trinity, and then made the best of my way to the
river.

"I knew that for miles, up and down, the banks were bluffs
and fifteen or twenty feet high. Where I struck the river they
were fifteen. I knew if my mare wouldnt take the leap I had to
do it without her. She stopped an instant and snorted once or
twice; but, hearing the savages yell close behind, she took the
jump. Down, down we went, full fifteen feet, plump into the
deep water. We both went under for a second, then she rose,
and struck out for the opposite bank with me on her back. Poor

creature, she got about two-thirds across, and then gave out under me with a groan. I tell you I fairly loved that animal at that moment, and hated to leave her as bad as if she had been human.

"I swam the rest of the way and crawled out on the bank pretty well used up. But I was safe. I saw the howling and disappointed savages come to the bank I had left. But not one of them dared to take the leap. And the distance was too great for them to shoot. So I rested awhile and then made the best of my way to the settlement."*

* Lawrence's leap is, perhaps, equalled in American annals only by that of Major Sam McCulloch down Wheeling Hill (West Virginia) in 1777.

# CHAPTER VI.

hen the sun rose New Year's day, 1833, it was confidently hoped by all, and believed by most of the struggling colonists that it ushered in what was to be a new and brighter era for Texas. It was known that Santa Anna as President and Farias as vice President of Mexico, would be inaugurated in April as victorious champions of democratic-republican principles and pledged to the restoration of the federal constitution of 1824 in letter and spirit. It was thought that centralism had been trampled in the dust and blood of the battle field, never to arise again, that liberty was secure, and that all other good things would follow—including a separate state government for Texas. The people at this time, viewed the Mexican flag with real affection, indulging the vain hope that it might forever remain their national ensign, guiding the destinies of their descendants.

But alas! All was soon changed. The mask had now been so far removed from the face of Santa Anna, as to show him the arch-traitor he was, and every promise made to the people of Texas at the beginning of this year was broken before its close.

And now it was that the spirit of revolution began to assume form. "About this time," says Burnet, "small clouds, the bigness of a man's hand, appeared, heaving up from the political horizon of Mexico, and portending changes which time alone could comprehend or develop." The little portentous clouds gradually expanded and gathered blackness, until the year 1835, when the storm broke violently upon the confederacy; and Texas, resolute to resist the imposition of a military despotism, was driven to her final and well consummated declaration of independence in 1836.

Viewing the events of this period from the vantage point of today, they are seen to be the seeds from which sprang the wonderful future that followed.

Briefly noting the records of this year, we find that both the American and the Mexican population of Texas were clamorous for a separate state government: Jose de la Garza, Angel Navarro, Jose Casiano, Manual Ximenes, Jose Angel Seguin, Jose M. Zambrano, and Tignacio Aracha, all prominent and influential citizens of San Antonio, addressed a memorial to the Congress of Coahuila and Texas, in which they called attention to the necessity for a separate state government for Texas, and reform of the land laws; and at some length reviewed conditions with regard to Indian hostilities. They said that Bexar (San Antonio,) was founded in 1693, and La Bahia (Goliad,) and Nacogdoches in 1717; that in the time that had elapsed, the presidios of San Saba, San Marcos, Trinidad and other military settlements on the rivers Brazos, Colorado, and Guadalupe, had been formed and later disappeared with the settlements that surrounded them, in some instances every soul being murdered by the savages, the Government having utterly failed to redeem its pledges to protect those who would undertake to people and civilize the wilderness; that since the year 1821 ninety-seven citizens of Bexar, La Bahia and the new town of Gonzales, had been killed by Indians, exclusive of soldiers who perished in various expeditions; that further west, settlements had suffered more, and that all were threatened with destruction by the Comanches, who were taking advantage of all troops having been withdrawn from Texas, in consequence of military operations in Mexico. The memorialists further said that the only body of soldiers in Texas consisted of seventy men supported by voluntary contributions of citizens of San Antonio.

The memorial to the Federal Congress drawn up and adopted by the American settlers of Texas in convention assembled at San Felipe de Austin, in April 1833, and forwarded to the capital by commissioner Stephen F. Austin, painted even a darker picture: "The history of Texas, from its earliest settlement to the present time exhibits a series of practical neglects and indifferences to all her peculiar interests on the part of each successive government which has had control of her political destinies. . . . Bexar, the ancient capital of Texas, presents a faithful, but gloomy picture of her general want of protection, and encouragement. Situated in a fertile, picturesque, and healthful region, and established a century and a half ago, (within which period populous and magnificent cities have sprung into existence), she exhibits only the decrepitude of age—sad testimonials of the absence of that political guardianship which a wise government should always bestow upon the feebleness of its exposed frontier settlements. A hundred and seventeen years have elapsed since Goliad and Nacogdoches assumed the distinctive name of towns, and they are still entitled only to the diminutive appellation of villages. Other military and missionary establishments have been attempted but, from the same defect of protection and encouragement, they have been swept away, and scarcely a vestige remains to rescue their locations from oblivion.

"Bexar is still exposed to the depredations of her ancient enemies, the insolvent, vindictive, and faithless Comanches. Her citizens are still massacred, their cattle destroyed or driven away, and their very habitation threatened by a tribe of erratic and undisciplined Indians, whose long continued aggressions have invested them with a fictitious and excessive terror. Goliad is still kept in constant trepidation; is paralyzed in all her efforts for improvement; and is harassed on all her borders by the predatory incursions of the Wacos, and other insignificant bands of savages, whom a well organized local government would soon subdue and exterminate."

But we must desist, lest this should assume the proportions of a disquisition, involving the reader in the labyrinths of Mexican politics. Rather our purpose is to recount the more stirring episodes of border warfare—horrible and atrocious as are the details in most instances.

## SCALPING OF WILBARGER.

Many incidents in Texas history illustrate the verity of the saying that, "Truth is stranger than fiction," but none perhaps, so forcibly as the circumstances of the scalping of Wilbarger— since their dramatic interest includes an occurrence as remarkable, if indeed not as mysterious, as any to be found within the range of spiritualistic and psychological literature.

Among the sturdy emigrants to Austin's Colony, was Josiah Wilbarger, a native of Bourbon county, Kentucky, who came with his young bride and his father-in-law, Leman Baker, from Lincoln county, Missouri in 1828.

In March, 1830, after a couple of years spent in what is now Matagorda and Colorado counties, Wilbarger located his head-right league ten miles above Bastrop on the Colorado, and with his wife, baby, and two or three transient young men, removed to that then extreme and greatly exposed section, and erected his cabin. Here, for a time, he was the outsider settler, but soon other fearless pioneers located along the river, some below, others above—the elder Reuben Hornsby becoming, and for several years remaining, the outside sentinel of American civilization in that direction. "Mr. Wilbarger," says Brown, "located various lands for other parties in that section, it being Austin's second grant above the old San Antonio and Nacogdoches road, which crossed at Bastrop."

Early in August, 1833, Wilbarger, in company with Christian, a surveyor, and three young men, Strother, Standifer and Hanie, rode out from Hornsby's to look at the country and locate lands. On reaching a point near Walnut Creek, some five or six miles northwest of where the present capital city now stands, they discovered an Indian on a neighboring ridge, watching their movements. He was hailed with signs of friendship, but as the party approached, the Indian rode away, pointing towards a smoke rising from a cedar brake to the west. After a short pursuit, fearing they were being decoyed into a large camp of hostile Indians, the whites halted, held a short consultation, and at once determined to return to Hornsby's. On Pecan Spring

Scalping of Wilbarger

Ad Lawrence's Famous Leap

branch, some four miles east of Austin, and in sight of the present dirt road leading from Austin to Manor, they stopped to refresh themselves and horses. "Wilbarger, Christian and Strother unsaddled and hoppled their horses, but Hanie and Standifer left their animals saddled and staked them to graze." While the men were eating, they were suddenly charged upon by about sixty savages, who had quietly stolen up afoot under cover of the brush and timber, leaving their horses in the rear, and out of sight. The trees near them were small and afforded but little protection. However, each man sprang behind one and promptly returned the fire. Strother had been mortally wounded at the first fire, and now Christian was struck with a ball, breaking his thigh bone. Wilbarger sprang to the side of Christian, set him up against his tree, primed his loaded gun, and jumped again behind his own tree—receiving in the operation a flesh wound in the thigh and an arrow through the calf of his leg; and scarcely had he regained the protection of his tree, when his other leg was pierced with an arrow. Meantime, the steady fire and deadly aim of the whites had telling effect, causing the Indians to withdraw some distance and out of range. Up to this time Hanie and Standifer had bravely helped to sustain the unequal contest, but now, seeing that Strother was dying, Christian perhaps mortally, and Wilbarger badly, wounded, they took advantage of the opportunity to secure and mount their horses. Wilbarger, seeing himself thus deserted, and his horse having broke away and fled, implored the two men to stay with him and fight; but if they would not, to allow him to mount behind one of them. Just then, however, seeing the enemy again approaching, they fled at full speed, leaving Wilbarger to his fate. "The Indians," says Brown, "one having mounted Christian's horse, encircled him on all sides. He had seized the guns of the fallen men, and just as he was taking deliberate aim at the mounted warrior, a ball entered his neck, paralyzing him, so that he fell to the ground and was at the mercy of the wretches.

With exultant yells the Indians now rushed upon, and stripped him naked, and passing a knife entirely around his head, tore off the scalp. Though helpless and apparently dead, the poor man was fully conscious of all that transpired, and afterwards, in recounting the thrilling experience, said that while no pain was perceptible, the removing of his scalp sounded like the ominous roar and peal of distant thunder. The three men were stripped, Christian and Strother scalped and their throats cut, and all left for dead; after which the savages retired.

Wilbarger lay in a dreamy, semi-conscious condition till late in the evening, when the loss of blood finally aroused him. Crazed with the pains of his numerous wounds, and consumed by an intolerable thirst, he put forth the little remaining vitality in an endeavor to reach the spring nearby, which he at last accomplished, dragging himself into the water, where he lay for some time, till chilled and quite numb, he crawled out on dry land, and fell asleep. When he awoke he found the flow of blood from his wounds had ceased, but, horrors! exposed in the hot sun, the detestable "blow flies" had infested and literally covered his scalp and other wounds. Again slaking his thirst from the limpid little stream and partially appeasing his hunger with a few snails he chanced to find, he felt refreshed, and as night approached, determined to travel as far as he could in the direction of Hornsby's. But poor man, he did not realize his enfeebled condition from pain and loss of blood. After many efforts he arose and staggered along for perhaps a quarter of a mile, when he sank to the earth thoroughly exhausted, and almost lifeless, at the foot of a large post oak tree. Here, naked and exposed to the chilling night air, he lay, suffering intensely from cold, and unable to move, till revived by the warm sunshine of the following day.

On arriving at Hornsby's, the two men, Standifer and Hanie, told how the Indians had attacked and killed all three of their companions; and how they had narrowly escaped. A messenger was at once despatched to warn the settlers below, and also for aid, which however, could not be expected before the following day.

And now we will relate a most marvelous coincidence of

circumstances—incidents at once so mysterious and supernatural as to excite credulity of belief, were it not for the high character and known veracity of those, who to their dying day, vouched for their truth:

During the night—that long and agonizing night—as Wilbarger lay under the old oak tree, "in a state of semi-consciousness, visions flitting through his mind bordering on the marvelous and the supernatural," he distinctly saw, standing before him, the spirit of his sister, Mrs. Margaret Clifton, who had died the day before in Florisant, St. Louis county, Missouri.* Speaking gently, she said: "Brother Josiah, you are too weak to go in alone! Remain here and friends will come to aid you before the setting of another sun." And then moved off in the direction of the settlements, Wilbarger piteously calling, "Margaret! Stay with me." But the apparition vanished.

That night and about the same hour—midnight—Mrs. Hornsby awoke from a most vivid and startling dream, in which she beheld Wilbarger, alive, scalped, bleeding and naked, at the foot of a tree. Her husband assuring her that dreams were always unreal; and the utter impossibility of this one being true, she again slumbered—till about three o'clock, when she again awoke, intensely excited, and arose saying, "I saw him again! Wilbarger is not dead! Go to the poor man at once;" and so confident was Mrs. Hornsby, she refused to retire again, but busied herself preparing an early breakfast, that there might be no delay in starting to Wilbarger's relief. As the nearest neighbors arrived in the morning, Mrs. Hornsby repeated to them her dual vision and urged them in a most serious manner, to go to Wilbarger in all haste. The relief party consisted of Reuben Hornsby, Joseph Rogers, John Walters, Webber, and others. After quite a search from the vague directions of the two excited men who had escaped from the scene, they finally found the

---

* John Henry Brown says: "Mrs.Clifton died the day before at Florisant, St. Louis county, Missouri. From the county post-office kept by my uncle, Capt. Wm. Kerr, I bore the letter, marked "In haste", written by Mr. Clifton to her father informing him of her death."

bodies of Christian and Strother; and presently discovered a most ghastly object—a mass of blood—causing them to hesitate and clutch their guns; whereupon the overjoyed man arose, beckoned, and finally managed to say—"Don't shoot, friends; it's Wilbarger, come on." As they approached he sank down and called out, "Water! Water!" and when revived, spoke of his sister who had visited him during the night and so kindly had gone for help which he knew would come—firmly believing he had seen and conversed with her in reality. With the sheets provided by Mrs. Hornsby for that purpose, the bodies of Strother and Christian were wrapped and left till the following day, when the party again went out, and buried them. In another sheet Wilbarger was wrapped and placed on a horse in front of Mr. Hornsby, who, placing his arms around him, sustained him in the saddle and bore him to the hospitable home and tender cares of Mrs. Hornsby, that saintly mother and ministering angel of the frontier. His scalp wound was dressed in bear's oil, and after a few days of tender nursing, the great loss of blood preventing febrile tendencies, he was sufficiently recovered to be placed on a sled and conveyed to his own cabin.

Rapidly Wilbarger recovered his usual health, and lived for eleven years, prospering, and accumulating a handsome estate. But his skull, bereft of the inner membrane and so long exposed to the sun, never entirely covered over, necessitating artificial covering, and eventually caused his death, hastened, as his physician, Dr. Anderson, thought, by accidentally striking his head against the upper portion of a low door frame of his gin house, causing the bone to exfoliate, exposing the brain and producing delirium. He died at his home in 1845, survived by his wife and five children. His widow, who afterward married Tolbert Chambers, was the second time bereft, and died a widow in Bastrop in 1896. The eldest son, John Wilbarger, a most gallant ranger under Col. "Rip" Ford, was killed by Indians in the Nueces River country, in 1847. Harvey Wilbarger, another son, lived to raise a large family. One married daughter lives at Georgetown, and another at Belton, Texas. Of the brothers and sisters of Josiah Wilbarger, who came to Texas in 1837,

J. W. Wilbarger, (Author of "Indian Depredations in Texas") died near Round Rock in 1890, and "Aunt Sallie" Wilbarger, long resided at Georgetown, where she died several years since. Another sister who became the wife of Col. W. C. Dalrymple, died many years ago, and still another—Mrs. Lewis Jones,— died on the way to Texas. Mathias, a brother, was a noted surveyor, and died of smallpox at Georgetown in 1853.

William Hornsby died in 1901, near Austin, and his parents many years before. The beautiful home and fertile Hornsby farm is still owned by surviving members of the family.

So far as we can ascertain, this was the first blood shed in that part of the State (in what is now Travis county), at the hands of the implacable savages, but it was "the beginning, however," says Wilbarger, "of a bloody era which was soon to dawn upon the people of the Colorado."*

"The vision," continues Wilbarger, "which impressed Mrs. Hornsby, was spoken of far and wide through the colony fifty years ago; her earnest manner and perfect confidence that Wilbarger was alive, in connection with her vision and its realization, made a profound impression on the men present, who spoke of it everywhere. There were no telegraphs in those days, and no means of knowing that Margaret, the sister, had died seven hundred miles away, on the day before her brother was wounded. The story of her apparition, related before he knew that she was dead—her going in the direction of Hornsby's and Mrs. Hornsby's vision, recurring after slumber, presents a mystery that made then a deep impression and created a feeling of awe, which, after the lapse of half a century, it still inspires. No man who knew them ever questioned the veracity of either Wilbarger or the Hornsby's, and Mrs. Hornsby was loved and revered by all who knew her.

---

* Recalling the days of childhood," says John Henry Brown, in writing of Josiah Wilbarger and other worthy members of the family in Texas, "when the writer often sat upon his lap and received many evidences of his kindly nature, it is a pleasure to state that in 1858 he enjoyed and embraced the opportunity of naming the county of Wilbarger jointly for him and his brother, Mathias, a surveyor."

"We leave to those more versed in the occult the task of explaining this mystery. Surely such things are not accidents; they tell us of a spirit world and of a God who 'moves in a mysterious way His wonders to perform.'"

Other incidents of border warfare occurring this year are of minor importance and without exact date or details: as the murder of Alexander, a trapper, near the Ledbetter-La Grange road on a small streamlet since called Alexander's Branch in Fayette county; and the killing of one Earthman on Long Prairie, near the present post-office hamlet of Nechanitz in the same county; the adventures of Tom Alley while out hunting horses in the Cummings' Creek community—unexpectedly riding into a camp of Indians, who fired upon and severely wounded him, as he put spurs to his steed and fled. Settlers followed these Indians toward the head of Cummings' Creek, where the trail was lost in consequence of the grass being burned to elude further pursuit.

In the spring of this year a band of Keechi Indians raided the Cummings' Creek settlements, in Fayette county, committing various depredations. Hastily collecting a company of twenty settlers, Captain John York pursued, attacked and killed eight or ten of them, dispersing the others. This was, so far as known, their last, and perhaps only really hostile demonstration against the settlers. The Keechis were comparatively a small, insignificant band, of beggarly and thieving propensities, and early lost their tribal existence, affiliating with other tribes.

During the same year a traveller named Reed, stopped at Tenoxtitlan, Falls of the Brazos, now in the lower part of Falls county. At that time a small party of friendly Tonkawa Indians were camped nearby, and with one of whom Reed "swapped" horses, and it is said, drove a shrewd bargain, which he refused to rue. A few days later, as the stranger left the vicinity on his return to the United States, he was waylaid and murdered by the exasperated Tonkawas, who appropriated his horse and equipments and fled. The old Caddo chief, Canoma, who was about the settlements a good deal, and then at the "Falls," with some of his warriors, went in pursuit and on the eighth day, returned with seven "Tonk" scalps, Reed's horse and other trophies—receiving the substantial commendation of the settlers. The sad fate of Canoma at the hands of the whites to whom he was ever friendly and faithful, some two years later, will be related in the order of its occurrence.*

"Other matters of interest," says John Henry Brown, "occurred in and about 1833. The colony of De Leon had increased considerably by the incoming of a good class of Mexicans and quite a number of Americans, including several Irishmen and their families from the United States, the younger members being natives of that country, and among whom were the following: John McHenry (a settler since 1826), John Linn, and his sons, John J., Charles, Henry and Edward, and two daughters, (subsequently the wives of Maj. James Kerr and James A. Moody), who came in 1830-31; Mrs. Margaret Bobo, afterwards Wright, (who came in 1825), Joseph Ware and others. From about 1829 to 1833-34, the colonists of Power and Howitson, with headquarters at the Mission of Refugio, and McCullen and McGloin, of which San Patricio was the capital, received valuable additions in a worthy, sober, industrious class of people, chiefly from Ireland, a few of Irish extraction, born in the United States, and others who were Americans. They were more exposed to Mexican oppression than the colonists farther east and equally so to hostile Indians."**

Glancing at the history of colonial Texas about this period, one can but wonder at the signs of substantial and permanent growth, despite all restrictions and obstacles: The spirit of colonization was abroad, and fearless emigrants were constantly

---

* The Tonkawas ever professed friendship to the whites, and being hereditary enemies of the Comanches, often joined the settlers and rangers in expeditions against this tribe, rendering valuable and valiant services. Kenney says, "This is the solitary instance of hostility by the Tonkawas in their long and trying experience of more than fifty years contact with the white people from the first settlement of Texas."

** It is of interest to note that 26 of these colonists signed the Goliad Declaration of Independence, Dec. 20, 1835, and four of them signed the regular Declaration of Texas Independence, March 2, 1836.

arriving overland by the various highways*—menaced though they were by lurking savages, who often lay in ambush to pounce upon the new-comers. "In 1833," says Pease, "the tide of emigration from the United States, which had been interrupted during the administration of Bustamente, began again to flow into the country."

"The history of frontier expansion in the United States" says Thrall, "shows that it is no easy task. In Texas the difficulties were very great. It was remote from other settlements—in a foreign country, with a government and institutions entirely different from those of the North; and the country was preoccupied by Indians. Considering all these circumstances, the success of Austin and others in introducing Anglo-American colonists, was wonderful. If we inquire into the grounds of this success, we shall find it in the character of the men. They were brave, hardy, industrious men, self-helpful and self-reliant. They asked no favors of the Government, and that Government let them severely alone. Their stout arms cultivated their farms and protected their homes from the incursions of the savages. Volumes might be written, detailing instances of individual bravery—of hardships cheerfully endured by old and young, male and female colonists."**

* The late venerable pioneer, I.D. Parker, says: "My father's family came to Texas in 1833. At that time the San Antonio road was the only highway running through Texas. It led from Nachedoches, in Louisiana, to San Antonio, and thence to the Rio Grande—via Nacogdoches, Tenoxtitlan on the Brazos, Mina (now Bastrop) on the Colorado, and thence to San Antonio, crossing the San Marcos near the mouth of the Blanco. James Gaines kept a ferry on the Sabine River, Joseph Durst on the Angeline, Leonard Williams on the Neches, Nathaniel Robbins on the Trinity, Jeremiah Timson on the Navasota, and Wm. Boren on the Brazos. The La Bahia (Goliad) road left the San Antonio road three miles west of the Trinity River, crossing the Brazos at the site of the present town of Washington, where Jack Hall kept a ferry, and thence to Goliad."—Unpublished "Reminiscences of Pioneer Life in Texas." MS. p.1
** Pictorial History of Texas," pp. 171-2.

## THE MADDEN MASSACRE.

The Madden family came to Texas in 1832, locating near the Trinity in Houston county. To better secure themselves in case of an attack from Indians, some three or four neighboring families, as was frequently the case in those days, had joined together and built a strong double log cabin with entry between, and where they all resided, opening and cultivating small fields near by.

The awful, bloody and heart-rending tragedy we must now relate—the one of only two such instances on record in which the fair name and courage of Texas pioneers has been disgraced with cowardice—occurred in the fall of the year, and during the moonlight nights, the time usually selected by the red men for making their raids.

On the fatal night, four men, eight women and several children were occupying the house. For a time all were in one room, but the men, leaving their guns, went into the adjoining room, and kindling a fire, busied themselves molding bullets. Meantime the lurking savages, a party of Caddos, had crept up and around the buildings, cautiously peering in and ascertaining the defenseless situation of the unsuspecting inmates. As the full orbed moon arose, casting its soft and tranquil flood of light upon the scene, the stillness of the night was suddenly rent by war whoops and yells fiendish enough to chill the strongest heart, and indeed strike terror to helpless women and children; at the same time forms, hideous as those of the under world, arose from brush and covert and rushed from every direction into the hallway, and most of them, in upon the terrified women and children, one powerful and hideous demon, guarding the doorway by spreading his arms and legs from side to side and grasping the lintels with his hands, all the while yelling and gloating rapturously over the bloody, sickening scene of death wrought within. Mrs. Madden was first attacked and soon fell apparently lifeless, but regaining consciousness crawled under a bed followed by one of her little sons. Another lady was tomahawked and fell dead into the fireplace, her life's blood flowing so profusely as to extinguish the flames, and leave the fiends to complete the slaughter in semi-darkness. Taking advantage of this, and the engrossed attention of the door guard, Mrs. Madden with her little son succeeded in crawling out of the room, and making her way to an unoccupied negro cabin a short distance away, where she secreted herself and child and thus escaped. Meanwhile, with tomahawk and scalping knife the savages completed their diabolical work, killing in all seven women and children.

As to the four men—we only refer to them through necessity of completing the narrative—it is said that as soon as the dying groans of their wives and children reached their ears, they dashed out of the room and escaped.

Securing the guns of the whites, the Indians now set fire to the building, which consumed it, with the bodies of their victims. Nearby they threw down their own inferior guns and left the settlement without pursuit.

After a long and doubtful illness, Mrs. Madden recovered and lived several years.

# CHAPTER VII.

he year 1834 we are told, was ushered in by a "freezing" norther—fitting precursor of the cold indifference with which the Mexican nation looked upon their American colonists in Texas. Political events had assumed a still worse complexion in Texas at this date.

Santa Anna, having received the support of the army and church, went over to the centralist party, dissolved the constitutional congress, convened one composed of his creatures, and became virtually the dictator of Mexico.

In the spring Santa Anna assembled a council, composed of Stephen F. Austin, Lorenzo Zavala, three members of the congress of Coahuila and Texas, and seven Mexican officials, to consider affairs in Texas. Austin made a strong plea in favor of the memorial of the Texas convention of 1833. The three members of congress, all of whom were from Coahuila, opposed it. Santa Anna announced his decision to be that Texas should have a separate government, and that four thousand troops should be stationed at San Antonio for the protection of the country—to which Austin strenuously objected, but without effect. This opposition of the part of Austin, doubtless had much to do with the continuance of his imprisonment.

An attempt to change the seat of government of Coahuila and Texas from Saltillo to Monclova, led to commotions that resulted in rival governors and legislatures being installed at the two places, and the Mexican part of the State being divided into two factions. These difficulties were referred to Santa Anna in December, who decided that the capital should remain at Monclova, and ordered new elections.

There were two parties in Mexico—the centralist and republican, the latter not being completely crushed. There were also two in Texas—one favoring immediate and determined action for separate state government and co-operation with the patriot republicans of Mexico; the other favoring acquiescence in the existing status, at least until Austin's release and return to Texas, and until it should definitely appear what Santa Anna's policy was to be. The latter party in Texas prevailed for the time being.

This year did not pass away without the usual outrages by Indians. No historical record has been preserved of many of these events, but ample evidence has been left that proves the Indians annoyed the colonists more or less. Speaking of the Comanches and alluding incidentally to other tribes, Kenney says: "During 1833 and 1834 their name does not appear in the hostilities ascribed to known tribes; but Indian hostilities in general would blacken many pages."

Pioneer Dewees, in his "Letters from Texas," writing under the date, "Colorado River, Texas. Oct. 31, 1834," says: "The first storm of Mexican wrath is lulled; but the Indians, who have ever been our enemies, still continue to annoy us. They will fall upon small parties of men, and kill them, and also steal our horses and cattle. Indeed such a thing as being free from the molestations of the Indians has never been known in the history of Texas, and doubtless, will not be known for many years to come."*

While the records supply materials for accounts of thrilling incidents that transpired within the limits of Austin's and DeWitt's Colonies, little reliable data is obtainable that relates to Indian troubles in the early settlement of Red River county, and the northeastern part of the State.

* Decree No. 278 of Coahuila and Texas, enacted April 19, 1834, authorizes the governor to organize and employ militia against hostile Indians, places 400 sitios of land at his disposal for distribution to militiamen as remuneration for their services on such terms as he might establish, and appropriates $20,000.00 to further aid in the accomplishment of the ends proposed.

"Although dim vistas appear," says John Henry Brown, "of inroads by Indians—robbers and occasional murders by Cooshatties, Tehuacanas, Wacos, and other tribes—it is lamentable that not one of those early settlers ever wrote, or caused to write, an account of such events until age impaired the memory. Hence the narrative we gather, lacks that certainty and definiteness, so desirable in such matters."

These observations are emphasized by the confused and conflicting stories that have been preserved concerning the killing of Judge Gabriel N. Martin and the capture of his little son in May or June, 1834.

## MURDER OF JUDGE GABRIEL N. MARTIN—CAPTIVITY AND RECOVERY OF HIS LITTLE SON—SOME CORRECTED HISTORY.

The accounts published by Thrall, Wilbarger and Sowell, mention only one expedition for the recovery of the boy, and place it in the year 1834. They differ as to what officer commanded the United States military force, some saying Leavenworth, and later Dean, and others, Col. (in after years Gen.) Dodge. Radical discrepancies exist with regard to the circumstances attending the killing of Judge Martin, and whether a negro was captured with the boy. One version is that the hunting party had mounted the rise of a hill and while watching a herd of buffalo, was charged upon by the Indians; and that Judge Martin and son fell behind and the Judge was killed, and the boy and negro man were made prisoners.

Others give a wholly different recital—one saying the Indians were Pawnees and that Judge Martin and a negro man were killed in camp. Careful sifting of the evidence, renders it certain that there were two expeditions for the recovery of the boy—one in 1834 and the other in 1836, and that the United States dragoons in the first year were commanded by Dean, and in the latter year by Dodge. Sowell possibly confuses and blends together as happening in 1834, events that occurred in both years.

That Martin was killed in May or June, 1834, and that the
boy was recovered in 1836, mainly through the instrumentality
of Col. Dodge, are the main points, and about which there is
little or no doubt.

Fortunately, through access to the official itinerary of Col.
Henry Dodge, in command of the United States cavalry, or
"mounted rangers,'" and then on an observation and treaty-
making tour among the "wild Indians of the far west;" supple-
mented and corroborated by the "notes" of Catlin, the artist,
who accompanied this expedition, we are enabled to give the
reader an elaborate and reliable narrative of this notable affair.

Judge Martin was one of the early and prominent citizens
of Pecan Point, in Red River county, Texas, and a son-in-law of
that still earlier and staunch pioneer, Claiborne Wright, who
landed at Pecan Point after a most hazardous keel-boat voyage
of six months down the Cumberland, the Ohio and the Mississippi Rivers, to the mouth of Red River, and thence up that
stream, arriving at his destination on the 5th day of September,
1816.

Martin was of a bold and fearless nature, fond of hunting
and outdoor life. In the latter days of May or first part of June,
with a small party composed of himself, his little son, Matthew
W., a negro playmate of the latter, Daniel Davis, James and
Robert Gamble, Zack Bottom, (a negro servant who had been
partly raised among the Indians), and a few other companions,
went out on a hunting and pleasure trip, higher up Red River,
pitching camp on a small stream—Sowell says Glass Creek—
presumably in the upper portion of what is now Grayson
county.

They had been here several weeks undisturbed, when they
became careless and scattered, as each saw fit, from day to day,
to hunt. On such an occasion, when none but the elder Martin,
the little negro, and Bottom, the servant, were in camp, a party
of Indians suddenly attacked them, killed the Judge and negro
boy—"because he fought so desperately and screamed so
loud"—plundered the camp and retreated. Zack Bottom, the old
servant, escaped, barefooted, and eventually, after much suffer-

ing and almost famished, reached the settlements.

The other members of the party, including Martin's son, it appears, discovered the Indians after the killing and, as they were retreating, in this way: while on the prairie-divide between the Washita and Red Rivers, they noticed a herd of excited buffalo coming over the ridge and at once suspected they were disturbed by Indians. As they reached the top of the ridge the Indians were in full view and not far away. Cutting loose their buffalo meat and game, they ran at full speed for Red River, and all affected their escape and made their way to the settlements— all save young Martin, who became separated and was soon overtaken and captured.

Writing from the mouth of False Washita, July, 1834, Catlin, the artist, says: "The cruel fate of Judge Martin and family has been published in the papers, and it belongs to the regiment of dragoons to demand the surrender of the murderers and get for the information of the world, some authentic account of the mode in which this horrible outrage was committed.

"Judge Martin was a very respectable and independent man, living on the lower part of Red River, and in the habit of taking his children, and one or two servants with him, and a tent to live in, every summer, into the wild regions, where he pitched his tent upon the prairie and spent several months in killing buffalo and other wild game for his own private amusement. The news came to Fort Gibson, but a few weeks before we started, that he had been set upon by a party of Indians, and destroyed. A detachment of troops was speedily sent to the spot, where they found his body horribly mangled, and also one of his negroes; and it is supposed that his son, a fine boy of nine years of age, had been taken home to their villages by them, where they still retain him, and where it is our hope to recover him.

"Camp Washita, July 4, 1834 Gen. Leavenworth declares his intention of sending Col. Dodge with 250 men to the Pawnee village.

"Under the protection of the United States dragoons, I arrived at this place three days since on my way again in search of the 'Far West.' How far I may this time follow the flying phantom, is uncertain. I am already again in the land of the buffalos and the fleet bounding antelopes. We are at this place on the banks of Red River, having Texas under our eye on the opposite bank. We are encamped on the ground on which Judge Martin and servant were butchered, and his son kidnapped by the Pawnees or Comanches, but a few weeks since; and the moment they discover us in a large body, they will presume that we are relentlessly seeking for revenge, and they will probably be very shy of our approach. We are over the Washita—the 'Rubicon is passed'—we are invaders of a sacred soil. We are carrying the war in our front, and 'we shall soon see what we shall see.'

"July 22.—At the Toyash village, Col. Dodge and several of his officers met, agreeably to previous notice, the Toyash chiefs and warriors in council. Council being in order, Col. Dodge proceeded to speak as follows: 'We are the first American officers who have ever come to see the Pawnees; we meet you as friends, not as enemies, to make peace with you, to shake hands with you. The great American captain is at peace with all the white men in the world; he wishes to be at peace with all the red men in the world; we have been sent to view this country, and to invite you to go to Washington, where the great American chief lives, to make a treaty with him, that you may learn how he wishes to send among you traders, who will bring you guns and blankets, and everything that you want.'

"As the council proceeded Dodge referred to the foul killing of Judge Martin, and the capture of his little son—also the capture of one Abbe, a ranger, the previous year. Evading reply as to the killing of Martin, the chief, Water-ra-shah-ro, a very dignified warrior of more than seventy years, replied that he had learned 'the Indians who lived near St. Antonio,' in Mexico (Texas), captured Abbe, and that they killed him on Red River; the white boy is here.' To which Col. Dodge replied: 'I wish the boy brought to me,' at the same time informing the chiefs that, as an evidence of his friendly intentions towards them, he had on starting, purchased at a very great price, from their enemies, the Osages, two Pawnee and one Kiowa, girls, which had been held by them some time as prisoners; and which he had there ready to deliver to their friends and relatives, in exchange for white prisoners held by the Pawnees. The little boy was now brought in from the middle of a corn field where they had hid him. The little fellow was entirely naked, except the scant dress worn by the children of the tribe. He was a very bright and intelligent lad of eight or nine summers. His appearance caused considerable excitement and commotion in the council room, and as the little fellow gazed around in great surprise, he exclaimed, 'What; are there white men here?' to which Col. Dodge replied by asking him his name—'Matthew Wright Martin'—was the prompt reply. He was then received into the arms of Col. Dodge, and the captive Indian girls brought in and soon recognized by their overjoyed friends and relatives, who embraced them with the most extravagant expressions of joy. From this moment the council, which before had been a very grave and uncertain one, took a pleasing and friendly turn. The heart of the venerable old chief was melted at the evidence of the white man's friendship. He at once embraced Col. Dodge and each of the officers in turn, with tears streaming down his cheeks."

Further quoting Catlin: "August 13th . . . reached the settlements at the north fork of the Canadian . . . informed by a citizen, that the mother of little Martin has recently offered $2,000 for his recovery; she will soon be made happy by his restoration, without ransom or reward.

"The little boy of whom I have spoken, was brought in, the whole distance to Fort Gibson, in the arms of the dragoons, who took turns in carrying him; and after the command reached there, he was transmitted to the Red River settlements by an officer, who had the enviable satisfaction of delivering him into the arms of his disconsolate and half-distracted mother."*

---

* Judge Martin left a widow, who afterwards married a Dr. Bason, and two sons, Matthew W. and William, and one daughter, Louisiana. Both the sons made good citizens, and the daughter a most estimable lady.

Thus we have the true version of Judge Martin's death and
the rescue of his little son from captivity—honoring those to
whom honor is due. Other matters co-incident with and forming a part of the sad story, though without concert of action or
knowledge of results, have not been noticed. We refer to an
expedition or party of neighbors and settlers led by Captain
Stiles, and which left for the scene of the tragedy, and in search
of the captured son, soon after the sad news reached the settlement. Brief knowledge of the movements of this fearless little
party of settlers, boldly penetrating far into the country of
numerous hostile bands and tribes, is obtained from an unpublished narrative prepared by John Henry Brown from data
supplied by Geo. W. Wright, one of the party, afterward a
prominent citizen and representative, and a brother of Mrs.
Martin, the account, however, all too brief and lacking dates and
details:

"On learning of the murder of Judge Martin and the capture of little Matthew Wright Martin, thirty brave men, assembled, chose Captain Richard Stiles as their leader, and guided
by Hardy, the colored man, repaired to the camp, buried Judge
Martin and the little colored boy, and then followed on the trail
of the Indians—how far and under what circumstances, does
not clearly appear. It is certain, however, that north of Red River
and west of the Washita, they encountered a large party of
Indians and were compelled to fight heavy odds, in which they
defended themselves with the loss of one man and one horse

*(footnote continued from previous page)*

Among the traditions of the Wright family, is a story that while residing
at Pecan Point, to avoid night attacks from the Indians, the family would
move across the river each night and secrete themselves until morning,
when they would all return to the cabin. The ferry consisted of drift logs
lashed together as a raft. The mother and daughter (afterwards wife of
Judge Martin) and a negro girl were placed upon the raft, which was then
towed across the river by the older brother and father swimming by the
side of it and pulling it along with them, while the two smaller boys, Travis
G., and George W., (afterwards prominent citizens of Paris, Texas) swam
along behind the raft, holding on to it. To prevent the children talking and
attracting the attention of the Indians, they were always kept separated in
the cane.—Encyclopedia of the West," p. 372.

killed, and one man had a thigh broken. Though more or less
annoyed by the enemy they retreated to, and crossed the
Washita, near which they fell in with Capt. Dean in command
of a company of United States dragoons, with whom they
camped for several days, and then returned home.

"The wounded man was taken in charge by the U. S.
surgeon, conveyed to Fort Gibson and recovered; but Mr.
Wright failed to give either his name, that of the man killed, or
of any other of the thirty one men, excepting Capt. Stiles and
himself. In my view of pioneer life each of these men was a hero
and entitled to be so remembered. Doubtless some of their
children and grandchildren are in the country now and ignorant
of these things. Such is fate. Aggregate achievements and deeds
of the many, as too much professed history goes, are awarded
to a lucky few. Not, truly, by design, but by a carelessness almost
criminal, in not giving, after so great a lapse of time, the names
of the men composing such daring parties in those early days.
Mr. Wright wrote in '74 of this daring expedition in '34, in which
he participated; yet he failed to name a single comrade, fix a
single date, the number of days occupied in any portion or all
of the expedition, or to definitely fix a single locality that could
be identified. Had he written earlier, his narrative would have
supplied these omissions, for he was a clear headed, just man,
personally familiar with the settlement of that country from its
inception onward. From Mr. Robert E. Frazier, I have learned
that 'Hardy,' the brave old Indian-trained negro, was the guide,
and that Zack Bottom, who escaped when Martin was killed,
was in it, as I am quite sure the ever faithful Henry Stout was."

## FRONTIER TROUBLES.

We cannot better close the narration of events of border
warfare in 1834, than by the introduction of a highly interesting
letter penned by one of the early pioneers—John T. Townsend,
and addressed to the old ranger chief, Capt. John S. Ford. The
letter is quite reminiscent, and sheds much light on the frontier
history of Texas at that early day—anticipating briefly, as it

does, some of the thrilling events that will be narrated in detail, in the order of their occurrence. But to the letter:

Eagle Pass, Texas, Jan. 20, 1893.

Col. John S. Ford: Dear Sir:

Remembering your request for something in regard to events of olden times in Texas; and being somewhat in a reminiscent mood after meeting and conversing with some of the descendents here of the oldest settlers of Texas, I write you a short statement of some notable incidents that I have never known published in any Texas history.

In 1834 or 1835, I am almost sure the latter, the Comanches came down. They passed our settlement on Cummings' Creek on their way down. In Austin county, on Mill Creek, they stole some horses. The Americans collected to follow them. My father, Stephen Townsend, and his brothers accompanied them in the pursuit. They left my mother, a sister of mine, who is now the wife of Hon. James C. Gaither of Falls county, myself, a negro woman and her little son, two or three years old. The Americans had left my grandfather's, John. G. Robinson's, three or four miles distant from us, a few days previously, and we were at the Robinson place. My mother and grandmother, feeling assured that the Texans were between us and all danger from the Indians, sent the negro woman to our place for some clothes. She carried her little boy with her. On her return the Indians met her on the road, killed her and carried off the negro boy as a prisoner. They opened the bundle she was carrying but took nothing from it. This occurred exactly on the spot where the town of Round Top, Fayette county, now stands. The bones of the negro woman lie under an oak tree near the center of the town. This occurred previous to 1836.

The Rev. Mr. Thrall in his history of Texas, gives a very short account of my grandfather and his brother, Walter Robinson, being killed in the spring of 1837. Judge Sam Lucky, who died in your city, San Antonio, was once chief justice of that county, and also represented it in the congress of the Texas Republic. He came from Georgia with Walter Robinson, and was at my grand father's house when the killing took place.

"He was a gentleman of ability and undoubted courage. He was one of Colonel Jack Hays' company of rangers. When Col. Hays was sent forward to bring on an engagement with the Mexicans under General Woll, Judge Lucky was shot through the body. He lived a number of years afterwards, but never recovered from the effects of the wound. The Authoress of "Beulah" and other works, Mrs. Augusta J. Evans, was his niece. She was one time a resident of San Antonio.

Joel W. Robinson was one of the party which captured General Santa Anna the day after the battle of San Jacinto and delivered him to General Sam Houston. He lived to a good, ripe old age. He was respected by all classes of Texas citizens.

Another matter happened not far from the time mentioned above. There lived about sixty miles below La Grange, a man named Ross. He traded with the Tonkaway Indians for horses they stole from the Comanche Indians. This was the cause of trouble between the white settlers and the Comanches, and was considered the cause of those Indians becoming hostile. Ross paid very little for a horse. He carried them to the United States and sold them. He came back with goods and sold them at immense profits to the Tonkaways. In their war with the Comanches they had not been successful, and had been so weakened by losses that they came inside the Texas settlements for protection from their enemies. They had a permanent camp near Ross' place. A crowd of from thirty to eighty men was raised. They intended to drive away the Tonkaways, and to notify them to stop the theft of Comanche horses for the reasons already set forth. Ross was drinking when they approached his house. He was a reckless, desperate man. He began firing on the Americans as they came within rifle distance. He continued to do so until shot down. My father and grandfather were with the company of Americans, but took no hand in killing Ross. This affair occurred in 1834. Desperate as the remedy was, it failed to cure the disease. The Comanches had become so incensed that they proceeded at once to stealing horses and killing men and women wherever they found them unprotected. Up to this time they had been friendly with the whites or at least inoffensive. This state of things continued until long after the annexation of Texas to the United States. In fact, until Texas become sufficiently settled by Americans to enable them to protect themselves.

One of the movements detering the Indians from sending expeditions into Texas was the killing off of the numerous herds of buffalo grazing upon the staked plains. When the outside world became conscious that the slaughtering of buffalo was going forward, and was perpetrated only for the skins, the bodies being left untouched to become food for the wolves or to rot, the conductors of newspapers denounced the proceeding as cruel and inhuman. The writer looked at results from a different standpoint. The Comanches had been enabled to use the buffalo in their robbing expeditions upon the people of Texas. If these animals were some distance from a settlement, they were driven down the country a proper distance and left to graze. The red gentlemen could tell pretty well where the drove could be found in a given number of days. They would visit the settlements, murder and rob. When they returned, they traveled at great speed until the herd of buffalo was reached. At that point they would eat, sleep and recruit. After the animals had been slaughtered, the Comanches had no commissariat. The journey to a settlement was long and tedious with but little to eat on the way. After the advent of the cattlemen it was a hazardous undertaking. Brave men with repeating rifles and pistols stood in the way. The destruction of the vast herds of buffalo effected as much for the security of Texas as a large standing army across the country from the Red River to the Rio Grande, could have done.

For many years we confidently expected the Comanches to come among us every full moon, in consequence of which, every man who had any patriotism, prepared himself and was ready at a moments warning to go after them.

There was a small remnant of a tribe led and controlled by a very sensible Indian, named Canoma, who always held himself ready to serve the whites as guide and spy. He was not to be found on one occasion, when the Americans were going out on a campaign against the Comanches. After they had gone some distance they found Canoma with some horses that had been stolen. He declared that he had taken them from the Comanches and intended to return them to their owners. He insisted that if the Americans would give him a chance he would take them to the Comanches and thus demonstrate his innocence. As is often the case, some of the Americans were so incensed that they killed Canoma. Some of the men on the spot—my father and John Rabb—were among those who opposed the killing. When they found it impossible to prevent it they left the company rather than witness what they deemed murder. I have often heard them speak of it when I was a boy with the deepest regret.

John T. Townsend.

# CHAPTER VIII.

iewed from the historian's standpoint, 1835 marks a most important epoch—the great turning point in the history of Texas. The revolution that achieved Texas independence began in this year—not, however, with that end in view, but as a movement to overthrow the despotism established by Santa Anna and to restore constitutional government. So distinguished a writer as Ex-President Roosevelt has fallen into the error of charging that the separation of Texas from Mexico, was deliberately planned by the restless and resistless American settlers. The people of Texas did not make the issue. It was forced upon them. They had to choose between resistance, or submission to a tyranny—to free-born, liberty-loving Americans—worse than death. Referring to the conquest of Texas, Mr. Roosevelt strikes the key note of truth, however, when he says: "The Government of the United States had nothing to do with winning Texas for the English-speaking people of North America. The American frontiersmen won Texas for themselves, unaided either by statesmen who controlled the politics of the Republic, or by the soldiers who took their orders from Washington."*

"A self-reliant people," says Thrall, "whose interests and liberties are imperiled, will not long lack the means necessary for concert of action. Texas was threatened with invasion by a government to which it had a right to look for protection. Again, the Indians were more or less troublesome. Ostensibly to provide for protection against these savages, committees of safety

---

* Theodore Roosevelt's "The Winning of the West." Page 186.

were organized in different municipalities. It was the business of these committees to collect and disseminate information, to secure arms and ammunition, and in case of necessity, to call out and drill the militia."*

In presenting the facts leading up to the revolution, historian Brown, says: "The situation was rendered more gloomy by evidences of increased hostilities on the part of the savages along the whole line of frontier from the Red River to the extreme southwest."

## MASSACRE OF THE TRADERS —FIGHT ON THE SAN MARCOS.

Following the second and successful, settlement of Gonzales, after its tragic breaking up in 1826, the town and community prospered—escaped further serious incursions; the Indians, over-awed doubtless by the exhibition and occasional firing of a four pound brass cannon,** presented by the Mexican authorities in 1831, to the citizens of that exposed hamlet for protection. As DeWitt's Colony now gave evidence of permanency, settlers continued to arrive, a few of the more venture-

---

* Prior to the meeting of the Consultation, the committee of vigilance, safety and correspondence at Nacogdoches, with the central council, took action to conciliate the civilized Indians, assuring them that the Consultation would recognize and safe-guard their rights. They also sent mounted rangers to the border of the territory occupied by the wild tribes.

"Great uneasiness was felt at this time," says Morrell, "relative to Indian depredations. There were fears of a general outbreak, predicated upon the amount of horse stealing going on through the country since the war between the Americans and Mexicans. The Mexicans were evidently encouraging all the wild tribes to exterminate the colonists.

General Houston now had use for all his ingenuity among the Indians to evade the fatal catastrophe. The war between the Indians and colonists was also being hurried on by the land speculators, as their lands were valueless without an increase of population in this part of the State."
—Morrell's "Fruits and Flowers, or 46 Years in Texas," page 42.

**This was the coveted gun demanded by Captain Castenado in 1835—causing the first collision or opening flurry of the Texas War of Independence.

some locating some distance out, westward—greatly exposed to numerous hostile bands of Indians constantly visiting that section. As these incursions were generally from the west, these intrepid pioneers bore the same relations as the advance-guard of an army, receiving the first blow or warning; and, on swift horses, alarming the people farther east of the threatened raid, or approaching danger.

"In the autumn of 1833," says John Henry Brown, "John Castleman, a bold and sagacious backwoodsman, from the borders of Missouri, with his wife and four children, and his wife's mother, settled fifteen miles west of Gonzales, on Sandy Creek, on the San Antonio road. He was a bold hunter, much in the forest, and had four ferocious dogs, which served as sentinels at night, and on one occasion had a terrible fight with a number of Indians who were in the yard endeavoring to steal horses tied around the house. The dogs evidently inflicted severe punishment on the savages, who left abundant blood marks on the ground, and were glad to escape without the horses. In doing so, in sheer self defense, the Indians killed the dogs. Castleman, in his wanderings, was ever watchful for indications of Indians, and thus served as a vidette to the people of Gonzales and persons traveling on that exposed road. Many were the persons who slumbered under his roof rather than camp out at that noted watering place."

One afternoon in the spring of 1835, Geser, a French trader, his two partners, and ten Mexican cart drivers and muleteers arrived at Castleman's.* Inquiring for a suitable camping place, they were pointed to a large pool of water not far from the house,

---

* The two principal authorities on this affair are at variance on some minor details. Brown says the caravan was from Natchitoches, Louisiana, enroute to Mexico, and arrived in the forenoon. Sowell, on the authority of his father, Asa J. Sowell, and four uncles, Andrew, William, Lewis and John, all early and prominent pioneer settlers in and around Gonzales, previous to, and at the time of the tragic occurrence, affirms the party reached Castleman's "just before sundown, with a large lot of costly goods brought from Mexico, and were going east among the American settlers to dispose of them."

but at the same time, Castleman informed them he had that morning discovered signs of Indians nearby, and advised the traders they had best camp by his house: "I have plenty of wood and water, and you can have all you need; you will be safe, as my house is enclosed by strong palisades, and in case of trouble, you can come inside and I will help you to defend yourselves and your property." Thanking the settler for his generous hospitality, and assuring him they were well armed and could defend themselves in case of an attack, they moved to the water-hole, unpacked, making the usual preparations for the night, and retired—little thinking they were sleeping to their awful doom at the morrow's dawn.

Castleman, too, making everything secure for the night, retired, but not without apprehensive forebodings of danger. Just at daylight he was aroused by the firing of guns and the yelling of Indians in the direction of the pool. Hastily springing out of bed and clothing himself, he unbarred a small port-hole like window and looked out. The traders had improvised breastworks of their carts, packsaddles, and bales of goods, and were fighting with great desperation—the loud and regular reports of their escopetas (smooth-bore cavalry guns) ringing out and commingling with the exultant yells of the savages, on the crisp morning air. The sun arose and still the fight raged, lasting some four hours—the Indians charging in a circle, firing and falling back. Again and again was this repeated, narrowing the circle each time; the traders as often repelling the attack with considerable loss to the enemy. But the besieged had also sustained loss and were despairing. Taking advantage of this fact, and rendered the more desperate by their own losses, the infuriated Comanches now made a combined and determined onslaught from three sides—maneuvering so as to draw the fire of all the party simultaneously, and leaving them unloaded, when they rushed in and with exultant yells, fell upon and soon despatched their victims.

Witnessing this last charge from his window, Castleman,* it is said, drew a long breath, excitedly exclaiming: "They are gone! wife, that charge will wind them up, those whoops are for victory." It was so—a short hand to hand struggle and all was over.

After scalping and mutilating their victims, disposing of their own dead, and packing all the booty they cared for on their horses and the captured mules, the victorious Comanches leisurely moved off up the country. Castleman said he counted eighty warriors as they slowly passed in single file, each shaking his lance or shield at his house, but making no further demonstrations.

"As soon as he thought it was safe after the Indians left," says Sowell, "Castleman visited the battle ground. It was a terrible sight; the Mexicans had piled up their goods, saddles and other camp equipage around them, and the whole surrounded by their carts. Inside this little square or circle, they lay horribly mutilated and drenched in blood. Geser had many wounds on him and had evidently fought bravely, and exposed

* "Castleman could," says Brown, "many times, have killed an Indian with his trusty rifle from his cabin window, but was restrained by his wife, who regarded the destruction of the strangers as certain, and contended that if her husband took part, vengeance would be wreaked upon the family—a hundred savages against one man. He desisted, but as his wife said, 'frothed at the mouth,' to be restrained from action on such an occasion. Had he possessed a modern Winchester, he could have repelled the whole array and saved both the traders and their goods." To which Sowell adds: "At the foot of the hill, 100 yards or more from the house, stood a large tree, upon which Castleman had tacked a piece of white paper to serve as a target when he felt disposed to rifle practice. This paper caught the eye of an Indian as he was scouting around, separated from his companions, and he came to the tree to see what it was. The settler saw him, and at once raised his rifle to take aim, as this was too good a chance to lose of killing an Indian. He had often hit the paper target at that distance. Before he could fire, however, his prudent wife laid her hand on the gun and implored him to desist; that if he killed one of them, the Indians would be almost sure to attack the house, otherwise they might leave without molesting them. The Indian in question did not long remain as a mark for the pioneer, for, as soon as he discovered the bullet holes in and around the paper on the tree, he turned and looked toward the cabin, and taking in the situation, ran behind the tree, and using it for cover, beat a hasty retreat."

his person more than any of the others.

"The ground was almost covered with arrows, some broken, others transfixed in boxes, saddles and carts. The Indians threw their dead in the pool of water—how many could not be ascertained. There were many bloody spots on the ground outside of where the Mexicans lay. Castleman now returned to the house, and taking his family, hurriedly departed for Gonzales to carry the news. The Indians went back towards the west, and no doubt had been on Geser's trail some time, knowing the nature of the rich booty which he carried. There were no white settlements from Castleman's on to the Rio Grande, and over this vast territory the Comanches then roamed at will, and often captured trains of Mexican carts and trade caravans."

## THE FIGHT ON THE BLANCO.

The sequel to the above tragic affair will now be given as condensed and reconciled, from the two principal accounts—Brown's and Sowell's both Texas pioneers, and each an acknowledged authority on matters pertaining to our border history.*

When Castleman reached Gonzales with the news, it spread rapidly, and by daylight on the following morning, a party of about thirty men were in the saddle and enroute to Castleman's. Among these volunteers the following names—

* As in the preceding affair, Brown and Sowell are at variance. We give preference to the latter, since he obtained his information from surviving participants in the engagement, supplying details. Sowell says twenty-seven men composed this expedition, and places them under command of Bartlett D. McClure. Brown says: "In a few hours a band of 29 or 30 volunteers, under Dr. Miller, were on the trail and followed it across the Guadalupe and up the San Marcos, and finally into a cedar brake in a valley surrounded by high hills, presumably on the Rio Blanco"; and adds, "This was on the second day after the massacre." "It is painful to add," continues Brown, "that this Dr. Miller, later in the same year, became a tory, and left the country, settling in Michigan, never to return." His name has sometimes been confounded with that of the patriotic Dr. James B. Miller, of Fort Bend, long distinguished in public life under the province and Republic of Texas.

several of whom afterward won fame on other fields, or figured prominently in the fiery history of Texas—are preserved: Matthew ("Old Paint") Caldwell, Dan McCoy, Jesse McCoy, James C. Darst, Ezekiel Williams, John Davis, "Wash" Cottle, Almaron Dickinson, (martyr of the Alamo), Andrew J. Sowell, Sr., Dr. James C. Miller, Wm. S. Fisher, (of Meir Expedition fame in 1842), David Hanna, Landon Webster, Jonathan Scott, John Castleman, Tom Malone, ____ White, and Bartlett D. McClure—the latter being chosen captain.

The trail of the Indians (from Castleman's ranch) led up the south valley of the Guadalupe, crossing that river at a place now called "Erskine's Ford," within the present limits of Guadalupe county, and some twelve miles from Seguin. After crossing Darst Creek, about twenty-six miles from Gonzales, and just below the "French Smith Ranch," the Indians, it seems, amused themselves by securing spools of thread to their horses' tails and letting it unwind across the flats and prairies as they traveled. The dropped strands thus served the settlers to follow the trail at a more rapid gait, but the Indians evidently apprehended no danger of pursuit. They now bore to the northwest and to the headwaters of Mill Creek, passing out across the York Creek divide. Though traveling slowly on account of their heavy booty, the Indians moved steadily by day and night, while the pursuers could only keep the trail in daylight—"two ravens," says Sowell, "followed in the wake of the Indians picking up the offal from their camps, and would fly up and follow on at the approach of the white men."

After breaking camp on the third day out, and some two miles ahead, the whites came upon the first regular camp of the enemy, on a high ridge, south of, and overlooking, the present town of San Marcos, in Hays county, and where in a circle round a pole, the Indians had tramped down the grass—performing their customary scalp dance, the night previous.

From here, the Indians having entered the mountains, the trailing was more difficult and the pursuit slackened, the men making their last outward camp in the brakes of the Rio Blanco. The signs now indicated that they were close upon the enemy, causing the whites to move with more caution. Just as they were entering a valley the heavy morning fog lifted, and suddenly the yell of an Indian was heard on a mountain across the river. Captain McClure now ordered a rapid advance, but soon entered such dense brakes, they were compelled to dismount (leaving their horses), and proceed on foot. Scouts were now sent forward to reconnoiter,* while the others slowly followed in single file, stooping and crawling as they went. "Finally they came out into an opening near the river where three or four could walk abreast, and at this instant bang! bang! came the sharp report of two rifles and the yelling of Indians near at hand. 'Charge, boys!' shouted McClure, as he sprang in front. 'Here they are!' Pell-mell, in a foot race that had it been timed, might have proved famous, came the scouts closely pursued by a party of yelling savages, who were pulling arrows and adjusting them to their bow strings. Springing to one side as their spies flew past, Captain McClure raised his rifle and fired at the foremost red skin to come in range; Castleman shot the next one who fell

* Sowell says two scouts, Almaron Dickinson and James Darst, were sent ahead to locate the Indians; Brown says three—Matthew Caldwell, Dan McCoy and Ezekiel Williams—went forward to reconnoiter, and adds a thrilling and amusing, but conflicting incident: "Following the newly made path of the Indians through the brake, in about three hundred yards, they suddenly came upon them dismounted and eating; they speedily retired, but were discovered and, being only three in number, the whole crowd of Indians furiously pursued them with such yells as, resounding from bluff to bluff, caused some of the men in ambush to flee from the apparent wrath to come; but of the whole number of 29 or 30, sixteen maintained their position and their senses. Dan McCoy, the hindmost of the three scouts in single file, wore a long-tailed coat. This was seized and held by an Indian, but Old Dan, as he was called, threw his arms backward and slipped from the garment without stopping, exclaiming, 'Take it, d—n you!' Caldwell sprang first into the glade, wheeled, fired and killed the first Indian to enter. Others unable to see through the brush till exposed to view, rushed into the trap till nine (?) warriors lay in a heap. Realizing this fact, and such unexpected fatality, the pursuers raised that dismal howl, which means death and defeat, and fell back to their camp. The panic among some of our men prevented pursuit. It is a fact that among those seized with the 'buck ague,' were men then wholly inexperienced, who subsequently became distinguished for coolness and bravery."

across the lifeless body of the first. Several other shots were fired, and a third Indian had his bow stick shot in two while in the act of discharging an arrow. Thus surprised, the other pursuers beat a hasty retreat towards the river, yelling loudly as a warning signal to their comrades, of the danger encountered. By this time most of the men had gotten clear of the brush and charged with their captain across the open ground."

"Near the river" says Sowell, "they met about fifty Indians, and the fight became general. The yelling of the Comanches almost drowned the report of the firearms, and echoed far up the Blanco valley. But the Indians soon gave way, evidently fighting more in an attempt to cross their packs over the river. Another sharp fight took place at the river, some of the Indians halting in the water to shoot, but the unerring rifles of the whites again caused them to flee in disorder—across the river and into the brakes beyond, leaving most of their spoils."

Thus the whites were victorious, without any serious or fatal casualties and were glad enough to abandon the pursuit without crossing the river. Sowell says, "The Indians made a very poor fight and seemed rattled at the very commencement, shooting wild and running at every volley from the whites. They had evidently shot most of their arrows in the fight with the Mexicans. Those killed had but very few in their quivers— some even none."

Regaining their horses and carrying part of the more valuable goods, the militant colonists returned home without further incident. The remaining spoils with many bows, shields, blankets and buffalo robes were cached on the bank of the river, and a party afterward went back for them, but they had been badly damaged by sun and rain.

---

## MURDER OF CANOMA.

Catching the thread of narrative, dropped for the sake of chronological order in 1833, the reader will now learn the sad story of Chief Canoma's fate.

The Wacos, Tehuacanas, Ionies, Anadarkos, Towash, and

other kindred tribes of the Caddoan confederation, inhabiting the Upper Brazos and Trinity Rivers, and known as the "Wild tribes," were now openly hostile—especially toward the settlers of the Colorado, regarding them as a separate "tribe" from the people of the Brazos.*

* "In the first settlement of Austin's colony," says Kenney, "some unscrupulous white men stole horses from the Caddos and brought them into.the settlement at the 'Falls' of the Brazos. But the settlers there, not relishing such freebooter proceedings, took the horses from the thieves and returned them to the Indians with explanations, which made a very favorable impression on the savages. The settlers on the Colorado were already involved in a war with the wild tribes, and the return of the stolen horses persuaded the Indians that they were different tribes, one disposed to be friendly, and the other hostile." A Comprehensive History of Texas, Vol. 1, page 746.

Issac Duke Parker, an early emigrant to the eastern part of Texas, writing of affairs prevous to and about this period, says: "At that time all the Indians east of the Brazos river were peaceable (?), and were located as follows: The Cooshatties and Alabamas lived on the Trinity, in what is now Polk county; the Beedis on Beedi creek, south of the 'Laborde' road, in what is now Madison county; the Wacos lived where the city of Waco now is; the Tehuacanas at the site of the present Tehuacana High School, Limestone county; the Ionies on Ioni creek, where the line between Houston and Anderson counties now runs; the Kickapoos on the Neches and north of the San Antonio road. They were all peaceable with the people east of the Brazos river, but most of them regarded the people west of the Brazos as a different race of people, and would commit depredations, killing and robbing west of that river, while maintaining friendly attitude towards the people east of the Brazos."—Reminiscences of Pioneer Life in Texas, MSS. page 1.

Writing of the Texas tribes, Captain George B. Erath says: "There is one thing that we particularly noted about their superstitions, they always believed the people of Texas to be of entirely different origin from the people of the United States; and they had the same ideas about a difference of tribes in Texas before Texas was separated from Mexico. Even after they made their treaties in 1845 they believed that the white people of the Brazos were altogether different 'tribes' from those on the Colorado and west of that stream. They claimed to be at peace on the Brazos, while depredating on the Colorado. And this was the idea of all the wild Indians in Texas, excepting, perhaps, the Tonks, who, from their total difference, and from the hatred against them by the other Indians, were compelled to occupy ground within the borders of white settlements. A small band or subdivision of Caddos also maintained friendly intercourse with the settlers about the Brazos and did not participate in this wild idea, but, knowing that the people on the Colorado made no distinction between Indians, they kept aloof and refrained from going westward of the waters of the Brazos, confining their hunting and camps within that scope. Friendly and fear-

During the spring of this year, the faithful and intelligent old chief, with his band of some thirty friendly Caddos, was still about the settlements, and village of Tenoxtitlan. Assured of his faithfulness to the whites and appreciating his influence with the wild tribes, the Americans about the "Falls" employed Canoma to go among the hostiles and invite them to come in for a friendly talk and treaty; and particularly to recover two white captives then held—children of a Mr. Ross.

Canoma, leaving two of his children as hostages, left on this peace embassy, and in due time returned, reporting that the tribes visited would treat with the Brazos people, but that a majority were irreconcilable and very bitter against the settlers on the Colorado—even then a party of the hostiles were leaving on a foray in the direction of that settlement.

A messenger rode rapidly from the "Falls" to give warning of this danger, but unfortunately, arrived too late the wily foe having slipped in, murdered a settler, stole a number of horses and left—eluding the quick pursuit of a small party of citizens under Edward Burleson.

Meantime some travelers, halting at the "Falls," lost some horses—strayed away—and employed Canoma to recover them, furnishing him with written authority for that purpose. The aged chief with his wife and son, following the track of the straying animals westward, found them near the Three Forks of Little River. "If he had returned at once to the settlements" says Kenney, "it would have saved the life of himself and son, and spared the historian a painful duty; but, being in no hurry, he stopped to hunt, and while in camp was found by the party from

less, they were regarded as protectors to the settlers of the Brazos.

"This produced, about the years 1834-5, an antipathy between the people on the Colorado and Guadalupe, and the people of the Brazos, some going so far as to charge the settlers on the Brazos side with conniving at the outrages committed out west, and buying the stolen horses. The wild Indians in doing mischief, would if possible, pass out through the camp of these more civilized bands, and, when followed, it would thus implicate those who were disposed or actually friendly and innocent—finally producing the general indiscriminate war."—"My Knowledge of the Aborigines of Texas", MSS. Page 5-6.

Bastrop, who were pursuing the marauders."

Canoma produced his credentials, which must have been convincing, since it was plainly impossible for him to have forged them. But, finding they were deliberating about taking his life, he begged them to go with him to the "Falls," thirty miles away, where the owners of the horses were, to verify his state-ment—a request which could not with any reason be refused; but it was left to a vote, and a fatal majority condemned the plainly innocent man to death.* Canoma and son were tied to trees and shot—the squaw being spared to find her way in alone to her people. Though not censuring the Brazos people, the report of this cold-blooded act greatly incensed the remainder of the band, who now left the settlement under their second, or war-chief, Choctaw Tom, for the Indian country—themselves declaring war against the Coloradoans.

Thus the smoldering sparks were being fanned, and as the settlers continued to push out further, and bolder, disregarding the fancied rights and privileges of the different tribes, the flames of savage warfare were being kindled along the entire frontier.

---

## ROUTING THE KEECHIS.

In May of this year, in consequence of some depredations; and suspecting the small tribe of Keechis, a company of about thirty Cummings settlement men armed, mounted, and left Washington-on-the-Brazos, against these Indians. Arriving at their village on Boggy Creek, a tributary of the Trinity in what is now Leon county, they were met by the head men of the tribe, who professed surprise, stoutly declaring their innocence and

---

* Brown, somewhat apologetically, says Burleson and party were not aware of the old chief's faithfulness, but that Burleson was disposed to honor his credentials. His men, however, "already incensed, and finding Canoma in possession of the horses under such suspicious circumstances, gave rein to unreasoning exasperation—ever lamented by the chivalrous and kind hearted Burleson." But the tainted page cannot be expunged from our history.

friendship; and in proof exhibited a treaty with them signed by the empresario Sterling C. Robertson.

"We were about to depart without molesting them," says Joel W. Robinson, who was in the expedition, "when some of our men, in looking about the village, saw and recognized several horses which had been stolen from the settlements on the Colorado. Finding they were detected, the Keechis seized their arms. We fired on them, killing two of their number, when they took refuge in a thicket contiguous to the village, which was afterwards burned. None of our men were injured. Papers were found in the village which were known to have been on the person of a young man named Edwards who was killed by the Indians twenty miles below Bastrop, a few months previously.

"We immediately collected about thirty head of horses and started homeward. As we expected the Indians would pursue us and make an effort to recover the horses, a strong guard was placed around our camp the ensuing night. At a late hour one of the sentinels fired off his gun and ran into camp crying 'Indians!' The night was unusually dark, and the men, suddenly aroused from sleep, mistook one another for the enemy. Some clubbed their rifles and knocked down their messmates. Several shots were also fired, and one man (Benjamin Castleman) was killed and another wounded, before the mistake was discovered. I think it probable that the sentinel really saw Indians, but they did not molest us. We returned home without further mishap. Both Major Oldham and Capt. John York claimed the command of this company, and were constantly quarreling about it, but neither of them was ever fully recognized as such by the men."

## COLEMAN'S FIGHT—MOORE'S EXPEDITION.

Following this summary chastisement of the Keechis, Captain Robert M. Coleman, of Bastrop, with a company of twenty-five, three of whom were Brazos men and well known to many of the Indians, crossed the Brazos at Washington, on the fourth of July, enroute to the Tehuacana village, at the famous springs of that name, now in Limestone county.

The purpose of this expedition, it is said, was to hold council and form a treaty with the tribe, but spies gave warning of an armed force approaching, and taking it for granted that their intentions were hostile, the Indians took strong position in their rifle pits, dug in the ground, firing upon the whites as they came within range. A desperate fight now ensued in which a number of Indians fell, but they were obstinate and held their ground, repelling all efforts to dislodge them from their strongholds; and in the end compelling Coleman and his small force to retreat, with the loss of one man killed and four wounded.

Halting at Fort Parker, two and a half miles from the present town of Groesbeck, Coleman sent messengers to the settlements for re-inforcements, and was soon joined by three volunteer companies, under Captains Robert M. Williamson, (the gifted, dauntless, eloquent and eccentric three-legged Willie) George W. Bennett and _____ Caheen.

The whole was under the chief command of Col. John H. Moore, with Joseph C. Neill (a soldier of the Horseshoe) as adjutant; the combined forces immediately marching to the village, but the Indians had timely warning and fled.

Thus foiled in their plans to retaliate and punish the wily Tehuacanas, the forces now scoured the country to the forks of the Trinity, near the subsequent site of Dallas, passing over to and down the Brazos; crossing that river where old Fort Graham later stood, and returned home after a trip of several weeks. But few Indians were encountered on the trip—one warrior who was killed, and a few women and children who were captured, carried into settlements, and sold for slaves—the only instance in all the Indian wars of Texas.*

Although failing to engage the enemy and to strike them a decisive blow, these expeditions and military demonstrations

* "The same experiment," says Kenney, "had been tried in all the States, but it had always proved a failure, as it did in this instance. The Indians would not work even in slavery, and, unfortunately, not in any other condition."

were not without their results—says Yoakum: "This seasonable display of force on the frontier was of great service, as it over-awed the Indians, and also tended to discipline the volunteers, and prepare them for the toils and triumphs that awaited them at home. As expressed in the somewhat pompous language of one of Austin's 'original 300,' 'this campaign on the frontier was of great service, as it gave the Indians an idea of what the Texans could and would do if they continued to bother them.'"

---

## HEROIC DEFENSE OF THE TAYLOR FAMILY.

Besides serving as a connecting link in the long and bloody chain of our frontier history, the following incident is of further consideration as illustrating the wonderful heroism of the pioneer women of Texas.

As early as 1833-4 the brave and hardy pioneers of Robertson's Colony, or "Milam Land District," as it was afterwards known, had pushed as far west as the present county seat of Bell county. Among the first—truly advance-guards, and for some time thereafter the outermost inhabitants in that direction—were the Taylor family, who settled near the Three Folks of Little River, in what is now known as "Taylor's Valley," some three miles southeast of the present city of Belton, and almost the same distance above the "Falls."

The home was a double log cabin with covered but un-floored, passage between—a door to each cabin opening to the passage; the shutters of riven slats, failing to reach to the top and leaving an opening of several inches.

The family consisted of Joseph Taylor and wife; two grown daughters, and two sons, Stephen, the oldest, 13 or 14 years of age—all the children by a former, deceased husband, Mr. Frazier.

In the night of November 12th, 1835,* on the light of the

---

* News, however important the event, did not travel so fast in that pioneer time, as now. There were no telephones; no telegraph, to flash the occurrence of this affair to the only newspaper then published in all Texas, that

Heroic Defense of the Taylor Family

Massacre of the Traders

moon, and after the family had retired—the parents and girls in one room; the two boys in the other—a party of eleven Kickapoo Indians attacked the house. The first intimation of danger was the fierce barking of a faithful watch-dog which, however, was soon silenced with an arrow. Approaching nearer, the Indians in broken English accosted Mr. Taylor, demanding to know how many men were in the house: "We have a plenty of men, well armed and ready to fight," answered Taylor. "You lie, one man!" shouted the red skin as he peered through a small crack. Whereupon Taylor thrust him with a board causing his hasty retreat.

Meantime Mrs. Taylor threw open the door and called the boys to her room, which they reached unharmed amid a shower of balls and arrows. At this moment and just as Mrs. Taylor succeeded in barring and securing the door with a heavy table, a powerful warrior violently shook the shutter, demanding admittance, saying "Me poor Indian. Want tobacco—no fight." To which Mrs. Taylor boldly replied: "No admittance, and no presents for red devils." The attack now commenced in earnest, the brave Mrs. Taylor commanding the forces within. Placing a table against the door, she armed and mounted the youngest boy, only twelve years old, with instructions to shoot the first Indian that came in range, while the two girls were set to moulding bullets, that the supply might not give out. For once the boy on the table found the opening over the door shutter, a convenience. Procuring an axe from the wood-pile, one of the fiends started for the door and had reached the covered passage-way, when the brave little boy fired and the Indian dropped dead. Seeing the fate of his comrade, another demon rushed up and attempted to drag the dead one away, when with the same accuracy as the boy, Taylor fired, felling the second Indian, mortally wounded, across the first one. The redskins were now more cautious, resorting to strategy rather than hazard the dangers of direct attack. The farthest end of the vacated

its readers might scan the headlines or read the details of this thrilling event. Just twenty days elapsed before the matter found its way into print.

room was fired, and as the flames made rapid headway, the exultant fiends danced and indulged in most demoniacal yells, which fell heavily on the ears of the besieged and now seemingly doomed inmates. And now it was that Mr. Taylor, considering their fate sealed, became very much dispirited, and suggested to his wife that they rush out and surrender. "They will doubtless kill me, but make you and the children prisoners. In that event you must drop bits of clothing on the way so that friends can follow and recapture you." But the heroic wife and mother with great earnestness and resolute determination responded: "No! I had rather perish in the flames; had rather die a thousand deaths, and see my daughters killed, rather than they should suffer the shame and agonizing tortures of captivity in the hands of such merciless and savage fiends! No! you must take courage and fight. We must defend ourselves to the last, and if the worst come, die bravely together!" This brave hearted matron infused her dauntless spirit into all.

Meanwhile the flames were making rapid headway in the roof, and the fate of the family now indeed seemed sealed, the fire would soon consume them, or force them to leave the house to meet a worse fate at the hands of the relentless foe, unless it was checked. But the heroic Mrs. Taylor in her desperate determination to save her loved ones, was equal to the emergency, declaring they would yet win the contest and all be saved. Fortunately there was a small barrel of home-made vinegar in the room, and the usual supply of milk. With these she declared she could put out the fire, and suiting her action to the resolution, and with a degree of courage evinced by few,* she mounted

* Afterwards, in relating this feat to Capt. Shapley Ross, Mrs. Taylor said she thought not of personal danger from the arrows of the Indians, abusing them all the while. In the covered passage-way already described, there was suspended by bear grass thongs, a quantity of "jerked" buffalo and bear meat. As the heat and flames reached this part of the roof, the fat "bacon" was ignited and began to fry—the intensely hot grease streaming down on the wounded Indian, virtually cooking him alive, and causing him to utter the most hideous and agonizing yells, greatly to the delight of Mrs. Taylor, who looked down upon the squirming wretch and pro-

a table and ascended the log wall to the roof. Removing the "weight poles" and quickly clearing away the boards or riven shingles, making an opening in advance of the fire, and then baring her head and chest to the constant fire of the enemy, she coolly and judiciously distributed the fluids as they were passed up to her, quenching and arresting the further spread of the flames. And surely old Mars smiled on this Spartan-like matron as she regained the floor unharmed, but with several bullet holes in and through her clothing. While these scenes were transpiring, Mr. Taylor and the eldest son were not idle. A horse was tied near the house in the yard; an Indian attempted to secure the animal; Mr. Taylor fired and the thief fled, wounded. About the same time the boy, Stephen Frazier, secured aim and wounded another. The contest was now varying somewhat in favor of the besieged. But the enemy were loath to give up the contest. The vigilant eye and ear of Mrs. Taylor now discovered one of the Indians in the outer chimney corner, endeavoring to start a fire and at the same time peering through a considerable hole burnt in the dirt and wood "jam," for a shot. Securing a large wooden shovelful of live coals and embers, she threw them full into his face and bosom, causing the red devil to spring away with an agonizing "waugh! ugh!"—to which Mrs. Taylor somewhat facetiously ejaculated: "Take that you yellow varmint, it will help you to kindle your fire!" This "heroic," ocular treatment, it was afterwards learned, partially destroyed the Indian's sight.

Thus discomfitted and foiled, the Indians withdrew, and after a short consultation, gave up the attack and left.

An hour or so later, the heroic family decided to leave their dismantled home—first secreting their bedding and some other valuables in the Leon bottom, one of the boys serving as sentinel from the house top while this was being done—and make their way to their nearest neighbor, Capt. Gouldsby Childress, who

claimed: "Howl, you yellow brute! You are not fit to feed to hogs! But we'll roast you for the wolves!!"

had built a cabin on Little River, about seven miles below, and near the present town of Rogers, where they arrived soon after daylight.

In the forenoon of the same day, George W. Chapman, in command of a small company of rangers stationed at the "Falls" of the Brazos, arrived at the Taylor cabin and were greatly surprised to find it dismantled and deserted, and naturally supposed the family had been carried into captivity, or murdered. The rangers cut off the heads of the two dead and charred Indians, stuck them on long poles, and raised them as a gruesome warning to other hostiles that might pass that way.

Reverting thus far into the misty past—this thrilling episode occurred full three quarters of a century ago—today a beautiful and substantial city, in point of numbers equal almost to the then combined white population of Texas, burst upon the vision of the writer—enlivened by the shrill whistle of locomotives and the humming spindles of busy factories—as he stands upon the spot once covered by the Taylor home. A marble shaft should be reared to commemorate the heroism of this noble family of pioneers—the prominent figure of which should be a woman—the heroic Mrs. Taylor, rifle in hand, in fighting attitude.

All the participants in this affair have passed away—Mr. Taylor soon thereafter; the noble Mrs. Taylor, "in 1851 or '52," says Capt. Shapley Ross, "re-occupied the old homestead, the scene of her desperate experience, in Taylor's Valley, in Bell county, and is said to have died there." Mrs. Chapman, the eldest daughter, survived till a few years ago.

A few years before his death, the gallant ranger chief, Col. "Rip" Ford, in response to the author's request for data on this affair, wrote:

"During 1888 the writer was at Pleasanton, Atascosa county, where he met Mrs. Chapman, the widow of Capt. Geo. W. Chapman, as brave an Indian fighter as ever set foot on Texas soil—winning his first spurs as lieutenant in Capt. Shapley Ross' ranger company; and who died in 1879. Mrs. Chapman was the eldest daughter of Mrs. Taylor and participated in the thrilling episode referred to. At that time Chapman made his home with the Taylor's, but was absent when the fight occurred.

"Mrs. Chapman explained the cause of the difficulty. A party of Tonkawa Indians were camped near Taylor's house. A party of Kickapoos were known to be in the vicinity. The Tonkawas informed Mr. Taylor they were going to steal the horses of the Kickapoos. Mr. Taylor insisted they should not, because their proximity to his home might implicate him. They agreed to move away, but failed to do so, till they had stolen the horses and maneuvered so as to cause the Kickapoos to blame Taylor. Preparations were made for defense in case of trouble—Taylor had only two guns; Chapman had gone to Nashville to procure more. He reached the Taylor home about daylight, and finding it partly consumed and vacated, and naturally supposing the inmates had been murdered, perhaps burned or carried off captives, he hastened back to Nashville and told the sad news. A company of rangers and citizens was quickly enroute to the scene—they met the Taylor family on the way. The fugitives were in a sad plight; their clothing almost torn to pieces from contact with the bushes and briars; in reality they were almost naked from the waist down.—Said Mrs. Chapaman: 'All of us were in a state of undress. My two brothers were almost without clothing. We were much fatigued, and hungry; everything to eat had been burned. When we reached the house of Mr. Childress, we were well treated. After we had been there sixteen days our dog came to us, but he never recovered from his wound.' As the Kickapoos surrounded the house, Mr. Taylor talked with them and asked them to desist till he could explain; that he would go with them to the Tonkawa camp next day and prove his innocence; but they refused, saying he was a party to the theft. The beleaguered family understood the situation. There was no chance to escape. It was fight, and the chances were to die. Mrs. Taylor advocated fighting to the bitter end. True heroine, she deserves a monument, not of marble alone, but a place in the heart of every one who admires undaunted courage—mortal and physical—and which menacing dangers cannot shake nor time abate."

"P. S. 'Captain Chapman, my late husband,' says Mrs. Chapman, 'came to us at the home of Mr. Childress. He had been to our house. The bodies of the two Indians were being eaten by the hogs. Both the rooms of the house were burned. He supposed the hogs were feasting on the dead bodies of the Taylor family, and knew no better till he reached the house of Mr. Childress.'"

Briefly referring to "The Taylor Fight" in a note to the Belton (Texas) Journal in 1886, the Hon. Geo. W. Tyler, himself the worthy son of a noble Texas pioneer—Judge Orville T. Tyler—said: "Mrs. Chapman visited her friends in Bell county some nine or ten years ago, when I called upon her and obtained a very full account of the whole affair, which I reduced to writing at the time in the form of notes, but they were destroyed when my office burned in 1879. She was a mere child when the fight occurred, but her recollections of the minutest details were vivid, accurate and interesting. Mrs. Chapman lives in Atascosa county. Her husband, Geo. W. Chapman, now deceased, was a brother of Mr. W. S. Chapman of Temple. He lived formerly in Bell county, and was, as I understand it, a justice of the peace at the first organization of the county, for one of the county precincts. There is a story among the old settlers to the effect that when he held his last term of court, a difficulty arose among the bystanders, and the constable attempted to restore order, whereupon the crowd ran the constable away, and there was therefore, no officer present to make proclamation of the adjournment of 'His Honor's' court, and that said court has remained open ever since."

To the late Capt. W. T. Davidson—one of the very early residents of old Nashville—we are indebted for many valuable notes on the Taylor fight and other early incidents in that section. He says: "I write entirely from memory, and after the lapse of many years, but in the main think I am accurate. The Taylor family and my mother with her family of five children (the Comanches having murdered my father in 1836), lived after the incident at the town of Nashville on the Brazos, and some twenty five miles below the scene of Taylor's fight; and I have heard Mrs. Taylor relate the affair to my mother on many occasions.

* * * * *

"There were many stirring events taking place all the time; one in which Joe Taylor, of Taylor's Valley fight fame, participated. He was carrying the mail between Nashville and Independence, and was returning after night when within about two miles of town he discovered five or six Indians just above the road sitting on their horses. Taylor hailed them, and at the same time put spurs to his horse with Indians right at his heels. On and on they came like a whirlwind into town. One big, stalwart fellow came right alongside and tried to grapple his bridle reins. Taylor, who was carrying a rifle, but being so closely pursued, was unable to use it up to this time, struck the Indian over the head and landed him on the ground. The people of the town soon collected around Taylor and wanted to know what he was making all that noise about—hollering 'run here boys, run here boys!' He then related his experience and showed a wound he had received at the hands of the red devils."

The "Three Forks of Little River," constituted by the juncture of the Leon, the Lampasas and the Salado, and designated by the Mexicans as well as the early American settlers, as the "San Andres," was a notable locality in the colonial and pioneer period of Texas, many stirring episodes occurring in and around the vicinity. Speaking of the Lampasas, (Water Lily) and the Salado, (Saltish) it may be of interest to know the names of these two streams were, in some way, perhaps by blundering geographers, transposed—the original nomenclature being characteristic, of the two waters, while the unfortunate change is noticeably incongruous. In like manner were the "Brazos" and "Colorado" misnomered.

In September of this year surveying parties were fitted out by Thomas A. Graves, for locating lands in the then rapidly settling Robertson's Colony. While working on the San Gabriel they were surprised by a band of depredating Indians—two of the party killed, and the others barely escaping by flight.

---

## TRIALS OF EARLY EMIGRANTS.

In November following, the same month in which occurred the Taylor attack, and in the same locality, W. C. Sparks, his negro man, Jack and Michael Reed, with an ox wagon loaded with corn, left the now unknown, but then important point called "Tenoxtitlan," to seek a camping place and ultimate home on the "Rio San Andres" (now Little River) about ten or twelve miles southeast of the present city of Belton. The sequel is best given by John Henry Brown, an acknowledged authority on matters of Texas border history: "Sparks, Reed and Jack arrived and pitched camp at a point on Little River on what has since been known as the Sparks League. They on the same day, constructed a pen in which to place their corn. As the night approached, Mr. Reed crossed the river and passed his first night on Little River in the camp of a newly arrived emigrant named John Welsh. Outside of the Taylor family that entire country was then a vast, but beautiful and lovely solitude. In most other outside localities, as at Bastrop, Gonzales, Tenoxtitlan and elsewhere, families congregated for the time being in a special settlement and had their temporary fields around them, whereby all the available force could be rallied in a moment for defense. But these men on Little River had no such nucleus. They took life with all its hazards and moved in the very heart of an Indian country.

"On this first night the Indians attacked the lonely camp of Sparks and Jack. Many shots were fired and were heard by Michael Reed and John Welsh on the opposite side of the river. Sparks and Jack, in the dark, sought refuge in a thicket. The Indians seemed afraid to attack the camp and retired. In the morning Sparks and Jack struck out for Tenoxtitlan, on the Brazos. Michael Reed and John Welsh on visiting the camp and finding no one, took up their effects and returned to the Brazos. On their way and near where Brushy Creek enters the San Gabriel, Sparks and Jack met two men, brothers, named Riley, with two wagons, their effects, wives and children, destined for the Little River settlement. They appraised them of the previous night's happenings and advised them to return, but they would not, and moved on. Inside of a mile the Indians appeared, professed friendship and claimed only to be following Sparks and Jack. Thereupon the brothers Riley countermarched. But as they were entering the bottom at Brushy Creek the Indians appeared on each side of the wagons. As they entered the creek one savage jumped on the lead horse, cut loose his hames, and was about to whirl around for offensive measures, when one of the Riley brothers shot him dead. Then began a vigorous fight. A young man of the party, with the women and children, fled to the brush and kept on fleeing until, in about two days, they reached the settlements on the Brazos. Very soon one of the Rileys was mortally wounded, but before dying killed two—so that the deceased brother and five Indians lay dead in the bed of the creek, within a few feet of each other. The attacking party, in view of such mortality, fled, and left the field to the surviving Riley. Nothing daunted, he took from one of the wagons a mattress, on which he laid his dead brother—covering him in sheets and quilts, to keep the wolves from mutilating his body— then mounted one of the horses and next day arrived at the settlement of Yellow Prairie, now in Burleson county. He returned with a party and buried his brother. Soon afterward, the Rileys left Texas and returned to Mississippi."

Both Reed and Sparks have relatives yet living in that vicinity; all honorable and worthy—William, a son of Michael Reed, having served as first sheriff of Bell county. Sam Sparks, a most estimable and worthy descendant of W. C. Sparks, is now holding the office of State Treasurer.*

Numerous other tragedies and incidents of border warfare occurred during this year—the exact dates, and in most instances reliable details of which are lacking.

* Resigned in 1912.

## MURDER OF THE RANCHEROS.

In the course of some excavations being made in the courthouse yard at Corpus Christi in 1902, eighteen human skeletons were unearthed. The gruesome discovery excited much curiosity and speculation till the mystery was cleared away by Mr. Frandalig, one of the oldest inhabitants of the coast country, and residing in the vicinity as far back as 1835. "In 1835," he said, "there resided a short distance west of the site of Corpus Christi, a ranchman Alejandro Garcia, who had in his employ about twenty peons. The Lipan Indians, about one hundred strong, made a raid on the ranch, and recognizing his inability to hold out against so formidable a band of Indians, Garcia and his peons fled for their lives in this direction. They were pursued and overtaken near the present site of Corpus Christi, and though they made desperate resistance, were finally overcome and most, if not all, massacred. After the Indians had retreated, Mexican soldiers from San Antonio and rancheros from intervening points, came and buried the unfortunate victims at or near where they fell, and, to the best of my recollection, that point is about where the present court house stands." This is the account in brief—the key that unlocks the past and reveals the fate of the participants in one of the many bloody, but unwritten scenes by which this "fairest spot of God's creation,"* now peopled with a generation who know the red man only as some legendary being, was wrenched from as cruel and relentless a

* DeCordova says: "Depredation after depredation continued, innumerable parties of frontiersmen were fitted out, who, whenever an opportunity offered, did good service; yet the Indians were seldom to be seen, although the settlers, to their sorrow, often felt their presence. No sooner was a murder committed, or horses stolen, than, even before the alarm could be given, the savages had traveled far upon the way to their homes; and, with the characteristic cunning and skill which they ever displayed on their predatory incursions, it was difficult for the white men to follow their trail. Besides, their power of endurance of fatigue and want of food were far beyond those of their pursuers. It is well known that these hardy sons of the forest have repeatedly traveled more than one hundred miles over hill and dale, swimming creeks and rivers, without food or rest."

race, when roused to resentment, as ever inhabited any portion of the globe from the day it was first flung untamed, uncultivated, from the creative hand of God.

---

## FATE OF PETER MERCER.

The Mercers, (Peter and Jesse) were the first settlers on the San Gabriel. They built a rude cabin on the bank of the river, and cleared a small farm in the bottom near what is now San Gabriel post-office. Jesse Mercer's wife was dead and he and his children lived with Peter Mercer, who was married, but had no children. One day when Jesse* was absent, a party of Indians approached the house, but manifesting friendship, surrounded the settler in his yard, when they seized his gun and discharged its contents into his body. In the agonies of death he ran some distance and sprang from a bluff, lodging in the underbrush below, a corpse. While the Indians were engaged in a futile search for his body, Mrs. Mercer with the children and a negro boy, fled down the bottom, and reached the slightly flushed river, which was crossed with some difficulty—tying a grapevine around the waist of the negro boy, and holding the other end while he carried the children across, one at a time. After other adventures and much suffering from hunger, the fugitives made their way down to the settlement on the San Gabriel, in what is now Milam county.

---

* In his series of "Frontier Sketches," published in the Fort Worth Gazette, 1884-5, pioneer Frank M. Collier wrote interestingly of this same Jesse Mercer—then married, though somewhat unhappily, a second time—as one of the first settlers on Mercer Creek six miles south of the present town of Comanche, in 1851, and adds: "Mercer was an old Texan, having emigrated from Georgia in 1835, and had assisted in surveying most of the Leon Valley from Gatesville up, and was the owner of several tracts of land on South Leon and Mercer creeks.

## OTHER ENCOUNTERS.

Enroute from Fort Marlin to the Falls of the Brazos, and when about midway their journey, David Ridgeway, recently from Tennessee, and another man whose name is not given, were ambushed by a party of Caddos. Ridgeway fell mortally wounded at the first volley of arrows, but his companion fortunately escaped by the fleetness of his horse. Citizens pursued, but failed to overtake these marauders. "Quite a number of people about this time" says Wilbarger, "were killed around Fort Marlin and the settlement robbed of an immense amount of property—the Indians doing all they could to break it up." "For some reason," continues Wilbarger, "the Indians fought harder to retain the Brazos country than any portion of the State. The soil of no State in the Union has been crimsoned with the blood of so many brave defenders as that of Texas—not even excepting Kentucky, the 'dark and bloody ground.'"

In the summer of this year, James Alexander, one of the early and valuable citizens of Bastrop, and his son, a youth of sixteen, were murdered by Indians at the head of Pin Oak Creek, on the Wilbarger "trace," near its intersection with the old La Bahia (Goliad) road. They were freighting goods in ox wagons from Columbia to Bastrop, and halted to "noon," when the Indians, under cover of a ravine, crept up and fired at such close range as to powderburn the clothing of the two unsuspecting men. After scalping and horribly mutilating the bodies of their victims, killing the oxen, and plundering and destroying the wagons and contents, the fiends left, going in the direction of the "Falls."

The bodies of the unfortunate men were discovered by parties traveling the road a few hours later, when the alarm spread, a party was soon organized, and in pursuit, following the trail of the savages to Little River where it was lost. However, the party continued to scour the country, and when some fifty miles above the "Falls" of the Brazos, they found a Caddo Indian who was captured and forced to guide them to his camp some five miles away, where they found four other warriors, and two squaws. The whites killed the five warriors, but spared the women—an act that at least palliates to the favor of the whites, since the Indians make no distinction in such instances; sparing neither men, women nor children.

No statement has been preserved alleging that goods or any other evidences were discovered in the camp of these Indians implicating them in the murder of the Alexanders.

Briefly, in closing this period, we mention a few of the many incidents and tragedies occurring in 1835: A Mr. Albright was killed by Indians on his farm near Fort Houston; James Boazman (or Boozeman), was killed at Boozeman's Ferry on the Trinity—he had driven his wagon into the river to soak and swell the wheels, when Indians killed him and carried away his horses; about the same time and perhaps the same Indians, (a foot party of ten or twelve) killed Mr. Bradley Davis. Davis and a Mr. Leathers were out bee tree hunting—Leathers escaped after a hard race; Tom Green was waylaid and killed by Indians on Keechi Creek in what is now Leon county; two families named Rity were moving west, on the old San Antonio road, and were near the Navasota River, when they were attacked by Indians. They corralled their wagons and prepared for defense—one of the men was killed at the first fire, but the other, aided by the women, made it hot for the red skins, causing them to finally withdraw. These emigrants retraced their steps back east; the Indians stole some horses on San Pedro Bayou and were pursued by a small party of men. In the charge James McLane and Isaac Sheridan were killed and the remainder of the party forced to retreat; at another time horses were stolen and a party of settlers went in pursuit, overtaking, and killing some of the Indians on the Trinity. In the fight Wm. Foster was killed.

At this period scouts were kept in the woods most of the time watching for trails and signs of Indians and to give alarms.

# CHAPTER IX.

hough ushered in amid dark and ominous war-clouds, followed by a series of the bloodiest and most appalling disasters that ever stained the history of any land, the year 1836—most memorable in the annals of Texas—soon evolved from its slough of despair.

The campaign of 1835 was settled by such brilliant and complete success for Texan arms, as to render wholly unexpected the disasters that befell them in 1836 up to the very moment that, with the suddenness of a transformation wrought by Prospero's wand, the clouds of defeat were dispelled, April 21, by the signal victory of San Jacinto, and the star of Texas, no longer obscured by lurid vapors, blazed forth steadily and serenely from a clear sky, as a new orb in the galaxy of nations.

## BIRTH OF THE LONE STAR REPUBLIC.

The siege and fall of the Alamo; the destruction of Grant and his command beyond the Nueces; the defeat and annihilation of Johnson's force at San Patricio; the killing of King and his followers, and the capture of Ward and his men at Refugio; the surrender of Fannin and his troops, and their subsequent massacre, together with that of Ward and his men and other prisoners of war, held at Goliad; the retreat of Gen. Houston from Gonzales to the Colorado, and thence to the Brazos, exposing to the devastating and sanguinary fury of Mexican soldiery, all the settlements in Texas, save those on Red River and about Nacogdoches and San Augustine; and the sweeping forward of

Sam Houston

S. F. Austin

Dec^r 18. 1836

a powerful Mexican army across Texas in three divisions, from the western frontier toward the Sabine, like a drag net, constituted a series of calamities of the most appalling nature. Apparently they portended that the tragedy enacted on the plain of Guadalupe, in Zacatecas, was to have a dreadful sequel in Texas, that would leave the despotism of Santa Anna firmly enthroned from the western confines of the United States to the Pacific Ocean, and southward to the Caribbean Sea. It seemed probable that the only visible reminders that would remain of the effort made by Anglo-American civilization and liberty, to plant themselves in the beautiful and pleasant land, and change it from a wilderness into a well ordered and populous commonwealth, would be the graves of patriot heroes, who had tried and failed.

When Gen. Houston fell back from the Colorado, the greater number of the volunteers with him, left the army to hurry to their homes and remove their families eastward, before the Mexicans reached them.

Panic-fear among the defenseless women and children, spread like fire in flax, resulting in what is known to history as the "Runaway Scrape." Nothing could allay it. Thousands of women and children, with and without escort, thronged all the routes of travel, hurrying afoot, horseback, and in vehicles in the direction of Louisiana. Women gave birth to children by the roadside with no one to care for them. Many of the sick and feeble died by the way. Back of those who constituted the anguished, scattered, scurrying throngs, were their homes, and all the property they had accumulated by years of toil and hardship. The Mexican troops reduced many of these habitations to ashes, and they wantonly destroyed thousands of cattle and horses.

In addition to all this, the Indians took advantage of the confusion and weakened power of resistance, to wage fiendish warfare, attended by murder and robbery.

Parties of refugees were several miles east of the battle ground when they heard the booming of cannon at San Jacinto. They halted to await news of the issue of the contest. Couriers dashed along the roads next day and gave intelligence of the splendid and decisive triumph. A few more days, and it was known that Santa Anna had been captured at San Jacinto, and that, under a treaty entered into with him, all the Mexican troops in Texas, except those captured at San Jacinto, were on the march back to Mexico, followed by a Texan force that buried the remains of the victims of the Goliad massacre, and saw that the terms of the agreement were observed.

An election was held in September, at which the constitution framed by the Plenary Convention in March, was adopted, and a president and vice president, members of congress and other officers, were chosen. Congress met in October, and General Sam Houston, as president, and Mirabeau B. Lamar, as vice president, were inaugurated; and the Republic of Texas was launched upon its glorious career—extending to the time that Texas became a state of the American Union in February, 1846.

The charred bones of the martyrs of the Alamo were collected by Seguin from the ashes of the pyres upon which their bodies had been consumed, and were interred at the Cathedral of San Fernando in San Antonio. The people bent themselves to the accomplishment of the new destinies that opened before them, and the constructive work of building a noble commonwealth, consecrated to liberty, order, peace, prosperity, enlightenment and progress, was begun in earnest, and has been continued to this day—with results that prove that the blood that was shed, the sacrifices that were made, and the sufferings that were endured, were not in vain.

The Texas people of 1836 mourned that Travis, Bowie, Bonham, Crockett, Fannin and a host of others were gone, and were not with them to enjoy the fruits of victory; this sorrow, too, was made more poignant by the untimely loss of the great Stephen F. Austin, also the noble patriot, Lorenzo de Zavalla. But their sorrows were tempered with the proud joy that they had won renown and deathless fame, establishing for Texas, memories and traditions that conserve patriotism and civic virtue to remotest times. "A land without memories and traditions of patriots is a land without liberty."

The Texan war for independence in some respects is without a parallel, and the final victory at San Jacinto will ever rank as one of the astonishing feats of military history. The great leader in that campaign and victor at San Jacinto, Sam Houston, (he needs no title), was yet long spared to the people. And he it was that so well and faithfully guided and guarded the destinies of the dearly bought new land of liberty—the Lone Star Republic.

The matter of the Cherokee claims came before the Plenary Convention, but was not finally acted upon, owing to the haste, confusion and alarm that prevailed.

The Cherokees considered their rights secure, in view of the action taken by the Consultation in 1835, and of the treaty entered into with them in January, 1836. They, therefore, remained quiet. But Sam Houston was the factor that kept these Indians pacified and in check. Other and hostile Indians glutted, as far as they could, their lust for revenge, blood and plunder, and the Texas people had to fight them with one hand while they fought combined Mexico with the other.

Morfitt's report to Secretary Forsyth in 1836, gave the following estimate of the number of Indians in Texas at that time: Wacos, 400; Tehuacanas, 200; Tonkawas, 800; Cooshatties, 350; Alabamas, 250; Comanches, 2,000; Caddos, 500; Lipans, 900; smaller bands, 800; Cherokees and their associate bands, 8,000, a total of 14,200.

---

## FAILURE OF BEALE'S COLONY.

Noting the futile efforts of the few English colonists under Dr. John Charles Beale, to exist on the extreme borders of Texas, or rather, at that time, within the limits of the state of Tamaulipas, between the Nueces and Rio Grande, we find its sequel in a most sad and bloody tragedy.

In 1832 Dr. Beale, a native of England, but then resident in the city of Mexico—having married the widow of Richard Exeter, an English merchant, and whose maiden name was Dona Maria Dolores Soto—in partnership with one or two other

gentlemen, secured a contact or permit from the State of Coahuila and Texas for colonizing a tract of three million acres
between the rivers Rio Grande and Nueces.

Omitting many interesting details incident to its establishment and brief existence, we shall briefly trace the history of
this colony as gleaned principally from Kennedy's "Texas"—
closing with the sad sequel.

The first and so far as we can find, only English colony—
fifty-nine men, women and children—sailed from New York on
November 10th, 1833, in the schooner Amos Wright, Capt.
Monroe, for Aransas Bay, and where after a tempestuous voyage they arrived and disembarked on the 12th of December,
going into camp, and remaining through most inclement
weather, till the end of the month. On the 3rd of January, 1834,
Dr. Beale having procured teams and means of transportation
from Goliad, the party left overland for the interior. The weather
continued very wet and cold, and much suffering was experienced by the "new comers" on the route. Crossing the San
Antonio River and leaving Goliad with fresh oxen on the 20th,
they arrived at the "Rancho" of Don Erasmo Seguin at noon on
the 31st of January. Borrowing of the Don five yokes of oxen,
they pounded on.

"February 4th, made an early start reaching a small brook
called the Salado, twelve miles distant, where we formed our
camp with great precaution, as this place is famous for the
murders committed by the Tahuacanas, being one of their usual
resting places."

About noon on the following day the travel-worn emigrants drove into San Antonio. "Bexar is one of the poorest, most
miserable places in this country. The Indians steal all their
horses, rob their rancheros and nearly every week, murder
some one or two of the inhabitants. From want of union and
energy, they tamely submit to this outrage, which all admit is
inflicted by a few Tahuacanas."

Resting here till the 18th of February, the now more cheerful colonists left Bexar with fifteen carts and wagons for their
final destination near the Rio Grande. Ten days travel from San

Antonio brought them to the Nueces River—which they crossed "with the English and Mexican flags flying and the people cheering most enthusiastically"—and for the first time entered the lands designated as Beale's Colony; and in commemoration of which event one of the party, Mr. Little, carved upon a large tree on the west bank: "Los Primeros Colonos de la Villa de Dolores pasaron el 28 de Febrero, 1834," the English rendition being: "The first colonists of the village of Dolores passed here on the 28th of February, 1834,"—many of them, alas, never to pass again.

After exploring the country in various directions and arranging other preliminaries, the little band of colonists finally halted, March 16, on the Las Moras Creek, below the present town of Del Rio and some ten or twelve miles from the northeast bank of the Rio Grande; and where they chose the site for the proposed village of Dolores—a name bestowed by Dr. Beale in honor of his absent wife. Municipal officers were now elected, the corner stone of a church laid with much ceremony, tents, huts, and cabins erected, streets and plazas platted, and the foundation for a permanent town laid—including the building of a brush wall around it for protection against the wild Indians, who then, as for generations before and for fifty years afterwards, were a terror to the Mexican population of that frontier. "But the settlement at Dolores did not prosper," says Kennedy, owing to a variety of causes; of which the principal, apparently, was the absence of proper qualifications of the colonists themselves. A drouth prevailed and, without irrigation, the colonists failed to raise crops; the frequent murders of rancheros by Indians caused the colonists much apprehension and uneasiness, lest they should be attacked by the savages. As time passed conditions grew worse, and much dissatisfaction arose, causing parties of the settlers to leave for Monclova, and other Mexican towns, Santa Pisa, San Fernando and other places, and still others for the coast to seek vessels and return passage to their native land—till finally on the 17th of June, 1836, the settlement was entirely abandoned, the last to leave being Mr. Palmer and seven others who went to San Fernando where we lose sight of them. And thus perished the bright hopes and persevering efforts of those ardent, but unfortunate men and women, to sustain themselves and acquire a home and heritage in the wilds of the new world. In the language of historian Kennedy, himself an Englishman, and chronicling the trials and failures of his own countrymen: "And though Dolores obtained a place on the map, it had no pretentions to the name of a successful settlement—further supplying evidence of the superiority of the Anglo-American in forming colonies. The North Americans are the only people who, in defiance of all obstacles, have struck the roots of civilization deep into the soil of Texas. Even as I trace these lines, I reflect upon their progress with renewed wonder and admiration. They are, indeed, the organized conquerers of the wild, united in themselves the three fold attributes of husbandmen, lawgivers, and soldiers."

## THE SAD SEQUEL.

And now, passing over the truly pathetic, revolting and heart-rending parts, we must briefly narrate the sad, saddest of all, sequels—the murder of the last twelve colonists; capture of Mrs. Horn, Mrs. Harris and their children; a story replete with cruel torture and sufferings that must elicit deepest sympathy, and cause even the maudlin sentimentalist to burn with rage and indignation.

Among other discouraged settlers were a party of eleven men, including John Horn, wife, and two little sons, John and Joseph; a Mr. Harris, his wife and three months old girl baby, probably the only child born at Dolores—in all sixteen souls—who left the fated settlement on the 10th, of March, 1836, hoping to reach the coast by way of San Patricio on the lower Nueces, and obtain passage by water to other and more favored lands. They reached the Nueces, and camped for several days in a secluded spot near what they supposed was the road leading to San Antonio. They purposely kept from view, as they had learned of Santa Anna's invasion of Texas. They heard teams, and men on horseback passing, and supposed them to belong to the Mexican army. The party resumed their journey April 2. Two days later while camped near a small lake, they were surrounded and attacked by fifty or sixty Comanches, who killed all of the men outright, except Mr. Harris and a young German whom they left for dead, made prisoners of the women and children, and secreted such effects of the colonists as they desired to appropriate, and destroyed the remainder. They later returned to the scene and got the property they had cached. At the same time they found Mr. Harris and the German alive and dragged them to camp and murdered and scalped them in the presence of the agonized prisoners. A savage also amused himself by tossing Mrs. Harris's infant in the air and letting it fall upon the ground until it was dead. The Indians were part of a force of four hundred Comanches who were operating in the rear of the Mexican army, plundering and murdering without regard to nationality. After killing several Mexicans and Americans, the entire body of Indians moved northward, out of Texas, after the battle of San Jacinto, and to their base of operations on the head waters of the Arkansas.

To follow these two unfortunate daughters in their multiplied sorrows and tribulations; to tell of the hellish tortures endured and fiendish treatment experienced—all the while weeping and agonizing over the fate of their innocent little children—beggars belief, and would cause bitter and burning tears to well up thick and fast. Better, a thousand times better, that they had shared the fate of their husbands and fathers on that fatal April day, and that their bodies had been left to devouring vultures and coyotes, and their bones to bleach on the lonely prairies of Southwest Texas. Reader! We will draw the veil of silence.

\* \* \* \* \*

On the outgoing trip, while camped near Red River, Col. Holland Coffee, founder of Coffee's Trading House, near where Denison now stands, on Red River, visited the Indian camp, and made every effort possible to rescue by purchase the two poor women—offering their captors any amount of goods or money; but without avail. The tenderhearted and noble man, it is said, wept bitterly over his disappointment. Col. Coffee was a brave and good man, and a valuable pioneer of Northeast Texas, and it is sad to reflect that he died at the hands of an assassin a few years later.

Finally, in June, 1837, Mrs. Harris was ransomed by American traders, acting under instructions from William Donaho, a philanthropic Santa Fe merchant. At the same time they tried to buy Mrs. Horn, but without success. A little later, however, Sept. 19, 1837, she was purchased at San Miguel, N. M., by a Mexican acting for Donaho. But in a few days a grasping and heartless merchant of the place, disgracing the fair name of Hill, set up a claim that he had furnished goods for her release and that he should have her as a servant. He obtained a judgment in his favor from the alcalde, and kept her in brutal slavery for a short while—allowing her barely sufficient food to sustain life. Hearing of her pitiable condition, a Mr. Smith, who lived at the mines, some distance away, sent an armed party, who brought her to his house, where his family tenderly cared for her. She was now soon conveyed from Taos, N. M., to Independence, Mo., by Messrs. Workman and Rowland, in 1838, and in October of that year became for some time, a guest of Mr. David Workman and family at New Franklin.

In the autumn of 1837, Mr. Donaho escorted Mrs. Plummer (one of the captives taken at Parker's Fort in 1836), and Mrs. Harris to Missouri. He left Mrs. Harris with his mother-in-law, Mrs. Lucy Dodson, in Pulaski county, Mo., took Mrs. Plummer to her relatives in Texas; and then in 1838, returned to Santa Fe. Mrs. Horn was ransomed during his absence, which accounted for his not being present to take charge of her when she was released by the Indians. He went to Taos to see her, but learned that she had recently departed for Missouri with Workman and Rowland, and several other persons bound for Independence. During the year Mr. Donaho wound up his business at Santa Fe and went to Missouri, where he resided until 1839, when he located at Clarksville, Texas, which was thereafter his home until the time of his death. Some of his descendants are still residing there and in Red River county. When he came back to Missouri, Mrs. Horn went to see him, learned who it was that had restored her to freedom, and thanked him with words such as only a poor captive could utter—simple words but sweeter to have than all the incense that has ever floated upwards from golden censers. Neither she nor Mrs. Harris lived long after their restoration to civilization.

Mrs. Horn published a small pamphlet giving an account of her life up to the time she was recovered from the Indians. But one copy of this rare pamphlet is know to be in existence.

Some of the experiences that she details are such as to dry whatever tears one might be disposed to shed over the fate of the Indian.

A single incident will suffice to indicate the rest.

On one occasion, while crossing a ford, her little son Joseph, slipped from the back of the mule into the water. An Indian, enraged at the accident, struck him with a lance, inflicting a severe wound, and knocking him into the water, none of the other Indians interfering. The child swam to the bank, "bleeding like a slaughtered animal." Mrs. Horn upbraided the Indian for his conduct. He made the boy travel on foot and drive a mule for the rest of the day, and at night called Mrs. Horn to him and gave her an unmerciful beating with the whip.

She says: "When the savage monster was done whipping me, he took his knife and literally sawed the hair from my head. It was quite long, and when he had completed the operation, he tied it to his own as an ornament. . . . At this time we had tasted no food for two days, and in hearing of the moans of my starving children, bound as on every night, mothers may judge, if they can, of my repose. The next day a wild horse was killed and we were allowed to partake of the flesh.

"During the same day the Indians amused themselves by throwing the two boys into a stream, time and again as fast as they swam out, until the children were partially unconscious and unable to stand. Their bodies were badly bruised and water came from their stomachs in gurgles. Little Jospeh's wounded face was swollen almost beyond recognition."

What became of the children was never known. They disappeared in the devouring darkness, like characters of Victor Hugo in Les Miserables, and baffled fancy seeks to follow them in vain.

## MURDER OF DOUGLAS AND DAUGHERTY FAMILIES.

Among other belated settlers who were hastily improvising means of conveyance with which to join in the wild flight—"the runaway scrape"—across Texas in advance of the Mexican army of invasion, in March, 1836, were two Irish families, John Douglas, wife and children, and ____ Daugherty, a widower with three children—the parents, natives of Ireland, but more recently of Cambria county, Pennsylvania, where their children were born, and from whence they had removed to Texas, in 1832, settling together in a somewhat isolated section, on Douglas or Clark Creek, some twelve miles from the present site of Hallettsville, in Lavaca county.

Ere they had completed sleds on which to transport their household effects, most of the families in that section had already left for the east. Ready to start on the morning of March 4th, Augustine and Thaddeus Douglas, aged respectively fifteen and thirteen, were sent out in the range for the oxen designed to draw the sleds. Returning in the afternoon, and when near home, they were horrified to behold the cabins in flames and surrounded by a band of painted warriors, whose yells mingled with agonizing death screams, told only too plainly of the massacre that was in progress. Unarmed and helpless, the two boys could only seek their own safety, which they did by hiding in a dense thicket, where they remained till night. Under cover of darkness, they cautiously approached the spot—once a home of life and happiness, now a scene of death and multiplied grief. A brief examination revealed to them the awful, shocking tragedy—the home and effects in smouldering ruins; their father, mother, sister and little brother; Mr. Daugherty, his son and two daughters, all dead, scalped, mutilated and lying naked in the yard—eight souls thus brutally snatched from earth. "Imagination," says John Henry Brown, "especially when assured that those two boys were noted for gentle and affectionate natures, as personally known to the writer for a number of years, may depict the forlorn anguish piercing their young hearts. It was a scene over which angels weep."

The two boys, having some idea as to course, now set out with bleeding hearts for the little settlement in the vicinity of what is now Hallettsville, but finding all had retreated, continued down the Lavaca some thirty-five miles further, to where their older sister, the wife of Capt. John McHenry, and a few others lived, but found that they too, had left. Thus nonplussed, fatigued and almost famished, the heart-broken youths plodded their way along the old Atascosa road, and when near the crossing on the Colorado River, they were picked up by some Mexican scouts and carried in to General Adrian Woll's camp, where they related their sad story. The boys were treated kindly and were soon placed in the care of one Auguste, a Frenchman, and a traitor to Texas, and who had, with a band of confederates, mostly negroes, "rounded up" the cattle of retreating citizens, and rendezvousing on Cummings Creek, was supplying Woll's army with beef at exorbitant prices. Here they remained, virtually as captives, till after the battle of San Jacinto, and the retreat of the Mexican army.

Again quoting Brown's narrative: "Auguste, mounting Augustine Douglas on a fine horse, sent him down to learn when Woll could start. In the meantime a party of Texans, headed by Allison York, who had heard of Auguste's thieving den, hurried forward to chastise him before he could leave the country with his booty. He punished them severely, all who could, fleeing into the bottom, and thence to Woll's camp. When York's party opened fire, little Thaddeus Douglas, not understanding the cause, fled down the road, and in about a mile met his brother returning from Woll's camp on Auguste's fine horse.

With equal prudence and financial skill, they determined to save both themselves and the horse. Thaddeus mounting behind, they started at double quick for the Brazos. They had not traveled many miles, however, when they met the gallant Capt. Henry W. Karnes, at the head of some cavalry, from whom they learned for the first time, of the victory of San Jacinto, and that they yet would see their only surviving sister and brother-in-law, Mrs. and Capt. McHenry. In writing of this incident in De Bow's Review of December, 1853, eighteen years after its occurrence, I used this language:

'These boys, thus rendered objects of sympathy, formed a link in the legends of the old Texans, and still reside on the Lavaca, much respected for their courage and moral deportment.'

"This was said thirty-four years ago. It is a still greater pleasure to say now that they ever after bore honorable characters and were both living a short time since, as I think their sister is; but the noble old patriot in three revolutions—Mexico in 1820, South America in 1822, and Texas in 1835—preceded by gallant conduct at New Orleans in 1815, when only sixteen years old—the honest, brave and ever true son of Erin's Isle, Capt. John McHenry, died a few years ago, leaving a memory sweetly embalmed in many thousand hearts."

---

## PIONEER TIMES IN ROBERTSON'S COLONY—TRIALS OF THE FIRST SETTLERS ABOUT THE "THREE FORKS" OF LITTLE RIVER.

During the latter half of 1835, and throughout 1836, the Indians—Tehuacanas, Wacos and Comanches—if not combining, vied with each other, as it were, in the frequency of their depredations and deviltry, being exceedingly hostile towards the settlers of Robertson's Colony, especially to those more exposed about the Falls of the Brazos, Nashville, about the Three Forks of Little River, and on the San Gabriel.

"In the month of February, 1836," says De Cordova, "a

company of rangers were stationed as high up the country as the Waco village, . . . but, from the scarcity of provisions and the difficulty of conveying the small quantity of the necessaries of life, (and few indeed were they that these efficient frontier soldiers required), they were forced to fall back to the "Falls"; and, notwithstanding all these exertions, during the months of April, May and June, innumerable were the acts of cruelty, and immense were the depredations, committed by the savages. And, in consequence of the poverty of the government, these rangers were disbanded, and for a time the magnificent region of country between the Colorado and the Brazos was deserted by the white man. But, as the settlers had for a time deserted this region of country, and as there was no further inducement for the savages to steal, they, too, retired to their villages on the Brazos, as they deemed themselves more secure higher up the country, where they could enjoy and revel in the fruits of their predatory excursions, unmolested."

For two or three years after the introduction of its first settlers in the early 30's, Robertson's Colony received but few accessions. However, the beauty and fertility of that section soon attracted the attention of home-seekers, and from about 1834-'5 they commenced to arrive and to locate on the more desirable, but also more exposed, sections, especially in and around Nashville, the capital of the colony, near the mouth of Little River and along that stream as high up as the "Three Forks." Among other families were the McLennans, Davidsons, Crouch, the Childers brothers, Rileys and Taylors; special mention of which has already been or will be made.

Following the return from the army and the "runaway scrape," after the victory at San Jacinto, April 21, most of these settlers repaired to their abandoned homes and claims.

"During the previous winter," says Brown, "each head of a family and one or two single men had cleared about forty acres of ground on his own land, and had planted corn before the retreat. To cultivate this corn and thus have bread, was the incentive to an early return."

Temporarily, the families of most of those who returned to

cultivate their crops, remained, for safety, in the town of Nashville, then the highest up settlement and refuge on that frontier.

---

## KILLING OF CROUCH AND DAVIDSON.

Thus matters stood till about the first week in June, when
two messengers, John Beal and Jack Hopson, arrived at the
"Three Forks" from Nashville, bringing the sad news of Parker's
Fort massacre, on the 19th of the previous month; advising these
toiling men of their great peril and urging them to leave at once,
as numerous parties of hostile Indians were traversing the
country and were in that vicinity. Heeding this advice, immediate preparations were made to retreat in a body to Nashville.

The entire party consisted of Capt. Gouldsby Childress,
wife, four sons, Robert, Frank, and two small boys, two grown,
and one eight year old daughter; Rhoads (an old gentleman
living with the family), Ezekiel Robertson, Orville T. Tyler, Rev.
Jasper Crouch, Dr. Robert Davidson, _____ Shackelford, the two
messengers, Beal and Hopson—in all seventeen souls, of whom
but ten were really able to bear arms. Their only vehicle was a
wagon to be drawn by a single pair of oxen—they had some
horses but not enough to mount the entire party.

Starting on the third day of June, their first day's journey
brought them to the cabins of Henry Walker, James (Camel
Back) Smith and Monroe, on Walkers Creek, about eight miles
east of the present town of Cameron, in Milam county; and
where they camped for the night. The three last named families
not being ready, the original party left on their journey early the
following morning, hoping to reach Nashville by the close, or
in the night, of that day. But they were doomed to disappointment—some alas! never to reach their destination and loved
ones.

On that fatal June morning, and when about three miles
from Walker's, enroute via the Smith crossing of Little River—
"Davidson and Crouch about three hundred, Captain Childress
about one hundred, yards ahead, and two or three men perhaps
two hundred yards behind, driving some cattle"—a party of

perhaps two hundred mounted and painted Comanche warriors dashed upon them. Childress, calling to Davidson and Crouch, regained his wagon, and hasty preparations were made for defense. Keeping well out of rifle range, the Indians commenced encircling the apparently doomed party, at the same moment discovering Davidson and Crouch, who had failed to join their comrades, a large party attacked them. Being poorly mounted, the two unfortunate men made a bold stand and a brave fight, killing one or two of the enemy, but were soon overpowered and both slain, scalped and mutilated. "Then followed," says Brown, "great excitement among the Indians, apparently quarreling over the disposition of the scalps and effects of the two murdered men. This enabled the main party to reach a grove of timber about four hundred yards distant, where they turned the oxen loose and only sought to save their lives."

At this critical moment, and just as the savages were returning en masse to renew the attack, the two young men, Beal and Hopson, seized with panic, succeeded in making their escape.

Again the Indians circled around, yelling, firing and maneuvering to "draw a fire from the little band," but they presented a bold front and reserved their charges. Shackelford, who could speak the Comanche tongue, challenged them to charge at closer quarters, but believing the brave little party well armed and determined, the wily Comanches kept aloof and eventually gave up the attack, moving off to the west. In close order the besieged now retreated, changing their course to "the raft," four or five miles distant on Little River, on which they crossed, swimming their horses, secured a favorable camp for the night, and arrived at Nashville early next day.*

---

* "During the next day," says John Henry Brown, "Smith, Monroe and Walker, with their families, arrived. Immediately on leaving the other party, the Indians had attacked the three families in Walker's house and kept up a fire all day without wounding either of the defenders, who fired deliberately through port-holes whenever opportunity offered. While not

Robertson's Colony played a most prominent part in the settlement and development of Texas—its outer settlements truly constituting the advance guards of civilization, but the growth of the colony during its first years was slow and of uncertain permanency. In 1833, there were only five persons settled within its limits above the Yegua, west of the Brazos. In 1834, the town of Viesca at the Falls of the Brazos, was laid off by Sterling C. Robertson, its name being afterwards changed to Fort Milam. Nearby was Fort Sullivan, afterwards called, "Bucksnort." Early in 1835 considerable additions were made to the colony—small settlements commencing on Pond Creek and on Little River. Tenoxtitlan, first as a noted crossing of the old San Antonio and Nacogdoches road, then as an important Mexican military garrison, and in the '30's, as a colonial hamlet, was some twenty miles below Nashville on the Brazos. The place is now defunct and almost forgotten.

Nashville, as the capital of the colony, and about central with reference to the colony limits, was situated on a most lovely and eligible site, a beautiful prairie plains on the south bank, overlooking the Brazos, about two miles below the mouth of Little River, and five miles northwest from the present town of Hearne, in Milam county—The International and Great Northern railroad bridge spanning the river a few hundred yards below the site of this now dead town. A number of bold springs gushed forth from the bluff, "the landscape o'er" was most picturesque, and it is no wonder that settlers were attracted, and would want to locate in and around this beautiful, once colonial capital. Its exact incipiency is not known, but certain it is that the empresario Robertson viewed the site in the middle '20's, he and his partner, Alex S. Thompson, were there in 1831—the

assured of killing a single Indian, they were perfectly certain of having wounded a considerable number. As night came on the Indians retired, and as soon as satisfied of their departure, the three families left for Nashville, and arrived without further molestation."—"Indian Wars and Pioneers of Texas," p. 44.

latter locating with his family, and doubtless erected the first cabin. But very few residents were there in the early 30's. A few settlers came as early as 1834, and early in 1835, and more in the summer and fall of this latter year.

The town was regularly laid out in the fall of 1835 by Gen. Thos. J. Chambers, who had previously located an eleven league grant, covering the site. This grant was long in litigation, during the days of the Republic, but it is not remembered how the suit was finally settled. At no period of its existence, according to the memory of Frank Brown, was the place very populous—perhaps not over 15 or 20 permanent resident families—"There were many comers and goers from time to time."

Here the records were kept and the business of the colony transacted, and later, as the capital of Milam Land District, from 1837 to 1846, it became quite an important place—till Cameron finally rivaled, and became the permanent county seat of Milam county. It continued as a post-office, at least till about the beginning of the Civil War.

## CAPT. HILL'S FORTUNATE SCRAP.

Late in August Captain Hill, scouting with a small company of rangers on the San Gabriel, discovered the trail of foot Indians, near the mouth of Brushy Creek, leading toward the lower country. After a rapid pursuit without halt or rest, of about twenty-four hours, the enemy—twenty Caddos—were overtaken and a desperate fight ensued—the odds for a time in favor of the Indians, who had taken favorable position in a dense thicket. In the end, however, several of the red men were killed and wounded and the others routed in confusion, leaving their camp equipage—among other trophies a large number of scalps taken from white people of both sexes and all ages. By this timely action the sparse and unprotected settlers at a point in the post oaks between the Yegua and Little Rivers and in what is now Burleson county, was no doubt saved from a serious visitation.

## MURDER AND CAPTURE OF THE McLENNANS.

Prominent among the early frontier settlers of Texas, were the McLennans, and one of the most tragic episodes to be recorded, is the fate which befell one of these families.

Neil McLennan, Sr.,* was a native of the Highlands of Scotland, born in the year 1777, and emigrated with a large family and relatives to America in 1802, settling in the state of North Carolina, where they remained till about 1820, "When, impelled by a brave, and adventurous spirit, in company with one companion, he determined to explore the wilderness of Florida. Without a path or guide, they penetrated and explored the dense forests of west Florida, traveling on foot, burdened with their guns, axes, provisions and blankets." To this, then terra incog., the McLennans soon removed, halting there until the year 1834, "when, having heard of the great and peculiar advantages of Texas, he, together with his brothers, a few friends and their families, removed to that country." "They purchased a schooner at Pensacola," continues a biographer, "loaded her with their worldly goods and navigated her themselves," arriving safely at the mouth of the Brazos on January 14, 1835. Proceeding up that river to a point in what is now Fort Bend county, they struck a snag, sinking the frail craft, but succeeded in saving most of their household effects and provisions. Procuring oxen and improvising carts they slowly continued up country reaching Robertson's colony early in April—settling near the mouth of Pond Creek in what is now

* "Neil McLennan," says Capt. Davidson, who as a boy, knew him at the village of Nashville, "was the soul of honor, and a most useful citizen— When a couple wanted to get married they would always send for "Squire" McLennan. Have seen him unite several couples—the occasion always being one of much frolic and feasting and one looked forward to with much anticipations of pleasure by those pioneer people of few and simple pastimes. I knew the McLennans well, and can truly say that among the early pioneers of Texas there was not to be found a grander or nobler gentleman than Neil McLennan."—Davidson's Letter—3-26-1907.

Falls county."

Misfortunes, it seems, beset these colonists almost from the very day they reached their destination—this "land of promise." Not satisfied with the Pond Creek country, one of the McLennan's, more venturesome than prudent, in the latter part of 1835 or early 1836, loaded his effects, and with his wife, two small boys, and an infant, removed to a more desirable location on the San Gabriel, at a point in what is now Williamson county. Arriving at this new homeplace, it was found they were out of meat. Mr. McLennan, taking his gun and the oldest boy, went in search of game, leaving his wife and two other children, to "keep camp." Becoming lost, he did not return until dark, when he found the camp plundered and his loved ones gone. Indians had discovered the "new comers" and visited them, capturing the mother and her two children. In fiendish glee they stripped their captives of every vestige of apparel and tied them fast, while they plundered the camp. Breaking open a large trunk they found a "looking glass"—apparently a great curiosity to the Indians, who became very much absorbed, performing many antics over and around the mirror. Taking advantage of this, and at a time when the Indians were some little distance away, Mrs. McLennan untied herself and child, and taking her infant, quietly moved off, motioning her little boy to follow. Reaching the San Gabriel bottom she found a sheltering rock under which she concealed herself and children. So absorbed were the Indians in plundering the camp and playing with the mysterious glass, they did not miss their captives until late; a hurried search was made, but the hiding refugees fortunately, escaped the vigilant observations, the Indians leaving as night came on.

Naturally supposing his wife and babies had been captured, and perhaps murdered, McLennan, with his little son, set out for the settlements many miles below. The refugees remained in hiding all night, suffering much from cold, and in the morning a few remnants of clothing were found, also a little corn scattered in the dust, and which was their only sustenance. In this terrible condition, almost famished and naked, these helpless beings remained for several days, until the husband and father returned from the settlement, with a small company raised for the purpose of pursuit and the hope of rescue.

Approaching the camp, Mrs. McLennan was discovered scratching in the dust in search of grains of corn, but thinking the men were Indians she fled, in wild fright, and had to be run down and caught. Poor woman, though overjoyed when realizing deliverance, she was almost crazed from exposure and hunger, and so emaciated that her husband could scarcely realize the change. Thus providentially spared worse misfortune, the family were glad to find a home in a less exposed section.

## MURDER OF THE LAUGHLIN McLENNAN FAMILY—"INDIAN JOHN," McLENNAN.

In the winter of 1835-'6, when most of the settlers had retired from this exposed frontier, in consequence of the hostility of Indians, these brave families remained on their little farms. In the spring of '36 their first and saddest misfortune overtook them. While splitting rails, a party of Indians, probably Wacos, surprised and killed Laughlin and his wife and captured their three small children—Laughlin's aged and feebled mother, unable to walk being burned alive in the house. Two of the captive children soon died. The other, John, a fine little fellow of seven years, was adopted and remained with the Indians some years till recovered through treaty stipulations in 1846—Neil McLennan attending the council high up on the Brazos, and bringing his nephew back to the village of Nashville. Now a grown young man, unable to speak a word of English, dressed in the Indian garb and with all the propensities of that race, he was indeed "the very picture of a wild warrior," and it was no ordinary task to win "this young savage" to civilization. It was very hard to get him reconciled to his relatives and their modes and manners, "but with the return of his mother tongue he became more civilized and contented." "My mother" says Capt.

W. T. Davidson, "made the first garment he would wear, out of red cloth, and besides provided him with a straw hat with a red ribbon band streaming down about a yard, of which he was very proud." During the lifetime of his adopted Indian mother, we are told he often visited her, being always loaded with such presents as he knew would gratify her—thus showing his gratitude for her care and attention to him during his boyhood. Eventually he became entirely reconciled, married happily and settled down on Hog Creek, in Bosque county, where he resided till his death in 1866.

Thus admonished by this terrible tragedy, of the dangers to which they were exposed on that then extreme frontier, the McLennans removed down to the frontier village of Nashville, where they remained till the spring of 1837, when Neil Sr., ventured back to his farm and commenced a crop, and when the Indians again made an attack, the father and his son, John, (afterwards sheriff, first of Milam and then of McLennan county) barely escaped, and a negro man was captured—but soon to effect his escape and return to his master.*

* "McLennan's faithful old negro servant, Alf for that was his name, in telling of the attack and his capture by Indians," says Capt. W.T. Davidson, "told me the first intimation he had that the Indians were anywhere about, he saw them jumping over the field fence where he was at work. He broke for the timber, but a big stalwart fellow pursued him, running up behind and slapped his hand on his shoulder, with the exclamation: 'Whoop!' They carried him off a prisoner and kept him for some time. Alf was a great character and was the only negro fiddler in the town of Nashville, and always played for the young people to dance about once a week. They would pay him in dressed deer skins, old clothes, shoes, and as much corn whisky as he could drink. They danced nothing but the reel or 'breakdown' in those days, and Alf would play: 'Give the fiddler a dram, give the fiddler a dram, and let him drink it and be d—ed,' or 'We will dance all night till broad daylight and go home with the gals in the morning,' and always accompanied the music with song. Those were great days—good old times—and were enjoyed by those brave and happy 'folks,'—a great deal more than the present times and (of) modern dances."—Letter 3, 26, 07.

# FALL OF PARKER'S FORT—THE HORRIBLE MASSACRE. FATE OF THE CAPTIVES. A THRILLING STORY.

Settlers at Parker's fort participated in the "runaway scrape" in the spring of 1836, and went as far east as the Trinity which they were unable to cross, as the river was so swollen by heavy rains. While encamped on its western bank, they were informed of the victory of San Jacinto, and at once started back to the fort, which they reached without unusual incident.

Parker's Fort was located near the headwaters of the Navasota, one half miles northwest of the site of the town of Groesbeck, in Limestone county, in the heart of what was then a wilderness, but now a fruited and thickly populated region divided into farmsteads and dotted with villages and towns.

Fort Houston, situated a mile or two west of the site of Palestine, on land now included in the John H. Reagan farm two miles west of Palestine, in Anderson county, was the nearest white settlement. Others were distant sixty miles or more.

Parker's fort consisted of cabins surrounded by a stockade. A large double gate afforded access to the enclosure. The outer walls of the log cabins formed part of the walls of the stockade. Their roofs sloped inward. At one or more corners of the stockade were block houses. The walls around the entire quadrangle were perforated with loop holes. The fortification was bullet proof, and, like others of the kind, could not be taken by Indians if defended by a few well-armed and determined men. It was built for the purpose of being occupied by the families living in the vicinity, when there was danger of attack by Indians. Most of the farms—some of them near-by and others a mile or so away—were provided with cabins where the tired colonists occasionally spent the night.

The patriarch of the settlement was Elder John Parker, seventy nine years of age. His aged wife, "Granny" Parker, was, perhaps, a few years younger. He was a Virginian by birth; resided for a time in Elbert county, Ga.; chiefly reared his family in Bedford county, Tenn.; afterwards lived for several years in

Cole county, Ill.; and then moved, in 1833, to Texas where Parker's fort was erected in the following year. Some of the family came to Texas prior, and others subsequent, to that time.

The little group consisted of the following persons: Elder John Parker and wife (Granny Parker); James W. Parker (son of Elder John), wife, four single children, married daughter, Mrs. Rachel Plummer, and her husband, L. T. M. Plummer, and fifteen months old son, James Pratt Plummer, and one daughter, Mrs. Sarah Nixon, and her husband, L. D. Nixon; Silas M. Parker (son of Elder John) and his wife, and four children; Benjamin F. Parker (an unmarried son of Elder John); Mrs. Nixon, Sr., (mother of Mrs. James W. Parker); Mrs. Elizabeth Kellogg (daughter of Mrs. Nixon, Sr.); Mrs. Duty; Samuel M. Frost and his wife and children; Robert Frost; G. E. Dwight and his wife and children; David Faulkenberry and his son, Evan; Seth Bates and his son, Silas H.; Elisha Anglin and his nineteen year old son, Abram, and old man Lunn—in all thirty-eight persons.

On returning to Parker's fort from the Trinity, the little band busied itself with gathering together its scattered stock and in preparing the fields for putting in crops, all unconscious of the fearful massacre that was to extinguish, so soon, the bright hopes they entertained of the future, and the lives of many of their number; and an unspeakable mental anguish and physical sufferings upon others of the survivors.

Early on the morning of May 19, 1836, James W. Parker, Nixon and Plummer left the fort, and repaired to a farm a mile from there, and David Faulkenberry and his son Evan, Silas H. Bates and Abram Anglin went from the fort to their fields a mile farther away.

Seth Bates, Elisha Anglin, and old man Lunn either slept at their cabins the night before, or left the fort prior to 9 o'clock the morning of the 19th.

At that hour from five hundred to seven hundred Indians (Comanches and Kiowas) appeared on the prairie two or three hundred yards from the fort, displayed a white flag, and sent forward one of their number, who said that they had no hostile intentions, and merely wanted some one to come out from the fort and direct them to a spring which they understood was near-by, and to be furnished a beef.

Subsequent events justify the belief that this Indian acted as a spy, noticed that nearly all the men were absent, and reported the practically defenseless condition of the occupants of the fort. Benjamin F. Parker went out to the Indians and, after returning, stated that it was his belief they were hostile and intended to attack the fort. He said that he would go to them again and try to dissuade them. His brother, Silas M. Parker, urged him not to go, but he went, nevertheless, and was immediately surrounded and killed.

While this tragedy was in progress, Elder John Parker, "Granny" Parker and Mrs. Kellogg, fled from the fort in one party, and Mrs. James W. Parker and children by themselves; Silas M. Parker and Mrs. Plummer ran outside the stockade. Everyone tried to escape.

As soon as the Indians appeared, Mrs. Sarah Nixon left for the farm where her father, husband and Plummer were at work, to tell them of the imminent peril the occupants of the fort were in.

The savages kept up terrific shouting and yelling while they were murdering Benjamin F. Parker—the peculiar blood-curdling Comanche scream (once heard, never forgotten) rising above the less distinctive cries of the Kiowas. Most of them rushed upon the fort, the gate of which was open; the remainder went in pursuit of the parties of refugees that were still in sight.

The main body of Indians first encountered and killed Silas M. Parker just outside the fort, where he fought to the last, trying to protect Mrs. Plummer. This opposition necessitated the attention of some of the Indians, who killed and scalped Silas M. Parker, knocked unconscious with a hoe and captured Mrs. Plummer, after fierce resistance on her part, and then poured into the fort, where they joined their companion fiends, and helped to murder Samuel M. and Robert Frost, who fought and fell as true men should. Mrs. Nixon, Sr., Mrs. Duty and all the other women and children, managed to get out of the fort before and during the melee.

Shrieks of victims rent the air. Hundreds of brazen throated savages shouted and screamed war-whoops, curses, and taunts. The thud of blows delivered with war-clubs and tomahawks, and the sharp reports of firearms resounded. Blood and death were everywhere. Murder, with bat-like wings, brooded over the scene infernal, and drank in the babel of piteous and fierce sounds that rose from it.

Elder John Parker, "Granny" Parker, and Mrs. Kellogg were captured when they had gone three-fourths of a mile. They were brought back to a spot near the fort, where Elder John Parker was stripped, speared and killed, and "Granny" Parker was stripped of everything except her under-clothing, speared, outraged, and left for dead. The Indians kept Mrs. Kellogg as a prisoner.

When Mrs. Sarah Nixon reached the field to tell of the coming Indians, she found her father, James W. Parker, and Plummer. Her husband had gone down to the other farm. Plummer at once hastened to the latter place to convey information of the danger. James W. Parker started immediately for the fort. Enroute he met his wife and children, and others.

Plummer reached Nixon first and told him that the fort was surrounded by Indians. Without waiting for the other men to come up, Nixon, though unarmed, ran toward the fort. In a few moments he met Mrs. Lucy Parker (wife of Silas M. Parker) and her four children, just as they were overtaken by Indians. They compelled her to lift behind two mounted warriors, her nine-year-old daughter Cynthia Ann, and little boy, John. The foot Indians then took her and her two younger children back to the fort, Nixon following. She passed around, and Nixon through the fort.

At the moment the Indians were about to kill Nixon, David Faulkenberry appeared with his rifle and leveling it, caused them to fall back. Thereupon Nixon left in search of his wife and overtook Dwight and family, and Frost's family, and with them, met James W. Parker and family and his own wife, Mrs. Sarah Nixon. This group hastened to the Navasota bottom and hid in a thicket.

Faulkenberry ordered Mrs. Lucy Parker to follow him, which she did, carrying her infant in her arms and holding her other child by the hand. The Indians made several dashes toward them, but were brought up standing each time by Faulkenberry turning upon them and presenting his rifle. One warrior, bolder than the rest, rode up so close that Mrs. Parker's faithful dog seized his horse by the nose, whereupon horse and rider somersaulted into a gully. At this time Silas H. Bates, Abram Anglin and Evan Faulkenberry, armed with rifles, and Plummer, unarmed, came up, and the pursuing Indians, after making further hostile demonstrations, retired. While this party of refugees were passing through Silas M. Parker's field, Plummer, as if awakened from a dream, asked where his wife and child were, and taking the butcher knife of Abram Anglin, went in search of them. Seth Bates and old man Lunn were met a little farther on, and the party proceeded to a hiding place in the creek bottom.

At twilight Abram Anglin and Evan Faulkenberry started back to the fort. On reaching Seth Anglin's cabin, three-fourths of a mile from their destination, they found "Granny" Parker. She had feigned death until the Indians left and then crawled there, more dead than alive. When Anglin beheld her, he thought he was looking at a ghost. In his account of the incident he says, "It was dressed in white, with long white hair streaming down its back. I admit that I was worse scared at this moment than when the Indians were yelling, and charging us. Seeing me hesitate, my ghost now beckoned me to come on. Approaching the object, it proved to be old 'Granny' Parker.

"I took some bed clothing and carrying her some distance from the house, made her a bed, covered her up, and left her until we should return from the fort. On arriving at the fort we could not see a single individual alive, or hear a human sound. But the dogs were barking, the cattle lowing, the horses neighing, and the hogs squealing.

"Mrs. Parker had told me where she had left some silver, $106.50. This I found under a hickory bush, by moonlight. Finding no one at the fort, we returned to where I had hidden

1. Issac Parker  2. I.D. Parker  3. Cynthia Ann Parker
4. Quanah Parker

Scene at Parker's Fort Massacre

'Granny' Parker. On taking her up behind me, we made our way back to our hiding place in the bottom, where we found Nixon."

Next morning Silas H. Bates, Abram Anglin and Evan Faulkenberry went back to the fort, where they secured five or six horses, a few saddles and bridles and some meal, bacon and honey; but, fearing that the Indians might return, did not tarry to bring the dead.

With the aid of the horses and provisions, the party with David Faulkenberry made its way to Fort Houston. They did not then know what had become of James W. Parker and those with him.

The people with James W. Parker, consisting of G. E. Dwight and nineteen women and children, reached, after traveling six days, Tinnin's, at the old San Antonio and Nacogdoches crossing of the Navasota, emaciated by starvation, with nearly all their clothing torn off of them by thorns, and that which remained reduced to shreds, their bodies and limbs lacerated and their feet swollen and bleeding. Messrs. Carter and Courting learned of their approach, went out to meet them with five horses, and brought them in.

The settlers at Tinnin's, themselves but recently returned from the "runaway scrape" and poorly supplied with necessaries, divided their little all of food and clothing with the sufferers, and cheered and comforted them as best they could.

There were hearts of gold in Texas in those days—of the kind of gold that is in the heavenly city, and not in the fated fane of Mammon.

A party of twelve men went up from Fort Houston and buried the dead. "Granny" Parker did not live long after reaching Fort Houston. Most of the Parker's Fort settlers later returned to that location.

Upon leaving Parker's fort after the massacre, the Comanches and Kiowas traveled together until midnight, when they halted, went into camp, tied their prisoners so tightly hand and foot that blood welled up from beneath the cruel cords, threw the prisoners on their faces, built fires, erected a pole, and engaged in a scalp dance around it that lasted until morning.

The savages seemed drunk with the horrors they had perpetrated, and abandoned themselves without restraint to the
frenzy of the dance.

They chanted and shouted themselves hoarse, leaped into
the air, contorted their bodies, and re-enacted the murders they
had committed until even the limit of their physical endurance
was exceeded.

The maddened demons tramped upon the prisoners and
beat them with bows, until they were covered with blood and
bruises.

The orgie ended at last, leaving Mrs. Kellogg, Mrs. Plummer and the children more dead than alive.

When the Indians parted they divided the prisoners among
them. Mrs. Plummer was separated from her little son, James
Pratt Plummer, he being taken by one band and she by another.

Mrs. Kellogg was sold to the Keechies and by them to the
Delawares, who, about six months after her capture, carried her
into Nacogdoches and surrendered her to Gen. Sam Houston,
who paid them $150.00, the amount they had paid the Keechies,
and all they demanded.

While she was being conveyed from Nacogdoches to Fort
Houston by James W. Parker and others, a Mr. Smith wounded
and disabled an Indian, whom she recognized as the savage
who scalped Elder John Parker. As soon as she made known the
fact, Parker, Smith and others of the party killed the man—rid-
dling his carcass with bullets, and leaving it where it fell for
wolves and buzzards to dispose of.

Six months after she was captured Mrs. Plummer gave
birth to a boy baby. She begged an Indian woman to tell her how
to save the child, but the squaw turned a deaf ear to her plead-
ings. One day, while she was nursing the infant, several Indians
came to her and one of them tore the child from her, strangled
it with his hands, tossed it in the air and let it fall on the ground
until life seemed extinct, and threw it at her feet, while the others
held her, despite frantic struggling. The bucks then left her. In
her printed narrative she says, "I had been weeping incessantly
whilst they were murdering my child, but now my grief was so

great that the fountain of my tears was dried up. As I gazed on the bruised cheeks of my darling infant, I discovered some symptoms of returning life. I hoped that if it could be resuscitated, they would allow me to keep it. I washed the blood from its face, and after a time it began to breathe again. But a more heart-rending scene ensued. As soon as the Indians ascertained that the child was still alive, they tore it from my arms and knocked me down. Then then tied a plaited rope around its neck and threw it into a bunch of prickly pears, and then pulled it backward and forward until its tender flesh was literally torn from its body. One of the Indians, who was mounted on a horse, then tied the end of the rope to his saddle and galloped around in a circle until my little innocent was not only dead, but torn to pieces. One of them then untied the rope and threw the remains of the child into my lap, and I dug a hole in the earth and buried them."

The Indians killed the child because they thought that caring for it interfered with the mother's work. Afterwards she was given to a squaw as a servant. The squaw, after much cruel treatment, attempted to beat her with a club. Mrs. Plummer wrenched the club from the Indian woman's hands and knocked her down with it. The Indian men, who were at some distance, ran, yelling, to the scene. Mrs. Plummer expected nothing less than to be killed by them. Instead, they patted her on the back, exclaiming "bueno! bueno!"—good! good!

After that she was called the "fighting squaw," and was much better treated. After a captivity of one and a half years, she was ransomed by Mr. William Donaho, a Santa Fe merchant-trader—the same generous, tender-hearted and noble gentleman through whose efforts the unfortunate Mrs. Horn and Mrs. Harris were rescued from savage captivity, as previously related.

The Indian camp in which she was found was so far north of Santa Fe that it took seventeen days travel to reach that place. Mr. and Mrs. Donaho took her with them to Independence, Missouri. There she met her brother-in-law, L. D. Nixon, who brought her to Texas, where she crossed the door sill of her father's home February 19, 1838. She wrote, or had written, an account of her Indian captivity. Her death occurred February 19, 1839. The 19th day of months seems to have had an occult significance for her. She was born on the 19th, was married on the 19th, was captured on the 19th, was ransomed on the 19th, reached Independence on the 19th, arrived at home on the 19th and died on the 19th.

She died without knowing what had become of her son, James Pratt Plummer. He was ransomed late in 1842 and taken to Fort Gibson, and reached home in February, 1843, in charge of his grandfather, and became a highly esteemed citizen of Anderson County.

## CYNTHIA ANN PARKER—JOHN PARKER—CHIEF QUANAH PARKER.

Many efforts were made by their relatives to trace and recover Cynthia Ann and John Parker, and Texan and United States government expeditions kept a sharp lookout for them; but without avail, until Cynthia Ann was unexpectedly captured at the battle of Pease River, in 1860.

There is a fairly authenticated story to the following effect: In 1840 (four years after her capture at Parker's fort) Col. Len Williams, _____ Stoal (a trader) and a Delaware Indian guide, named "Jack Henry" found her with Pa-ha-u-ka's band of Comanche Indians on the Canadian River. Col. Williams offered to ransom her, but the Indian into whose family she had been adopted said that all the goods the Colonel had were not sufficient to get her, that she would not be surrendered for any consideration. Col. Williams requested the privilege of talking with her, and she was permitted to come into his presence. She walked quietly to him and seated herself at the foot of a tree, but could not be induced to utter a word, or make a gesture that showed whether she did or did not understand what he said to her. She was then thirteen years old. Some years later she became the squaw of the noted Comanche chief, Peta Nocona, and bore him several children.

Victor M. Rose says: "Fifteen years after her capture a party of white hunters, including some friends of her family, visited the Comanche encampment on the upper Canadian, and recognizing Cynthia Ann, probably through the medium of her name alone, sounded her in a secret manner as to the desirableness of a return to her people and the haunts of civilization. She shook her head in a sorrowful negative, and pointed to her little naked barbarians sporting at her feet, and to the great, lazy buck sleeping in the shade near at hand, the locks of a score of scalps dangling at his belt, and whose first utterance upon arousing would be a stern command to his meek, pale faced wife. Though, in truth, exposure to sun and air had browned the complexion of Cynthia Ann almost as intensely as that of the native daughters of the plain and forest. She said,'I am happily wedded. I love my husband, who is good and kind, and my little ones, too, are his, and I cannot forsake them.'"

If, indeed the entire account given by Rose is not apochryphal, it is certain that Cynthia Ann did not employ, in her reply, the set of words attributed to her, and that she did not speak in her mother tongue.

When recaptured, the veneer of savagery that covered her was so thick that it took time and unremitting, loving care to remove it.

Young Lawrence Sullivan Ross, then a dashing ranger Captain; in after years to win much renown as a Confederate Brigadier-General; Governor of Texas, and later, President of the A. and M. college of Texas till his untimely death, in command of a company of Texas rangers, a sergeant and twenty United States dragoons, and seventy citizens from Palo Pinto county under Capt. Jack Curington, came upon an Indian village at the head waters of Pease River. Most of his men were some distance in his rear, their horses being much jaded by travel and want of food. With him were the dragoons and twenty of his own men. With these, he charged immediately. The Indians, although surprised, fought with more than usual bravery, their women and children and all of their possessions being with them. They could not hold their ground against such an attacking force, however, and, after many had been killed, the survivors tried to escape to the mountains, about six miles distant. Lieut. Thomas Kellihuir pursued one, and Capt. Ross and Lieut. Somerville another. Somerville was a heavy man, and his horse fell behind. Ross dashed on and overtook the Indian he was after. A fierce combat followed, resulting in the death of the Indian, who proved to be Peta Nocona, chief of the band.

Kellihuir captured the supposed Indian he was after, and who proved to be Cynthia Ann Parker. She had in her arms a girl child about two and a half years of age, Topasannah—"Prairie Flower." It was not known at the time who the captured woman was. She spoke no word that tended to clear the mystery. Lieut. Sublett picked up a Comanche boy. Capt. Ross took charge of him, named him Pease, and reared him at Waco.

On returning to the settlements, Capt. Ross sent for Isaac Parker, thinking it possible that the woman might be Cynthia Ann Parker. Thrall says: "The venerable Isaac Parker, still in hopes of hearing of his long lost niece, went to the camp. Her age and general appearance suited the object of his search, but she had lost every word of her native tongue. Col. Parker was about to give up in despair, when he turned to the interpreters and said very distinctly that the woman he was seeking was named 'Cynthia Ann.' The sound of the name by which her mother had called her, awakened in the bosom of the poor captive emotions that had long lain dormant. In a letter to us Col. Parker says: 'The moment I mentioned the name, she straightened herself in her seat and, patting herself on the breast, said, 'Cynthia Ann, Cynthia Ann.' A ray of recollection sprang up in her mind, that had been obliterated for twenty-five years. Her very countenance changed, and a pleasant smile took the place of a sullen gloom.'

"Returning with her uncle, she soon regained her native tongue. It was during the war, and she learned to spin and weave and make herself useful about the house." Her uncle took her to his home in Tarrant county. Soon thereafter she was carried to Austin and was there conducted by a party of ladies and gentlemen into the hall where the State Secession Convention was being held in Austin, in 1861. She appeared to be greatly distressed. Inquiry revealed the fact that she thought the assemblage was a meeting of war chiefs, convened for the purpose of deciding her fate, and was apprehensive that they would condemn her to death.

An act of the Texas Legislature, approved April 8, 1861, granted Cynthia Ann Parker a pension of $100 a year for five years, dating from January 1, 1861, and required the county court of Tarrant county to appoint a guardian for her, the guardian to give a bond, "conditioned for the faithful application of the pension, and for the support and education of her child." Another act of the Legislature, in the same year, donated to her a league of land.

An act of the Legislature, approved January 8, 1862, contained the following: "Silas M. Parker, of Van Zandt county, is hereby constituted as agent of Cynthia Ann Parker, formerly of Tarrant and now of Van Zandt county, and, on his giving bond in the sum of $400 to the Chief Justice of Van Zandt county, for the faithful application of said pension to the support of said Cynthia Ann Parker, and for the support and education of her child, Topasannah, the State Treasurer shall pay said pension to the said agent, or his order."

The last appropriations to pay the pension were for the years 1864 and 1865, and are contained in the general appropriation act passed by the Tenth Legislature, approved December 16, 1863.

Topasannah (little Prairie Flower) died in 1864, and during the same year the soul of the mother winged its way to the spirit land. Cynthia Ann was buried in the Foster graveyard, Henderson county, Texas where her remains reposed for forty-six years—till late in December, 1910 through the efforts of the adoring son, Chief Quanah Parker, they were exhumed, conveyed to Lawton, Okla.; and, after much ceremony, re-interred in the Indian family cemetery at Post Oak, in the Wichita mountains. And thus briefly traced, closes the history of this unfortunate woman, far famed in the border annals of Texas.

Cynthia Ann Parker had two other children, besides "Prairie Flower"—both sons, and both with the Comanches. One of the boys died not long after her own demise; the other, Quanah by name, who long survived and acquired renown as the head chief of all the Comanches. Aged, and beloved by both the red and white man, the famous chief died at his tribal home, on Thursday, February 23, 1911, and was buried as he had so desired to be, by the side of his mother, "Preloch,"—Cynthia Ann Parker.

The death of Quanah Parker marked the passing of the last of the great Indian chiefs—Sitting Bull, Red Cloud, Crazy Horse, Chief Joseph and Geronimo having preceded him some years to the "happy hunting grounds."

John Parker, brother of Cynthia Ann, grew to manhood among the Comanches, and participated in their forays as a Comanche brave. During a raid into Mexico, a Mexican girl was captured. Shortly thereafter he was stricken with small-pox. The tribe fled from him in consternation, and left him to die without attention. The Mexican girl remained with and nursed him back to health. Disgusted with his former comrades, he followed the girl's advice, and went with her to her people beyond the Rio Grande. He served in a Mexican company in the Confederate Army during the war between the states, but would not leave the soil of Texas, refusing even to cross the line into Louisiana. The last heard of him, he was living on a ranch in Mexico. He, too, has long since gone to his reward.

---

## DEATH OF McSHERRY AND STINNETT— KILLING OF HIBBINS AND CREATH AND THE CAPTURE OF MRS. HIBBINS AND CHILDREN—HEROISM OF THE LITTLE SON.

Of the many, very many, pathetic episodes already chronicled, and yet to be recounted, the dual—triple; yea, four-fold tragic misfortunes of Mrs. McSherry—Hibbins—Stinnett—Howard, must certainly claim precedence, and in fact, are with-

out a parallel in border annals. Recording the multiplied incidents of the story (extending over a period of "13", to her,
unfortunate years) at this juncture, and to connect the thread of
narrative, we much revert a few years—closing with sad sequels.

"In 1828," says John Henry Brown, "there arrived on the
Guadalupe River, a young couple from the vicinity of Browns-
ville, Jackson county, Illinois—John McSherry and his wife,
Sarah, whose maiden name was Creath. They settled on the
west side of the Guadalupe, in DeWitt's colony at a place in what
is now the lower edge of DeWitt county, near a little creek,
which, with a spring, was some two hundred yards in front of
the cabin they erected—wild and isolated, but one of the love-
liest spots of the Southwest. Their nearest neighbor was Andrew Lockhart, ten miles up the river, and one of a large family
of sterling pioneers on the Guadalupe, bearing that name.

"Mrs. McSherry was a beautiful blonde, an excellent type
of the country girls of the West in that day, very handsome in
person, graceful in manner and pure of heart. Mr. McSherry was
an honest, industrious man of nerve and will. They were happily devoted to each other.

"Early in 1829 their first child, a son, was born, comple-
menting the full measure of their connubial bliss—but alas! soon
to be blighted with a most direful calamity."

"Later in the same year," continues Brown, "about noon on
a pleasant day, Mr. McSherry went to the spring for a bucket of
water. As he arose from the bank, bucket in hand, a party of
Indians, with a wild yell, sprang from the bushes, and in a
moment he was a lifeless corpse. His wife, hearing the yell,
sprang to the door, saw him plainly and realized the peril of
herself and infant. In the twinkling of an eye, she barred the
door, seized the gun, and resolved to defend herself and baby
unto death. The savages surveyed the situation and maneuvered to and fro, but failed to attack the cabin, and soon disappeared. Thus she was left alone, ten miles from the nearest
habitation, and without a road to that, or any other place. But
truly, in the belief of every honest person of long frontier experience, the ways of Providence are inscrutable. About dark, John

McCrabb, a fearless and excellent man, well armed and mounted, but wholly unaware of the sad condition of matters, rode up to the cabin to pass the night. Hearing the recital, his strong nerves became stronger, and his heart pulsated as became a whole-souled Irishman. Very soon he placed the young mother and babe on his horse, and by the light of the stars, started on foot, through the wilderness, for the house of settler Lockhart, reaching it before daylight, where warm hearts bestowed all possible care and kindness on those so ruthlessly stricken in the wilderness, and so remote from all kindred ties."

Here in this hospitable home the bereaved lady remained, till she met, was wooed, and married John Hibbins, a worthy man, who settled on the east side of the Guadalupe, in the vicinity of where the town of Concrete, in DeWitt county, now stands.

Again happy and prosperous, in the summer of 1835, with her little boy, John McSherry, and an infant by Mr. Hibbins, she visited her kindred in Illinois—returning in company with a single brother, George Creath, in boat, via New Orleans, and thence to Columbia, on the Brazos, "where, early in February, 1836, Mr. Hibbins met them with an ox-cart, on which they began the journey home." From Beason's Crossing on the Colorado, they proceeded to the Navidad, and thence along the old La Bahia road, reaching their last camp on Rock Creek, six miles above the subsequent village of Sweet Home, in Lavaca county, and within about fifteen miles of their home, where they were suddenly attacked by thirteen Comanche Indian warriors, who immediately killed Hibbins and Creath, made captives of Mrs. Hibbins and her two children, took possession of the effects, and leisurely moved off, passing up through the Peach Creek timbered region, between the Guadalupe and the Colorado. At their second camp, Mrs. Hibbins' suffering little babe, crying from pain, was seized by one of the fiends and its brains dashed out against a tree, before the eyes of its shrieking, frantic, but helpless mother.

For an account of this lady's further sufferings, providential escape, and rescue of her little son, on this occasion, we quote from the Reminiscences of the octogenarian pioneer, Noah Smithwick, who wrote from personal knowledge—prefacing with the providential, or at least fortunate fact that, on account of the numerous and alarming depredations of the Indians all along that frontier, Capt. John J. Tumlinson had been commissioned with a small company of rangers—the first ever raised under the revolutionary government of Texas—for protection, and was at that time in close proximity to this band of marauders. Says Smithwick, one of the company: "We were assigned to duty on the headwaters of Brushy Creek, some thirty miles northwest of the site of the present capital, that city not having been even projected then. The appointed rendezvous was Hornsby's station, ten miles below Austin, on the Colorado, from which place we were to proceed at once to our post, taking such materials as were necessary to aid us in the construction of a block house. . . . Just as we were preparing for our supper, a young white woman, an entire stranger, her clothing hanging in shreds about her torn and bleeding body, dragged herself into camp and sank exhausted on the ground. The feeling of rest and relief on finding herself among friends able and willing to help her, so overcame her overtaxed strength that it was some little time before she could give a coherent explanation of her situation, name, and sad misfortunes. . . .

"The scene of the attack being a lonely spot on a lonely road, the cunning redskins knew there was little risk of the outrage being discovered till they were beyond the reach of pursuit; so when a cold norther met them at the crossing of the Colorado, about where the city of Austin now stands, they sought the shelter of a cedar brake on Walnut Creek, and encamped. Confident that Mrs. Hibbins could not escape with her child, and trusting to her mother's love to prevent her leaving it, the Indians allowed her to lie unbound, not even putting out guards. It was bitterly cold, and wrapping themselves in their buffalo robes, they were soon sound asleep. But there was no sleep for Mrs. Hibbins—heroic woman, she resolved to escape and to rescue her child. There was no time to lose, as another day's travel would take her far beyond the settlements and the possibility of successful escape and procuring help before the savages reached their stronghold. Assured by their breathing that her captors were asleep, and summoning all her courage, she carefully tucked the robe about her sleeping boy—her first-born, and now her only child—and stole away, leaving him to the mercy of the brutal barbarians.

"She felt sure the river they had crossed was the Colorado, and knew there were settlements below; how far down she had no idea, but that seeming to offer the only means of escape, she made straight for the river, hiding her tracks in the icy waters, and hurried away as fast as the darkness would permit. Once she thought she heard her child call, 'Mamma! Mamma!' and her heart stood still with fear that the Indians would be awakened and miss her. She momentarily expected to hear a yell of alarm, and not daring to leave the shelter of the bottom timber, she meandered the winding stream, sometimes wading in the shallow water along the edge, and again working her way through the brush and briars, tearing her clothing and lacerating her flesh, never pausing in her painful journey till late in the afternoon, when she came upon the first sign of civilization— some gentle milk cows feeding along the river bottom, and felt that she must be near a white settlement, but dared not call for assistance, lest the Indians be in pursuit. Surmising the cows would soon be going home, she secreted herself nearby and waited till they had finished their browsing, and followed them in to the station—having spent nearly twenty-four hours in traveling a distance of only ten miles.

"Fortunate beyond hope, in finding the rangers there, she implored us to save her child, describing the mule he rode, the band of Indians and the direction they were traveling. Hastily dispatching our supper, we were soon in the saddle, and, with a trusty guide, Reuben Hornsby, traveled on till we judged we must be near the trail, and fearful of crossing it in the darkness, we halted and waited for daylight. As soon as it was light enough, our scouts were out, and soon found the trail, fresh and well defined. Cautiously following, we came upon the Indians about 10 o'clock in the morning, just as they were preparing to break camp. Taken completely by surprise, they broke for the shelter of a cedar brake, leaving everything except such weapons as they hastily snatched as they started."

In the quick charge and pursuit, four warriors were killed before they could reach the almost impenetrable cedar brakes. Two of the rangers, Elijah Ingram and Hugh M. Childress, were wounded, while a number of thrilling, and some narrow, escapes occurred—Captain Tumlinson having his horse shot and killed, himself narrowly escaping death.

"But," continues Smithwick, "we got all their horses and other plunder, and, to crown our success, we achieved the main object of the expedition, which was the rescue of the little boy, though the heedlessness of one of our men came near robbing us of our prize in a shocking manner. The Indians, careful of the preservation of their little captive—they intended to make a good Comanche of him—had wrapped him up warmly in a buffalo robe and tied him on his mule, preparatory to resuming their journey. When we rushed upon them, they had no time to remove him, and the mule, being startled by our charge, started to run, when one of our men, not seeing that the rider was a child, gave chase, and putting his gun against the back of the boy, pulled the trigger. Fortunately the gun missed fire. He tried again with like result. The third time his finger was on the trigger, when one of the other boys, perceiving with horror the tragedy about to be enacted, knocked the gun up. It fired clear, sending a ball whistling over the head of the rescued child. Providence seemed to have interposed to save him."

Gathering up the spoils, and with their precious charge, the rangers now returned in triumph to their camp. Of the affecting scene, the joyous meeting here, we let Captain Tumlinson tell: "Lieut. Rogers* presented the child to its mother, and the scene which here ensued beggars description. A mother meeting with

* Lieut. Joseph Rogers was a brother of Mrs. Gen. Edward Burleson, and was killed in a surprise attack by Indians near Hornsby's on the Colorado the following year.

her child released from Indian captivity, rescued, as it were, from the very jaws of death! Not an eye was dry. She called us brothers, and every other endearing name, and would have fallen on her knees to worship us. She hugged the child—her only remaining treasure—to her bosom as if fearful that she would again lose him. And—but 'tis useless to say more."

Near the same time—perhaps by the same tribe, if not same party, of Indians—and only about ten miles distant from the spot where Hibbins and Creath were killed, and Mrs. Hibbins and children were captured, occurred the murder of the Douglas and Daugherty families, already related.

But other tribulations were yet in store for this seemingly fated woman; who, however, survived forty or more years afterward—passing through other horrors—finally to meet a peaceful death, mourned by her fourth husband, Phillip Howard, in Bosque county. Gleaning the further facts of her extraordinary career we quote from Brown's detailed narrative, who, as neighbor to Mr. Howard in 1846, received the main facts from her own lips: "Thus the mother and child, bereft of husband and father, and left without a relative nearer than Southern Illinois, found themselves in the families of Messrs. Harrell and Hornsby, the outside settlers on the then feeble frontier of the Colorado—large hearted and sympathizing avant-couriers in the advancing civilization of Texas. The coincident fall of the Alamo came to them as a summons to pack up their effects and hasten eastward, as their fellow citizens below were already doing.

"The mother and child accompanied these two families in flight from the advancing Mexicans, till they halted east of the Trinity, where, in a few weeks, couriers bore the glorious news of victory and redemption from the field of San Jacinto. Soon they resumed their weary march, but this time for their homes. In Washington county Mrs. Hibbins halted, under the friendly roof of a sympathizing pioneer. There she also met a former neighbor, in the person of Mr. Claiborne Stinnett, an intelligent and estimable man, who, with Captain Henry S. Brown (father of the writer of this) represented DeWitt's Colony in the first deliberative body ever assembled at San Felipe, October 1, 1832.

After a widowhood of twelve months, Mrs. Hibbins married Mr. Stinnett and they at once (in the spring of 1837) returned to their former home on the Guadalupe. In the organization of Gonzales county, a little later, Mr. Stinnett was elected sheriff. Late in the fall with a pack-horse, he went to Linnville one day, to buy needed supplies. Loading this extra horse with sugar, coffee, etc., and with $700.00 in cash, he started home. But instead of following the road by Victoria, he traveled a more direct route through the prairie. When about night, near the Arenosa creek, some twenty miles northeast of Victoria, he discovered a smoke in a grove of timber, and supposing it to be a camp of hunters, went to it. Instead, it was the camp of two "runaway" negro men, seeking their way to Mexico. They murdered Mr. Stinnett, took his horses, provisions and money, and, undiscovered, reached Mexico. The fate of the murdered man remained a mystery. No trace of him was found for five years until, in the fall of 1842, one of the negroes revealed all the facts to an American prisoner in Mexico (the late Col. Andrew Neill) and so described the locality that the remains of Mr. Stinnett were found and interred.

Thus this estimable lady lost her third husband—two by red savages and one by black fiends—and was again alone without ties of kinship, except her child, in all the land. Yet she was still young, attractive in person and pure of heart, so that, two years later, she was wooed and won by Phillip Howard. Unwisely, in June, 1840, soon after their marriage, they abandoned their home on the Guadalupe and removed to the ancient Mission of San Juan, eight miles below San Antonio. It was a trip of 100 miles through a wilderness often traversed by hostile savages. Hence they were escorted by seven young men of the vicinity, consisting of Byrd Lockpart, Jr., (of that well known pioneer family) young McGary, two brothers named Powers (one of whom was a boy of thirteen, and both the sons of a widow) and three others whose names are forgotten. On arriving at the mission in the forenoon, their horses were "hobbled" out near by and little John McSherry, (the child of Mrs. Howard, recovered from the Indians in 1836, and at this time in his eleventh year) was left on a pony to watch them; but within half an hour a body of Indians suddenly charged upon them, captured some of the horses and little John barely escaped by dashing into the camp, a vivid reminder to the mother that her cup of affliction was not yet full. In a day or two the seven young men started on their return home. About noon next day, a heavy shower fell, wetting their fire-arms, but was soon followed by sunshine, when they all fired off their guns to clean and dry them. Most imprudently they all did so at the same time, leaving no loaded piece. This volley attracted the keen ear of seventy hostile Comanches who otherwise might not have discovered them. In a moment or two they appeared and cried out that they were friendly Tonkawas. The ruse succeeded and they were allowed to approach and encircle the now helpless young men. Six of them were instantly slain, scalped and their horses and effects, with the boy Powers, carried off. During the second night afterwards, in passing through a cedar brake at the foot of the Cibolo mountains, he slid quietly off his horse and escaped. In three or four days he reached the upper settlements on the Guadalupe, and gave the first information of these harrowing facts.

Thus again admonished, Mr. and Mrs. Howard removed down on the San Antonio River, below the old Mexican ranch of Don Carlos de la Garza, in the lower edge of Goliad county, confident that no hostile Indians would ever visit that secluded and far down locality. But they were mistaken. Early in the spring of 1842 marauding savages made a raid in that vicinity, stole a number of horses, killed stock, murdered settler Gilleland and wife in a most brutal manner and carried off their little son and daughter, but a party of volunteers, among whom were the late Maj. Alfred S. Thurmond of Aransas, and the late Col. Andrew Neill of Austin, over-hauled and defeated the Indians and recaptured the children, the boy Wm. M. Gilleland long a prominent citizen of Austin and the little girl, Mrs. Rebecca Fisher, still surviving, and a prominent member and leader of the Daughters of the Republic—a story full of pathos and tragedy, to be recounted hereinafter.

Following this sixth admonition, Mr. and Mrs. Howard at once removed to the present vicinity of Hallettsville, in Lavaca county, and thenceforward her life encountered no repetition of the horrors which had so terribly followed her footsteps through the previous thirteen years. Peace and a fair share of prosperity succeeded. In 1848 Mr. Howard was made County Judge, and some years later they located in Bosque county, where she died and where he is believed to be now living, probably a little past four-score years.

\* \* \* \* \*

Other incidents without exact dates, but all occurring during this year, in different sections of the country—mostly within the limits of Austin's colonies will be briefly noticed. Mainly, these are small affairs, in view of greater ones, but deserving of notice—illustrating at least, in the eminent degree, too, the tremendous hazards taken, and trials suffered, by the early pioneers of Texas in their struggles to secure and retain homes for themselves and their children, in this fair, but blood-bought land.

## THE HARVEY MASSACRE.

Among other brave and worthy pioneers, were the Harvey family, emigrating from Alabama, and settling near Wheelock, in what is now Robertson county, Texas, in 1835. In November of the following year, while the happy family were enjoying the frugal evening meal—little thinking of near danger—a party of Indians, cautiously approaching, attacked the house. Mr. Harvey attempted to secure his gun, in a rack over the door, but was struck in the neck by a bullet and instantly killed. His wife concealed herself under one of the beds in the room, but was discovered, dragged out and after a desperate resistance, killed and horribly mutilated—the savage fiends cutting her heart out and placing it on her breast. The son, a lad of about ten years, was also killed—"with many wounds"—his coat containing more than twenty holes. Securing the scalps of their victims the savages now departed, carrying away as captives the little nine year old daughter, whose arm was broken during the massacre, and a negro servant girl.

Finally, after more than a year's search, and the expenditure of considerable money, the daughter was found and ransomed by an uncle, James Tolbert, who carried her to his home in Alabama—removing thence to Texas.

"They settled," says the Rev. Morrell, "near where her parents and brother were killed. She has since married, and when recently (1873) heard from, was living. I have often been at her house, and used the family Bible at worship, owned by her father; and which yet has upon its pages the blood of her parents, spilled by the hands of the Indians on that fearful night."—"Flowers and Fruits, or Thirty-Six Years in Texas," pp. 68, 69.

## CAPTURE OF MRS. YEARGIN AND CHILDREN.

In the night, a few weeks before the battle of San Jacinto, a party of Comanches attacked the Yeargin home, on Cummings Creek, in Fayette county. This family was one of the few that had not joined their neighbors in the "runaway scrape." Mrs. Yeargin and her two little sons were captured—the aged husband and father escaped after pursuit, running afoot, it is said, ten miles, from the effects of which he soon died.

After a captivity of some three months, the mother was reclaimed by relatives, at Coffee's trading house on Red River—the ransom paid being $300. But the Indians steadfastly refused to sell the two little boys, and they were never after heard of. Eventually recovering from the effects of exposure and ill treatment at the hands of her cruel captors, but ever mourning the loss of her loved ones, this estimable lady survived many years, dying at her old homestead a few years since.

## FATE OF THE REEDS.

Joseph and Braman Reed, brothers, were natives of Vir-

ginia, emigrating to Texas in 1829, and first locating in the
Bastrop community, removing after a short time to what is now
Burleson county, settling on Davidson's Creek, where they
followed the business of stock raising. One day in the spring of
this year, Joseph Reed rode out on the range, looking after his
cattle, and when about half a mile from home, was suddenly
attacked by a party of forty or fifty Indians. Amid a perfect
shower of arrows, Reed put spurs to his horse and fled for his
home, pursued by the yelling savages. Mortally wounded, the
poor man fell from his horse just as he reached his yard gate.
His heroic wife, determined he should not be scalped and
mutilated, now rushed out and, under the excitement of the
occasion, actually lifted her dead husband to her arms and
dragged him into the cabin, which she succeeded in reaching
unharmed, although the target of many arrows.

Fortunately, the Indians did not attack the house, but left,
camping, however in the vicinity. The brother of the dead man,
arriving on the scene, spread the alarm, and soon collected a
small party of settlers, who attacked the Indians in their camp.
In the hard fight, Braman Reed, too, was killed, and several
others wounded; and for a time the situation of the whites was
desperate, but finally the chief fell, when the Indians fled,
leaving their dead on the field. Though seldom following the
harrowing practice of the savages, so exasperated were the
whites on this occasion, we are told, they scalped the dead chief.

In Travis county, in May of this year, depredating Indians
plundered the house of Nathaniel Moore, who, with his family
was absent, and on the following morning at Thomas Moore's,
killed Conrad Rohrer, from ambush, as he was saddling his
horse to ride out after his team. Showing themselves now, to the
number of ten, they threatened to attack Moore's house, but
desisted on the appearance of several men, who happened to be
stopping over night at Moore's.

## KILLING OF EDWARDS.

About the same time, and in the same section, John Edwards, one of the early pioneers of Texas, was killed by Indians. In company with Mr. Bartholomew Manlove, he was traveling from the town of Bastrop to Washington. Approaching under the guise of friendship, the Indians shook hands with Edwards, and then fell upon him, spearing him to death. Manlove had fled at the first sight of the enemy and after a hard race of several miles, effected his escape.*

On one occasion, three men—John Marlin, Jarrett and Lanham Menifee, repaired to the vicinity of a beetree they had discovered. Walking single file along a narrow, wooded trail, they suddenly discovered an Indian aiming at them, but his gun missed fire, when Marlin and Lanham Menifee both fired, "each killing the same Indian." Reloading their guns, the settlers proceeded but a few paces further, when they were fired upon by other Indians in ambush. The fire was quickly returned with fatal effect—killing two more Indians and causing the others to retreat to a dense thicket. Joined at this moment by another settler, who chanced to be riding in that direction, the two remaining Indians were attacked, one being killed and the other escaping.

## TROUBLES IN THE HORNSBY SETTLEMENT.

Hornsby's on the Colorado, some ten miles below the present city of Austin, was one of the earliest, and outside, settlements in Austin's upper colony, and at this date consisted of the Hornsbys, Harrells and a few other brave families.

In the spring of 1836, these families, escorted by Williams, Hoggett and Cain, three young men detailed by Captain Tumlinson, then in command of a small ranger force in that vicinity, fled like others, before the Mexican army of invasion, toward the Sabine. On arriving at the old town of Nashville, they heard the glorious news of Santa Anna's defeat at San Jacinto, and at

* Wilbarger, p. 231.

once returned to their homes, and to the tilling of their fields. "They had only been home a few days (says Wilbarger) when about ten o'clock one bright morning in the early part of May, while Williams and Hoggett were in one part of the field, hoeing and thinning corn, and the Hornsby boys and Cain were working in another portion, about one hundred Indians rode up to the fence near where Williams and Hoggett were at work, threw down the fence and marched in, bearing a white flag hoisted on a lance—the wily redskins thus throwing the young men off their guard. As they rode up, forming a circle, they shook hands with the two young men, and almost at the same moment commenced their bloody work, spearing one of them to death, and shooting the other dead as he attempted to flee."

At this juncture the Hornsby boys, Billy, aged 19; Malcolm, 17; Reuben, Jr., about twelve years of age, and the young man Cain, witnessing the attack upon, and fate of their two companions in the adjoining field, fled for the river bottom, crossed and went up the steam some distance, recrossing about the present Burdett ford, and then traveled down through the thicket brush of the bottom to within about a mile of their home, where they concealed themselves until after dark, when they cautiously ventured in—expecting perhaps, to find their parents and others slaughtered, and the house plundered or burned. But the murderous fiends, "after riding around and firing off a few guns, had departed, carrying with them all the stock they could gather in the neighborhood," amounting to some seventy-five or one hundred head of cattle, some of which got loose from the Indians and came back home about three weeks afterward. "The joyful meeting," continues Wilbarger, in telling of the return of the five boys, "can better be imagined than described, for up to this time neither party knew what had been the fate of the other."

In this same vicinity, in the fall, two other men were killed by the Indians. Blakely, Harris and one other, name now forgotten, came up from Webber's Prairie, some six or seven miles below, and stopped over night at Hornsby's, leaving next morning to hunt for wild stray cattle—"mavericks"—of which there were a great number ranging on the river at that time—common property and "free to whoever might be lucky enough to kill them." Having crossed the river and entered the range, and just as Harris and the unknown man were ascending the bank of a small ravine, they were fired upon and killed. Blakely, who fortunately was some distance in the rear, wheeled, put spurs to his horse and succeeded in escaping by fast riding. The murdered men were scalped and disemboweled, their entrails strewn upon bushes, their arms chopped off and hearts cut out. "Such," says Wilbarger, was the unsettled state of affairs in the Hornsby settlement in 1836; nor did the Indians cease their murders in this section for many years afterward, as late as 1845—as will be shown further on.

* * * * *

Note—The following letter from Hon. W. T. Davidson, (lately deceased) gives further details of the murder of his father and of Crouch, his companion, by the Indians. The statements can be relied on as true. The letter follows:

Belton, Texas, March 25, 1907.

Mr. J. T. DeShields,
Farmersville, Texas.

Dear Sir: At your request I send you a short account of the killing of Robert Davidson, my father, by the Comanche Indians in 1836. Mr. Davidson was born in Kentucky on July 1, 1799. Married Rebecca Landis in Ohio in 1825; settled in Illinois and from there moved to Texas in 1833. First stopped in Burleson county on Davidson's Creek, near the present town of Caldwell, and set up the body of a log house, but never did finish it, and moved from there up to Nashville on the Brazos, and from there in the fall of 1834 moved with his family up to the Three Forks of Little River, settled on his headright league of land, and built a log cabin in the bottom of the river bank, for protection against the Indians. In 1835 he cleared about four acres of land and put it in corn and pumpkins. The Indians having become so bold and troublesome, my father moved his family back to Nashville in the fall of 1835, but in the spring of 1836, he went back to his home on Little River to plant a crop, but before he got through, Santa Anna had invaded Texas, butchered the defenders of the Alamo, and then the settlers having been notified by couriers, sent from Nashville up on Little River, to fall back to Nashville, as the country was being over-run by Mexicans and Indians. My father, Jasper Crouch, Gouldsby Childers, O.T. Tyler, _____ Shackelford, Jno. Beal, Jack Hopson, Ezekiel Robertson and probably two or three others, on receipt of this information, made immediate preparations to retreat in a body to Nashville. Their only vehicle was a wagon to be drawn by a single pair of oxen. They had some horses but not enough to mount the entire party. On the morning of the first day they arrived at Henry Walker's on Walker's Creek, about 7 or 8 miles north of the present town of Cameron. There they found Henry Walker, Campbell Smith and _____ Monroe. On the next morning the party started on their journey to Nashviille, and father and Crouch concluded the party was out of danger from the Indians, and their families being down at Nashville, told the balance of the party they would go on ahead, and reach Nashville that evening, but they had got about 300 yards ahead of the main party, when about 200 Indians, coming up in their rear, passed by the main party without making any halt, and pushed ahead and attacked my father and Crouch, who made a bold stand, but were both slain by the merciless savages, after losing one or two of their number.

This occurrence took place in the month of March according to my recollection of the event; others say as late as June, 1836.

My father had studied medicine before moving to Texas, and brought some valuable medical works with him, but not being sufficiently settled, he never practiced in this country. Jasper Crouch, who was killed with my father, was a Missionary Baptist preacher, he and my father were close friends, and were both buried in the same grave on the prairie where they were slain about 7 or 8 miles north of the present town of Cameron.

They were buried the next day by friends who came up from Nashville. Judge O. T. Tyler and a few others performed the last sad rites. Years after I went on the ground where my father and Crouch were murdered, for the purpose of finding their grave, if possible, that I might give them a more decent burial. The land having been put in cultivation, and all plowed over, I soon found that I would never be able to find it. So gave up the idea with a sad heart. I am the only member of the original Davidson family that moved to Texas in 1833, now living. And Mrs. O. T. Tyler, Hon. Geo. W. Tyler's mother, is the only member of the original Childers family, left, and she is living in Belton, loved and respected by all. Robert Childers after living a long and useful life, died near Temple on his farm.

Robert Childers related the following incident to me as having occurred on the first day's march of the party down to where they camped the first night: As the party in the wagon stayed close together, my father traveled near them trying to kill a deer for supper. Finally he succeeded, and when he overtook the party, he told them he had seen an Indian, when one of the party remarked, "Davidson is scared!" Another one replied saying, "when Davidson gets scared, the rest of us had better look out."

A few years after my father's death, my mother married L. M. H. Washington. There were three children by this marriage, namely, Elizabeth, Jennie and Annie, and all of them are still living and have interesting families.

In 1846, my mother's family moved from Nashville to Austin, but after several changes, went back to her old home in Illinois to visit her brother, Fred Landis, who has two sons in Congress, and one a United States District Judge, in Chicago. My mother died very suddenly while on that visit, May, 1874, at Mt. Pulaski, Ill., at the home of one of her nephews.

Hoping you may be able to use this hastily prepared sketch of my father and his death, I remain,

Yours truly,
W. T. Davidson

# CHAPTER X.

The flow of events in Texas history has now reached into a distinctive era—that of the Lone Star Republic—and henceforward the affairs and destinies of Texas are under the guidance and control of its patriot fathers, who had heroically battled for and won this independence. But many breakers were yet to be encountered. A predatory and menacing Indian warfare had now been carried on for fifteen years—a strife but yet in the incipient stage and which was to increase in fierceness and bloody atrocity as the Republic's emboldened and increasing population expanded her borders, and pushed further into the Indian country.

## AFFAIRS OF STATE—INTERNAL MATTERS.

At the first general election in the Republic, on Monday, the first day of September 1836, Gen. Sam Houston was chosen President and Mirabeau B. Lamar, Vice President. The First Congress convened at Columbia, Oct. 3, and on the 22nd the President and Vice President-elect were inaugurated. The Cabinet was composed of the following famous and talented men: Stephen F. Austin, Secretary of State; Henry Smith, Secretary of the Treasury; Thos. J. Rusk, Secretary of War; S. Rhodes Fisher, Secretary of the Navy; James Pinckney Henderson, Attorney General; and Robert Barr, Postmaster General.

Though the Texas Congress at its first session in 1836 refused to pass a resolution authorizing the liberation of Santa Anna, President Houston assumed the responsibility of discharging him from custody and sending him and Col. Almonte, to Washington, D. C., in charge of George W. Hockley, (Inspector General of the Texas army) and an escort consisting of Gen. Barnard E. Bee and Maj. W. H. Patton.

Santa Anna left Texas in December, 1836; arrived in Washington January 17, 1837, where he had an interview with President Jackson; later sailed from Norfolk, Va., for Vera Cruz, where he disembarked February 23, 1837; was defeated in the Mexican presidential election March 1, 1837, and retired to his magnificent hacienda—Mango de Clavo.

Santa Anna regained popularity by his loss of a leg in an action at Vera Cruz during the blockade of that port by a French fleet in 1838. He was later elected President of Mexico. After the capture of the city of Mexico by Gen. Winfield Scott in the war of 1846-8, between the United States and Mexico, Santa Anna fled the country, and was subsequently formally banished. He returned in after years; experienced a slight rise to favor; was again compelled to leave; and was finally permitted to return and end his days in Mexico.

Although Mexico had repudiated Santa Anna's treaty and declared she would never recognize Texas independence, but little serious fears were entertained of a second invasion—for awhile at least. The invincible Texans had taught the Mexicans a lesson not to be soon forgotten. But a more stubborn, cunning and determined foe was yet to be subdued and banished.

Comanche chiefs are said to have visited the seat of government in the latter part of January and had a friendly talk with President Houston.* If they did, they scarcely got back to their

---

* It will be interesting to note in this connection the cheerful—but it proved erroneous—view, which the first British Minister to the Republic of Texas—Jas. T. Crawford—writing his government under date, May 29, 1837, entertained regarding Indian affairs in Texas. "Texas has several companies of Rangers on the various frontiers to check the Indian tribes. These however, have but little occupation, as the policy of Gen. Houston has been conciliatory and he has very lately entered into treaties with the most influential chiefs, who were at the seat of Government on a 'Big Talk' and returned well satisfied."

camps before they and their followers murdered in February, Hon. John G. Robinson, representative of Fayette county in the house of the First Texas Congress, his brother, and others—incidents that will be detailed in their proper sequence.

March 1, 1837, W. H. Secrest,* living on the Colorado, wrote to President Houston, telling of the murder of the Robinson's, Fortran and two children. In the course of the letter he says: "They are killing and stealing all of our stock, and we can't help ourselves. We are so few in number that we can't leave our homes to rout them. I am here the same as both hands tied—four women to guard—so that I can't get out to see about them. If you can't do something for us, we are in a bad situation and will be, no doubt some of our women and children massacred the next time you hear from us."

The Independence of Texas was recognized by the United States March 2, 1837—the anniversary of its declaration by the Plenary convention.

"During the spring of 1837," says Yoakum, "a party of Mexicans visited all the Indian nations on the frontier, making to them the most seductive offers to induce them to make war on the Texans. They promised them arms, ammunition, and the plunder and prisoners—women and children included—taken during the war; also peaceable possession of the country then held by them. At the same time, these emissaries succeeded in persuading them that, if the Texans were successful in the war then pending between the latter and Mexico, they would seize the country then occupied by the different tribes, and drive them from the land of their fathers. Thus many of the prairie tribes were induced to join the Mexicans."

Maj. Le Grande, who was sent to have a talk with the Comanche Chief, Chiconie, reported him as saying that so long as he continued to see the gradual approach of the whites and their habitations to the hunting grounds of the Comanches, so

---

* Texas Archives—State Library.

long would he believe to be true what the Mexicans had told him, and so long would he continue to be the enemy of the white race.

At the beginning of 1837 there was a small ranger force in the field. It was divided into detachments, which were established at the Falls of the Brazos, the Three Forks of Little River, Walnut Creek, and the Trinity River.

During the early part of the year, while there was no defacto Texas army, parties of cavalry under Wells, Seguin, Cook, Karnes, and Deaf Smith, rendered valuable service against the Indians—Deaf Smith, on one occasion, scouting as far west as the Rio Grande and defeating a superior force of Mexicans and Indians.

The appointment of Albert Sidney Johnston to the command of the Texas army, with the rank of senior Brigadier-General, reduced Gen. Felix Huston from first to second place, and was followed by Huston challenging Johnston. In the duel that followed, Johnston was dangerously, and for a time, it was thought, mortally, wounded.

His wound incapacitating him for the discharge of the duties of the position, Gen. Johnston devolved the command of the army on Col. Rogers May 7, and went to the United States to recuperate his health. On May 18, following, President Houston furloughed all the army (a total of 1,800 or 2,000 soldiers of all arms) except six hundred man, who, unpaid and ill-supplied, personneled the mere semblance of a military force, which soon dwindled almost to the vanishing point, owing to the men quitting the service as fast as they could.

The First Congress reconvened May 1, 1837. It passed an act, approved June 12, 1837, providing for a corps of rangers, to consist of an aggregate of six hundred white men, and a spy company of Shawnee, Delaware or other friendly Indians. The act appropriated no money to carry its provisions into effect, hence it was inoperative, and remained so until the Second Congress passed an act, approved December 28, 1837, appropriating $25,000 for the creation and maintenance of the corps. No protection resulted from the measure during 1837.

The First Congress doubtless relied on the President being able to negotiate at least some part of the $5,000,000 loan (or rather, "borrow") he had been given authority to consummate in the United States. It leaned on a broken reed, with the usual result. The financial panic that convulsed the United States at that time rendered it impossible for anybody to secure ready money on even much better security than Texas had to offer.

One vessel of the Texas navy was captured after an engagement with a Mexican brig, and two other vessels foundered, leaving only one schooner in the service—and it was fit for, and only used as, a receiving ship.

It was with the greatest difficulty that a ranging force was kept in the field. It could not have been maintained for a month, if the officers and men had been actuated by mercenary motives.

The Mexican navy swept along the coast, and the Indians met with but slight and inadequate resistance. Yoakum says, "Every day or two during the year 1837, some murdered citizen or stolen property attested the hostile feeling of the Indians."

On the first Monday in September an election was held, at which members of the house of Representatives and one-third of the Senators of the Second Congress were chosen. That body was convened in extra session by President Houston September 26, 1837, and enacted much important legislation—passing a land law (providing for opening the land office in 1838) and some other measures over the President's veto. The growing opposition to President Houston's "stand-pat" policy with regard to hostilities with Mexico, and his policy of conciliation with regard to the Indians, became crystalized and was given expression to in the Second Congress.

During the year, rumors of an invasion of Texas by Mexico, came near producing another "runaway scrape" such as that of 1836. The only reason they did not, was because the invasion did not occur. Texas was totally unprepared for not only offensive, but defensive measures.

Gen. Houston believed that if treaties of peace were entered into with the Indians and they were dealt with kindly and justly, hostilities would cease, and the two races could and would live peaceably side by side. The defect in his reasoning was that the points of views, the habits, aims, desires, and real interests of the Indians and the white people, were radical and necessarily antagonistic, and it was beyond diplomacy or any other human power to harmonize them. War—continual war—ending in the survival of the fittest—was inevitable and irrepressible, was perhaps, the only solution possible. Still, the motives that actuated him were philanthropic and noble. As means to the ends he had in view, he exerted himself to obtain treaties with various tribes. Congress co-operated with him to the extent of passing an act providing that commissioners to the Indians should be paid five dollars a day for their services.

September 14, 1837, Secretary of War Thomas J. Rusk and Gen. K. H. Douglass issued written instructions* to Jesse Watkins to proceed, with Lewis Sanchez as interpreter, to the prairies and have a talk with the chiefs and head men of the Keechies, Caddos, Tonkawas and Ionies, with a view to making a treaty of amity and commerce with them. The letter of instructions directed him to tell them that "we are disposed to be at peace with all our red brethren; that we are disposed to break our long knives and bury our tomahawks with them, and to open a wide road between the house of the red and white man; that all that we shall require of them will be to give up the prisoners they have of ours, to bring back all of the property they have stolen, and not to murder and steal any more, and to prevent other Indians from doing so where they may know of it—to all of which, if they will agree, you may promise them that we will make a treaty of peace with them which shall last forever.

"These presents which are furnished you, you may distribute as you may think proper, and you may make such arrangements about the chiefs coming in as is most satisfactory to the Indians. We would like it well if they could be brought down to the seat of government; but, for fear that cannot be done, we will ask the President to nominate two Commissioners here who can treat with them and who will be furnished with the proper instructions. In your talk with them you will be careful not to promise them lands at any particular place; and be cautious that you make no promise, however slight, that cannot be strictly complied with."

Henry W. Karnes concluded a treaty of peace and commerce with the Tonkawas at San Antonio, November 22, 1837, under the terms of which Nathaniel Lewis was to be trading agent among them and they were to buy articles from, and make sales to no other person.

During the latter part of the year Noah Smithwick induced five Comanche chiefs to go with him to Houston, where some sort of agreement was entered into with them, but it was lived up to by neither party.

Texas Indians considered themselves as the real lords of the soil under the old regime, and Spaniards and Mexicans as tenants at will. They regarded the Anglo-Americans as intruders, who were robbing them of that which was rightfully theirs. Indians from the United States who had effected lodgment in Texas believed they had rights which were being criminally trampled under foot by the white people.

The white man on their part, did not recognize the right of savagery to pre-empt so beautiful and fertile a domain as Texas, and unflinchingly demanded and conquered it, with the design that it should afford a theatre for the development of a high and splendid civilization that would bless all who participated in it, and contribute to the happiness of mankind.

Furthermore, there were "bad Indians" and "bad white men" who poured oil on the flames of warfare, every time they burned low, till the last tepee crumbled to ashes and the last brave (nearly fifty years after the time covered by this chapter) retreated from the confines of Texas, never more to return.

The picture of 1837 as further revealed by history, is seen not to be made up solely of sombre colors.

The seasons were remarkably propitious, and abundant

cotton and food crops were raised. The cotton crop amounted
to more than 50,000 bales and was sold for good prices.

The Mexican ranch owners, who formerly dwelt between
the Nueces and Rio Grande, and who abandoned that region in
1836, left behind them immense herds of cattle. People living
farther east "rounded up" and appropriated this stock, which
gave them a good supply for breeding and other purposes—in
some instances, from two hundred to six hundred head to the
cowboy.*

The sale of lots on Galveston Island, (under authority of an
act of Congress) resulted in the establishment and rapid growth
of the town of Galveston. A fine line of sailing packets was
established between New York, New Orleans, and Texas.

Congress, by the act of November 4, 1837, appropriated
$280,000.00 for the establishment of a new Texas navy, to consist
of six armed vessels—one ship, or brig, eighteen guns; two
barques, twelve guns each; and three schooners, seven guns
each.

New counties and towns were created. A stream of desirable immigration flowed steadily into Texas during the year,
with augmenting volume; industrial enterprises were introduced in a small way and some of them successfully operated;
the mechanism of government was adjusted and set in motion;
and the commonwealth girded itself for, and started sturdily
forward upon the high career it has since pursued.

The shadows that lay upon the land, served but to heighten
the beauty and add to the cheering effects of the sunshine that
was mingled with them, and that rested upon it like a benedic-
tion.

Brave hearts and true, met the dangers and difficulties of
the present unflinchingly, and pressed on to the future with
confidence and enthusiasm. It was not a "phantom of hope" or

---

* The term "cow-boy" is said to have been first used in Texas to designate
these cattle hunters.

"delusion of fancy" that led them on, but the Spirit of Progress, which had selected them for nation builders, and nerved them for and kept them at their task.

---

## MURDER OF THE GOTCHER FAMILY—CAPTURE OF MRS. CRAWFORD AND THREE CHILDREN.

Among the valuable and prominent accessions to Austin's Colony, was James Gotcher,* a native of Alabama, who emigrated in 1835, settling with his family and son-in-law, Crawford, at a point on Rabb's Creek, near the present town of Giddings, in Lee county.

Erecting comfortable cabins, opening farms, and accumulating ample and increasing stocks of cattle, horses and hogs, these settlers were prosperous and happy. Other families soon located in the vicinity, and for a time all went well. But alas! they, too, were destined to meet a fate—the common fate befalling so many of the brave pioneers in the settling and reclaiming of Texas.

On the same day, and by the same party of Indians who had murdered Congressman Robinson and his brother, the Gotcher home was attacked. At the time, Mr. Gotcher, with one son, and Crawford, were away, cutting and hauling wood from the bottom. The Indians approached the house in two parties, one of which came upon a little son and daughter of Mr. Gotcher near the dwelling, killing and scalping the boy, and making a prisoner of the little girl. In the house were Mrs. Nancy Gotcher, her married daughter, Mrs. Jane Crawford, and several children. Seeing that they had only to contend with women and

---

* Gotier, pronounced Gotcher by Texans of that day, and so spelled in some accounts. Enroute from the lower colony, they first marked, and afterwards cut out, the trail or road since known as the "Gotcher Trace"— once much traveled.

children, the Indians disregarded their usual mode of attack and rushed directly upon the cabin, expecting to meet with little or no resistance. They were mistaken in their calculations. Both the women inside, seized the few guns that were there, and discharged them, one after another, into the midst of the yelling mass of assailants. There was no time to reload. The savages burst into the room, and one of them, armed with a gun, shot and killed Mrs. Gotcher, whose body was already dotted with arrows that had been fired into it. Mrs. Crawford was overpowered and she and her two children (one of them two months old) were made captives. A little son of Mr. Gotcher attempted to make his escape but was seized, as he turned the corner of the house, by an Indian. He caught one of the Indian's thumbs in his mouth and bit it until the warrior forced him to let go by beating him with a ramrod.

Mr. Gotcher, and his son, and Crawford, ran to the house when they heard the firing; but in the excitement of the moment forgot to bring their guns with them from the woods. They arrived upon the scene while the tragedy was being enacted. There was neither time nor opportunity for them to return for their weapons, their dear ones were being murdered, or taken prisoners, and were appealing to them for succor.

They made a bold and desperate dash for the house, intending to secure the guns there, and make battle. The chance was not only a forlorn, but a hopeless one, and fighting gallantly as best they could, they soon fell beneath the fire and spear thrusts of the Indians, before going many steps. The son fought desperately, almost amputating the throat of a warrior with his teeth. Another son, after being mortally wounded, crawled to a clump of trees, unobserved, pillowed his head on a rock, and expired. Thus the bloody tragedy was soon over. The Gotcher home, being somewhat isolated, the occurrence was not known for some days later when casually visited by Gen. Ed. Burleson, too late for successful pursuit of the Indians.

But the news soon spread far and near, filling every heart with indignation and horror. "This," says Wilbarger, who furnishes the only details of the horrible affair, "was indeed one of the bloodiest tragedies that had ever occurred up to that time in the settlement. A father, wife, son and son-in-law and two children, lay cold in death, and mingled together their kindred blood, where but a few hours previously, they had assembled in fancied security, within the walls of their once happy home."

But, gentle reader, the sad story stops not here. After plundering the house and mutilating their victims, the fiendish murderers departed, carrying as captives, Mrs. Crawford, her two children and the little daughter of Mrs. Gotcher. They suffered, as the prisoners of Indians usually did, all the hardships and indignities their barbarous captors could inflict.

The Indians, annoyed by the crying of Mrs. Crawford's two months old babe, threw it into a deep pool, to drown. The desperate mother plunged into the water, seized the child, and swam with it to the bank. Again and again they seized and tossed it back, and as often the determined mother rescued her child. For a time this was sport for the cruel fiends, but tiring of their deviltry, a brave lifted the child in his hands and bending back its head, told a companion to cut its throat. As the knife was raised, and the diabolical deed about to be consummated, the frantic mother felled the fiend with a billet of wood. As the Indian lay motionless at her feet, as a result of the blow she had dealt him, she expected only death as her fate. But instead, the Indians merely laughed at their fallen comrade, and expressed much admiration for her bravery, and now returned the child, saying, "Squaw too much brave. Damn you, take your papoose and carry it yourself—we will not do it."

After a captivity of two or three years, during which time Mrs. Crawford was subjected to the most shameful treatment, she and the children were brought into Holland Coffee's trading house on Red River. Here Mr. Spaulding, a trader, formed an attachment for the unfortunate lady and purchased the captives—the ransom being 400 yards of calico, a large number of blankets, a quantity of beads, and some other articles. Mr. Spaulding married the widow and brought them all back to Bastrop county. Children born of this union yet survive in Texas.

## LIEUT. WREN'S FIGHT.

Early in the spring of this year, Lieut. Wren with a detachment of fifteen rangers from Coleman's Fort, attacked and defeated a party of Comanche warriors near the site of the present city of Austin. They were surprised in their camp just at daylight, and one of their number killed by Joe Weeks, at the first fire. The Indians took shelter in a ravine and fought bravely, but the rangers rapidly moved down upon them, pouring in a heavy fire which caused the enemy to scatter and seek safety in the adjoining cedar brakes—leaving their camp equipage and a caballado of stolen horses to the whites. But the joy of the victory was saddened by the loss of one of the rangers, Phillip Martin, who was shot in the mouth and instantly killed.

---

# MURDER OF CONGRESSMAN ROBINSON AND HIS BROTHER.

In February of this year a party of thirty or forty Comanche Indians came down into Fayette county on a horse stealing expedition, and on their way out, met and murdered the Hon. John G. Robinson and his youthful brother, Walter.*

Judge Robinson was one of Austin's colonists, coming in 1831, and settling on his headright league, on Cummings Creek within the present limits of Fayette county. He was an educated

---

* Neal Robinson, of Fayette county, son of Joel W. Robinson (or Robison) says the family have always spelled the name Robison. It appears as Robinson in the recollections of his father in Vol. 6, of the Texas Historical Association Quarterly, and as it is more familiar to Texas readers in that form, it is not altered to the correct spelling in this article. Joel W. Robinson was one of the men who captured Santa Anna after the battle of San Jacinto, and prior to and subsequent to that time, took part in many expeditions against the Indians. Both he and his father participated in the attacks upon and capture of the Mexican fort at Velasco in 1832. He also took part in the storming and capture of San Antonio in December, 1835, under Milam and Johnson. The family came to Texas from Georgia in 1831.

gentleman, filling valuable positions, and his death was greatly deplored. At the time of his death, he was a member of the First Congress of the Republic, which convened at Columbia, in the fall of 1836.

During the session he bought a supply of groceries and sent them to a house of a Mr. Stevens, a neighbor living some five miles south of his home.

In February, 1837, soon after his return from Columbia, Judge Robinson and his brother went with a team to bring home the supplies. They were to stay over night with Stevens, and no uneasiness was felt by the family till the next morning, when it became known that Indians had visited the settlement. We quote details as given by the son, Joel W. Robinson: "At that time I was at my father's on a visit—my residence being at Washington on the Brazos. Very early in the morning after father left home, I started down to Mr. Breeding's about eight miles below on Cummings Creek, purposing to go thence to Washington. When I arrived at Breeding's, I learned that the night before, the Indians had stolen all his horses. Knowing that my father and uncle intended starting home early that morning, and that they were unarmed, I was instantly siezed with a presentiment that the Indians would fall in with and murder them. I returned as speedily as possible to my mother and told the news. She was very uneasy. It was about noon. I armed myself and proceeded on the road toward Stevens'. I had scarcely gone a mile, when, in the open post oak woods I found my father's cart and oxen standing in the road. The groceries were also in the cart. But neither father nor uncle were there. I had now no doubt of their fate. The conviction that they were murdered shot into my heart like a thunder bolt. Riding on a few yards further I discovered buzzards collecting near the road. My approach scared them away and revealed to my sight the body of my father, nude, scalped and mutilated. I dismounted and sat down by the body. After recovering a little from the shock I looked around for uncle. I found his body, also stripped, scalped and mangled, about fifty yards from my father's remains. His body was small and light and I carried it and laid it by the side of my father. The vultures, in black groups, were perched on the trees around, and I knew they would quickly devour the bodies if I left them exposed. I covered them with a coat and saddle blanket and piled brush upon them. I then hurried back with the woeful news to my aged mother." And as this narrative closes, we leave the reader to picture the pathetic, heart-rending, scene between that suddenly widowed mother and orphaned son.

## LITTLE RIVER FORT —ERATH'S FAMOUS FIGHT.

Late in 1836, in accordance with a previously agreed plan looking to the special protection of Robertson's Colony, Capt. Coleman, in command of ranger forces, proceeded to locate a block house station or log fort about the "Three Forks" of Little River. Lieut. George B. Erath was detailed with a small force to erect the buildings and to protect that point. Of the thrilling events that soon occurred, Erath himself, tells in a graphic narrative prepared expressly for this work: "On returning from the army after the battle of San Jacinto, I became attached immediately to Robertson's company operating against the Indians, and in July was transferred to Capt. Hill's company operating between the Brazos and Colorado—participating in an engagement on the Yegua in August. On the first of October I enlisted in a corps of rangers then commanded by Col. Coleman, serving as lieutenant under Captain Barren. I may here mention that the men in this service were promised 1280 acres of land, which they received, and $25.00 a month, which was paid after a time, in depreciated currency—Texas 'red backs.' The men were to be furnished with rations of every kind. This was generally a failure, though the government furnished us ammunition to kill game with, which was our principal support. The First Congress passed a law authorizing the raising of five companies, who were to provide their own horses and arms, but be furnished everything else. About half the men had horses, and some had very poor guns, borrowed or pressed from citizens. Those of us who had horses performed by far, the greater part of the service, but there was no distinction in pay, or in rations.

"In the early part of November, 1836, I was placed in command of a few over twenty men detached from Barren's company, and stationed at a point on the Leon about one mile from what is known as the 'Three Forks' of Little River—having cut out, marked and measured, a road from the Falls of the Brazos to that place. Col. Coleman, who had accompanied us with a few men, after planning for improvements, left, measuring and working a road to his fort on Walnut Creek, about six miles east of where Austin now stands and about eight miles above Hornsby's, the highest settlement on the Colorado.

"Settlements had been attempted in the surrounding country the winter before, and here and there patches of corn were planted in the spring, mostly without fence, and by a prolific season, some corn, not eaten by the buffalo or wild stock, matured. Thus I was enabled to procure a few bags of corn, which I issued to my men—a 'nubbin' a day; and which had to be ground on a steel hand mill to be made into bread. For meat, we depended on wild game—then plentiful—while honey was obtained from numerous 'bee trees,' and kept in rawhide or deerskin sacks, made with the hair outside. Coffee was scarce and used sparingly.

"The details of operations up to Christmas, are unimportant. By that time I had up seven or eight houses, well covered, with wooden chimneys to them; buffalo robes for carpets or floors. One of the soldiers—Collins—having a family, had one of the cabins to himself, and Gouldsby Childers, a settler, with his family, occupied another. Thus we were not idle, besides my men had to dress deerskins to make themselves clothes, especially moccasins.

"And now to the operations. As already alluded to, Congress reorganized the ranger corps. Most of the old officers were retained, new ones added, and some of the inferiors promoted. The commander, Col. Coleman, was deposed by Gen. Houston and Major Smith appointed—the effect of which took place about Christmas. Lieut. Curtis was sent to Little River Fort about that time to take command, with orders for me to hold myself in readiness at any moment to proceed (under additional special orders to be sent) to Colorado Fort (Coleman's Fort) to inaugurate the new system and notify Col. Coleman to depart. This new and special order did not arrive till the 4th of January, 1837, when it was delivered by Lieut. McLochlin. But the information of greatest consequence he brought, was that he had seen the tracks of some dozen Indians on foot, going down the country about twelve miles from the fort, on the waters of Elm Creek. All was now excitement and bustle in quarters, as we determined to intercept and prevent these Indians reaching the settlement below and doing mischief. Lieut. Curtis, now properly in command and ranking officer, refused to make pursuit and at first objected to the horses being used—suggesting that I proceed with eight or ten men on foot. During the night, a cold rain set in and continued with heavy downpour through the next day. Finally, arrangements having been made, about 10 o'clock in the morning of the 6th, we left on the scout. My force consisted of fourteen men, rank and file: Sergeant McLochlin, the rangers, Lee R. Davis, Daniel Clark, (an elderly man) Empson Thompson, Jack Gross, Robert Childers, and his boy brother, Frank, Jack Houston (volunteers) John Folks, Lewis and Maurice Moore, Green McCoy—the three latter also were boys—and Leishly, a prospector. Four of our number had never been in battle before. Besides, four young men from the settlements below, whose parents had lived in the vicinity before the 'runaway scrape' in 1836, and who had been sent back to look after stock and other property that had been left behind, decided to accompany us so far as we traveled in the direction of their homes at Nashville, some sixty miles below—but my course soon deflecting they parted company and continued alone.

The trail was soon struck—"but behold!" continues Erath, "instead of a dozen Indians, signs showed nearer one hundred, all on foot and leading toward the settlements below. Following for two or three miles, we came to their camp of the previous

Erath's Fight with an Indian

1. Judge O.T. Tyler, 2. Capt. John Harvey,
3. Hon. W. T. Davidson and 4. Col. Wm. F. Henderson

day and night, and where they had constructed temporary brush and grass shelters from the rain. The signs were fresh—the camp fires still burning. The moccasin tracks were numerous—enough to deter the bravest, but we pushed on. Indians, and Indian hunters can tell by the cast of the moccasin soles to what tribe the wearer belongs, but not possessing that experience we were compelled to advance without knowing whether we were to encounter prairie tribes warriors with bows and lances or Caddos and other semi-civilized Indians armed with rifles—all brave and expert marksmen."

At nightfall the little force halted in close proximity to the enemy, whose position they reconnoitered. The Indians were encamped in a small horse-shoe like bend, some twenty three miles east of the fort and within about eight miles of a small settlement near the present town of Cameron, in Milam county. Resting till four in the morning, the horses were saddled, and tied to trees—ready to mount in case of retreat—and the men advanced afoot under cover of the creek bank.

As the Indians arose and commenced to build fires, Erath shifted his forces to a position within twenty five yards of the foe, and as soon as it was light enough to see sights on guns, delivered a well aimed volley, which tumbled eight or ten redskins to the ground—some of them falling into the fires. The Indians were taken completely by surprise and were thrown into confusion. Had the whites been supplied with repeating arms, (then unknown) they could have charged and kept the enemy on the run. As it was, however, they had to stop and re-load their pieces by the slow, old time process. This delay enabled the savages to recover in a measure, from their consternation. Some of them leaped behind trees and returned the fire, while others moved to the right and left flank to positions where they could look into the creek bottom, see the numerical strength of the whites, and enfilade them.

The engagement now became desperate, the enemy being Caddos, all well armed, mostly with rifles. David Clark and Frank Childers were mortally wounded, and all being greatly exposed, now shifted to the opposite bank and the protection of some small trees—Erath remaining behind to watch movements. He says: "As the men got posted, the Indians came charging with a terrific yell. I retreated to the other side of the creek channel, but found myself under a steep bank six or eight feet high. The Indians jumped down the bank of the creek. One had his gun within a few feet of me, and fired, but missed me. I could not miss him,* and he fell right before me. This caused the others to dodge back a few feet behind trees."

As the Indians continued to advance, and fire in combined force, Erath ordered a retreat. This was successfully accomplished by alternation—one half the men covering the retreat of the other half for thirty or forty yards at a time, so that half of the guns were alternately loaded and fired. In this way, and favored somewhat by a number of elm trees and saplings, the men reached their horses at the edge of the prairie. In the retreat, a number of narrow escapes and thrilling adventures occurred. Continues Erath: "At this juncture my left had reached the bank of the gully we had just descended into. There was a big thicket on the other side. The Indians charged us with great fury and terrific yells. We could not be blamed for seeking shelter, but it extended my line, and seeing Indians on my right dashing up to us, McLochlin and myself took to a big tree standing on the extreme right. McLochlin presented his gun, but it was broken and would not fire. I had my gun loaded and took aim at a bunch of Indians close by, who were maneuvering obliquely, but advancing. I had no time to see the effect of my shot, but ran to another thicket with McLochlin, the Indians getting between us and the other men and keeping up their yelling. Fifteen or twenty steps more, we reached the ravine that went square up the creek. Here we found Clark going up the bed of it, just about exhausted and sinking. He said something about fighting to the last or we would all be killed.

---

* It is vouched for by his own men that at the report of his gun, Erath fell, but immediately arose to his feet. A ranger cried "George, are you hurt"? "No I'ish not hurt: my gun knocks down before and behind"!

"I halted a few moments with poor Clark, who was now down and his life fast ebbing, but as half a dozen Indians were rushing towards us, I continued on up the gully, reloading my gun as I went, and soon rejoined my men."

On reaching Clark, the Indians yelled and danced around in great glee, butchering up their unfortunate victim in a horrible manner. But they never found poor Frank Childers, who, unable to join in the retreat, had sank down at the foot of a tree in a secluded spot, and expired within twenty steps of where the hottest of the fight had been going on.

Fortunately, the Indians made no further attack and soon collected at their camp, where they set up a terrible howl over their dead. "I knew they would soon leave," continues Erath, "and proposed that we remain and look after our dead, but I could not blame my men for refusing—several of them told me that but for impeachment for cowardice and insubordination, they never would have gone into the affair."

Earth's reason for making the attack against such fearful odds, was that he and his men were employed to protect the citizens. "But for this engagement, this large body of Indians would very soon have been in the settlements below, killing, burning and stealing; for they never came down in such large numbers in those days, without desperate ends in view."

The rangers now returned to the fort and reported. Erath, on the following morning, Sunday, leaving under previous orders, for Coleman's Fort—never again visiting the scene of his hard fought battle. A burial party of fifteen, sent out under Sergeant McLochlin on the 8th, failed to find Childers, and his remains were not discovered till eight days later.

Summed up, the casualties of this engagement, were the loss of two gallant rangers, while according to their own admission, later, the Indians lost ten warriors whom they carried about a mile from the field and threw into a big hole of water. There were several narrow escapes during the action—some of the men receiving slight wounds, and balls cutting the clothes of nearly every one. Sergeant McLochlin seems to have been a special mark—one ball breaking his ramrod, another the lock of his gun, a third bursting his powder horn, a fourth passing through his coat, and a fifth through the handkerchief worn as a turban on his head.

The news of this engagement with such a large body of marauding Indians, so near the settlements, caused general consternation and alarm, and preparations were rapidly made for pursuit by a combined force from the forts, under Smith. But a very heavy and severe snow storm and sleet set in on January 9th, delaying and preventing further operations.

## KILLING OF THE FAULKENBURYS AND ANDERSON—NARROW ESCAPE OF ANGLIN.

Members of the dispersed Parker Fort Colony were soon to suffer further trials and to meet sad fates at the hands of Indians. On January 28, 1837, Abraham Anglin, David and Evan Faulkenbury, James Hunter, Anderson and Douthit left Fort Houston for the Trinity bottom in search of strayed hogs. Finding some on the east side, they sent them back by Hunter and Douthit, who promised to return the next day and bring a canoe in which to cross the river. Becoming impatient, the remaining party improvised a log raft, crossed over, and after spending the forenoon in unsuccessful search, returned to the river to await their companions with the canoe.

We give the sequel in Mr. Anglin's own language:* "To our surprise we found plenty of fresh moccasin tracks along the margin of the river, but supposing them to have been made by friendly Indians known to frequent that vicinity, soon dismissed any apprehensions of danger. Being much fatigued and chilled, we sought shelter from the wind beneath the river bank and lay down to rest, falling asleep. But they were soon aroused by the war whoops and firing of a party of about thirty dastardly red skins, who had crept up within fifteen feet of them, and opened

---

* Abraham Anglin, in Groesbeck Argus.

fire with rifles and bows and arrows. David Faulkenbury and Anderson were mortally wounded, but both leaped to their feet, and plunged into the river—Faulkenbury exclaiming, 'Come on boys its time to go,'—and swam across." As Anglin arose to his feet, he received a gun shot in the thigh, the ball passing through his powder horn and burying part of the horn in his flesh. He said Evan Faulkenbury sought protection behind trees, and the Indians behind a bluff. Seeing the enemy were more advantageously posted, and with no hope of dislodging them, Anglin, throwing his gun in, took to the river. "As I was swimming," continues Anglin's narrative, "the Indians were discharging their arrows, and while climbing out on the opposite bank, I received several other slight wounds. Weak and exhausted, however, as I was, I reached the bank, where I found David Faulkenbury too badly wounded to travel. He told me to escape if I could and hasten back relief. Poor fellow, I knew he would soon be gone, but I did not know that I would survive him long. Fortunately, on going about four hundred yards, I met Hunter returning with the canoe, and mounting behind him, we rode as rapidly as possible for the fort."

A relief party was soon made up and started out that night. They found David Faulkenbury—but dead. He had cut the long grass near a pool of water, and made a bed on which to die. Some two miles from the scene of attack, they found the lifeless body of Anderson, with two arrows sticking through his neck. He had run that distance after swimming the river, and fell dead. Evan Faulkenbury's footprints were traced from the tree behind which he had last fought, to the river and down the bank a short distance to where they disappeared. The stream was sounded for his body, but it was not found and nothing more was ever heard of him, except an Indian tale—that he fought like a demon, killing two of his assailants, wounded a third, and when scalped and almost cloven asunder, jerked away from them, threw himself into the river and swam as far as midstream, where he sank from view.

Anglin recovered from his wounds and lived to participate in other conflicts with the redskins, joining a ranger force in

March of this year. He was a native of Kentucky, born Dec. 28, 1817, and emigrated with his parents to Illinois in 1818; thence, in 1833, with the Parker family, to Texas. He long resided in the vicinity of Fort Houston and Parker's Fort, leading an honorable and useful life till his death in 1875 or 1876.

---

## TRAGIC DEATH OF JAMES CORYELL.

Numerous fancy sketches—all more or less unreliable—of this noted frontiersman and his tragic death, have been given the public from time to time. We give the facts as narrated by one from personal knowledge—says pioneer Newton C. Duncan:

"James Coryell, for whom Coryell county was named, came to Texas in 1828 or 1829 from Ohio, coming down the Ohio and Mississippi River to New Orleans, from there to the mouth of the Brazos and on to San Antonio. He remained at San Antonio some time, and the next I knew of him he had joined a company under Bowie, going to hunt the silver mines at San Saba. This I think was in 1831. Coming back from this trip he stayed in San Antonio awhile, then he came to that part of Robertson's Colony, near where the town of Marlin now stands. While staying in that part of Texas he made his home with the family of Mr. Andrew Cavitt (father of Mr. Volney Cavitt). In 1835 Mr. Coryell went with Mr. Cavitt and they located the land still owned by the Cavitts in Coryell county, also locating land for Mr. Coryell on what is now Coryell Creek.

"After this, in the fall of 1836, Mr. Coryell joined a company of soldiers under Capt. Thomas H. Barron. I knew him personally at that time, having come with my mother from Tennessee in the early part of 1836.

"The Indians had troubled us so much that we had all gone into Robertson's headquarters at Viesca. While here, Coryell, with some companions, had gone about half a mile on the road to Perry Springs, on what is now Perry's Creek, where there lived a lawyer named Judge Albert G. Perry. Here they had found and cut a bee tree and were sitting around eating the honey and talking. Mr. Coryell had told the other men that he could not run, if the Indians came, as he had been sick and was not able to run. In a short time they heard a noise as of sticks breaking, when they looked and saw twelve Caddo Indians right near them, too near for them to try to get away. Mr. Coryell rose to his feet. One of the guns in the party was empty, one failed to fire, and, as there were only three guns in the party, Coryell's was the only one left. The men who had no guns ran. Three of the Indians took aim at Coryell and he fired at the same time. Coryell fell grasping some bushes and pulling the tops off as he fell. He was scalped by the Indians, but it is thought he wounded one of them, as the feathers from his cap were found, also some blood. Mr. Berry, an old friend of Coryell's, stood and snapped his gun, trying to fire, until he saw the Indians pull Coryell down and begin to scalp him, then Berry ran and escaped, Coryell being the only one of the party killed. This party consisted of James Coryell, Sam Burton, Mr. Berry, Michael Castleman, Ezra Webb and one other, whose name I do not remember.

"Ezra Webb was the first one of the party to reach the settlement. Coming to the house of Capt. Barron he found a crowd of ladies gathered awaiting the orders of Capt. Barron, as they were expecting to be ordered to the block-house for protection. When Webb ran in with great haste and fright, and breathless from his run, he fell on the bed, past speaking. The ladies gathered around, anxious to know what had happened. After a little time he was able to whisper 'Indians! Poor Coryell!'

"Coryell was truly a frontiersman—an excellent woodsman, an agreeable companion, a brave soldier, and an admirable gentlemen—beloved by all who knew him. At the time of his death he was forty years old. A short time before his death, while out on a scout, he explored a region of country now known as Coryell county, and being a man of acute judgment, was struck with the beauty and eligibility of the country near the mouth of Coryell Creek. He there selected his head-right of one quarter of a league which was located after his death by his executor and thus gave his name to that stream. So far as I know

Mr. Volney Cavitt and I are the only two men now living who knew Coryell in 1837".*

At this time Erath, with his little company, had been withdrawn from the Little River fort, and stationed, with other forces, at the Falls of the Brazos, where it was deemed advisable to concentrate all the rangers in that section, as they could be more advantageously utilized against the numerous bands of Indians then constantly raiding that section of country. At that time, however, Capt. Erath and most of his men were absent on a scout west of Little River—all the rangers being out on scouts—and thus the Indians who fell upon Coryell effected their retreat without pursuit.

---

## CAPTURE OF WARREN LIONS —SKIRMISH BETWEEN SETTLERS AND INDIANS —RECLAIMING THE CAPTIVE —TRUE ACCOUNT OF THIS NOTED EPISODE.

Late in 1837, LaGrange, on the Colorado, was an outpost, Bastrop being the only settlement above. Northeast and west to the Gaudalupe the country was still an unbroken wilderness. Southwest from LaGrange, some sixteen miles, and near the present line of the Sunset railway, lived the Lions family—early emigrants to Austin's Colony from New York State—consisting of the father, mother, a married daughter (Mrs. Wm. B. Bridges) and four sons Seymour, George, DeWitt and Warren, a boy thirteen years old. Some twenty miles further to the southwest, on the same road, from LaGrange to Texana and Victoria, and in the vicinity of the present town of Hallettsville, there were a number of settlers near the Lavaca, among them the names of Hallett Foley, Zumwalt, Heath, Kent and Jesse Robinson—comrades in arms and adventure of Capt. Henry S. Brown in 1828-'9.

In the summer of this year a raiding party of about thirty

---

* Paper read at Reunion of Old Settlers, Belton, Texas, Sept. 4, 1903.

Comanches, were discovered in the vicinity, descending from the mountains on their usual route toward Victoria, their trail being some fifteen miles west of the Lavaca settlement. The alarm spread, and a party of 12 or 15 was hastily made up, without any leader, who struck and followed the Indians' trail. In a very few miles, on the waters of Little Brushy, perhaps twenty miles southwest of Hallettsville, and in an open forest, they suddenly came upon the savages, who had camped, "staking out" some of their horses and "hobbling" others. It was raining at the time, and hence their approach was undiscovered till they charged with a view of stampeding the Indians' horses. With their bowie-knives some of the party cut the ropes by which some of the horses were staked, while others sought to secure the hobbled animals. But the Indians outnumbering their assailants two to one, soon rallied and charged furiously to recover their horses. Against odds, and in the absence of a leader, confusion ensued. Two or three Indians were wounded, and Stiffier killed. The whites effected a retreat with a few of the horses, but the Indians followed them in, and at Zumwalt's recaptured a portion of the animals during the night.

While admittedly suffering defeat, the settlers at least prevented an intended raid on Victoria. But the Indians, somewhat emboldened, sought another field for their operations. Deflecting to the northeast and rapidly covering the intervening distance of about forty miles, they suddenly appeared just after daylight at the Lions place, Mr. Lions and his son Warren having arose and entered the cow-pen to milk, while other members of the family were yet in bed. In a moment they killed and scalped the father, made captive the son, and gathering up a number of horses belonging to Mr. Lions, left for their mountain fastnesses.

Ten long years rolled by and beyond vague, unreliable, rumors, no tidings were received of the lost boy. Relatives and friends gave him up and mourned him as one forever lost to civilization, perhaps dead—all but the hoping and praying mother. She "dreamed dreams" and had visions of her darling baby child, and ever believed he would come back to her—believing that Providence, in some way would restore her treasure.

In 1847, pending the Mexican war, a party of Comanches appeared at San Antonio on a trading expedition. It leaked out that among them was a young warrior, believed to be an American. Two near neighbors of Mrs. Lions happened to be in San Antonio, and hearing of this rumor, determined to investigate the matter. In the young warrior of twenty-three they found such a resemblance to the Lions brothers as to convince them he was Warren Lions. An interview through an interpreter soon removed all doubt. They resolved, if possible, to take him home, but this required several days and much diplomacy. Warren well remembered his mother, but believed she was dead. He had two young wives and did not wish to leave them. Numerous presents were made to him, but still he remained obdurate till about the third day when his consent was won by a present of two very fine red blankets—one for each wife, with which he adorned them with the pride of a true knight. He, however, only promised to visit his mother, and then return to his wives and his tribe. With that understanding he accompanied the gentlemen home, in the full garb of a wild Indian.

The Lions home stood just as he had left it, a double log house, on a prairie ridge, and visible from the west two or three miles. Warren recognized it. When about two hundred yards from the house, the unsuspecting old mother stepped out in the yard in plain view of the approaching party. Her long hair, originally of flaxen color, had only assumed a whiter hue. Warren instantly recognized her and dashed forward, uttering the wild man's "wail of joy."* Abruptly halting and dismounting, he sprang into the yard, weeping, wailing and gyrating in

* "When he came near the lot where his father was killed," says Wilbarger, "he pointed it out and said: 'Dar me fadder kill—dar me take off,' and as soon as he saw his mother he cried out: 'Dar me mudder! Dar me mudder!!' Thus showing that through the long years of his wild, nomadic life—in the chase and on the warpath—the tragic scenes of that morning ten years agone were vividly remembered, and that the mother's features had been indelibly impressed on the mind of the youthful captive."

a manner so wierd as to unnerve the dear old mother, till the two neighbors shrieked to her: "It is Warren, your lost boy!" Then she shouted praise to God, and sought to encircle Warren in her arms, while he expressed his delight in Indian style, involving dancing, gesticulations and those guttural indications of joy peculiar to the wild tribes.

Warren was resolved to fulfill his promise and return to his wives, but the whole country round joined in schemes to detain him, but all to no avail till his brother, DeWitt, induced him to accompany him and join a company of rangers in Southwest Texas, to fight the Mexicans. To this he assented, and this service gradually weaned him from his Indian habits, and reconciled him to civilization, ending in his marriage and domestic life; not, however, till he had participated in several engagements with the Indians, in which, like his brothers, he developed the characteristics of a courageous soldier.

## INDIANS AMBUSH THREE SETTLERS.

Some negroes belonging to Mr. Beesan, of Columbus, on the Colorado, having run away from him, his two sons, Collins and Leander Beesan, accompanied by a Scotchman named Steele, went in pursuit, in the summer of 1837, hoping to intercept them before they made their way to Mexico. The three young men traveled along the San Antonio road, without mishap, until they crossed the Guadalupe River at Gonzales. As they ascended the bank of that stream on the western side, they rode into an Indian ambuscade, and were received with a rifle volley that killed Collins Beesan, crippled and disabled Steele and shot Leander Beesan's horse from under him.

Leander Beesan ran to the river, threw his gun as far out into it as he could, and swam back to the other side, with bullets whistling about his ears and ricochetting uncomfortably near him. As he buffeted the current he heard some one swimming behind him, but did not turn to see who it was, either while crossing or after he reached dry ground. As he ran from the border of the river into the timber, he heard a groan, which led him to surmise that the person who had followed in his wake across the river was Steele. Finding that his heavy, water-soaked boots impeded his progress, Beesan divested himself of them, and made his way home—arriving there some days later in a pitiable condition.

A company of ten men, including W. B. Dewees, was immediately assembled and leaving their families almost entirely unprotected, started for the Guadalupe. A gentleman who had just left the army and who was at Mr. Dewees' house sick, loaned them a spy glass.

When the party was within fifteen miles of Gonzales they saw, with the naked eye, a large number of horses at a distance through the timber. Dismounting and bringing the spy glass into requisition, they discovered that Indians were astride the horses, and were apparently awaiting the approach of the whites.

After a brief consultation, it was decided to attack the redskins. Slightly deflecting their course and concealed by timber and a hill, Dewees and his companions emerged into the open from an unexpected quarter and charged the Indians, taking them completely by surprise, routing them, and sending them scurrying as fast as their mustangs could be made to travel. The Indian loss is not stated by Dewees.* The pursuit was kept up for a short while. On arriving at the river the rescue party found and buried the body of Collins Beesan, but saw nothing of Steele. It was afterwards learned that the head of Steele was seen in the camp of the Indians, about three quarters of a mile above Gonzales.

## THE "STONE HOUSE" FIGHT.

October 7, 1837, Capt. Eastland, then in command of Coleman's Fort, departed from that station with all, or the greater

* Author of Dewees' Letters.

portion, of his force, and made a reconnaissance up the Colorado river to the mouth of Pecan bayou, and up that stream to
its source. He desired the entire command to return to the fort;
but a party under Lieuts. Benthuysen and Miles (in all eighteen
men) either disobeyed his orders, or secured permission from
him, and kept on farther west to the vicinity of the rock mound,
called the "stone house," near Caddo Peak, in what is now
Callahan county, and had a desperate and disastrous battle with
a force of one hundred or more Indians (Wacos, Caddos, and
Keechies), near the latter land mark, while a body of Delawares
looked on, from a distance, as passive spectators.

Noah Smithwick says that a large Indian encampment,
occupied by the members of several tribes, including some
Delawares, was found at the "stone house." While at that point
one of the rangers, Felix McClusky, gave chase to and killed a
lone Indian, scalped him, and rifled his pockets, though the
Delawares tried to prevent him. His fellow rangers upbraiding
him for the deed, he exhibited a chunk of tobacco that he had
taken from his victim's pocket, and declared that he "would kill
any Injun for that much tobacco."

The Delawares warned the whites that Indians of the murdered man's tribe and others in alliance with them, would
avenge the atrocious crime.

When the rangers came in sight of Caddo Peak, they were
suddenly confronted by the avengers, who demanded the surrender of McCluskey,* which was refused. He possessed no
atom of that spirit of self-sacrifice, that has sometimes led men
to accept death in order to save the lives of others. There was
nothing to do but fight. The whites took position in a ravine and
the Indians in a grove, and the battle opened, sans ceremonie,
and raged with great fury and deadly effect for an hour and a
half. The men of both sides were armed with rifles, were expert
marksmen, and tried to waste as little time and ammunition as

* Survived the engagement, but was afterwards killed in a drunken brawl.

possible. Four of the rangers were killed, and it is believed, a large number of the Indians, before the scales of victory were depressed in favor of the savage warriors by a stratagem they adopted. They set fire to the tall, dry grass that covered the prairie and that extended into the ravine. The wind was blowing in the direction of the white men, and the flames raced toward them, preceded by a dense and blinding volume of smoke. The rangers glanced in one direction for a route by which to escape, but saw the Delawares sitting there, apparently for the purpose of cutting off their retreat. Lieuts. Benthuysen and Miles then ordered their men to follow them in the opposite direction down the ravine, and, emerging from the depression, shot and cut their way through the encompassing Indian line, and fought to the timber, a distance of about eighty yards. While this movement was being executed, eight white men were killed, Lieut. Miles among the number.* The six survivors, some of them severely wounded, were not pursued through the woods, and made their way to the site of the present city of Dallas, where they found a large encampment of Kickapoo Indians, who treated them kindly and allowed them to return to the settlements.

---

* Much controversy, and a diversity of opinions, has existed as to who was the real captor of Santa Anna. Without attempt to disparage the names and fame of others, we subjoin the following "Obituary Notice of Lieut. A.H. Miles"—printed in the Telegraph of issue Saturday, Dec. 16, 1837; and which has passed without reply or direct attempt to dispute ever since:

"Killed in an engagement with the Indians, Lieut. A.H. Miles, formerly of the city of Richmond, Va. This young man, at the first call for volunteers, gallantly came forward to assist the sinking and apparently desperate cause of Texas. He was at the battle of San Jacinto, and was the real capturer of Santa Anna. His modesty while living induced him (together with the fact that he believed he had only done his duty) silently to see others reap the honor of the capture. He had, however, in his possession certificates of the late Secretary of War, and Adjutant General of the Army, of the above facts. He left to mourn his loss an affectionate mother and sister, together with a numerous circle of friends and acquaintances. They, however, will find consolation by knowing that he died struggling for the weal of his adopted country.—S."

## MURDER OF THE KELLOUGH FAMILIES IN
## EAST TEXAS.

In 1837 the Indians became so hostile in the territory now
constituting Cherokee county, that the settlers moved to Nacogdoches. In the fall of that year a number of white families went
back to their former homes. On the way they were met by an
old and friendly Indian who told them that the region to which
they were journeying was filled with hostile Indians, and urged
them to retrace their steps to Nacogdoches. They disregarded
his advice. They found their fences burned, most of their stock
driven off, and their crops greatly damaged. They also saw
many Indians roving about, but took them to be Cherokees and
members of the bands associated with that tribe, all of whom
professed to be friendly. The white people determined to stay
long enough to gather what remained of their crops. One day
while busily engaged in this work, they were attacked by a large
force of Indians, with whom there were a few Mexicans. The
male members of the Wood, Kellough and other families were
murdered, and women and children made prisoners. Nothing
was ever after heard of the captives, save vague rumors regarding a little son of Mrs. Wood. It was said that the child became
an Indian warrior and chief of the tribe into which he was
adopted, but this is only vague tradition.

There were two Kellough families. The first family, consisting of Allen Kellough, wife and five children, were all killed.
Old man Kellough, wife, and two sons, comprised the other. The
old man and his sons were slaughtered. His aged wife ran into
the yard, and told the Indians to kill her. They refused. Mexicans, who were with them, cursed her and told her to go back
into the house, which she finally did. There were two other
ladies in the house. Neither she nor they were molested. Neither
were two other families. The miserable survivors of the massacre, left everything behind them and fled from the accursed spot
to Nacogdoches. En route they were joined by a band of
Cherokees who accompanied them into the town, ostensibly as
an escort. The Cherokees vehemently denied that they or Indi-

ans associated with them had anything to do with the massacre; but evidence was adduced that satisfied many minds that they and their confederates perpetrated the murders.

John Henry Brown says that the butchery "led to the battle of Kickapoo, and was one of the impelling causes that led to the expulsion of the Cherokees and associate bands from the country."

## KILLING OF SETTLER McCULLOM AND CAPT. ROGERS — ADVENTURE OF THE HORNSBYS.

In November, 1837, Capt. McCullom, who had recently come to Texas from Alabama, and who was stopping at the home of Capt. James Rogers, in Bastrop county,* went with a son of Capt. Rogers to a creek for the purpose of building a wolf pen, or trap. While they were cutting the necessary timber, McCullom was fired on by Indians, who were attracted to the spot by the sound of the axes. He called to Rogers, telling him to make for the house, and then ran in that direction himself, forgetting to take his gun, which he left standing by a tree. The two men speeded down a new cut road leading to Wilbarger Creek, and crossed ahead of their pursuers; but as McCullom mounted the farther bank, he was shot in the back and instantly killed. Young Rogers kept on, passed below the ridge, plunged into the undergrowth, and escaped.

Subsequent to the foregoing incident, Capt. Rogers, Craft and a man whose name is not remembered, went to Coleman's Fort to procure ammunition for settlers on the Colorado River. While they were crossing the open prairie in Hornsby's bend, on their way home, they were chased by two parties of Indians—one riding toward them from the rear and the other from the right. Craft and the stranger, who were well mounted, escaped; but Rogers, who had an inferior horse was overtaken,

* Father of Ed. and J.B. Rogers of Travis county.

killed and scalped. The Indians proceeded to the residence of Reuben Hornsby. He was at work on the farm. They attempted to cut him off from the house; but fortunately his son saw them, and reached him on a fleet horse in time for both of them to escape to the house, where they barred the doors, presented their rifles, and bluffed the Indians. The redskins were not in a mood to come to close quarters and rode off, after yelling, circling about the place, and making daring demonstrations.

When young Hornsby left the dwelling to take the horse to his father, Mrs. Hornsby and children who were with her, ran to the river bottom and concealed themselves. They remained there until after the departure of the Indians and then returned to the habitation, endeared to her by so many sorrowful and happy associations.

## POST OAK SPRINGS MASSACRE.

From several sources—all reliable, but conflicting as to date etc.—we gather meagre details of a horrible affair, which occured, presumably in May of this year, at a place then known as Post Oak Springs, now called Ad Hall, in Milam county.

Preparatory to withdrawing the small ranger force from Little River Fort, Lieutenant Erath it appears had sent five of his men, Dave Farmer, Aaron Collins, Clabe Neil, Sterrett Smith and Jesse Bailey, to Nashville for wagons and teams with which to move household effects etc., of the two or three families residing at the fort.

On their return trip with the wagons and teams, and just as they approached an island or grove of post-oaks in the prairie, they were ambushed by a party of Comanche Indians* and all killed.

Overdue to return, a scout was dispatched and soon came

* Newton C. Duncan's paper read at Old Settlers Reunion, Belton, Texas, 1903.

upon the horrible scene. All the evidences of a desperate fight
were apparent. The bodies of Collins and Smith, says Sowell,*
were found in one of the wagons, and the other three were
scattered on the prairie between the wagons and mott of timber.
The particulars of this struggle cannot be given as none were
left of the white men to tell the tale. "But it is likely," continues
Sowell, "the Indians discovered them some distance off and hid
their forces in or behind the mott, and when they charged out
and cut the rangers off from this position, they had made a
desperate effort to fight their way through the Indians to it. It is
likely also that there was some confusion and there was no
concert of action, as the scattered position of their bodies would
show. The Indians secured all the teams, guns, pistols, etc., and
retreated."

## GEN. JNO. B. HOOD'S BRILLIANT VICTORY.

One of the most severe engagements of this year was
Lieutenant, afterward the famous Confederate General, John. B.
Hood's fight with a party of Comanches and Lipans near the
head of Devil's River, Texas. On the 5th of July, the gallant
young Lieutenant in command of twenty-five men of company
G, 2nd Cavalry, left Fort Mason on a scout against depredating
Indians. Provided with thirty days rations, an Indian guide and
a compass, and actuated by youthful aspiration, the little party
scoured the country to the head of the Concho.

Near the mouth of Kiowa Creek a trail was discovered and
rapidly followed to a water hole near the head of Devil's River.
From here he hurried on, though his horses were very much
worried, and traveled over the bluffs and mountains down the
river, but keeping some three miles from it. Late in the afternoon
of the 20th of July he left the trail, and went in towards the river

* A.J. Sowell—on authority of James A. Boales—in "Texas Indian Fighters", p. 229.

to get water, as his men were very thirsty. About a mile from the trail, and some two and a half miles from his party, on a ridge he discovered some horses and a large flag waving. The orders in Texas at that time were to attack any Indians found away from the government reservation, but of course to respect a white flag. Without going to water, and leaving eight of his company with the pack mules and supplies, Lieutenant Hood, with seventeen of his men rode towards the flag. Halting near the Indians, Hood signaled them that he was ready to fight or talk. As Hood's men advanced five of the Indians came forward with the flag, but when within about thirty paces the treacherous foe suddenly threw down the flag and setting fire to a lot of rubbish they had collected commenced a desperate attack, at the same moment about thirty warriors arose from among the tall grass and "Spanish leaganets," within ten paces of the soldiers. Twelve had rifles, the rest bows and arrows; besides which 8 or 10, mounted on horse back, attacked with lances. Hood's men went at them with a yell—thus the struggle commenced and continued in a most desperate and determined hand-to-hand struggle, with the odds in favor of the Indians. Hood's little force wavered and fell back, but were soon rallied by their brave young leader, and making a most desperate and dashing charge with their revolvers, the Indians gave way—thus the fight continued till dark when the Indians gave up the contest and gathering up their dead and wounded moved off toward the Rio Grande—much to the relief of the soldiers who had exhausted about their last round of ammunition. This was a most serious affair in which two of the scouting party were killed and several wounded, among them Lieutenant Hood, who had his hand pinned to his bridle with an arrow. It was afterwards learned that the Indians lost nineteen warriors killed on the field and fatally wounded. Hood made his way to Camp Hudson, where he obtained supplies and medical aid for his wounded— then returned to Fort Mason. General Twiggs, commanding the department, complimented this brave little company on their exploit, saying in his official report: "Lieutenant Hood's affair was a gallant one, and much credit is due to both officer and men."

This gave Hood much eclat as a brave soldier and established his reputation for gallantry.

Soon after his return from this fight he was promoted to the rank of First Lieutenant and stationed at Camp Colorado. In 1858 he established Camp Wood, on the Nueces river, at which post he remained till 1860 when he was called to Washington and commissioned as chief of Cavalry at West Point—a position he filled till the breaking out of the Civil War.

During this year there was a severe encounter with Indians on Maine's Prairie, Anderson county, the particulars of which are not at hand. Also, Nunley, Stifflen and Smothers were killed in Lavaca county, and a Mr. Davis was killed sixteen miles east of Gonzales, by Indians.

The blood of brave men shed upon the soil of Texas during this year was alone enough to render it holy ground, and the sufferings that the women and children experienced were sufficient to consecrate the land to high ideals. But the year stands not alone in these particulars. Grouped with it are others. United they call to the Texans of today and of the future. "Guard well the noble heritage that you enjoy and that cost such a price."

# CHAPTER XI

he year of 1838 opened well for Texas. A heavy and desirable emigration that began in the latter part of 1837, continued, while land values and taxable wealth increased steadily. New towns, farms and ranches were established, and settlements pushed westward—along Red River to Fannin and Grayson counties.

Galveston had taken on new life through the efforts of Colonel Menard, and others, and grew rapidly to a town of importance, being adorned by handsome buildings, and having in its harbor frequently as many as fifteen or twenty ships and vessels at a time. Houston, the seat of government, also increased in population and wealth and became a commercial depot—communication being maintained between the two towns by a line of four steamboats. Let the reader remember those were days of small things and sparse population.

## PROGRESS AND PROSPERITY—TREATIES WITH THE INDIAN TRIBES.

The French blockade of the coast of Mexico and political convulsions in that country, prevented invasion of Texas in force, and left the seas open for development of Texas commerce, which expanded until it included trade with England, France, and other foreign countries.

President Houston by his rigid rules of economy, if not replenishing the empty exchequer, was at least restoring confidence in the credit of the rising young Republic. The country had been blessed with prolific crop yields the previous year. Thus the people were prosperous, and might have been entirely happy, but for the redoubled continuation of Indian hostilities, which "lit up the whole frontier with the flames of a savage war."

The General Land Office of the Republic of Texas, according to previous enactment, was opened January 4th of this year, and was immediately followed by land claimants, with surveying parties, invading Indian territory, and battles with, and fierce and sanguinary reprisals on the part of, the Indians. Yoakum attributes the immediate cause of increased hostilities to the opening of the land office. "Surveyors and locators, desiring to select the best lands, had gone out beyond the settlements, and begun their operations. The Indians, seeing them at work, were not slow to believe what the Mexicans had told them—that the white people would take all their hunting grounds, and drive them off. Their attacks upon the frontiers were in resistance of this movement."*

President Houston's Indian policy was continued, and tested to the utmost.

January 18, 1838, a treaty of peace was signed at Live Oak Point, by James Power, acting for the government of Texas, and Culegasde Castro, chief of the tribe, representing the Lipans. It was stipulated that the Indians were to be given $250.00 worth of presents; that trading houses were to be established among them; and that neither Indians nor white people were to take redress of grievances into their own hands.

Emanating from the War Department, a little later, we find the following conciliatory order:

Houston, Feb. 4, 1838.

To Gen. A. Sidney Johnston, Col. Lysander Wells.

Gentlemen: By order of His Excellency,the President, you are hereby empowered as commissioners to meet and hold

* History of Texas, Vol. 2. p. 248.

conference with the Comanche Indians.

You are to meet them so soon as practicable, assure them of our friendly feelings toward them, and of our earnest desire to cultivate with them a trade for our mutual advantage, and to this end, trading houses shall be established for their convenience, by which means they will find a market for their mules, buffalo robes, etc. Invite seven or eight of their chiefs to visit the Executive and both houses of Congress at the next session, say about the 21st of April next. Also have an understanding with them that they are at all times to co-operate with us against our enemies.

We rely upon your good judgment and discretion in saying to them all which shall be necessary to convince them of our friendship to them. Assure them also that the President has now gone to Nacogdoches to enter into an arrangement with the Cherokees.

Barnard E. Bee.

Col. Henry W. Karnes was appointed as a colleague of Johnston and Wells, to assist in the mission. His letter of instructions, under the date of April 12, 1838, suggests that he must use great caution in discussing the question of territory limits with this tribe—"That you must manage in this way. You must say to them that they will continue to hunt where they have game, and if they find our people in their hunting grounds with the passwords, to treat them kindly, as our people will do should the Comanches come into our settlements."

"After a delay of some two months, a band of about 150 Comanches, led by two chiefs, Essowakkenny and Essomanny," says Gen. Johnston's biographers, "came in to hold the 'talk.' The chiefs were about twenty-seven or twenty-eight years old, and about five feet eight in height; Essomanny was rather a bull-headed fellow, with a firm and sensible expression; Essowakkenny had a more intelligent countenance."

It had been the immemorial custom of the Comanches, after plundering the country, to ride at their leisure into San Antonio to trade, or for ransom. On such occasions, to relieve themselves

from the care of their horses, these fierce warriors conde-
scendingly committed their caballado to the custody of the
commandant, from whom they required a scrupulous return of
their chattels when they should be ready to leave. On this
occasion, Essowakkenny, on meeting General Johnston, waved
his hand with a lordly gesture towards his horses, saying:
"There is our caballado. Take care of it." "Yes," replied General
Johnston, looking at him steadily, "I see your caballado. You
ride good ponies. I advise you to watch them well. All white
men are not honest. I take good care of my horses. Take care of
yours." By which the General meant to teach the Comanches
that he was not "A Mexican hostler in uniform." The chief
understood the irony, and that he had to deal with a warrior; he
smiled grimly, and detailed some of his own men to watch the
grazing herd.

A "big talk" was held, in which the advantages of a peace
truce were freely discussed, and with reciprocal assurances of
a desire for such. In the course of his "talk" General Johnston
suggested, that if so desired, trading posts would be established
among them. Essowakkenny rose, and said "that the Comanches had noticed that trading posts always seemed to
frighten the buffalo away, so that they did not want any in their
country; but they did not object to a line of posts along the
border of their country"—drawing an imaginary line with his
hand, so as to indicate a distance of about three miles from San
Antonio. Not caring to discuss the delicate subject of the boundary further, General Johnston, without alluding to the trading
posts again, dilated upon the benefits of peace. Essowakkenny
rejoined that his people had made peace with the Mexicans. "I
am glad of it," replied Johnston; "although the Mexicans are not
our friends, it is good for the Comanches to be at peace with
everybody." Essowakkenny added, with a humorous look, that
"he did not make peace with the Mexicans until he had stolen
all their horses." To the invitation and request that he visit the
President at Houston, Essowakkenny replied that he could not
go, but that his brother, Essomanny, who was a braver man than
himself, would go. He then declared sentiments of the strongest

friendship for the whites; presents of considerable value were distributed—eliciting many "grunts" and expressions of satisfaction—when the council was dismissed with the best of feelings prevailing.

On the strength of this talk, Colonel Karnes, supplying himself with a quantity of suitable goods, left with the band on a trading venture among the Comanches. And it is of record that "he was treated well and made much money." Encouraged by these results, a party of thirteen men afterwards left San Antonio with goods to trade with them; but as they were never heard of again, it was supposed they were treacherously murdered by the Comanches.*

A treaty of peace was concluded with the Tonkawas, at Houston, April 11, 1838, and signed by Secretary of War Barnard E. Bee and Col. George W. Hockley for Texas, and chiefs, Placido, Benavido, Campos and Oquin, for the Indians. It contained the following, among other provisions: "Art. 1. The Tonkawa Indians . . . being desirous of enjoying their hunting grounds and homes in peace and also, that their white brothers may be fully assured that they sincerely wish to love them as brothers, do agree and promise to bring to just punishment such individuals of their tribe as may commit any depredation upon the property or injure the person of any of the citizens belonging to the Republic of Texas.

"Art. 2. Hon. B. E. Bee and Col. G. W. Hockley, commissioners on the part of the Republic of Texas, being desirous that their red brothers, the Tonkawas, may not be cheated by bad men, will forthwith appoint an agent who shall superintend their business and protect their rights and see that this agreement is complied with by all.

"It was stipulated that five Tonkawa chiefs should visit the seat of Government twice a year and talk with the President and amicably adjust all differences."

* Wm. Preston Johnston's "The Life of Albert Sidney Johnston." p. 89.

An act of the Texas Congress, approved May 15, 1838, authorized the President to raise a corps of cavalry, to consist of two hundred men, enlisted for not less than one nor more than three years, for the protection of the southwestern frontier.

Following the "big talk" at San Antonio, it appears that the President succeeded in concluding a treaty of peace with the Comanches, at the Capital, signed on May 29, 1838,* by Secretary of State, R. A. Irion, and Dr. Ashbel Smith, for Texas, and chiefs Muguarroh, Muestyad and Muhy for the Indians. The Comanches were to quit stealing from, and murdering white people. The chiefs were to visit the seat of Government at stated times to discuss matters of mutual interest and to peaceably settle grievances. The following were some of the articles of the compact: "Art. 9. The Comanches bind themselves to make war upon all tribes of Indians that may make, or attempt to make, war on the traders.

"Art. 10. The Comanches promise that they will stand by the white man and be his friend against all of his enemies . . . and will not kill him or steal his property.

"Art. 11. Peace is never to die between the parties that make this agreement, they have shaken hands upon it, and the Great Spirit has looked down and seen their actions. He will curse all the chiefs that tell a lie before his eyes. Their women and children cannot be happy."

But the ink was scarcely dry on the instrument before it was violated by these faithless and fiendish savages, whom we soon find not only "raiding, robbing and scalping as of yore, but with the reckless abandon of back-sliders."

A treaty of peace was entered into with the Wacos, Tehuacanas, Keechies and Towash (Pawnee) Indians Sept. 2, 1838. It was negotiated by Holland Coffee near the mouth of the Washita in Fannin county.

However impractical Houston's policy may have been we

* Archives—Indian Affairs—State Library.

see that no efforts were lacking to conciliate the Indians. How far these measures served in preventing hostilities one cannot judge—since the catalogue of crimes and tragedies is seemingly most complete, as may be seen from a review of the history of this period.

---

## SURVEYORS FIGHT ON BATTLE CREEK.

One of the bloodiest and hardest fought battles that ever took place on Texas soil between white men and Indians was what is known in history as the Surveyors Fight, which occurred near the present village of Dawson, Navarro county, in October, 1838.

Omitting many details of thrilling incidents and acts of individual heroism in this celebrated encounter and fierce border drama, we shall give the principal facts of the affair as contained in a letter to the author from the late Gen. Walter P. Lane, one of the participants, and who escaped the fearful conflict with life and lived to participate in many other bloody battles—but none so hotly contested nor so fatal, considering numbers engaged and arms employed.

Marshall, Texas, May 18, 1885.

James T. DeShields, Esq.,
Belton, Texas.

Dear Sir: Your letter asking me to give you an account of the fight with the Kickapoo Indians, September 8, 1838, is just to hand. In answer I will say that I was in a fight with the Indians on Richland Creek, (afterwards called Battle Creek) but it has been so long ago I have forgotten most of the incidents.

We started—a surveying party of twenty-two men and a boy from Old Franklin, in Robertson county, Captain Neill commanding, and William Henderson, surveyor. We camped on the second day at Parker's Fort. Two years before that the Fort had been taken by the Comanches, the men killed, and the women and children taken into captivity.

When we reached Battle Creek it was day, so we encamped on the other side, some two miles beyond, where we found some 300 Kickapoo Indians killing buffalo for winter supplies. We got on very well with them till we commenced surveying. They tried to frighten us off by stating that the Ionies were coming down to kill us, and it would be laid on them. We would not go. The third day we came to camp in the morning to cook breakfast, when they begged us again to go. After breakfast we went back to resume our surveying where we left off. A mile from camp they ambuscaded us in a ravine; some fifty fired on us at forty yards. We charged them, when 100 more showed themselves in the timber behind them. At the same time 100 charged down upon us on horseback from the prairies. They rode around us, firing. We retreated to the head of a ravine in the prairie; its banks were some four or five feet high, with a few cottonwood trees growing on them. The Indians got seventy-five yards below us and commenced firing. This was about nine o'clock. Whenever one of our men would put up his head to shoot, twenty-five Indians would pull down on him. The Indians had climbed up in these cottonwood trees in order to shoot over into the creek. A gallant gentleman, Mr. Euclid M. Cox, got behind a lone tree on the bank, and fired for several hours, shooting at the Indians in the trees below, but exposing his body, he was shot through the spine. He fell from the tree, the Indians still firing at him. I ran up the bank, took him by the shoulder, and, under heavy fire dragged him to the ravine. Mr. Cox was still alive when his companions made their escape but realizing that his wound was fatal he urged them to save themselves and leave him to his fate. Button, one of his companions, proposed to stay and die with him; he told Button there was no chance for him, giving him one of his pistols and told him that if he made his escape to give the pistol to his wife; the other, he took in his hand and remarked that he would keep this one to defend himself with. Button made his escape and delivered the pistol as requested and it is now in the possession of Sheriff Cox of Hillsboro. Davis of San Augustine, who was well mounted, tried to break through but the Indians caught and killed him in

sight. We fought till twelve o'clock at night. We were waiting
for the moon to cloud over before we charged through them to
the bottom one fourth mile distant. At that time we broke
through. The Indians kept thirty steps in our rear, firing. We
would face around and fire. We had three horses left when we
retreated, with two wounded men on each. Captain Neill was
shot in the back and fell. He called to me to help him on a horse,
whose rider was just killed. Two of us got him on, but the horse
and rider were both killed before they got twenty steps. I had
got within one hundred yards of the timber when I was shot in
the leg, splintering the bone. I made out to reach a thicket in
company with Henderson and Button, the only two who were
not wounded. We got into a deep ravine that led to the creek. I
called to Henderson to stop and tie up my leg as I was bleeding
to death. He did so promptly. We went down some distance and
heard the Indians following us. We climbed on the bank and lay
down with our guns cocked. Twelve of them passed so close I
could have touched them. We got on the creek an hour before
day, and followed down till we found some muddy water. We
left the creek and went on the bank till we found a log reaching
to a brushy island. We crossed over it and lay hidden all day.
We could hear the Indians on the bank looking for us. At dark
we started. When I got to my feet the pain from splinters of the
bone was so great that I fainted. When I came to, I heard Button
tell Henderson to come on and leave me, for I could not get to
the settlements. I arose to my feet, cursed Button, and told him
I would beat him to the settlements—which I did. We traveled
two days without water before we reached Tehuacana Hill. A
party of Kickapoos found us at the spring (they did not know
of our fight with their tribe). They pointed to my bloody leg and
asked "Who shot you?" I told him we had a fight with the
Ionies, and we had got lost from our party going home. They
took us to their camp, gave us plenty to eat, and their squaws
treated us very kindly.

In two days after we got to Franklin the people raised a
company and went to Battle Creek and buried the bones of our
men. Summed up, sixteen killed, seven escaped five of whom

were badly wounded.

Mr. Violet had his thigh wounded in the edge of the timber. He ate green haws for two days and then struck out for Tehuacana Hill, distance twenty-five miles, on his hands and knees. The party we sent up found him nearly famished, brought him to the settlement, and cared for him.

Yours truly,<br>Walter P. Lane.

* * * * *

Further incidents occurring in the course of this fearful engagement and especially detailing the tragic fate of the brave Euclid M. Cox, are gleaned from a graphic narrative of this affair by Mr. T. H. Dixon who wrote from authentic data supplied by John P. Cox, a surviving son of the noble martyr-pioneer.

As Gen. Lane has stated, the little band of hardy pioneers were surrounded on all sides and quickly realized that to charge in any direction would be certain death. The enfilade of the Indians was already fierce. In this dilemma they discovered near them the head of a ravine, the bed of which was some five or six feet in depth, and to which they made way with their wounded in all possible haste. On gaining this refuge they managed to check the onslaught of the Indians and succeeded by cautious firing, bravery and alertness, in holding their position. But along the banks of the ravine no foliage appeared behind which they could conceal their position, other than a large and lone tree standing near the bank, and in order to shoot it became necessary for them to show their heads, and every time this was done a perfect fusillade of bullets whistled about them from the guns of the savages. Though partially protected by the friendly banks of the ravine the little band of brave and dauntless men were completely hemmed in on all sides by hordes of painted and yelling warriors.

"About noon (says Dixon) the daring and intrepid Euclid M. Cox conceived the idea of gaining the shelter of the oak above mentioned, and by the use of extreme caution he managed to secrete himself in its foliage and from this place of concealment he managed for nearly two hours to pour a continuous and deadly fire into the savage ranks. Unfortunately, however, in an unguarded moment, this hero exposed a portion of his body to the savages and they greeted its appearance with a perfect whirlwind of shot, one of which penetrated his spine causing him to fall to the ground, and the Indians noticing this, and believing that he was the leader of the party, redoubled their firing at that point. At the time of the fall of the brave man from the tree, Gen. Walter P. Lane, then in the prime and vigor of his early manhood, chanced to be in the ravine near by, and noting the imminent peril of his heroic and wounded companion, dashed from his place of refuge and with leaden missiles hailing all about him, seized Cox by the shoulders and pulled him to the bed of the ravine. This heroic conduct of Walter P. Lane was but in keeping with his subsequent deeds of valor upon full many a hard fought field.*

"The rescue of Cox's wounded body and the escape of Lane in safety back to the ravine appeared to arouse the fury of the savages to the utmost, and from that time forward until nightfall the hard pressed heroes found it a matter of extreme difficulty to hold the savages at bay. They realized that something must be done and that speedily, for they had been fighting hard all day without food or water, and their thirst was becoming unbearable. A consultation was held and it was decided that upon the going down of the moon at midnight, they would make a desperate attempt to charge through the savages and gain the shelter of the timber, about half a mile distant.

"Among the survivors in the ravine, was a man by the

* Gen. Walter P. Lane was the last survivor of this memorable fight. The grand old hero of several wars and many similar border affrays, finally died in peace at an advanced age on January 28, 1892, and his remains rest in "Old Marshall Cemetery" at Marshall, Harrison county, Texas. Peace to his ashes.

name of Davis, who hailed from San Augustine who being well mounted, determined to make an effort to reach the timber by charging through the savages single handed and alone in order to be in a position at midnight to aid his companions in their desperate resolve by opening fire upon the savages from the rear, hoping thereby to withdraw attention from the ravine until his companions could succeed in making considerable headway. He bade his companions good-by and started upon his desperate ride, but both horse and rider perished before they had gotten thirty yards. At last the moon sank to rest behind the horizon, and the little band began active preparations for their desperate charge. They had three horses left them and upon each they put two of their wounded who could ride.

"The brave and daring Cox realizing his position full well, and knowing that he had but a few hours to live, would not hear to his companions remaining behind with him, but insisted upon their taking their leave. One of the survivors, a young man who was in the employ of Cox, went to him and begged to be permitted to remain with him, but the dying hero would not hear to it, and taking one of the pistols from his belt, he handed it to his friend and requested that in the event of his escape he give the weapon to his beloved wife, then at their home in Washington county, and whose loved form he was destined never more to see upon this earth. This party was one of the few survivors of this massacre, and he carried out to the letter the instructions of his dead employer. Mr. John P. Cox of Hillsboro, who has been for nearly a fifth of a century the sheriff of Hill county, has that very pistol of his dead father in his possession to-day, and as he exhibited it to the writer his eyes beamed with pride and affection upon it. But let us proceed with the narrative.

"During that fearful midnight charge, all but three of the survivors of the day's fighting were killed or wounded, and among the latter was the heroic Walter P. Lane, who had his leg broken by a bullet, but managed to gain the timber in safety in spite of his wound. Smith, Button, and the gallant Col. W. F. Henderson were the three who escaped unhurt, but amidst

Walter P. Lane Rescues Euclid M. Cox

Monument to Heroes of Battle Creek Fight

great suffering. In the charge, the party became separated, and one of their number wandered through the country alone for days and weeks, but finally succeeded in reaching the settlements. Violet, who had his leg broken, also became separated from his companions in that fearful charge and crawled twenty-five miles in that condition to Tehuacana Springs, where he was rescued a week later in a famished and almost dying condition. Henderson and Button with the wounded Lane slowly proceeded toward the settlements.

"The Indians knowing well the route they had to take or would take on the journey and being desirous of killing the entire party proceeded ahead, and waylaid the route they expected them to take. But fortunately for those gallant heroes, Love and Jackson, chanced to discover the Indians while returning from the settlement with the compass, and after a short skirmish succeeded in routing them. They were surprised upon proceeding some distance further, to meet Henderson and Button with the wounded Lane slowly walking into the trap set for them by the wily savages, and it was here that they first learned of the sad fate that had befallen their party. After carrying Lane to the settlement a burial party was organized and they set out for the purpose of interring their dead.

"Upon reaching the scene of the fight they recovered and buried beneath the spreading boughs of the oak on the bank of the ravine, the dead bodies of seventeen heroes. They found the dead body of the heroic Cox near where they had left him at his own request to die alone in the darkness of the night, for the reason that he knew he had received his death wound, and that any attempt to save him would be useless. When they left this hero on that fateful night, life was not entirely gone from his body and a loaded pistol was left with him, but on their return it was gone, and near him were pools of blood, indicating that he had dealt the death wound to at least another savage prior to the flight of his soul to that other world."

\* \* \* \* \*

Should the tourist, seeking objects of historical interest, and shrines of hero worship chance to visit the vicinity of this desperate contest between white and red men in the long ago, he would behold beneath the boughs of a majestic, but a battle-scarred, oak, a beautiful shaft towering far above the surrounding undergrowth, and upon closer inspection he would find it chiseled with the names of the heroic dead who rest beneath it; the date and manner of their death, etc.—a fitting memorial erected a few years since, in commemoration of the gallant fight they made for the supremacy of the white man and civilization, by two loving sons of the gallant Euclid M. Cox; John P. Cox who has spent the best years of his life as a sheriff and in enforcing the laws of his country, and Rev. J. Fred Cox, a presiding elder of the M. E. church South, long laboring for the uplifting of man in Texas—a tribute of noble sons to the valor of their worthy sire and his equally gallant comrades who lost their lives in defense of this land against savagery. And reader, were you a stranger and knew not the legends of our border land, any Texan, with swelling pride and patriotic emotions, would tell you in substance the story here recounted—the traditions of our border history and the valorous deeds of our matchless pioneers that have been handed down, transmitted as it were, from bleeding sire to son.*

---

\*                                                        Hillsboro, Texas, February 14, 1899.
Mr. James T. DeShields, Farmersville, Texas.
Dear Sir: I send you herewith the photograph of the monument to the heroes of the Battle Creek, or Surveyors fight, also of my fathers pistol. My father, Euclid M. Cox, was born in Kentucky, near Bowling Green. He came to Texas in February, 1832. I have his passport from New Orleans to Texas, given by the Mexican Council. He was in the battle of Concepcion and the Grass fight in 1835, and served under Gen. Sam Houston in the campaign of 1836.
I append a list of those who were killed in the Battle Creek fight, and whose names appear on the monument: Euclid M. Cox, Tom Barton, Sam Allen, ___ Ingraham, ___ Davis, J. Hard, Asa T. Mitchell, J. Neal, Wm. Tremier, ___ Spikes, J. Bulloch, N. Baker, A. Houston, P.M. Jones, James

## FATE OF OTHER SURVEYING EXPEDITIONS.

Earlier in this year, perhaps two or three months before the occurrence of the Surveyors Fight, above narrated, the veteran surveyor, Col. Wm. F. Henderson, had led a surveying party from Old Franklin to the same vicinity and succeeded in doing some work on Pin Oak, a small tributary of Richland creek, in Navarro county. But the party experienced considerable trouble from Indians; one of the men—Holland—having been killed and the balance of the corps forced to desist from work and retreat to the settlements.

At the same time another surveying party conducted by Col. Richard Sparks from Fort Houston (now Palestine) penetrated the same section and attempted to survey lands—somewhat in conjunction with Henderson's party. But Spark's party also met with disaster—first, Berry, one of their men who became separated from his companions, was brutally murdered, and then the Indians attacked the party, killing Colonel Sparks and dispersing the balance, who escaped afoot and without food or arms with which to kill game, finally reaching the settlements in sad plight.

The sad and unsuccessful results of these and other expeditions, going out of Old Franklin, Fort Houston and that section of the country, completely broke up the Springfield and other more advanced settlements, and further efforts in that direction were not again attempted until about 1844-45 when the Indians were pushed back, effectual surveys accomplished and the country regularly located and permanently settled.

---

Jones, Dave Clark, J.W. Williams. The few to escape were Walter P. Lane, W.F. Henderson, ___ Violet, ___ Button, and ___ Smith.

I hope to read your history soon, for I am satisfied it will be fine.

Yours truly, John P. Cox

## THE PIONEER MOTHERS OF TEXAS.

During the winter of 1837-8, Indians were exceedingly hostile toward the people of the Brazos, depredating to such an extent that the few advanced settlers were compelled to remove down to the more populous settlements. Among those to abandon their newly acquired homestead was Wm. Smith and family, who had located in the Brazos bottom. While loading their household effects into a wagon for moving, they were attacked by a party of Indians. Barring the doors of their log cabin, they prepared for defense, but unfortunately found that most of their ammunition was in the wagon. The situation was critical, requiring quick and desperate action. The brave wife and mother was equal to the emergency—unmindful of her great peril—thinking only of protecting her loved ones—she opened the door, rushed to the wagon near by in the yard, and secured a supply of powder and lead, returned, with but slight wounds, amid a perfect shower of balls and arrows, and calmly set to work moulding bullets. Firing through the cracks with good aim as opportunity afforded, Mr. Smith withstood the fierce and prolonged attack, causing the savages to retire with their wounded. As soon as expedient, the family retreated with their effects into the settlements. The following year, Mr. Smith participated, as we have seen, in the famous Battle Creek fight, and escaped to render much service on the southwestern frontier. He was a brave, Christian gentleman. His heroic and noble wife, noted for her many virtues, lived to rear an interesting and worthy family of sons and daughters—one son, the late Prof. Smith of Old Salado College, being personally known to the writer.

Forever honored and exalted be the memory of the noble and matchless pioneer mothers of Texas. Brave, hardy, and suffering severest trials without shirking or complaint, the highest tribute should be conferred on them, because "a spirit so resolute, yet so adventurous, so unambitious yet so exalted—a spirit so highly calculated to awaken a love of the pure and noble, yet so uncommon, never before actuated the ancestral matrons of any land or clime."

The mothers of our frontier land!
Stout-hearted dames were they,
With nerves to wield the battle-brand
And join the border fray.
Our rough land had no braver ones
In the days of blood and strife—
Aye, ready for the severest toil,
Aye, free to peril life.

The mothers of our frontier land
Their bosoms pillowed men!
And proud indeed were they to stand
In hummock, fort or glen;
To load the sure old rifle,
To run the leaden ball,
To stand beside a husband's place
And fill it should he fall.

The mothers of our forest land,
Such was their daily deeds,
Their monument where does it stand?
Their epitaph! Who reads?
No braver dames had Sparta,
No nobler matrons Rome,
And yet who lauds or honors them,
In this their own green home?

## EARLY DAYS OF BASTROP.

Like Gonzales on the Guadalupe, and Nashville on the Brazos, Bastrop on the Colorado, was for some years an extreme outpost, and in consequence suffered greatly from Indian depredations. The town was first laid out by Stephen F. Austin in 1830, and named in honor of that early friend to the Austins and colonial Texas—the Baron de Bastrop. Some of the most prominent early defenders of Texas; as the Burlesons, the Wilbargers, the Wileys, the Hardemans, the Andersons, the Bartons, Robt. M. Williamson, Highsmiths, Robt. M. Coleman, John Caldwell, Dalrymple, Gilleland, Barkley, John W. Pace, Bartlett Sims, Jesse ("Buckskin") Billingsley, Cicero Rufus Perry, Geren Brown, John Eggleston, and many others of whom space forbids mention here, were residents of this town.

The municipality of Bastrop took an early and prominent part in the revolutionary movement for independence in 1835, being the first to organize a committee of safety.

Some of the stirring and bloody episodes occurring in and around this truly frontier town have already been narrated and other incidents will be briefly noted in this connection.

John Eggleston, an early settler and a worthy soldier in the Texas war of independence, was killed by Indians in the town of Bastrop. Wilbarger furnishes the following incidents of his tragic fate:

"Near Eggleston's residence, one of his neighbors, Carter Anderson, had picketed in a large lot for the safe keeping of his stock, the gate of which was fastened every night with a chain and padlock. One dark night in January, 1838, Eggleston happened to be walking on the street near Anderson's lot. Hearing a rattling of the chain at the gate and thinking probably some one was trying to enter it, he concluded to investigate the matter. As he approached he heard, as he thought, the grunting of hogs, and seeing several dark objects moving in the vicinity, he naturally supposed they were hogs and turned to retrace his step. Just as he did so an arrow struck him in the breast. Eggleston fled, crying out 'Indians' as he went. There were a few men on guard at the time, who heard his cries and hurried to his assistance, but they were unable to pursue the Indians, for the night was a very dark one, and they made their escape. Eggleston survived for three days in great agony."

Soon after this the Indians again entered the town at night, killing Messrs. Hart and Weaver, and escaped.

A little later, some three miles east of town, Messrs. Robinson and Dollar were riving boards, when they were surprised by fifteen Indians. Says Brown: "Each sprang upon his horse, near by, but Robinson was killed at the same moment, while Dollar was pursued and hemmed on a high bank of the river; but leaving his horse, he leaped down the bank about twenty feet, swam the Colorado and then hastened to town. Soon afterwards he started to leave the country and was never again heard of. No doubt was entertained, however, of his having been killed by Indians."*

In the winter of this year a citizen was killed by Indians in the streets of Bastrop. In fact scarcely a month passed that the town was not visited by some murdering band of Indians, but the details in most instances, are too meager for record.

---

## CAPTAIN HARVEY'S ADVENTURE.

Among the early and useful pioneers, personally known to the writer, was Capt. John Harvey, who long resided at the beautiful little village of Salado in Bell county; and where he died about 1886. He was another Tennesseean to Texas, born in 1810, and emigrating in 1834. He participated in the battle of San Jacinto, and afterwards joined several expeditions against Indians and Mexicans. Being a surveyor by profession and doing much work on the frontier, he had a number of adventures and escapades. The following incident, though not resulting in tragedy, will be of thrilling interest:

Harvey, accompanied by a party of twenty men, camped in the territory traversed by the San Saba, but several miles from the stream, for the purpose of surveying lands granted to German colonists.

His companions were inexperienced and he found it impossible to induce them to take ordinary precautions against surprise and attack by hostile Indians. The weather being sultry, the men dispersed in various directions for water, leaving

* Brown's Indian Wars and Pioneers of Texas.

Harvey in camp.

Becoming thirsty himself, some time after their departure, he struck out down a ravine, hoping to find a pool of water. After he had proceeded for a mile or more, he was suddenly surrounded and captured by Waco Indians, who rose from behind bushes where they had been crouching and awaiting his approach.

With their prisoner they started for camp. On the way they stole a pony from a Comanche camp and being very hungry, killed it and cooked and ate part of it. They then tied a hind-quarter of the animal—over one hundred pounds of meat—on Harvey's back and hastened on to their rendezvous. No halt was made there, but the entire band at once started on the retreat to their distant home. They traveled without pause until sunset, and then stopped for the purpose of camping for the night. Harvey had been compelled to carry his burden and keep up with them over mountains and across gulches and canyons, and was completely exhausted.

A moment later the pursuing Comanches dashed upon the scene and surrounded the camp. The Wacos offered no resistance.

In obedience to the command of the Comanche chief, they produced the Waco who had stolen the pony, and he was immediately tied and staked to the ground, and given three hundred lashes on the bare back with a rawhide whip.

He then asked who was responsible for taking the white man prisoner. The Wacos indicated their chief, and the Comanches immediately seized and bound him, and gave him the same kind of flogging.

They gave Harvey a butcher knife and told him to kill the Waco chief. He refused to do so. They then urged him to cut off the chief's ears. This he also declined to do.

The Comanche chief ordered the Wacos not to further molest Harvey or his men and departed, taking him with them and started him back to his own camp. For some reason, it seems, they considered him and his men, as being under their special protection.

## KARNES' FAMOUS FIGHT.

On August 10, 1838, Henry Karnes, with twenty volunteers, was halting on the Arroya Seco, a small stream west of the Medina, when they were suddenly and unexpectedly attacked by about 200 armed and mounted Comanches. Quick as possible the rangers secured their horses, and immediately prepared—somewhat protected by a ravine and the chaparral—for defense. Ten to one, the Indians were confident of success, and charged with exultant yells. The Texans were cool and determined, firing with deadly aim and in alternate platoons, by which one third of their guns were always loaded to meet the oft repeated attacks at close quarters. Again and again the Indians charged and were repulsed, till more than twenty of their warriors were slain, and as many more wounded, when they gave up the contest, retreating with their dead. Captain Karnes, greatly exposed, received a severe wound, (which two years later caused his death) besides nearly every horse belonging to his men was either killed or wounded.

This was a most gallant and successful defense against immense odds, the skill and bravery displayed, stamping every member of the little company a real hero.

## CAPTURE OF MATILDA LOCKHART AND THE PUTMAN CHILDREN.

In October, 1838, occurred the capture of Matilda Lockhart and the Putman children, one of the notable incidents of Texas border history. The following account is from the pen of A. J. Sowell, and is believed to be substantially correct:

"In the fall of 1838 there lived two families on the west bank of the Guadalupe river, two miles below the town of Gonzales, named Putman and Lockhart. They were industrious, good citizens and had just begun to get things into shape again around their homes after the terrible "runaway scrape," as it was called, and the battle of San Jacinto. Life ahead of them looked bright and cheerful, but alas for human hopes and aspirations, how soon was their cup of sorrow to be filled to overflowing and they compelled to drink to the bitter dregs! In the fall of the above named year Matilda Lockhart and three of the Putman children, two girls and a boy, James, the youngest of the party, went to the river bottom for the purpose of gathering pecans. For some time they gathered the nuts which were in abundance and their merry laugh ever and anon rang out through the gloomy forest. At last it was time to go home, their vessels were full and their exertions had given them a keen appetite for their dinner the hour for which had now passed. The girls got their bonnets and buckets and the merry group emerged from the bottom to the edge of the prairie, but what a sight now met the eyes of those merry ones, the laughing voices were hushed and the cheeks which a moment ago glowed with health and gay spirits now blanched and paled with terror. There, in a few yards of them, rode a band of wild painted Comanche Indians; the scourge of the Texas frontier. Escape was impossible. With a wild shout the Indians circled around them and all were soon captured and carried screaming away on the horses of the painted demons who dashed up the valley toward their hunting grounds in the great west. When the children did not come home at the proper time the parents became uneasy and repaired to the pecan groves to search for them. No pen can describe the agony of those parents when they came to the spot where the capture had taken place. A bonnet here, an overturned bucket there, and pecans scattered everywhere. Out in the prairie lay little Jimmie's hat. The ground was torn up by horse tracks and too well these pioneers knew what had become of their loved ones. No time was to be lost. Neighbors were notified, and soon a party was on the trail of the daring red men. Lockhart was furious and vowed vengence of the most direful nature as he spurred madly on the trail. Putman was more cautious but not lacking in courage. He had fought at San Jacinto. He advised the men to move cautiously and not rush into an ambuscade. The trail led up the river to the foot of the mountains and here it was lost. The last sign of the Indians was seen on a sand bar at the mouth of the Comal river where the town of New Braunfels now is.

Andrew Sowell who was one of the trailing party says they turned back here but against the wishes of Lockhart who wanted to go on into the mountains. After the return a larger force was raised and once more went in pursuit. This time they came upon the Indians in their village in the mountains and a battle was fought which was disastrous to the settlers, as they were greatly outnumbered. Lockhart was wounded and it was with difficulty that the men could get him away as he still wanted to fight. In 1840 a treaty was made with the Comanches in which Matilda Lockart was recovered, and later on James Putman who at the time was about 16 years of age and as wild as any Indian. He would not sleep on a bed or in a house, nor eat with a knife and fork. The oldest Putman girl became the wife of a chief and lived and died a wild life among the Indians.

"About 30 years after the capture of the children a man named Chenault who had been an Indian agent, moved to Gonzales from Missouri, bringing a lady with him whom he had bought from the Indians several years before. He had carried her to his home in Missouri and when he came to Texas brought her with him as a member of the family. This was the youngest Putman girl. She could not remember her name but said the Guadalupe valley was strangely familiar to her. Her father, who was still alive, hearing of the circumstance came to see her and by marks on her body identified her as his long lost child. How strange that she should be brought back almost to the very spot where she was captured thirty years before. James Putman lived for many years in Guadalupe county and died in Hays county in the early seventies. He married a widow Nash and had one daughter named Sarah. He said the Indians carried him all over Texas, New Mexico and Arizona and also parts of California. He saw them fight several battles with emigrants on the plains."

## IN THE SHADOW OF THE ALAMO—TRAGIC SCENES OF INDIAN WARFARE AROUND SAN ANTONIO.

Although the most populous and important town in the

province and the Republic of Texas, San Antonio, being the extreme, and isolated, outpost of civilization in that direction, was, from early times, and until a much later period than that of which we are now writing, greatly exposed to Indian forays.

After the fall of the place and expulsion of the Mexican soldiery, in December 1835, many of its Mexican residents, some of much worth and respectability, left, crossing over the Rio Grande. Thus depleted in population, but little life appeared in San Antonio from the campaigns of 1835-36 till on the eve of opening the land office and preparations for the survey of lands early in this year. These openings drew to the place various surveyors, holders of bounty warrants and head-right certificates, as well as many others, seeking either employment or adventure.*

At that date bands of Comanches, all professing friendship, frequented the vicinity—and visited the town renewing treaties, but at the same time protesting against surveyors exploring their country, marking the trees, and running off the game. One of the first surveying parties to go out, while on the Rio Frio, had some of their horses stolen by the Indians camped in the vicinity. Upon discovering and demanding the animals a fight ensued in which Mr. Campbell, the surveyor, was killed and Captain Cage severely wounded by a copper arrow in his cheek,** but narrowly escaped with his companions to town. This affair sufficiently demonstrated the necessity of larger and well armed parties in successfully prosecuting further work.

Accordingly, on the 21st of September, 1838, John C. (Jack)

---

* Among others appearing at San Antonio about this time and seeking employment as a surveyor, was a young man destined to perform a most important and meritorious service in the defense of the Texas frontier and to gain much renown as a fearless border chief and partisan leader—Jack Hays, the famous Texas Ranger.

** The copper arrow-head was skillfully extracted by the early and eminent Dr. Smithers of San Antonio—a soldier of Velasco in '32, who, with two companions, was murdered at the Cibola Sulphur Springs, in one of the raids of 1842.

Hays, in the double capacity of surveyor and commander, left with a force for the Leon, where they remained about a month, running three compasses and doing considerable work without serious hindrances.

About the middle of October another, but smaller, force was organized for work closer in. On the 18th of this month while camped at the Presidio crossing on the Leon, some seven miles from town, they were surprised by Indians and two of their number, Moses Lapham a soldier at San Jacinto, and a Mr. Jones, of Bastrop, were killed. Mr. Earnest and others escaped on foot to town. "A Mexican named Padre Goaner (says Thrall) was scalped, but succeeded in reaching the city, where he still (1878) lives."*

At the time, District Court (Judge James W. Robinson presiding) was in session, from which cause there were more persons than usual in town.

Hendrick Arnold, a disciple of Deaf Smith, took command of a few men, went out to reconnoitre, and had a slight skirmish. Others were anxious to go, but some lacked horses. Major Valentine Bennett, as quartermaster, partly supplied this want, in so far that Capt. Cage was soon enabled to leave in charge of nine others. A few more followed Cage on the Presidio road towards the scene of conflict on the Leon. Time passed, and the house tops in town were occupied by anxious persons scanning the west (for at that day the view was uninterrupted by bushes) for indications of the anticipated engagement; and while so engaged a party of Indians, in plain view, passed on the west side of town, killing a Mexican cartman and his oxen. Frightened Mexicans occasionally rushed in with wild reports and the interest became intense among those powerless to render suc-

---

* "On the same day, Francisco A. Ruiz and Nicolas Flores Ruiz were taken prisoners. Francisco Ruiz was well known to the Indians and that night one of the chiefs untied him and told him to escape. He now lives on the Medina River. Flores was probably killed, as he was never heard of afterwards."—Thrall's "Pictorial History of Texas."—Page 457.

cor. Among those who had gone out with Cage, or followed after, were Judge Hood,* Gen. Dunlap, (late of Tennessee) James Campbell, an Irishman, appropriately known from his volubility as "Talking" Campbell, ____ Bailey, ___ Lee, a young merchant from Houston, ___O'Boyle, Robert Patton and others whose names cannot now be given. On the way out, before reaching the Leon, the Indians appeared, the volunteers not yet being united, but in view of each other. Divided counsels prevailed. Some proposed occupying a grove not far off—others opposed. The enemy encircled them, but in doing so, Campbell, mounted on a fleet gray horse, broke for town, pursued by several Indians. Though closely pressed, he outran his pursuers, and was the first messenger to report. Cage and O'Boyle dismounted at a tree and called on the others to do likewise; but they preferred fighting on horseback. Hood and Bailey charged through the Indians and then back to their comrades, in which the former was wounded by an arrow. Bailey's gun then failed to fire and Hood had but one charge left. Cage and O'Boyle, on the ground, and Lee on horseback, were killed about this time, as were several others. Robert Patton was lanced in the arm and his horse wounded. Finally the Indians opened the way towards town, and the survivors, as their only hope, seized the opportunity of a race for life. Speed was their sole reliance. As they dashed forward the enemy closed in on their flanks and rear, and the chase only ceased as the survivors entered the town. Gen. Dunlap was lanced and his noble bay steed severely wounded. Some were killed as the retreat began. A Mexican, naked and terribly wounded, crawled in some time later.

On the 20th Capt. Carras (or Carracas), with a company of Mexicans and Americans (Wm. H. Hargis being of the party) went out, gathered up the remains of the ten unfortunate settlers who had fallen and conveyed them in. Coffins were improvised

---

* Judge Hood was killed by the Comanches in the Council House hand-to-hand fight in San Antonio, in the spring of 1840.

by Major Bennett, it being a time when lumber was very scarce, and on Monday, Oct. 21, 1838, after an eloquent address by Judge James W. Robinson, the deceased heroes were committed to earth in the American cemetery adjoining the Campo Santo of the town.

## INDIAN TROUBLES IN EAST TEXAS—FIRST STAGES OF THE "CORDOVAN REBELLION."

July 1, 1838, Capt. Seguin wrote President Houston that a messenger had just arrived in San Antonio, who reported having seen two men, a German and a Mexican, who had been killed by Comanches, and were lying by the road side four miles from town. Seguin said that he was about to start with a company in pursuit of the Indians. In conclusion, he urged upon the President the necessity for better armed protection for the frontier. The powerful pushing of the frontier line westward, with surveyors moving in advance of it as avant couriers, was not the only cause that stirred the Indians to deadly action in 1838; another equally potent one was the military policy adopted by the Mexican Government to keep alive its claim to Texas. It had in view the invasion and re-conquest of Texas by a Mexican army with the aid of the entire body of Texas Indians as allies.

To secure their co-operation, agents were sent among them to represent that they would be given fee simple titles to all the lands they claimed if they would begin at once and actively wage ceaseless, and murderous war upon the whites. They were told that it was folly to expect anything from the whites except expulsion, or extermination; and that if they stood by Mexico, it would stand by them. The white people suspected in a general way what was going forward, but the conception they entertained was so far short of the truth that they were amazed at the extent and diabolism of the actual plot when it was disclosed by papers captured in the following year, under circumstances that will be detailed in the next chapter.

The following is a statement of part of the contents of one

of the papers: A letter written by Vicente Cordova to Manuel Flores—and inserted here, for the reason that it renders more intelligible events that follow. The date of Cordova's letter is July 19, 1838. He says that he had been commissioned by Gen. Filisola to visit the Indians and induce them to become auxilaries of the Mexican national army of invasion; and had entered on his duties by inviting a meeting of neighboring tribes. Continuing, he says: "Being informed that you have been appointed for the same purpose, I would like to know what preliminary action you have taken, and for you to advance, with such force as you may be able to command, as far as you may judge proper . . . to hold with me verbal communication in order that we may have, in our respective stations an understanding . . . and that you will bring the pipe, of which I understand you are in possession, in order that the Indian chiefs may smoke it, of the Cherokee and other tribes who have promised me to unite as soon as possible for action, and who have, also, agreed that, in case our plan should be discovered in the meantime, they will commence operations with the force we have in hand, it is highly desirable that you should approach to give us, in such case, a helping hand."

August 4, 1838, citizens of Nacogdoches who were in search of horses that had been stolen from them, found the animals in a Mexican settlement. On the way home, with their property, the white men were fired upon and one of their number killed. They pursued the murderers a short distance; but coming into a large trail, returned to town.

August 7th, Capt. John Durst reported to Maj.-Gen. Rusk, commanding the Texas militia, that one hundred or more Mexicans were under arms and encamped on the Angelina river. Capt. Antonio Manchaca who went to the camp, reported that there were 120 Mexicans and 25 Biloxi and Ionie Indians.

Gen. Rusk issued requisition for men of the eastern militia brigade and, while waiting for them to assemble, stationed a company of sixty volunteers at the lower crossing of the Angelina. On the 8th, President Houston who was in Nacogdoches, issued a proclamation ordering the Mexicans and Indians to disperse and to return to their homes under penalty of being declared enemies of the Republic. On the 10th, it was learned that 300 Indians had joined the Mexicans. On that day President Houston, received a communication from Vicente Cordova, Nat Morris, Joshua Robertson, Juan Jose Rodriguez, C. Morales, J. Santos Coy, J. Vicente Micheli, J. Arriola and A. Corda, leaders of the insurgents, in which they refused to obey the executive order and made vague declaration as to their ultimate purpose.

During the day Cordova broke camp and marched in the direction of the Cherokee settlement. Maj. Henry W. Augustin at the head of a strong detachment, followed him, while Gen. Rusk with his main force advanced directly toward the Cherokee village. On reaching the Neches Saline, Gen. Rusk learned that Cordova's force had dissolved and the leader, with a few of the more desperate Cooshaties and Cherokees and some of his Mexican companions, had retreated in the direction of the Kickapoo village in the northeastern corner of Anderson county. Rusk followed him there and, forty miles further on to the Killough settlements, where he abandoned the chase, there being no hope of overtaking the fugitives.

Joined by a few of the Kickapoos at their village, Cordova now made his way to the headwaters of the Trinity, where he continued his fiendish machinations.

Thus the accidental circumstance of the search for stolen horses, precipitated a series of events that spoiled his plans for 1838. No army of invasion was moving from Mexico. Not even Flores was at hand with a force to co-operate. Yet the fierce anger of his Mexican fellow conspirators at the Americans, forced him to act, and he did so boldly and called upon the Cherokees to take the warpath. Those Indians had a great deal at stake. They were, also, more than ordinarily intelligent. They saw that the emute was premature, and would be a failure—they still hoped for justice from the Americans. President Houston was in Nacogdoches, and they had unbounded faith in the rectitude of his intentions, and trusted that he had power to give effect to them, hence they refused Cordova's overtures.

## DEFEAT OF THE KICKAPOOS.

In the meantime, taking advantage of the disturbed conditions in that section, the Kickapoos were depredating to such an extent as to call for prompt action. Accordingly, with a hastily collected company of 200 volunteers, General Rusk moved against them. Leaving Fort Houston on Oct. 14th, he arrived in the vicinity of the Kickapoo town (in what is now Anderson county) and at sunset on the following day made a furious attack. After an engagement of some fifteen minutes the enemy fled and were hotly pursued for some distance. No official report of this fight exists, but it is known that eleven warriors were left dead on the field and presumably a much larger number were wounded. Rusk had eleven men wounded but none killed.*

## ROUTING THE COMANCHES.

A few days later, on the 25th of this month, Col. John C. Neil with his force attacked a considerable party of Comanches at the Jose Maria Village (afterwards the site of Fort Graham) in Young county. After a fierce and bloody battle, the Indians were defeated and fled, "leaving many of their warriors slain." The casualties to the Texans are not known.

Such military demonstrations and summary dealings with the savages and Mexicans, at least served to overawe and prevent them from combining in their raids.

The citizens of East Texas, with arms in their hands and emboldened, under Rusk and other brave leaders, had nothing to fear; welcomed a challenge by the Indians to mortal combat, and were more than a match for their hated foes. But murders, such as the Hutchison massacre; the tragedies in the Eden's settlement, and other atrocious affairs, occurring in the eastern

* Indian Wars and Pioneers of Texas, p. 107.

part of the Republic about this period, chilled their hearts, not with a coward's terror, but an appalling one nevertheless, for they realized that courage and superior numbers, arms and discipline, furnished no protection against their occurrence. The frontiermen did not know but that, at an unexpected moment, death in its most appalling form, would obliterate all that they held dear.

## RUSK CHASES INDIANS ACROSS THE BORDER.

In a dispatch from headquarters at Fort Caddo, Dec. 1, 1838, Gen. Rusk gave account of crossing into Louisiana and compelling a large party of Caddo Indians to surrender their arms to the United States Indian agent at Shreveport and agree to remain quiet until the existing danger of hostilities subsided.

These Indians were to be fed by the Texas government until their arms were returned to them. He said that until after his arrival with militia and this action had been taken by him, the people of Texas west of the border-line, believed that the Caddos intended to march through the settlements to a junction with the prairie Indians, and there, in connection with them, turn back and murder and pillage. The white people abandoned their homes and assembled in the forts for protection.

It is difficult at this day to fully realize the excited and hostile state of the public mind in Texas in the latter part of 1838, with regard to Indians, further than that it was such as to wholly neutralize every fact and argument that was adduced in favor of any of them.

## LAMAR'S REIGN.

The general election for President, Vice-President, members of Congress and other officers of the Republic occurred September 3, 1838.

Mirabeau B. Lamar, James Collinsworth, Peter W. Grayson, and Robert Wilson were rival candidates for the presidency.

There were two well defined political parties—the Houston and Anti-Houston—that crystalized during the year.

The campaign was a very bitter one—so bitter that Grayson shot and killed himself, at Bean's Station, Tennessee, and Collinsworth leaped from a steamer and drowned himself in Galveston Bay before the day of the election.

They were too sensitive and proud to withstand the mudslinging and vilification that was indulged in as a matter of course in that day in Texas, and in the United States. Lamar received 6,995 votes and Wilson 252,—300 were scattering.

President Houston was not a candidate. The consititution provided that the first President should hold office for two years and each of his successors for three years, and that no President should be eligible for election for the term next succeeding that for which he was chosen.

Mirabeau B. Lamar, as President, and David G. Burnet, as Vice-President, were inaugurated December 9, 1838.

In his inaugural message, Lamar declared that the only means by which Indian hostilities could be brought to an end were the extinction or total expulsion of United States Indians who were domiciled in Texas. He asked that immediate legislative action be taken for the establishment of a line of military posts along the frontier and the organization and maintenance of a strong military force in order that the policy he declared might be given vigorous and immediate effect.

He declared that the boundaries of the Republic would be defined and made good by the sword; took ground against the annexation of Texas to the United States; favored the establishment of a national bank; and spoke noble words in favor of popular education.*

Gen. Albert Sidney Johnston was appointed Secretary of war December 13, 1838, and qualified December 16.

---

* During his term fifty leagues of land were set apart for the establishment of a university and three leagues to each county for school purposes.

Mirabeau B. Lamar

Albert Sidney Johnston

Congress responded promptly to the recommendations of the President, as a majority of the members had been elected as advocates of the principles and policies he declared.

It passed an act, approved December 21, that provided for a mounted regiment of 840 men rank and file to protect the frontier, and for the establishment of the line of posts proposed. The men were to be enlisted for three years, to be paid $16.00 per month and be given a bounty of $30.00 in money and a certificate for land.

An act approved December 29, provided for a corps of mounted rangers, to consist of eight companies of fifty-nine men (rank and file) each.*

All spoils that were captured (except recovered property of citizens of Texas) were to be divided among the captors. Troops who were already enlisted, under act of May 15, 1838, were to proceed forthwith to the Nueces.

A few days later an act was passed and approved, that provided for a mounted regiment of 472 men to serve for six months.

Despite all measures and every effort to keep the Indians in subjection and to prevent or intercept their hostile raids, depredations and murders increased to an alarming extent. The clouds of despair were gathering and soon hung heavy all along the frontier. As Gen. K. H. Douglas wrote Secretary of War Johnston, on Dec. 30, 1838, "the affairs of the Texas frontier were never in so critical a condition."

---

* The following number of men were to be stationed at the localities mentioned: At, or near, Red River, 56; at, or near, the Three Forks of the Trinity, 168; at, or near, the Brazos, 112; at, or near, the Colorado, 112; at, or near, the San Marcos, 56; at, or near the Cibolo, 56; at, or near, the Frio, 56; and at, or near, the Nueces, 124. A strongly garrisoned post was to be established at the upper settlements on Red River. The regiments were to be divided into two battalions, one of which was to operate east of and the other west of the Colorado. A military road was to be constructed from the mouth of the Kiamitia to the point where the regular highway from San Antonio to the Presidio de Rio Grande crossed the Nueces.

Thus the catalogue grows in volume and intensity, with tragic episodes that would extend many pages, did the limits of this volume permit. That which follows, and especially matters transpiring within the next two years—during President Lamar's turbulent reign—presents a still darker and sadder picture of pioneer life and border trials in Texas. And yet, to him who can see beneath the surface of history the mighty forces that are the soul of it, the records of 1838 are full of interest and food for pleasant reflection; of interest because it exhibits the growth of a healthy and complex social organization, and food for pleasant reflection for the reason that it justifies the belief that such growth is normal under free institutions such as the pioneers and patriot fathers of Texas established and partially developed under such confusing, adverse and painful conditions.*

Pistol that Euclid M. Cox, mortally wounded in the Battle Creek Fight, sent home to his wife.

* An important event affecting the affairs of the Texas Republic during this year was the death of Gen. John A. Wharton—an irreparable loss from the ranks of the great men of early Texas—a man whom Judge Burnett in a memorial oration pronounced "the keenest blade on the field of San Jacinto."

Another important matter was the creating of a navy for the Republic. September 17, 1838, Samuel M. Williams entered into a contract for Frederick Dawson to furnish Texas with the new navy, provided for by act of November 4, 1837, Dawson to receive as payment two bonds of the Republic for $280,000 each.

# CHAPTER XII

onditions on the Indian frontier at the beginning of 1839 were particularly threatening. Since 1831 the United States government had steadily pursued a policy of removing Indians from their ancestral homes in the "states" to the district between the Arkansas, Red River and the False Washita along the boundary line of Texas and Mexico. It was estimated that in a short time there would be concentrated on the frontiers of Texas 240,000 of these Indians, including about 45,000 warriors, some of whom would be certain to make thieving and murderous incursions unless prevented.

The Texas Indians were restless and most of them hostile. It was believed that the agricultural tribes located in the eastern part of the Republic were co-operating with the prairie Indians, and it was known that some sort of conspiracy was being hatched between the Mexicans and Indians to make a more united and determined effort to prevent extension of the frontiers into the Indian country and to retard settlement and, if possible, to make Texas untenable and undesirable to its Anglo-American inhabitants. The Comanches were at war with the Lipans and Tonkawas. The latter circumstance was a favorable one for the whites, as the Lipans and Tonkawas joined with them against the Comanches—the Lipans for the most part pitching their camps within the settlements.

## THE MORGAN MASSACRE.

And now we will chronicle some of the events occurring in

the course of border warfare history. The narrative of pathetic scenes immediately following are true as to details and not overdrawn as to extent of fiendish atrocity. The account of these atrocious crimes was prepared by John Henry Brown from data furnished by surviving participants and first published in an issue of the old Texas Almanac more than half a century ago. We follow Brown in substance:

On the east side of the Brazos, near the "Falls," the Morgans and Marlins, somewhat intermarried, constituted several families residing a few miles apart, some above and some a little below the site of the present town of Marlin. There was a considerable settlement along the river for some twenty miles, but the country beyond or above them was open to the Indians. The period to which reference is made was the winter of 1838-39.

On Sunday night, the 1st day of January, 1839, a part of the families of James Marlin and Mrs. Jones, and the family of Jackson Morgan, were together, passing the night with the family of George Morgan, at what is now called Morgan's Point, six miles above the town of Marlin. The remainder of the divided families were at the house of John Marlin, seven miles lower down the river. John and James Marlin were brothers; the others of that name were their children.

A little after dark the house of George Morgan was suddenly surrounded and attacked by Indians, who instantly rushed in upon the inmates, giving them no time for defense. Old Mr. George Morgan and wife, their grandson, Jackson Jones, Jackson Morgan's wife, and Miss Adeline Marlin, a young lady of sixteen, were all tomahawked and scalped in the house within the space of a few minutes after the first alarm. Miss Stacy Ann Marlin (afterwards the wife of William Morgan) was severely wounded and left for dead. Three children were in the yard playing when the attack was made. One of these, Isaac Marlin, ten years of age, secreted himself under the fence, and there remained until the tragedy was over. Another child, Wesley Jones, at once ran into the house, but seeing the Indians entering and tomahawking the inmates, ran out unobserved by the murderous demons, and was followed by Mary Marlin, another child. They both escaped together. The wounded lady retaining consciousness, feigned death, but was not scalped as all the others were. The Indians robbed the house of its contents and left. When they had gone, and silence again reigned, the heroic child first mentioned, Isaac Marlin—his name should be immortalized—crept from his hiding-place, and entering the house carefully and silently, examined the bodies to find which were dead. His wounded sister, supposing him to be an Indian, remained perfectly motionless until he had gone, when she crawled out of the house. Little Isaac then took the path leading to John Marlin's, and ran the entire distance, seven miles, very quickly,—a swift messenger of death to his kindred there assembled. Wesley Jones and Mary Marlin did not get in till daylight, and the wounded Miss Marlin not till noon the next day.

As soon as little Isaac arrived at John Marlin's house and narrated his pathetic story, that gentlemen, his brother, James, William N. P., and Wilson Marlin, Jackson and Geo. W. Morgan, and Albert G. Gholson, immediately hastened to the scene, and found the facts identical with the child's narration. Other relief arrived next day, and the dead were consigned to their graves amid the wailings of their grief-stricken relatives and friends.

## ATTACK ON MARLIN'S HOUSE.

Ten days later, the Indians, about seventy in number attacked the house of John Marlin and his son Benjamin (whose descendants still reside in Milam county) and of Jarett Menefee and his son Thomas. This time the whites were better prepared for defense. The Indians charged upon the four men, who made a stout and gallant fight, killing seven Indians and wounding others without receiving any injury themselves. Tired of that kind of reception, the savages soon withdrew, carrying off their dead and wounded. When the attack was made, Menefee's negro man, "Hinchey," was at a short distance from the house, but failing to reach it in time, he left in double-quick time for the settlements below, and made twenty-five miles in pretty fair saddle-horse time. "Hinchey" at once reported the attack, and a company was quickly gathered together, who lost no time in repairing to the scene of action, in order to relieve their besieged friends, but found the red-skins had retreated, as before stated.

## BRYANT'S FIGHT AND DEFEAT.

It was determined, however, after a discussion of the matter by those present, that they must pursue and fight the Indians, or abandon their homes and fall back into the more settled parts of the country. They chose the former alternative, and made their dispositions accordingly. The effective force available for pursuit was forty-eight men. Benjamin Bryant (of Bryant's Station, whose surviving family still reside in Milam county) was chosen to command.

On the next morning Bryant's party took the trail of the enemy, and pursued, crossing the Brazos near Morgan's Point. On the west side they found a deserted camp with fresh signs, and about a mile out came upon a fresh trail. At the river they counted sixty-four fresh horse-tracks and a trail of foot Indians, which crossed the river. Seeing the prairie on fire below, they supposed it to be Marlin's house, and hastened back, without finding the enemy, and then halted for the night. On the next morning, January 16, they started out again, and found that the Indians had been at the deserted houses two miles above and plundered them. Thence they traveled up six miles to Morgan's Point, and suddenly discovered the enemy in the open timber near a dry branch. The noted chief, Jose Maria, who was riding in front in perfect nonchalance, halted, slipped off his gloves, and, taking deliberate aim, fired at Joseph Boren, who was a few feet in advance, cutting his coat-sleeve. Jose Maria then gave the signal for his men to fire, and the action commenced. Bryant ordered a charge, which was gallantly made, though the captain received a wound at the same instant, which accident called Ethan Stroud to the command.

The Indians fired and fell back into the ravine. Simultaneous with the charge, David W. Campbell fired at Jose Maria, the ball striking him on the breast-bone, but failing to dismount him. Albert G. Gholson then shot the chief's horse, which died in the ravine. The Texans then charged up to the bend of the ravine and fired, when the Indians commenced retreating down the bed of the ravine towards a densely timbered bottom. Seeing this, a part of the whites rushed down below to cut them off. This caused the enemy to return to the first position and renew the defense, by which time, supposing the day to be won, our men had somewhat scattered and were acting each for himself. The result was that when the enemy reopened the fire several were wounded, and confusion and disorder at once ensued. To remedy this, the men were ordered to retreat to another point some two hundred yards distant, in order to draw the Indians from their concealment. This unfortunate order, from the prevailing confusion, was understood by some of the men to be an unqualified retreat. Panic seized some of them, which being discovered by the wily Jose Maria, he gave the command and charged in full force, making the welkin ring with hideous and exultant yells. Several of the whites fell, and the rout now became general. Without order, in utter confusion, and each man acting for himself, they were hotly pursued for four miles, their pursuers dealing death and carnage among them.

In the disaster some acts were performed which deserve mention. David W. Campbell, not at first observing the retreat, was about being surrounded by the savages when the brave Captain Eli Chandler, already mounted, rushed to his relief and took him up behind him. Young Jackson Powers, missing his horse, mounted on a pony behind William McGrew, his arm being broken at the same moment, as he was retreating. His brother William came up at this moment, mounted on a large horse, and requested him to leave the pony and ride behind him. Poor fellow! he dismounted, but, from his broken arm and the restlessness of the horse, he was unable to mount before the Indians had rushed up and tomahawked him, his brother only leaving him just in time to save his own life. William N. P. Marlin, before the retreat, was so severely wounded in the hip that he could not mount, and was about being left, when David

Cobb ran up and threw him on his horse amid a shower of balls
and arrows. Wilson Reed, a daring fellow, in the retreat was
knocked from his horse by the projecting limb of a tree, the
enemy being close at hand, when he sang out in a half-mirthful
tone, "Oh, Lord, boys, Mary Ann is a widow!" but some brave
fellow picked him up and carried him safely off. The loss of the
whites in this fight was ten killed and five wounded. The loss
of the Indians was about the same number; but they were
greatly elated by their success,* and became more daring than
ever until checked by that stubborn and destructive engagement, known as "Bird's Victory," in Bell county.

## FATE OF THE WEBSTER FAMILY.

In January the family of James Webster and twelve men
who were escorting them to their home in what is now Williamson county, were attacked by Comanches on the San Gabriel.
The white men formed their wagons in a hollow square, and
fought from sunrise until 10 o'clock a.m., when the last of them
were slain. Mrs. Webster and little daughter were made captives. She escaped with her child nearly two years later, and
reached San Antonio a few days after the Council House fight.

During January, Ben and Henry McCulloch, Wilson Ran-
dle, David Henson and John Walfen, accompanied by thirty-
five Tonkawas, defeated a band of Comanches and Wacos on
Peach Creek, in Gonzales county, killing five and wounding a
considerable number. The only loss sustained by the attacking
party was one Tonkawa killed.

* Jose Maria, so long the dread of the frontier, but afterwards the most
pacific and civilized Comanche chief on the government reserve, has
always acknowledged that he was whipped and retreating until he observed the panic and confusion among the Texans. Jose Maria visited
Bryant's Station years afterwards and offered Bryant his pipe to smoke.
Bryant insisted that Jose Maria should smoke first, as he had won the fight,
and the old chief proudly followed the suggestion.

In the same month a company of land locaters retreated from Uvalde Canyon to avoid being surrounded by Comanches who threatened to attack them. In doing so they were opposed by a small party of Indians stationed at the mouth of the gorge, but charged and routed them, killing three or four, and returned to San Antonio without loss.

## FAMOUS BIRD CREEK BATTLE.

This bloody engagement ranks as one of the notable Indian battles of Texas, and may be well termed a model fight between Rangers and Comanches. The narrative which follows is believed to be substantially correct, having been carefully prepared from statements and notes furnished by participants and others of authority.

On Sunday morning, May 27, 1839, the intrepid Captain John Bird, one of the early ranger chiefs of Texas, with a company of 31 rangers, well mounted and equipped, left Fort Milam at the "Falls" of the Brazos, on a scouting expedition against the depredating bands of Indians who were constantly making forays upon the unprotected settlements around Fort Griffin on Little River, which was at that time on the extreme frontier of Texas in that direction—the Bryants, Marlins, Morgans and a few others on the Brazos being their nearest neighbors. Capt. Bird arrived at Fort Griffin at 1 o'clock in the afternoon of the same day, and at once learned that Indians had been seen near the fort but a few hours before his arrival.

Without dismounting, the rangers proceeded to the point where the Indians had been seen. After a hurried march of some five miles upon the freshly made trail, they suddenly came upon 27 Comanches, dismounted and busy butchering buffalos. As the rangers charged down upon the unsuspecting redskins they quickly mounted and fled in different directions, the rangers following hard after the main body. After a flight of some three miles, the Indians again came together and forming in battle array, confronted their pursuers, ready for a fight. The rangers again charged upon them and after a sharp skirmish put the

Indians to flight, pursuing them for several miles but without again overtaking or engaging them.

The enemy having scattered in various directions and the horses of the rangers being considerably jaded, the chase was given up. But as the rangers were returning to the fort, and just as they were emerging from a skirt of timber on the south side of a small stream, since called Birds Creek, and at a point some seven miles northeast of the present town of Belton, they were surprised and almost surrounded by about forty Indians, who shot their arrows at them from every direction. The rangers dashed out of the ambush and made for a ravine some 600 yards in front, where, fortunately, there was a spring, which they succeeded in reaching, despite the determined efforts made by the savages to cut them off. The Indians now retired to the crest of a hill about 300 yards distant, and where a "council of war" was held and "signal smokes"—the Indian mode of telegraphing—sent up and answered from several directions. The little company of rangers now well knew the Indians would soon be reinforced and that the red devils would then swoop down upon them in large numbers. Orders were given and preparations were hurriedly made to defend their position, and, if finally overpowered with numbers, to sell their lives as dearly as possible—those must have been critical moments.

In about half an hour the rangers saw a large body of mounted warriors rapidly approaching in the direction of their confederates, and in a few minutes the hill top seemed to be literally alive with painted demons. Increased to about 300 in numbers, and led by the noted Comanche war chief, Buffalo Hump, the Indians now arrayed themselves in imposing battle order, and with some semblance of military display, while the chief, bedecked with his immense and grotesque buffalo hide war bonnet surmounted with horns, rode up and down the lines, giving orders and defiantly gesticulating and pointing toward the enemy. The Indians were confident of victory. The little band of rangers were cool and determined, but the odds were fearful.

Raising the Comanche war whoop all along their lines, the

savage red warriors charged down upon the whites in the ravine, uttering the most unearthly and exultant yells that ever greeted the ears of mortals, and at the same time pouring in a regular deluge of arrows. The brave rangers were cool and steady and gave them a most deadly reception, causing a number to reel and tumble from their mounts, and the balance to retire to the hill top without carrying off their dead and wounded. Again the enemy charged, in bold order, this time advancing to within fifty yards of the ravine, but under the galling fire of the rangers, they were again forced to beat a retreat, leaving a number of their braves upon the field. Once more, but somewhat less exultant, they were led in a charge, to sustain loss and be forced back.

Thus chagrined and discomfited, the maddened red warriors retired in a body from the hill top and out of sight—to council and plan for another and more effective attack. Meanwhile the little band of dauntless rangers were busy, comforting their wounded, improving their position and preparing as best they could for another onslaught, which they well knew would be made.

Ere long the Indians again appeared, this time in two circling companies, and immediately bore down and around in a fiercer attack upon the rangers than ever, this time closing in from either side, determined to rout the little company of whites from their position and to annihilate them at all hazards. The strife now became fearful and deadly. The gallant little troop of rangers in the ravine fought for life, and taxed their energies to the utmost. It was indeed a terrible battle against fearful odds— victory trembled in the balance—the rangers despaired but were determined to fight till the last breath. The red warriors were loudly exhorted, and repeatedly charged almost to the brink of the ravine, but were as often forced back by the deadly aim of the ranger rifles. The field was an almost open prairie, with but little to shield the contending foes against the shower of arrows, and the leaden hail which were incessantly being sent. The noble Captain Bird was killed early in the fight, and six other rangers were killed or wounded. The remainder, now reduced to only 25 in number, and exhausted by the fierce and protracted contest, seemed doomed to almost certain destruction, when brave James Robinett, a young German, and upon whom the command now devolved, swore to his comrades that he would kill the chief in the next charge, at the risk of his own life. Robinett had not long to wait before the Indians again charged, led by their brave chief. In his full war toggery, and mounted on a splendid American horse, he presented a conspicuous mark. Taking deliberate aim Robinett fired, and, true to his vow, succeeded in killing the chief. His lifeless body was immediately surrounded by ten or a dozen braves, who bore it out of sight, leaving their now infuriated comrades to avenge his death, and for a time the battle continued to rage, the rangers holding their position and successfully repulsing each furious assault.

Finally, night coming on, the savages sullenly retired to their hill top position—having sustained fearful loss in both men and horses—Nathaniel Brookshire in an official report of this affair, May 31, 1839, says the supposed number of Indians killed on the field was only thirty. Later evidence however proved that to be incorrect. The number slain was not less than fifty warriors. The rangers lost five of their number killed—their lamented captain, and Private Gales, Nash, Weaver, and one other whose name has not been given—two or three wounded.

Exhausted, and fearing the Indians lay in wait nearby, the rangers remained under cover of the ravine till morning, when they mounted their horses which had fortunately been secured and held in the ravine, and ventured forth, hastily making their way back to Fort Griffin. The story of the sanguinary engagement and the fate of their brave comrades was soon told. A runner was sent to Fort Milam for reinforcements, and with a rough coffin which had been prepared, the fresh force repaired to the battleground. Captain Bird and his unfortunate comrades were placed in the huge, uncouth receptacle and borne back by a detachment to the fort, where they were buried, while the main force took up the trail of the enemy and followed in hot pursuit as far as "Stampede Creek" where, having halted for a short rest,

Robinett Killing Chief Buffalo Hump

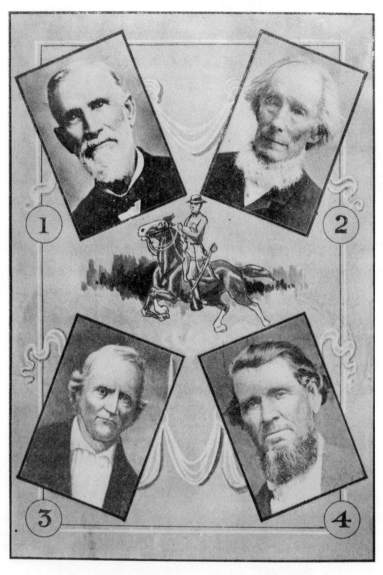

Rev. Andrew Davis, 2. Jno. W. Wilbarger,
3. Collin McKinney and 4. Abram Anglin

their horses were stampeded about midnight, leaving the rangers afoot, which circumstance gave name to the stream.

Old settlers tell of often visiting the scene of the Birds Creek battle; of gathering flint arrow points, and of viewing numerous bullet holes in the scattering trees. But the battle ground is now enclosed in a farm, and all evidence of the desperate struggle has long since disappeared, save the little spring in the ravine which still bubbles forth its sweet, sparkling, waters, as on that memorable May day seventy odd years ago, when it slaked the thirst of the besieged rangers and cooled the fevered brown and crisping lips of their dying comrades—murmuring an eternal requiem to the memory of those who so nobly perished to protect others and thus aid in redeeming a fair land from savagery. The site of old Fort Griffin is yet known, but the exact resting place of the brave Captain Bird and his comrades has been lost. A more patriotic duty could not be performed by the citizens of grand old Bell county than to erect at some point a suitable shaft to the memory of these fallen heroes.

## McCULLOCH'S PEACH CREEK FIGHT.

About the first of March, immediately following the notable "cold snap"* prevalent throughout southwest Texas during the latter half of February, 1839, Ben McCulloch and Henry E. McCulloch, with Wilson Randel, David Hanson, John D. Walfin, and thirty-five Tonkawa warriors—under the immediate command of their trusty old chief, "Capt. Jim Kerr" (a name assumed through friendship for pioneer James Kerr of DeWitt Colony, in 1826), left the Tonkawa village at the junction of

* This destructive sleet was the heaviest and most prolonged ever known in that part of the country—continuing for ten or twelve days, while the ice and snow shielded from the sun, lay upon the ground for a much longer period. Great trees were bereft of limbs and tops by the immense weight of ice, and bottoms previously open were simply choked to impassability by the fallen timbers.

Peach and Sandy Creeks, some fifteen miles northeast of Gonzales, on a campaign to the mountains—hoping to find in a winter camp and possibly rescue, the Putman children and Matilda Lockhart.

In the morning of the second day out, and some twenty-five miles higher up on the head waters of Peach Creek, "they struck a fresh trail of foot Indians, bearing directly for Gonzales. This, of course, changed their plans. Duty to their threatened neighbors demanded that they should follow and break up this invading party; for such inroads by foot Indians almost invariably resulted in the loss of numerous horses, and one or more—alas! sometimes many—lives to the settlers."

After a hasty pursuit of three or four hours, the invaders, a party of thirteen Waco and Comanche warriors, were sighted, but quickly disappeared into a dense thicket bordering a branch. As a last resort to dislodge or engage the enemy, the Tonkawa allies were stationed around the lower end of the thicket, with orders to intercept all retreat, while Ben and Henry McCulloch, with Randel and Hanson, ventured into the ambuscade. "Slowly they moved, observing every precaution till, one by one, each of the four had killed an Indian, and two or three others were wounded." Finally the survivors emerged into the branch, and protected somewhat by its banks, fled down and into a larger and almost impenetrable thicket. Thus foiled, and night coming on, the attack was not resumed.

Though having lost one of their comrades in the fight, the Tonkawas were elated over the victory, and after scalping the dead and dying Wacos and Comanches, cutting off their hands, feet, arms and legs, and fleecing strips of flesh from their thighs and breast, they were ready and anxious to return to their village and engage in their usual cannibal-like and mystic war dance. This, of course, prevented further operations, and here the expedition ended.

---

## COL. MOORE'S SAN SABA FIGHT.

Capt. John H. Moore, writing from LaGrange, March 10,

made the following official report* of a battle fought with the Comanches February 15, 1839:

"I herewith transmit the muster rolls of three volunteer companies which, in conformity to the act of Congress authorizing the raising of volunteer companies for the protection of the frontier, were organized on the 25th of January last, at the upper settlements of the Colorado and placed under my command to proceed against the Comanches on our northwestern frontier.

"From this place we proceeded on the morning of the 26th directly up the Colorado. On the 13th of February, our spies, who from the mouth of the Llano had been kept in advance, returned and reported that they had discovered an encampment or village of Comanches on a small stream called Spring Creek, in the valley of the San Saba.

"On the succeeding day we marched about an hour under cover of the timber of the Colorado bottom. We then deposited our packs and baggage in a place of security and proceeded onward, still seeking the cover of the timber and valley, to a place about ten miles from the village, where we remained until after sunset.

"After night, we proceeded to within a mile of the village, where we dismounted and tied our horses in a valley, and having put eight Lipans on horseback with orders to stampede the enemy's caballado, proceeded on foot to within three hundred yards of the town, still keeping our spies in advance.

"The LaGrange company, under Capt. Wm. M. Eastland, formed the right wing, the Bastrop company, Capt. Smithwick, the centre; and the Lipan's, under Castro, their chief, the left.

"The attack was made after daybreak by marching Capt. Eastland's company in advance, down between the timber and the village (whose skirts run parallel to each other) for the purpose of having the timber in our rear and driving the enemy

* Army Archives in State Library.

towards the prairie. When opposite the centre of the town we were discovered by the enemy, at which moment I ordered a charge, which was promptly obeyed and carried to near the centre of the village, the men throwing open the doors of the wigwams or pulling them down and slaughtering the enemy in their beds.

"It was now discovered that the opposite side, which had been supposed to have opened to the level prairie, was bordered by a meander of the bayou which formed a deep rut and secure place of retreat into which the savages had fled and in which they had already rallied and formed for defense. At this time the darkness, which previously had been such as barely to permit us to aim with tolerable accuracy, became greater in consequence of the smoke and, all our firearms having been discharged, it became necessary to retire for a moment to reload and wait for the darkness to dispel, to enable us to renew the attack. The disorder which had resulted from the eagerness of the men was another cause which rendered this movement necessary.

"We had barely time to form and reload when the enemy charged us in front and on both flanks to within a few steps, which attacks were repeated at short intervals until 10 o'clock a.m., after which the firing from the enemy continued, but from a considerable distance. Ten men were now dispatched by way of the bayou to reconnoitre, who returned soon after and reported the enemy very numerous. We continued in our position until half after 11 o'clock, when the enemy ceased firing, at which time, having abandoned the hope of being able with so few men to force them from the strong position they occupied, I ordered litters to be prepared for our wounded, and soon after retired to the place at which we had left our horses. In fifteen or twenty minutes after our arrival at this place we were surrounded by a large body of the enemy, who I believe were between 300 and 500 in number, who immediately opened a fire on us, but this was soon silenced, and a white flag (the same presented to them last summer at the seat of government by the President, Sam Houston) approached, carried by a woman, accompanied by a man. A parley ensued in which she stated that they had five white prisoners; one a woman about middle age, understood to have been captured on the Brazos river; a girl about fifteen years of age, supposed to be the daughter* of one of our company, Andrew Lockhart, captured on the Guadalupe; the other three children, captured at the same place a short time since. This information, I believe, was given because they were under the impression that we had some of their prisoners which they wished to exchange for, as some prisoners had been taken by the Lipans which they killed or otherwise disposed of without advice from me. They also made some statements relative to their great numbers which were constantly increasing and the co-operation of Shawnees who were near, to which was replied 'Our numbers are small; come on.'

"The attack was not repeated. The number killed on the part of the enemy it was impossible to know, but must have been very considerable.

"Our men were furnished with about three shots each, which, during the first attack upon the village, were discharged with great accuracy at only a few feet distance and in many instances by placing the muzzle against the object. Add to this their exposed position in their repeated attacks upon us and the unerring accuracy of our riflemen, justifies the belief that their loss must have been very great. In supposing their loss to have been thirty or forty killed and fifty or sixty wounded, I make an estimate much below what I believe to be correct. Loss on our side; killed, none; mortally wounded, one—since died; slightly wounded, six. We also lost a considerable number of horses, in all—including those which had previously died from various causes—forty-six.

"One of our men, Mr. Wilson, from Lagrange, was accidently wounded on our way up and dispatched homeward with two men; since died. Our force in the engagement con-

* Matilda Lockhart.

sisted only of sixty-three white men and sixteen Indians—total, seventy-nine.

"Taken by the Lipan Indians; ninty-three horses and mules, only forty-six of which have been received here. Much credit is due to Captain W. M. Eastland and Lieut. N. M. Bain, of the Bastrop company, and Adjutant Wm. Bugg, for strict and prompt obedience to orders and their general officer-like conduct, and to the men and officers in general for their bravery on the field of battle and their subordination and good conduct."

---

## MURDER OF CAPT. COLEMAN'S WIDOW AND CHILDREN—COL. BURLESON ENGAGES THE INDIANS.

Col. Burleson in an official report to Gen. Albert Sidney Johnston, writing from Bastrop county, says: "Immediately after my return home, I was informed of a body of Indians having been seen in the Big Prairie on Saturday, February 22, fifteen or twenty miles from Bastrop, supposed to be Northern Indians— i.e. Caddos, Wacos and Keechies. On Monday following, about 10 o'clock a.m., they attacked the house of the widow Coleman, twelve miles above Bastrop. They attempted to cut off a man and a boy from the house, who were plowing in the field and who, at the sight of them, broke for an adjoining thicket and made good their escape. In the meantime a party of the Indians fired at Mrs. Coleman, who was at work in the garden fifty paces distant from the house, and slightly wounded her in the neck with an arrow. She fled with all speed for the house and succeeded in reaching it. At the time of her entering the house there was in the room her oldest son, about twelve years of age, and three other small children. With the assistance of the boy, she was enabled to bar the door. The Indians followed her to the house and forced the door open wide enough to admit a man. They were fired upon by the boy, who killed one dead on the spot and is supposed to have wounded another. In attempting to defend the passage, the boy and Mrs. Coleman were killed.

The remaining three children, who were at the time in the room, crawled under the bed.

"The Indians, having received so warm a reception, desisted. . . . (They succeeded in cutting off a boy child from the house and carried him off captive).

"The Indians at the same time attacked and plundered the house of Dr. Robertson, situated about two hundred yards from the former. Fortunately, at the time the doctor's family was absent, or they would have shared the fate of Mrs. Coleman, as there was no white person on the premises to give them protection. The Indians took and carried off from the latter place one negro woman and four children, one old man, and a boy.

"A party of fifty men from above Bastrop went immediately in pursuit and overtook them twenty-five miles north of the Colorado, where a skirmish took place. The Indians having advantage of position caused the whites to fall back about three miles, with the loss of one man, at which place I fell in with thirty men. I immediately went in pursuit and overtook them; in the meantime, the Indians having changed their ground for a more advantageous position. On discovering me, they took a stand. I attacked them at about 1 o'clock p.m. I continued to pick them off at every opportunity until dark. The old negro man was found on the battle ground after night, with nine arrows shot into him; supposed to have been left for dead. He says he saw several killed; say thirty. From the quantity of blood seen on the ground, I am induced to believe that the above number is not an over-estimate. Our loss in the last attack was two killed and one wounded, who has since died.

"I remained encamped on the ground until next morning, and found that the Indians had left several guns, bows and arrows, all their camp equipments, one mule and several horses.

"I ordered, without delay, Capt. Billingsley, with thirty men, to follow on their trail, which he did three miles and found that they had dispersed to avoid further pursuit.

"Since the above took place there has been no more depredations committed on this frontier, except by some thieving parties. It is confidently believed that the Indians will renew hostilities on this part of the frontier early this spring.

"I request that those officers who have accepted their commissions and who are destined to recruit for the First Regiment of Infantry West of the Brazos, to be sent to such points as in your judgment are most suitable for that purpose, until I shall come down to Houston, which will be in about three weeks."

## THE CORDOVA REBELLION.

Our historians have not attached due importance to the motives of what they are wont to term this "strange" outbreak and the incidents of its quelling. Previous to 1836 the town and County of Nacogdoches contained a majority of Mexican citizens. These people had made small settlements in various parts of this then immense territory. Here, too, resided a large number of Cherokee and associate bands of Indians, who properly belonged in the Indian Territory and under the jurisdiction of the United States. They had been permitted, it seems, to occupy those lands as tenants at will, but the Mexican Government while maintaining friendly and favorable relations with these Indians, had studiously avoided granting them anything in the shape of title.

Although Texas had declared her independence and bravely won her liberty on the sanguinary field of San Jacinto in one of the most decisive battles of ancient or modern times— driving the enemy beyond her borders and concluding an honorable treaty of peace with the captive General and President, Santa Anna—Mexico never willingly relinquished claims to her lost province, and for nearly a decade, during which time the Lone Star Republic heroically maintained her proud position as one of the principalities of the world, a predatory and guerilla-like warfare was kept up against the more exposed border settlements of Texas.

One of the principal and most feasible schemes was to send emissaries through the country with instructions to arouse and incite the Indians to hostilities and open rebellion. Yoakum says: "Previous to the French attack at Vera Cruz, and the Civil war in Mexico, that Government had commenced a system, which, if it had been carried out as was intended, would have been most disastrous to Texas. Its object was to turn loose upon her all the Indian tribes upon her borders, from the Rio Grande to Red River." Of these facts the Texas Government received undoubted evidence a little later as will be seen.

At Nacogdoches early in August, 1838, it was found that a motley company of about 150 citizens, headed by Vicente Cordova an early, intelligent and somewhat influential Mexican resident of the settlement, had secretly taken up arms and encamped on the west bank of the Angelina. On learning these facts a proclamation was issued to the malcontents requiring them to return to their homes and lay down their arms, under the penalty of being declared enemies of the Republic.

To this proclamation the rebel leaders made the following bold and defiant reply: "The citizens of Nacogdoches, being tired of the unjust treatment, and of the unsurpation of their rights, can do no less than state that they are embodied, with arms in their hands, to sustain those rights, and those of the nation to which they belong. They are ready to shed the last drop of their blood; and declare as they have heretofore done, that they do not acknowledge the existing laws, through which they are offered guaranties (by the proclamation) for their lives and properties. They only ask that you will not molest their families, promising in good faith to do the same in regard to yours.

| | |
|---|---|
| Vicente Cordova, | A. Cordova |
| Nat Morris, | C. Morales, |
| J. Arriola, | Joshua Robertson, |
| J. Vincent Micheli, | Juan Jose Rodriques. |
| J. Santos Coy, and others. | |

August 10, 1838.

By this time other Mexican adherents with some 300 Indians and negroes had joined the enemy, augmenting their force to about six hundred, when they set out on their march, in the direction of the Cherokee nation. Meantime General Rusk had made an urgent and immediate requisition for men and a considerable force of volunteers was soon collected. Directing Major Augustin with 150 men to follow the trail, Gen. Rusk with the main force marched rapidly, and more direct to the headquarters of Chief Bowles, expecting to intercept and engage the enemy at that point. But the enemy had warning, no doubt, of these movements, and on arriving at the Saline it was found they had disbanded and dispersed, the insurgent leader and a few of his followers having hastily fled westward, to the wild tribes of the upper Trinity and Brazos, where they remained until the following spring, visiting and mingling with these several tribes and endeavoring with presents and promises to incite them to open hostilities, and encouraging them to wage a relentless war of extermination against the Texans; to burn their houses, kill their cattle, steal their horses and to lay waste the settlements; and for all of which, besides the spoils, they were promised aid and protection from the Mexican Government and fee simple rights for all time to come to the respective territories they then occupied. At the same time a regular correspondence was carried on through secret agents and discrete messengers with Commandant Canalizo as well as Manuel Flores—charged with diplomatic duties towards the Indians of Texas—at Matamoras, and plans were being discussed and perfected for carrying out the devilish designs of a concerted and general border warfare of rapine and murder against the settlers of Texas. To this end and looking to a better and more definite understanding and arrangement of plans, Cordova urged agent Flores to meet and confer with him at his rendezvous in the Indian country.

## CORDOVA'S DEFEAT.

Early in 1839 Gen. Canalizo succeeded Gen. Filisola as commander at Matamoras.

Wishing to confer with the new military chief, Vicente Cordova left his lair on the upper Trinity in March and started for the Rio Grande, accompanied by a force of seventy-five men—Mexicans, Indians, and negroes.

His camp was discovered at the foot of the mountains north of, and not far from Austin, and the news was conveyed to Col. Burleson at Bastrop.

At the head of eighty men, he went in pursuit and overtook the enemy on the 29th in an open body of postoaks about six miles southeast of Seguin and dismounted a portion of his men, who opened fire from behind trees. Cordova formed his followers, also using trees for protection and sought to stimulate them to determined and successful resistance. They stood their ground for awhile, although the Texans moved nearer and nearer to them, pouring in a steady and telling rifle-fire, but broke into pieces and fled when Burleson's Colorado volunteers leaped into the open and charged among them. The pursuit that followed extended to the dense jungles of Guadalupe bottom, where it was discontinued as twilight deepened into dark.

Burleson suffered no loss in killed, but several of his men were wounded. After the fight, he moved six miles up to Seguin, to protect the few families living there.

Cordova retreated during the night. Starting east of Seguin he moved northward as far as the present town of New Braunfels, crossed the Guadalupe, and then bore to the north and passed north of San Antonio to the Nueces where pursuit of him was abandoned by Capt. Matthew Caldwell and his company of rangers and a few citizen volunteers who had picked up his trail. Prior to the chase, Caldwell's rangers were scattered in several camps, scouting. Cordova came upon one of these detachments north of Seguin, and wounded three men—a circumstance that was immediately reported to Caldwell who concentrated his forces and went in pursuit.

Ignorant of what had transpired and desirous to meet and confer with Cordova, wherever he might be found—on the upper Brazos, Trinity or elsewhere—Manuel Flores, with an escort of about thirty Mexicans and Indians, supplies, ammunition, and official communications to, and instructions for contemplated Indian allies, set forth from Matamoras in the latter part of April and traveled into Texas along a route different from

that of Cordova's retreat and hence, missed him and got into a
trap.

He traveled slowly, crossed the road between San Antonio
and Seguin, May 14; crossed the Guadalupe at the old Nacogdoches ford (at the site now occupied by New Braunfels) May
15, and proceeded to a point on the San Gabriel, in the edge of
Williamson county, north of where the town of Austin was
established later in the year, and was attacked there and killed
and his force defeated and scattered. Two of his men were killed
and nearly all of those who escaped were wounded.

He displayed great coolness and bravery in the skirmish
however, and fell sword in hand, while trying to encourage his
men to stand to their arms.

Prior to the engagement with Cordova, Maj. Walters was
directed to raise two companies of six month's men and occupy
the Neches Saline so as to prevent communication between the
Cherokees and prairie Indians and afford protection to settlers.
The Saline was claimed as part of the property of the Cherokees.
Chief Bowles notified Maj. Walters that its occupancy would be
resisted by force of arms. That officer, acting on the advice of
the Texas Indian agent, Martin Lacy, did not make the attempt
and crossed to the west bank of the Neches and established a
camp.

The facts were communicated to Gen. Albert Sidney
Johnston, Secretary of War; and to be prepared for any emergency, he directed Col. Burleson, who was collecting a force on
the Colorado to operate against other Indians, to march lower
down and hold himself in readiness to enter the Cherokee
country on the shortest notice.

## EXPULSION OF THE CHEROKEES.

In May, President Lamar addressed a letter to Chief Bowles
in which he said that the Houston-Forbes treaty had never been
recognized and never would be, and that there should be no
division of sovereignty in Texas. He said that whatever equitable claims the Cherokees may have ever possessed had been

effaced by murders and robberies, by furnishing arms and supplies to prairie Indians, and by the treacherous and murderous coalition entered into with Cordova and other enemies of Texas. Alluding to Bowles' action with regard to Maj. Walters, he said that officer had been ordered again to take the post at Saline. Continuing, he said: "I deem it to be my duty . . . to tell you . . . that the Cherokees are permitted at present to remain where they are only because this government is looking forward to the time when some peaceable arrangement can be made for their removal without shedding blood; but that this final removal is contemplated is certain, and that it will be effected is equally so. Whether it will be done by friendly negotiations or by the violence of war, must depend upon the Cherokees themselves. If they remain at home quietly and inoffensively, without murdering our people, stealing their property or giving succor and protection to our enemies, they will be permitted to remain in the undisturbed enjoyment of their present possessions until Congress shall be able to make some final arrangements satisfactory to both parties for their return to their own tribe beyond Red River. But if, listening to the suggestions of bad men, equally the enemies of the red man and the white, they shall pursue such a course of conduct as to jeopardize the lives and property of our citizens, or to destroy the sense of security essential to the happiness and prosperity of our frontier, the inevitable consequence will be prompt and sanguinary war which can terminate only in their destruction or expulsion."

He urged them to show that they were friends and wait until the next Congress met and he would ask it to act so liberally toward them, as to leave the Cherokees and white people lasting friends. Continuing he said:

"If we were to give you all you ask—if this government were to acknowledge you as a free, sovereign and independent power to the fullest extent—your condition would not be the least improved by it. You could not live in peace with our people. You would be subject to perpetual and unavoidable annoyance and would have finally to sell out and leave the country. Surrounded, as you soon would be, by a strong population and daily harassed by bad men ever ready to take advantage of your ignorance or weakness, what security would you have for any of your rights? What redress of wrong? There would be none except the honor of this government. You would be powerless and have to rely upon the magnanimity of Congress. Then, why not rely upon it now? This government has no desire to wrong the Indian, or shed his blood; but, it will not hesitate to adopt the most vigorous and decisive measures for the defense of its rights and the protection of its own people."

After several papers captured from Flores were laid before the President and his cabinet, steps were taken to compel the departure of the Cherokees from Texas, with the least possible delay.

The Houston Telegraph of June 19, contained an editorial saying that the time had arrived for severe chastisement of the Indians who had lurked "like spirits of darkness on the borders" and who had "construed forbearance into weakness and indulgence into timidity." After alluding to the Houston-Forbes treaty of 1836 with the Cherokees, the article continues:

"We have neither time nor patience to discuss that treaty. It has never been ratified—has received no sanction except from the inexplicable fatuity of the commissioners who made it. To confirm it now would inflict irreparable injury upon Texas, and positive, palpable injustice on many of her citizens. The proposition is therefore idle.

" . . . . The Cherokees are, and always were, unwelcome intruders among us. If they will not return peaceably to their original tribe, it will become our duty—now that their stealthy machinations with Mexico have been fully discovered, to compel their retirement and perpetual alienation from the country . . . .

"The Cherokees have long been a source of inquietude and distrust to our eastern brethren. During the invasion of '36, the proximity of those wily savages to his homestead restrained many a strong hearted Red Lander from the field of battle, and kept him an idle and unwilling spectator of his country's struggle. Their insidious connection with Mexico, and their secret intrigues with the paltry tribes of the prairies, have already cost us much blood and suffering. . . . There should be an end put to these things."

Col. Burleson was ordered to increase his force to 400 men and to march into the Cherokee country, which he did, crossing to the east side of the Neches July 14, where he was joined by the regiment of Col. Landrum, composed of volunteers from Harrison, Shelby, Sabine and San Augustine counties. Gen Rusk was already on the ground with the Nacogdoches regiment and encamped near the Cherokee village.

Douglass despatched Capt. Kimbro's company of San Augustine volunteers to the village of the Shawnees to demand the surrender of their gun-locks to enforce neutrality. They were promptly delivered.

Vice-President, David G. Burnet, Thomas J. Rusk, J. W. Burton, James S. Mayfield and Secretary of War, Gen. Albert Sidney Johnston (the latter of whom was appointed at the instance of Bowles), as commissioners for Texas, were for several days previous to July 15 engaged in conferences with the Cherokee chiefs, trying to effect an amicable agreement.* They had been instructed to allow a fair compensation for improvements, payment to be made partly in money and partly in goods; but were not authorized to stipulate for payment of the Cherokees for their lands.

At noon on July 15, the commissioners came into camp and announced their failure to negotiate a settlement.

The troops were immediately put in motion and proceeded to the Cherokee village, under instructions not to fire until the Indians had been summoned to accept the terms of the government.

It was found that the Cherokees had retreated some hours before to a strong position near a Delaware village, five or six miles distant.

The Texas army followed them. The Indians opened fire.

---

* Official report of Secretary of War.

The engagement began late in the afternoon. The Indians were beaten.

Another battle followed the next day near the Neches, in which the Indians were hopelessly defeated and Chief Bowles* was killed. The Cherokees fled from the country after these affairs. Parties of them returned from time to time afterwards and committed murders and depredations alone or in conjunction with other Indians. Thomas J. Rusk and James S. Mayfield, as commissioners, entered into an agreement under which the Shawnees accepted terms of the government and left the country.

In the battle with the Cherokees at the Delaware village, Vice-President Burnet, Adjutant General McLeod, General Johnston, and Major David S. Kaufman were among the wounded.

Brig. Gen. K. H. Douglass, commanding the Texas army under date of "Headquarters, Camp Carter, 16th of July, 1839," made the following official report to Gen. A. Sidney Johnston, Secretary of War:

"On yesterday, the negotiations on the part of the commissioners having failed, under your orders the whole force was put in motion towards the encampment of Bowles on the Neches. Col. Landrum crossed on the west side of the Neches and up the river. The regiments under Col. Burleson and Rusk moved directly to the camp of Bowles, on reaching which it was found to be abandoned. Their trail was ascertained, and a rapid pursuit made. About six miles above their encampment, in the vicinity of the Delaware village, at the head of a prairie, they were discovered by the spy company under Capt. Carter and a

---

* Bowles was the son of a Scotch father and Indian mother. He was a man of unusual sagacity. It is said that he advised the Indians to accept the best terms they could get from the whites, but they refused to be guided by his advice, whereupon he told them that he would live or die for them as fortune might determine, and exhorted them to fight bravely. During the last battle he could be repeatedly heard encouraging them, and more than once urging them to charge.

detachment of about twenty-five from Capt. Todd's company led by Gen. Rusk. The enemy deployed from the point of a hill. Gen. Rusk motioned for them to come on. They advanced and fired four or five times and immediately occupied a thicket and ravine on the left. As we advanced, the lines were immediately formed and the action became general. The ravine was instantly charged and flanked on the left by Col. Burleson with a part of his regiment. The rest of Col. Burleson's regiment was led by Lieut. Col. Woodlief; a portion of Gen. Rusk's regiment charging at the same time, and another portion took position on a point or hill to the right and drove a party, who attempted to flank us, from that quarter—thus instantly driving the enemy from the ravine and thicket, leaving eighteen dead on the field that have been found and carrying off, as usual, their wounded as was seen by many of our men. Our loss in the engagement was two killed, one wounded mortally, and five slightly.

"Col. Landrum was not able, having so much further to march, to participate in the engagement, but has been ordered to join us this morning. All behaved so gallantly, it would be invidious to particularize. The action commenced about half an hour before sundown, which prevented a pursuit. Most of their baggage was captured; five kegs of powder, 250 lbs. of lead, many horses, cattle, corn and other property."

The action of July 16, began by Capt. Carter's spy company being fired upon. Col. Burleson, with the companies of Capts. Jordan and Howard of his regiment, advanced briskly to the support of Carter and drove the enemy's force in front to a ravine and thicket where the main body of the Cherokees were posted in a very strong position. Burleson's loss was one man killed and seven horses wounded.

Col. Rusk, leading the companies of Capts. Tipp and Todd, and followed by the second battalion of his regiment (companies of Capts. R. W. and Madison Smith) under Lt. Col. James Smith, moved up to the support of Burleson and took position as the center of the Texas line. Burleson obliqued to the left and engaged the enemy's right. Capts. Lewis and Ownsby of the other battalion of Burleson's regiment moved to the right of

Rusk and in front of the enemy's left wing.

Spirited firing continued for an hour and a half—the Cherokees evidently making a serious effort for victory. Then Gen. Douglass ordered a simultaneous charge, which was gallantly executed. The enemy were driven with slaughter for half a mile and took refuge in a swamp in the Neches bottom. They were again charged, Lt. Col. Woodlief leading the right, Rusk the center and Burleson the left. This time they offered no opposition, but broke and ran in every direction away from their assailants. Gen. Douglass then halted his men and ordered them to collect the wounded and form on high ground. According to his estimate, the Cherokee force consisted of 700 or 800 warriors. Their own report placed their loss in killed and wounded at 100. The Texan loss was two killed and thirty wounded.—three mortally: Maj. H. W. Augustin, Jno. S. Thompson, and Jno. Ewing.

Gen. Douglass says that Capt. Jordan was wounded early in the action and, while he was on the ground, continued to command his men. The General favorably mentions Drs. Booker, Brown and Towers and the other surgeons, Capt. Smith, Lieut. Corbin, Adjutant General McLeod, Brigadier General Snively, volunteer aides Davis and Morbett and Maj. Sturgiss and Capts. Milroy and Patton of his staff, and others.

He says, "Rusk and Burleson behaved with that gallantry and coolness that has so often distinguished them on the field of battle in Texas."

Also: "Important benefits are likewise acknowledged to have been derived from the active exertions of the Secretary of War and Vice-President, who were on the field in both engagements, and behaved in such a manner as reflected credit upon themselves."

On the morning of the 18th, the wounded were conveyed to Fort Lamar by Capt. Todd in command of a detail of eighty men.

The Texas army remained in camp for two days—until joined by the force under Col. Landrum which had been advancing up the east side of the Neches.

On the 21st the army went in pursuit of the enemy.

Gen. Douglass says: "The trail of the Indians bore westward to the headwaters of the Sabine, which was followed and brought us about 4 o'clock in the evening to some Indian huts and cornfields. Several villages and several hundred acres of corn were discovered. We encamped at one of them—destroyed their houses and cut down their corn.

"This devastating march was continued up to the 25th, until the entire Cherokee country had been traversed and Indian trails had disappeared. Houses were burnt and crops and improvements destroyed every day until none remained. All cattle and other stock were appropriated.

"On the 25th orders were issued for the companies to be marched home by different routes and mustered out of service, which was done."

## RIGHTS OF THE CHEROKEES—THE INGRATITUDE OF A REPUBLIC.

Yoakum's view that the Cherokees had a strong equitable, if not legal, title to the lands they claimed; that the Consultation was a private organic body that had the right and power to issue the solemn decree it did; and to authorize the negotiation of the treaty entered into by Houston and Forbes by direction of the Provisional Government of Texas; and that the white people were the first to break the terms of the solemn compact entered into with the Indians, is sustained by the facts of history.

But a breach had been created that it was impossible to bridge, as mutual confidence had been destroyed. The people at large regarded the Cherokees as enemies, and a greedy element hungered for their lands. Reflecting public sentiment, the Texas Senate rejected the Houston-Forbes treaty.

President Houston believed that the Cherokees were being made the victims of a cruel combination of circumstances, and made a noble but unavailing effort to save them.

It is not only possible, but probable, that, if the declaration of the Consultation and the treaty had been lived up to in letter and spirit by the people and government of Texas, the Cherokees would have proven faithful allies.

The action of the Consultation and the treaty if adhered to, would have cured its defects and given them defense and inviolable territory. Both were repudiated.

## LOCATING THE CAPITAL AT AUSTIN.

By October 1st, the seat of government was transferred to Austin. President Lamar and cabinet traveled overland from Houston. They were met outside the town and escorted in by a delegation of citizens, who gave a banquet and ball in their honor. Public buildings, including a wooden one-story capitol situated where the city hall now stands, had been erected during the summer.

The site of Austin was selected by Albert C. Horton, Louis P. Cook, Isaac W. Burton, William Menefee and J. Campbell, commissioners appointed under the act of January 14, 1839. Their action was bitterly criticised by those opposed to Lamar's administration, and enthusiastically supported by his adherents and all who favored the policy of driving the Indians westward as rapidly as possible and shoving the frontier line forward in their wake. A prime object was to open lands for safe settlement by immigrants and other homeseekers.

At that time Austin was on the extreme frontier. The nearest settlement on the west was San Antonio, about eighty miles away. "To Lavaca Bay, one hundred and fifty miles distant, the only settlements were Gonzales and Victoria. To Houston, a distance of two hundred miles, the only settlements were about Washington." To the settlements on Red River, nearly four hundred miles distant, was a region unoccupied save by roving and murderous bands of Indians.

# CAPT. HOWARD'S SKIRMISH.

Fort Burleson, Oct. 26, 1839.

To the Hon. A. Sidney Johnston, Sec. of War:

Sir—I have the honor to report that on the morning of the 26th inst., between San Gabriel and Little River, as I was riding accompanied by one of my command, about one quarter of a mile in advance of the wagons and their guard, I discovered a number of Indians at a distance, and leaving a man to watch their movements and endeavor to ascertain their numbers, I joined my company to put them in a position for attack or defense, as circumstances might require.

The scout came in and reported about 140 Indians. I then took a position in an island of timber, forming a breastwork with the wagons, which I had hardly completed when the enemy came upon us. There were from 15 to 30 riding around, and as I thought, endeavoring to draw me from my position.

Finding that impossible, they drew off to a point of timber about 250 yards distant. In order to ascertain their numbers with more certainty, I mounted and rode in their direction, when they withdrew into the prairie. As I found that their force did not exceed 20, and some of them had previously rode off in a different direction (probably to obtain reinforcements), I took up the line of march for the Falls, after instructing Capt. Moore and Lt. Lewis that I would endeavor to provoke them to an attack, and to hold themselves in readiness. I being the best mounted, pursued the Indians alone. On reaching the summit of a hill in the prairie, I discovered them in advance. They immediately turned and gave chase, hoping to cut me off before I could reach my force. I led them back towards the wagons, and on their arriving within 200 yards, Lt. Lewis and twelve men met me; we then charged them, (leaving Capt. Moore and the balance of the men to guard the wagons) and a skirmish ensued which lasted about fifteen minutes, when they retreated, leaving three men and three horses dead upon the field, besides several who rode off evidently wounded. The state of our horses was such that I could not pursue them, as they were mostly mounted on fine American horses, and having seen a very large trail near Brushy the day before, I thought it most prudent to proceed on my route. We sustained no injury, with the exception of one horse, which was badly wounded and left behind. I arrived here on Monday the 28th without futher interruption, but from the various trails and signs, I am convinced there is a large force hovering about the road from this place to Austin.

Lt. Alexander and several of the men are down with the fever, there is no surgeon within seventy miles of the post, and no medicines on hand.

I have the honor to be very respectfully your obedient servant.

Geo. T. Howard, Comd'g Post.
—Austin City Gazette, Nov. 6, 1839.

---

## INDIAN TROUBLES NEAR THE NEW CAPITAL.

During the fall of 1839, a young negro man owned by Hamilton White was killed and scalped by Indians in Walnut Creek bottom about six miles from Austin. White had a contract to deliver lumber at Austin, and started the negro for that place with a wagon load of lumber and $300.00 in money. The night before he was killed, the negro stopped with his team at Reuben Hornsby's. In the morning he said that he was afraid to go on to Austin, as it was known that hostile Indians were in the vicinity. Mr. Hornsby told him that he had better wait until he could get company. The darkey, replied that Mr. White expected him to reach town by a certain time, and he would have to take chances. He accordingly set forward, with the result stated.

The "Telegraph," published at Houston, says in its issue of Dec. 18, 1839:

"The combined tribes of the Lipans and Tonkaways were at Austin on the 11th inst. They were to accompany Col. Burleson on the expedition into the Comanche country. About 300 troops under this officer and 200 of the Indians were to leave the encampment near Austin on or about the 13th inst. for this purpose.

"The object of the expedition is to force the Comanches from the section of country near the San Saba and to establish a line of block houses from the Colorado to the Red River. These block houses, when erected and garrisoned, it is believed, will effectually shut out the prairie Indians from the country, and remove the frontier from 100 to 200 miles further northward. By this means an immense tract, the most fertile and healthy section of Texas, will be opened to the enterprising immigrants who are crowding into the country. The section of country to be thus wrested from these savage hordes, is exceedingly valuable, from the fact that it is peculiarly adapted to the culture of wheat and other staples of the middle states of the American Union."

---

## BURLESON'S ATTACK ON MIGRATING CHEROKEES —DEATH OF "THE BOWL" AND "THE EGG."

The year closed with an engagement on Christmas day with a considerable body of Cherokees who were trying to make their way across Texas into Mexico by traveling north of the settlements. They were led by John Bowles, son of Col. Bowles, or "The Bowl," as he was called by the tribe, (the deceased chief who was killed in one of the battles fought when the Cherokees were expelled from East Texas in July), and another chief called "The Egg."

Col. Edward Burleson, of the army, in command of a body of regulars, a few volunteers and Lipan and Tonkawa scouts was making a winter campaign between the upper Colorado and Brazos rivers.

During the afternoon of December 23, when he was about twenty-five miles east of Pecan bayou, his scouts reported that they had discovered a large trail of horses and cattle bearing south, in the direction of the Colorado river.

The trail was followed and some time in the afternoon of December 25, Col. Burleson and his men crossed to the west side of the river and approached within a short distance of the camp of John Bowles and "The Egg" before being discovered.

Burleson desired the Indians to surrender. They sent a messenger to him to parley and at the same time a party of them moved to his rear and took position in a ravine. Concluding that they were merely endeavoring to secure time to attack his force to best advantage, he detained the Indian messenger and gave orders under which his men began to deploy in such a manner as to be able to assail the enemy both in front and back.

Correctly interpreting what was transpiring, the Indians in the ravine opened fire, instantly killing Capt. Lynch and wounding several of the whites. The fire was returned by Company B, which immediately charged under Capt. Clendenin, and drove the savages out of the ravine and back upon the main force. At the same time the rest of Burleson's force charged the warriors under Bowles and "The Egg." Both of the chiefs and five other Indians were killed. The conflict was brief, the Cherokees breaking before the impetuous onset, and seeking cover in dense cedar brakes. All the surviving warriors, except the messenger, escaped. He and five women and nineteen children were made captives. Among the prisoners were the wife and two daughters of Col. Bowles and three children of John Bowles. Some months later the prisoners were sent to their kindred in the Cherokee Nation, west of Arkansas.

Col. Burleson continued his expedition to a successful conclusion, marching up Pecan Bayou, thence across to the Leon, and down the country to the settlements, frightening Indians out of the region. Several bodies of hostiles were reported by their scouts, but dissolved and disappeared on his approach.

Among those who accompanied him were Col. Wm. S. Fisher, Major Wyatt, Captain Matthew Caldwell, Lieut. Lewis, Dr. Booker, and Capt. (afterwards Dr.) J.P.B. January.

The end of the year found the Indian situation in Texas somewhat improved, the settlements rapidly extending, population and wealth largely increased, and security—the twin blessing of freedom—being afforded in larger measure to the people on the frontier and elsewhere than at any former time since the era of the Republic.

# CHAPTER XIII.

he year 1840, in the history of Texas, teems with interest. The stream of the nation's life, no longer a rivulet, was broadening and deepening into a noble river.

During the twelve months, the eastern, and a portion of the northern boundary of Texas were established by commissioners appointed for the purpose. The "neutral ground" on the eastern line was thus eliminated. The survey added a narrow strip of land to the northern portion of the Republic. The settlers in it were generously treated by Texas, being allowed the same quantities of land as emigrants.

Having no use for the navy, Texas leased the greater portion of it to Yucatan, in whose service it remained for two years. An attempt was made to establish a Republic of the Rio Grande by Mexican revolutionists, but failed. The effort would be unworthy of mention, but for the increase of fame added to Texas arms by Colonels William S. Fisher, S. W. Jordan and their comrades, who aided the movement and performed military exploits on Mexican soil that are not surpassed by any record of Texas soldiers.

In the latter part of the year the independence of Texas was formally recognized by Great Britain, France and Belgium, and the Republic's position as a sovereign state assured.

So much for general events and legislation. The main interest that attaches to the year centers in incidents that marked the working out of President Lamar's Indian policy, and in happenings that swelled the bloody tide of savage atrocities that continued to surge along the frontier.

# FAMOUS COUNCIL HOUSE FIGHT.

January 30, Gen. Albert Sidney Johnston wrote to Col. William S. Fisher, commanding 1st regiment of Texas Infantry, directing him to order three companies of the regiment to march immediately to San Antonio, and to proceed there himself and take command of the troops and station them in such advantageous position near the town as he might select. Gen. Johnston recited the contents of a letter received from Karnes and then, speaking of the Comanches, said: "If they come, in accordance with their agreements, bringing with them the captives and deliver them up, such voluntary release of their prisoners will be regarded as an evidence of their sincere desire for peace and they will, therefore, be treated with kindness and be permitted to depart without molestation.

"You will state to them that this government assumes the right, with regard to all Indian tribes residing within the limits of the Republic, to dictate the conditions of their residence, and that their own happiness depends on their good or bad conduct toward our citizens; that their remaining within such limits as may be prescribed, and an entire abstinence from acts of hostility or annoyance to the inhabitants of the frontier, are the only conditions for the privilege of occupancy that the government deems it is necessary at this time to impose."

He described that the Comanches be told that they must keep out of the settlements, and not molest persons locating lands, as citizens were entitled by law to make locations upon any vacant and unappropriated portion of the public domain.

He also commanded Col. Fisher to arrest and hold as hostages the Indians who came to the meeting, unless they brought in and surrendered all the captives held by Comanches; but to allow messengers to return to the tribe and report what had occurred, and that the Indian hostages would be released as soon as the white captives were produced.

Col. Fisher communicated with the Comanches in February, telling them not to come in without bringing all the prisoners.

They replied that they would arrive at the time appointed.

March 19th a party of Comanches, consisting of thirty two warriors and thirty-three women and children entered San Antonio, bringing only one prisoner, Matilda Lockhart. The girl's body was covered with bruises and sores, her hair had been singed to the scalp, and her nose had been burned off to the bone—evidently at some time considerably anterior to the meeting, as the wound had healed.

Twelve chiefs who accompanied the party, were conducted to the Court House, where they took seats on the platform at one end of the room with Col. Fisher, Col. Hugh McLeod, Adjutant General, and Col. William G. Cooke, Quartermaster General, and acting Secretary of war,* commissioners appointed to treat with them. In the room were also a considerable crowd of bystanders. Capt. George T. Howard was ordered up with two companies of soldiers, one of which was stationed in the Court House and the other near the building.

The Indian women and children were gathered in the yard and the warriors about the house.

The jail occupied the corner formed by the east line of Main Plaza and the north line of what is now Market street, and to the north of, and adjoining it, was the court house. Both buildings were of stone, one story, flat roofed, and dirt floor.

Col. Fisher opened the talk by asking the chiefs why they had not brought in all the prisoners, thirteen in number, which they were known to have. Muke-war-rah replied that they had brought in the only prisoners, and that the others were with bands over whom they had no control. Miss Lockhart was then questioned, and said that she had seen several prisoners in camp a few days previous, and that the policy determined upon by the Indians was to bring them in one at a time and thus extort large ransoms. She also told of the brutal treatment and indignities to which she had been subjected. The chiefs listened in haughty and defiant silence while she spoke, and as she left the

* Gen. Albert Sidney Johnston had refused the position of Secretary of War.

room they became restless and gave evidence of their feelings—trouble was imminent.

A message was sent Capt. Howard, and he marched into the room with the company that had been stationed in the yard, drew his men up in a line across the apartment, and stationed himself and sentry at the closed doors. Capt. Redd's company was ordered to the rear of the building, and had barely arrived there when the fighting began.

In the yard were Indian boys shooting with bows and arrows at marks, for small coins that Judge Robinson was offering them as prizes. Mrs. Maverick and other ladies were looking on through cracks in the fence.

When Howard's company had been brought to parade rest, Col. Fisher arose and addressed the chiefs. He reproached them with their former perfidy, and for violating the terms of the subsisting agreement. In conclusion, he asked them if they recollected murdering two white men while under a white flag.

A Comanche chief arose, and with an audacity and an insolence of tone and manner that could not be exceeded, replied, "No, we do not recollect," and seated himself, after the Indian fashion.

Silenced ensued. It was broken by the chief again arising, turning toward Col. Fisher with an air at once contemptuous and threatening, and demanding in a loud voice, "How do you like our answer?"

Col. Fisher replied: "I do not like your answer. I told you not to come here again without bringing in the prisoners. You have come against my orders. Your women and children may depart in peace, and your braves may go and tell your people to send in the prisoners. When those prisoners are returned, you and the other chiefs here present may likewise go free. Until then we will hold you as hostages.

The interpreter had to be told twice to report this declaration; protesting that a conflict would immediately follow. As soon as he uttered the words he left the room. True to his prediction, the chiefs strung their bows, and drew their knives.

In his official report, Col. McLeod says: "We told the chiefs that the soldiers they saw were their guards, and descended from the platform. They immediately followed. One of them sprang to the back door and attempted to pass the sentinel who presented his musket, when the chief drew his knife and stabbed him. A rush was then made to the door. Capt. Howard collared one of them and received a severe stab in the side. Howard tried to use his sword, but it was too long for service in a breast to breast struggle, and all he could do was to seize the Indian's wrist, which he held till faint from loss of blood. He ordered the sentinel to fire upon his antagonist, which he did and the Indian fell dead. Col. Fisher ordered, 'Fire if they do not desist.' The Indians rushed on and fought desperately, and a general order to fire became necessary.

"After a short, but desperate, struggle every one of the twelve chiefs in the council room lay dead upon the floor.

"The indoor work being finished, Capt. Howard's company was formed in front to prevent retreat in that direction; but in consequence of the severity of his wound, he was relieved by Capt. Gillen, who commanded the company till the close of the action."

The bystanders in the room had to fight for their lives as well as the rest. Judge John Hemphill (then District Judge and later Chief Justice of the Supreme Court) was one of them, and disemboweled with a bowie knife, one of the chiefs, who grappled with him.

The Indians outside the house fought like wild beasts. Capt. Redd's company coming up promptly in the rear of the building, drove them toward a stone building, which only one of them succeeded in entering. Several white men were killed and wounded. The Indian arrows with which they were struck were driven to the feathers. Several Indians were killed in adjacent streets and yards by citizens. A small number of the savages managed to reach the river, but were pursued and killed by Maj. Lysander Wells and a few other mounted men, only one of their party—a renegade Mexican—escaping. Three women and two boys, who took part in the fray, were slain.

Wishing to spare the warrior in the stone building, the

commissioners sent in an Indian woman to tell him to surrender and be spared. He refused the offer, and continued to shoot, wounding several persons. After dark, a Mexican crawled on top of the house, picked a hole in the roof, and dropped a large ignited ball of cloth saturated with turpentine into the room, for the purpose of lighting up the interior so the occupant could be seen. The ball fell on the Indian's head and stuck there, and he rushed into the street covered with flame. He was instantly riddled with bullets. Twenty-eight Indian women and children were detained as prisoners.

The Texan loss was, killed: Judge James W. Robinson; Judge Hood of San Antonio; Judge Thompson of Houston; Casey of Matagorda county; Lieut. W. M. Dunnington, 1st Infantry; Privates Kaminske and Whiting, and a Mexican. Wounded: Capt. George T. Howard, Lieut. Edward A. Thompson and private Kelley, severely, and Capt. Matthew Caldwell, and Mr. Higgenbottom and Deputy Sheriff Morgan and Private Carson, slightly. Col. McLeod says: "Over a hundred horses and a large quantity of buffalo robes and peltries remained to the victors."

By request of the prisoners, one squaw was released, provisioned and allowed to go to her people and say that the prisoners would be released whenever the Texan prisoners held by the Indians were brought in.

A short time afterward a party of Comanches displayed a white flag on a hill some distance from town, evidently afraid to come nearer. When a flag was sent out it was found that they had brought in several white children to exchange for their people. Their mission was successful and they hurried away.

The Telegraph and Texas Register gave an account of the following, among other incidents of the Council House Fight:

"Capt. Matthew Caldwell, 1st Regiment of Infantry, was in the street unarmed when the struggle commenced. He stepped into a house to see if he could procure a gun. No one was at home, and he passed into the back yard. There he was confronted by an Indian warrior, who made ready to shoot him. Caldwell stooped down and picked up a rock, which he threw, hitting the warrior on the forehead, slightly stunning him.

Caldwell continued to throw stones, hurling them so fast, that for dodging, the Indian did not get a chance to take aim and let fly an arrow. While this unequal combat was in progress John D. Morris, with only a three inch barrel, single shot pistol, came into the inclosure. Caldwell, who was nearly exhausted, called out, 'Go up and shoot him John, or he will get me. I will keep him on the jump with stones.'

"Morris did as requested, walking to within four feet of the Indian and shooting him through the heart.

"Deputy Sheriff Morgan (one of Deaf Smith's men) was standing in the back yard of a residence when three warriors scaled the wall and attacked him. Although wounded, he picked up a rock and fractured the skull of one of his assailants with it killing him. He then seized an axe and retreated into the house, where he stationed himself at one side of the open door. The two remaining Indians attempted to follow him, and he killed them with terrific blows, dealt with the axe."

A German doctor, who was a local celebrity and a man of scientific taste and attainments, came upon the body of one of the Indians killed by Morgan and, being impressed by the peculiar bumps on the head, took it for purpose of dissecting it. He was much disgusted to find that the protuberance were not natural developments, but due to the skull being fractured in thirty-two places. He later boiled one of the bodies, removed the flesh from the bones, and articulated the complete skeleton, which he placed in his cabinet. Incidently, he emptied the refuse into the Acequia, from which citizens procured drinking water. The fact becoming known, he stated that the deposit was made when everybody was asleep at night and the stream was completely purified before water was again taken from it for drinking or cooking purposes. Nothing but his popularity saved him from enforced emigration.

March 28th, two hundred and fifty, or three hundred, Comanches came close to San Antonio, and chief Isimanca and another warrior of their number, rode daringly into the public square, and circled around the plaza, then rode some distance down Commerce street and back, shouting all the while, offering to fight, and showering abuse and insults on the Americans. "Isimanca was in full war paint and almost naked. He stopped quite awhile in front of Bluck's saloon, on the northeast corner of the square. He shouted defiance, rose in his stirrups, shook his clenched fist, raved and foamed at the mouth. The citizens, through an interpreter, told him that the soldiers were all down at the Mission San Jose, and if he went there Colonel Fisher would give him fight enough."

He proceeded at once to the Mission and repeated his challenge. Col. Fisher was sick in bed and Capt. Redd was in command of the post.

Redd replied to Isimanca by saying that a twelve days truce had been entered into with the Comanches and he had orders not to break it, but if the chief and his warriors would return when the truce was at an end, they would be accommodated.

Isimanca denounced him and his men as cowards and finally left.

Yoakum says: "The Comanches hung about San Antonio in small parties brooding over their loss. The killing of so many of their chiefs was a severe stroke, and they were divided on the question of war. At length they retired to their homes, on the upper branch of the Texas rivers, to make serious preparations for a terrible visitation on the white settlements."*

Branch T. Archer was appointed secretary of War, and Col. William G. Cooke succeeded Col. Edward Burleson as Colonel of infantry.

In May, the Republic was aroused by rumors of an impending military invasion from Mexico, to be accompanied by Indians employed as allies of the Mexican troops.

Orders were issued under which a large force of Texas volunteers assembled for the purpose of organizing an army for

---

* March 26th, Mrs. Webster came into San Antonio with her three-year-old baby upon her back, having escaped from the Comanches by whom she had been captured the previous year when her husband and party had been killed on Brushy Creek, near Georgetown. She presented a most wretched and pitiable appearance and was almost famished. Friends cared for and ministered to her.

resistance.

Upon the receipt of other information that was deemed reliable to the effect that no such hostile movement was likely to take place—they were disbanded.

The incident was designated as the "Archer War" and provoked much adverse and undeserved criticism.

In the early days of July, Capt. Clendenin left San Antonio in command of a volunteer expedition against the Comanches, but afterwards returned to the town leaving Capt. J. R. Cunningham and a force of nineteen men on the Frio. In an official report by Cunningham he says that after they parted July 4th, he crossed the Frio (on the same day) and came upon a fresh Indian trail, which he pursued for several miles up the western side of the stream, expecting every moment to come upon the enemy. The trail finally bore away from the river, and he followed it without stopping to get water. After proceeding for some time, men and horses began to suffer greatly from want of water. It was not practicable to return to the river, without abandoning the chase. He and the men determined to go on. This they did, knowing that the Indians would stop at the first water hole and would probably make a stubborn fight for its retention.

Between 5 and 6 o'clock p.m., Antonio, a Tonkaway scout employed by the company, and who had been kept considerably in advance of the command, rode back and reported that the Indians—twenty warriors—were at a spring just ahead and were saddling their animals preparatory to resuming their journey. Cunningham and those of his men who were with him cautiously approached the place and took position within a short distance of the Indians without being perceived. He waited a few moments for his rear file to come up and dress into line before ordering a charge. While this movement was being executed one of his men accidently discharged a gun, and the Indians leaped into their saddles and applied the whip. He and his men charged at once, killing Indians right and left. The surviving savages labored to reach thickets some distance ahead. When all of them were wounded except three, the latter protected the retreat of the band in a manner that he repeatedly speaks of "as noble." He says that one of the three was under fire of ten or twelve of the best shots on the frontier, but acted with cool intrepidity to the last. A rifle ball finally shattered his leg, and he fell over on his horse, just as he and the remnant of the band reached cover. Cunningham captured all the effects of the Indians. He says that he made "a bon-fire of most of their trumpery" and divided the balance of their "plunder" among the volunteers by lot. The most important part of his capture was a caballado of horses and mules—a total of sixteen. He reached San Antonio July 7th.

## THE GREAT COMANCHE RAID—SACKING OF LINVILLE AND BURNING OF VICTORIA.

During the first week in August, following the Council House Fight, and other bloody affrays, narrated, occurred the Great Comanche Raid; in some respects the most formidable invasion ever made by Indians into Texas.

This raid was known to and encouraged, if not materially aided, by the Mexican authorities—especially Gen. Canalizo at Matamoras—and shows to have been well planned, with some degree of military strategy. The descent was sudden, but the alarm spread as if borne on the wings of the wind and the brave defenders of our frontier were soon collected under their favorite leaders and went in pursuit, overtaking, engaging, and routing the murderers.

This remarkable affair marks an important epoch in Texas history, and indeed most of our historians regard it as the turning point in affairs with the Indians. Many partial and often erroneous accounts of this bold uprising and its timely quelling, have been published. Fortunately we are enabled to give the facts as detailed by those in authority on matters pertaining to our border history.* It is not our purpose to enter into the details

---

* Much of the data used in the preparation of this narrative was furnished the author by the late Dr. Rufus C. Burleson a short time before his death, expressly for Border Wars of Texas.

of matters leading up to and resulting in this bold raid—that belongs to the history of Texas proper and has much to do with the political attitude of Mexico toward the struggling Texas Republic.

The unfortunate Council House tragedy doubtless hastened the movements of this expedition, the enraged Comanches, swearing to avenge the death of their fallen chiefs. The Indians to the number of about one thousand, began the descent from their stronghold in the mountains above the San Marcos and extending their raid across the country to Lavaca Bay on the coast, and back to Good's Crossing on Plum Creek, twenty miles south-west of Austin, where they were intercepted and routed, losing all their prisoners and property captured at Victoria and Linville.

The Indians passed down the country during the first days of August, leaving Gonzales seventeen miles to the west, and murdering a few families as they passed through the sparsely settled country,* they reached the quiet town of Victoria at 2:30 o'clock p.m. on August 6. The citizens were not dreaming of Indians. Children were playing in the yards, and on the streets, ladies were shopping and joyfully engaged in their domestic affairs, the men were at their usual vocations, when the bloody demons with horrid yells rushed into the streets and began their slaughter. Dr. Gray and a few others who attempted resistance were cut down. The citizens not killed, took refuge in their houses and fortified themselves as best they could. The Comanches then plundered the stores and private residences of everything valuable. They caught in the lots and pastures between two and three thousand horses and mules and loaded

---

* "At the time of this raid," says John Henry Brown, "the country between the Guadalupe and San Marcos, on the west, and the Colorado on the east, above a line drawn from Gonzales to La Grange, was a wilderness, while between that line it was thinly settled. Between Gonzales and Austin, on Plum Creek, were two recent settlers—Isom J. Good and John A. Neil. From Gonzales to within a few miles of Austin there was not a settler. There was not one between Austin and San Antonio. A road from Gonzales to Austin had been opened in July, 1839."

eight hundred or a thousand of them with the goods plundered. They started onto Linville. That night they kindled big fires and with fiendish joy danced and yelled around the scalps of murdered citizens and their plunder.

Next morning they hurried on to Linville, on the way capturing Mrs. Crosby, grand-daughter of the celebrated Daniel Boone of Kentucky, with her child and a nurse. About daylight, on August the 8th, while many of the citizens were in bed, the Indians entered Linville and throwing themselves on the sides of their horses and riding in this way, deceived the few early risers who saw them coming but thought they were some of the usual caballados of horses and mules brought into Linville for sale and shipment.

No language can tell the horror of the innocent people when they saw a thousand red demons suddenly rising in their saddles and with fiendish yells killing the defenseless citizens, some of them in their beds. Resistance was utterly useless and the terror stricken men, women and children rushed for the small boats lying in Lavaca Bay. The warwhoop of the wild Comanches, the cries of women and children and the groans of the dying, presented a scene of horror upon which the rising sun never before dawned. The bloody demons pursued the fleeing men, women and children into the water. Among those killed was Captain H. O. Watts, collector of customs. He and his beautiful bride were captured between the shore and the boats. He was killed and his young bride was ruthlessly dragged back to the shore and carried away as captive. The majority of the inhabitants escaped to the boats, but all others were murdered or carried away captives.

Linville was the shipping point for a large portion of Southwestern Texas and Mexico and was at that time well supplied with all sorts of merchandise. The exulting Comanches greedily sacked the stores and private residences and packed several hundred more horses and mules with every kind of merchandise, elegant dresses and bed clothes from private residences. They now bedecked themselves with red ribbons and gay clothing captured, and rode up and down the

Famous Council House Fight

Battle at Plum Creek

streets yelling like demons and fired the town, burning every house except one.

What language can express the horror of the innocent men, women and children as they stood on the boats in the bay and looked upon their once happy homes, burning to ashes, and remembering many of their loved ones lay bleeding in the streets!

## BATTLE AT PLUM CREEK.

The exulting Comanches, with three or four thousand horses and mules, many of them heavily packed with goods plundered at Victoria and Linville, began their retreat. They had glorious visions of the grand feasts and "War Dances" they would have when they reached their mountain home and displayed the scalps and the untold wealth, and the women and children they had captured.

But, says one, God gave Texas heroes and path-finders, who were ever ready to avenge such bloody raids. Among these were "Old Gotch" Hardeman, Henry McCulloch, John H. Moore, "Paint" Caldwell, Ed. Burleson and others.

The vigilant Ben McCulloch with a small force, was already in pursuit—and in fact had engaged the enemy. He sent Burleson the following dispatch: "General: The Indians have sacked and burned the town of Linville, and carried off several prisoners. We made a draw fight with them at Casa Blanco—could not stop them. We want to fight them before they get to the mountains. We have sent expressmen up the Guadalupe."

Messengers rode swift in every direction, and at a moment's warning, every man seized his gun, mounted and rushed to the place of rendezvous. Those near La Grange met at Col. Jno. H. Moore's, those near Bastrop met at Gen. Ed. Burleson's, those near Webberville at "Paint" Caldwell's, and all concentrated at the point suggested by Gen. Burleson, who ordered all to meet and attack the Comanches at Good's Crossing on Plum Creek, two miles from where the town of Lockhart now stands and twenty-seven miles below Austin. The grand old hero Paint Caldwell with eighty-two men, first reached the place of rendezvous August 1. Next morning the scouts reported a thousand Indians coming on the prairie with vast herds of horses and mules, and several women and children. But Burleson, nor Moore, nor McCulloch, nor Hardeman had arrived; was it safe for eighty-two men to attack a thousand Comanches? However, as they looked upon the awful spectacle, and saw them moving along with women and children, Caldwell could hold in no longer, but yelled out: "Boys, yonder they go and they have got our women and children—they are a thousand strong—but we can whip hell out of them! Shall we fight?" All shouted, "Yes, fight, fight!"

But at that time a courier came galloping up crying, "General Burleson with one hundred Texans and thirteen Tonkawas and old Placido are coming!" In the meantime Gen. Felix Huston arrived, and as Major General of the militia, took command.

The Indians were exceedingly anxious to defer the battle until they could get their packmules with the vast plunder and captured women and children beyond reach of the infuriated Texans. And General Huston was equally anxious to defer the battle until more recruits came. Several bluff old Indian fighters told him he knew nothing about fighting Indians, that he ought to resign and let Gen. Burleson command. But this was Gen. Huston's first chance for glory. The Indian chiefs did all in their power to intimidate the Texans and hold them back until they could get their plunder and captives far removed. Several of the Indian chiefs charged up in front of the Texans and hurled defiant arrows and spears at them. One of these daring chiefs rode a fine horse with a fine American bridle, with a red ribbon eight or ten feet long tied to the tail of his horse. He was dressed in elegant style from the goods plundered at Victoria and Linville, with a high-top silk hat, fine pair of boots, leather gloves and an elegant broad-cloth coat hindpart before with brass buttons shining brightly up and down his back. When he first made his appearance he carried a large umbrella stretched. He and others would charge upon the Texans, shoot their arrows, and retreat. This was done several times in reach of our guns.

Soon the discovery was made that they wore shields, and though our men took good aim, the bullets glanced. An old Texan, getting as near the place as was safe, waited patiently till they came up, and as the Indian wheeled his horse his shield flew up. The Texan fired and brought him to the ground. Several others fell at the same time. Then the Indians began their retreat, and would soon have been beyond the reach of the Texans.

Gen. Huston was now told by the gallant McCulloch and Gen. Burleson that the time had come when they must fight, and he reluctantly gave the order, "Charge!" Never was a command obeyed with wilder shouts. Every man was a hero, and the conscience-stricken, blood-stained Comanches were swept away like chaff before a tornado.

The Indians fled in wild confusion. Not one thought of saving anything but his own scalp. They abandoned their three thousand horses and plunder, and the captured women and children. But they could not forego the fiendish pleasure of murdering Mrs. Crosby, her child and nurse. They also shot an arrow into the bosom of the lovely young bride, Mrs. Watts, and left her as dead. But Rev. Z. N. Morrell and Dr. Brown heard her screams in a thicket and went to her assistance. They extracted the arrow, and she recovered and lived many years—never forgetting her awful experience—and died at Port Lavaca, in 1878.

The enraged Texans pursued the Indians, and killed them for twelve or fifteen miles out, till they finally gained safety in the brakes and mountains.

Thus ended the great raid of 1840—the most remarkable in our border annals so far as Indian affairs are concerned. It was a wonderful era in Texas history; indeed it was the turning point. Had the Comanches been successful, they confidently intended, with the horses, mules and materials captured, to equip a formidable war party of two or three thousand Indians for a grand re-raid down the Colorado to the Gulf, plundering and devastating the fairest portion of Texas. In the meantime Generals Canalizo and Woll, with some three thousand Mexi-

can cavalry, were to rush forward, capturing San Antonio and
Austin, with all booty. Chief Bowles and his Cherokees were to
move down and destroy the eastern portion of the state; the
Wacos, Apaches and allied tribes raiding down the Brazos, and
central Texas, thus utterly wiping out the Texans. "But in the
good Providence of God, we had heroes true and brave, who
quickly rallied, and uniting under their tried and chosen leaders, crushed out this diabolical purpose for the ruin of Texas.
The defeated and routed Comanches fled to their mountain
homes, overwhelmed with the conviction that the Texans were
quick of action, fearlessly brave, and invincible of purpose—
against any odds."

The savages were crestfallen and chagrined, and sullenly
retired to their mountain haunts to brood over defeat, and to
plan revenge—on their Mexican allies, who had failed to fulfill
their agreement, after inciting the Indians and promising to join
them with their forces in a grand re-raid of the whole country.
And for this breaking of faith it is said the Mexicans suffered
severely.*

## HUSTON'S OFFICIAL REPORT.

Many thrilling incidents and acts of individual bravery on
the part of the charging Texans might be related did space
permit. It is in justice to the subject that the official report of the
commander of the forces should be given—supplying, as it
does, important facts—and it follows:

* "In October (1840) more than 400 warriors penetrated into Mexico, some
400 miles; they killed, scalped, burned and destroyed everything they
could; their track could be traced for miles by the burning ranches and
villages. They carried off a great many female captives, and thousands of
horses and mules, and escaped safely to their strongholds in the mountains
with their booty. The State of Nueva Leon suffered the most severely from
this onset, having more than 700 inhabitants killed, and the State of
Coahuila nearly as many."—Captain Flack's "The Texas Rifle Hunter," p.
133.

On Plum Creek, 5 miles west of Good's.

August 12, 1840.

To the Hon. B. T. Archer, Secretary of War.

I arrived on yesterday evening and found Capt. Caldwell encamped on Plum Creek with about one hundred men. This morning I was requested to take the command, which I did, with the consent of the men. I organized them into companies, under the command of Captains Caldwell, Bird and Ward. About 6 o'clock a.m. the spies reported that Indians were approaching Plum Creek. I crossed above the trail about three miles, and passed down on the west side; on arriving near the trail I was joined by Col. Burleson with about one hundred men, under the command of Col. Jones, Lieut. Col. Wallace and Major Hardeman. I immediately formed into two lines, the right commanded by Col. Burleson, and the left commanded by Capt. Caldwell, with a reserve commanded by Maj. Hardeman, with Capt. Ward's company. On advancing near the Indians, they formed for action, with a front of woods on their right, (which they occupied), their lines extending nearly a quarter of a mile into the prairie. I dismounted my men and a handsome fire was opened—the Indian chiefs cavorting around in splendid style, on front and flank, finely mounted, and dressed in all the splendor of Comanche warfare. At this time several Indians fell from their horses, and we had three of four men wounded. Finding that the Indians were disposed to keep at a distance, and that a large body were assembled in the woods, I ordered Col. Burleson, with the right wing, to move around the point of woods, and Captain Caldwell, with the left wing, to charge into the woods; which movements were executed in gallant style. The Indians did not stand the charge, and fled at all points; from that time there was a warm and spirited pursuit for fifteen miles; the Indians scattered, mostly abandoning their horses and taking to the thickets. Nothing could exceed the animation of the men, and the cool and steady manner in which they would dismount and deliver their fire.

Upwards of forty Indians were killed—two prisoners (a squaw and a child) taken; and we have taken upwards of two hundred horses and mules, many of them heavily packed with the plunder of Linville and the lower country. There is still a large amount of good horses and mules which are not gathered in. Of the captives taken by the Indians below, we have only been able to retake one—Mrs. Watts, of Linville—who was wounded by the Indians with an arrow when they fled. Mrs. Crosby was speared, and we understand that all the others were killed. We have lost one killed and seven wounded—one mortally. I cannot speak too highly of the Colorado, Guadalupe and Lavaca militia, assembled so hastily together, and without organization. I was assisted by Major Izod, Colonel Bell, Captain Howard and Captain Neil, as volunteer aids, all of whom rendered essential service. Colonel Burleson acted with that cool, deliberate and prompt courage and conduct which he has so often and gallantly displayed in almost every Indian and Mexican battle since the war commenced. Capt. Caldwell, also a tried Indian fighter, led on his wing to the charge with a bold front and a cheerful heart. Colonel Jones, Lieut. Col. Wallace, Major Hardeman, and each of the captains commanding companies, acted with the utmost courage and firmness.

To conclude, I believe we have given the Comanches a lesson which they will long remember; near four hundred of their bravest warriors have been defeated by half their number, and I hope and trust that this will be the last of their depredations on our frontier.

On tomorrow I contemplate embodying as many men as I can, and if we have a sufficient number of good horses, pursue the Indians, in the hopes that we may overtake them before they reach the mountains. Colonel Moore joined us this evening with about 170 men, horses very hard ridden.

I have the honor to be,
Your most obedient servant,
Felix Huston,
Major-General, T.M.

# INDIANS ATTACK KINNEY'S FORT AND ARE REPULSED.

During August, Kinney's Fort on Brushy Creek, about eighteen miles from Austin, was attacked by Indians. They expected to take its inmates unawares, and would have done so had it not been for Joseph Weeks. He heard what he at first supposed to be owls hooting, but paid little attention to the sounds until he noted many answering hoots from various directions.

He listened attentively, until his practiced ear assured him that the cries were uttered by human throats, and then summoned his companions to arms, and started a messenger to the nearest settlement for assistance.

This action was taken none too soon, as the hooting was evidently a signal of attack, and the Indians immediately thereafter rushed on the place. They were met by a discharge of rifles that sent them reeling back. They fought from cover for some time, but finding that there was no possibility of taking the place without greater loss than they cared to sustain, drew off with their dead and wounded. Only one man in the fort was killed, and only one wounded.

The messenger reached his destination, and a company of fifty men arrived at the fort next day—too late to pursue the Indians.

Kinney was a soldier in the Texas army during the revolution; resided at Bastrop for some years, and later moved to Brushy Cove, where he erected the stockade that bore his name. The attack was probably made before news of the result of the battle of Plum Creek had spread among the Indians, for after it became generally known, they remained overawed for some time.

---

# JACK HAYS FIGHTS LARGE WAR PARTY.

In the fall of 1840 a party of about two hundred Comanches stole a large number of horses near San Antonio and drove them toward the Guadalupe River.

Capt. John C. ("Jack") Hays and twenty men went in pursuit, and came upon and charged the Indians at the crossing of the Guadalupe.

The redskins awaited the onset, expecting to easily overwhelm their assailants by mere force of numbers. The plans they laid for that purpose went "aglee". Hays and his comrades had a love of fighting that was untinged by fear, and that was fatal to those they encountered.

The head chief was speedily killed, and the Indians driven into complete rout. Hays and his men pursued them for several miles, killing a number of them and recovering most of the stolen horses.

* * * * *

Saturday, September 1, Michael Nash, a carpenter of Bastrop who had a fondness for hunting, killed a deer in the woods and started home with the carcass tied behind his saddle. While riding along, he was fired upon and killed by Indians, who scalped him and took his horse and its load of venison.

His body was found next day by friends who went in search of him. His eyes had been pecked out by buzzards and his body mutilated by the Indians, or by wolves, almost beyond identification.

## CAPT. ERATH'S SERVICES.

September 20, Gen. Felix Huston, as Major General of the Texas militia, transmitted to the Speaker of the House of Representatives a communication, accompanied by a report forwarded to him by Geo. B. Erath, captain of a spy company that he had placed in the field. After urging payment of Captain Erath and his men, and saying that the company had performed valuable service, he continues: "I allude principally to the discovery of the Indian trail above the Waco village, leading far into the mountains and, doubtless, to the homes of our savage enemy. This, you will immediately perceive, will greatly facilitate our army in carrying into effect what should be the only policy pursued towards our savage invaders—utter extermination."

Captain Erath, in his report, says that his company killed two Indians, and that various parties of Indians were seen by him, but fled upon the approach of his force, and burned the grass behind them. The information furnished by Erath induced the Texas Government to depute Col. Jno. H. Moore to lead an expedition to the home of the Comanches for the purpose of dealing them a crushing blow.

The Austin City Gazette, of September 23, says that an expedition against the Indians had been agreed upon, in accordance with a plan long projected by Gen. Felix Huston; that a total of 1600 men were to be raised in various counties, and were to invade the Indian country at different points; that the volunteers from the Colorado, Brazos, Trinity and Neches, would leave their respective places of rendezvous November 10, and that those from Red River would leave November 15. The paper says: "The General commanding was called to the honorable station he now fills by the free suffrages of his fellow citizens, and they will not now desert him." It declares that the war is to be one of extermination, and, commenting on the fact, remarks: "This is as it should be; for, once let the reds be taught to fear the whites and to respect their property, and peace and prosperity will reign supreme in Texas, immigration and wealth will flow to our shores, and the settlements will in a short time be pushed tens, aye hundreds of miles, above the present frontier."

## BEGINNING OF SAN MARCOS.

In an official report* dated October 1, Adjutant and Inspector General Hugh McLeod among other things says that the

* Army Archives.

detachment of rangers at San Antonio had been sent on an expedition, and that a company had been sent to the head of the San Marcos river to construct and occupy a fort, which was to be built of the best materials, as it was designed to control the pass through the mountains at that point. He says that a large number of settlers would locate near the fort, and if it was properly maintained, there would in a few years be a sufficient number of them to protect themselves. After speaking of the reinforcement and supplies forwarded to Col. Cooke, he says: "Col. Cooke will be enabled from observations on his present campaign, to report the most practicable line of defense and settlement on our frontier from the Colorado to Red River, and on his return be sufficiently early for the action of Congress. Any report at present might appear speculative and premature; but, in the absence of accurate information, I would suggest that the cross-timbers, being a wooded and well watered country, seems to present the most continuous line for settlements and communication from Red River to the Brazos." He asserts, and lays stress upon, the futility of employing volunteer forces enlisted for short periods—and, particularly, such forces when drawn from the floating population of towns, as they felt no interest in protecting the frontier, or the success of campaigns.

## MOORE'S GREAT VICTORY.

President Lamar determined to carry the war into the Indian country and to inflict upon the Comanches such slaughter as would leave them no longer sufficient power or courage to injure the whites. Accordingly Col. John H. Moore, with two companies of citizen-volunteers, aggregating ninety men, drawn mostly from Fayette county and captained by Thos. J. Rabb and Nicholas Dawson, with S. S. B. Field, a brilliant lawyer of La Grange, as Adjutant—Clark L. Owens of Texana, and R. Addison Gillispie, Lieutenants; and augmented by twelve trusty Lipan guides and scouts under their chiefs, Castro and Flaco—set out for an extended campaign far out into the Indian country.

Breaking camp on Walnut Creek, near Austin, on October 5, 1840, the company bore up the Colorado for a distance of some 300 miles to the vicinity of where Colorado City now stands. On October 23, the Indian trail was found on the Red Fork of the Colorado and dashing forward the Lipan spies soon located a considerable village of Comanches—60 wigwams and about 150 warriors—on the south bank of the river. Herding the beeves in a mesquite flat and leaving them to Fortune's chance, the Texans marched up in closer proximity to the enemy, halted at midnight and planned an attack to take place at dawn. A fierce "wet norther" was blowing. The unsuspecting Comanches slumbered comfortably under buffalo robes in their skin-covered teepees, while the Texans had only the blue sidereal dome for a covering and shivered in the chill light of the stars. As the first rays of light glimmered across the wild and wind-swept plains, the troops were ordered to mount, deploy and move rapidly to the onslaught—Lieut. Clark L. Owens with fifteen picked men as cavalry were deployed to cut off any retreat of the enemy; Capt. Rabb with his command to the right, and Capt. Dawson with his contingent upon the left; the Lipans being with the center advancing column. What happened when the village was reached is best told by Col. Moore himself:

"At the break of day, on Saturday, the 24th of October, I ordered the troops to mount and march. I soon ascended the hill, and ordered Lieut. Clark L. Owen to take command of fifteen men taken from the companies, to act as cavalry, to cut off any retreat of the enemy. I ordered Capt. Thomas J. Rabb, with his command, up the right, Lieut. Owen in the center, and Capt. Nicholas M. Dawson, with his command, upon the left. Just before reaching the village I had to descend the hill, which brought us within two hundred paces of the enemy. I then ordered Lieut. Owen with his command to the right of Capt. Rabb's command. I then ordered a charge of the whole upon the village, which was obeyed instanter. The enemy fled for the river, which was in the shape of a half moon, encircling the village. Immediately upon charging the village, a general, effective fire was opened upon the enemy, who soon commenced falling upon the right and left. After charging pretty nearly through their encampment, the men dismounted from their horses, and continued the fire upon the enemy, as they were retreating to the river. Many were slain before they reached the river, in which they took refuge—many of whom were killed or drowned. Some, however, succeeded in crossing the stream and making off thro' the prairie on the opposite side. At this time, Lieut. Owen crossed over and commenced cutting off their retreat. In this the gallant lieutenant succeeded admirably. During all this time, the fire was kept up most effectively at the river for the space of thirty minutes.

"When the enemy had reached the opposite bank, then it was that my troops displayed their skill in rifle shooting. Every man was deliberate and at the crack of his piece it was apparent that good aim had been taken. The river and its banks now presented every evidence of a total defeat of our savage foes. The bodies of men, women and children were to be seen on every hand, wounded, dying, and dead. Having found that the work of death and destruction had been fully consummated here, I accordingly ordered my troops to cross the river, and a portion to act in concert with Lieut. Owen. With the residue, I ordered a general charge in pursuit of the Indians who were attempting to effect their escape. My men were soon seen flying in every direction through the prairie, and their valor told that the enemy was entirely defeated. The pursuit ceased at the distance of four miles from the point of attack, and finding that the enemy was entirely overthrown, I ordered my men to the encampment.

"The number of prisoners taken and brought into camp in small parties amounted to thirty four, seven of whom escaped during a stampede of our horses on a very dark night, besides three I left behind.

"I instituted an examination into the number slain, and from the best information, there were 48 killed upon the ground and 80 killed and drowned in the river. This number is considered by the troops as being too small an estimate of the number actually killed and destroyed in the engagement. I had two men

Moore's Great Victory—Charging the Village

1. Ben McCulloch  2.  Henry McCulloch
3.  Col. John C. Hays "Jack",  and
4.  "Jack" Hays as a Regular in 1840

slightly wounded, Mr. Dougherty of Colorado county, and Mr. M. F. Jones of Fayette—two horses were also wounded in the engagement.

"At 10 o'clock my troops had all returned. I then ordered the village to be destroyed by fire, and in fifteen minutes the whole encampment, with all property of every description, including more than three hundred saddles, and a large number of skins of various kinds was in flames.

"I then ordered the troops to march, assigning a sufficient guard to herd and drive the immense caballado of horses which had been captured from the enemy, in number about five hundred, and then turned my course for this place, marching by the position where I had left my beef cattle. After herding my cattle, I marched about six miles and encamped for the night. The weather on my return was unfavorable—had to lie in camp two days on account of the north winds and rain. The distance from the city of Austin to the battle ground, I estimate at full three hundred miles, and from the best information I have been able to obtain from the Lipan Chief, and those of the Seratic tribe of Indians with whom we met, I would say that we penetrated more than half way to the city of Santa Fe. Upon my return, near the old Mission of San Saba, I fell in with a small party of Indians of the Seratic tribe, fifteen in number. After a consultation held between them and Castro, the Lipan chief, I concluded to bring in two of their captains, as they appeared friendly and desirous to treat with us, and to aid us in our wars with the Comanches, with whom they are also hostile. They represent their tribe as residing in the vicinity of the Rio Grande, between Santa Fe and Chihuahua, and that they have about eight hundred warriors.

"Two sprightly Mexican youths, between the ages of fourteen and sixteen, were recaptured during the battle, whom the Comanches had made captives in the vicinity of Camargo, on the Rio Grande, about three months since.

"Great credit is due Castro and his men, seventeen in number, who acted as spies during the campaign. They proved faithful and active throughout, and the Government should be

particular in retaining their friendship, for as spies, they are
unsurpassed.

"In conclusion, let me remark that too much credit cannot
be awarded to the officers of my command for their gallant and
officer-like conduct and bearing during the entire campaign,
and particularly during the engagement. And it affords me the
greatest pleasure to inform your Department of the manner in
which both officers and privates discharged their duties, always
ready and ever willing to obey any order however arduous the
performance might be.

"My men have returned in good health and fine spirits,
though much fatigued.

I have the honor to remain,
Your most obedient servant,
John H. Moore,
Col. Commanding Volunteers"
—Austin City Gazette, Nov. 11, 1840

* * * * *

October 21, Col. A. Somerville wrote to Capt. A. Neill
regarding the proposed grand expedition against the Indians in
November. He said that he had been informed that Neill intended to raise a company, and requests him to muster and
organize it and report with the command by November 10, at
Fort Dunnington, on Brushy Creek, the rendezvous designated
by Maj. Gen. Felix Huston.

Thomas G. Stubblefield, Texas government agent for the
Alabamas and Cooshatties, says in a letter* dated November 2,
addressed to Secretary of State, Abner S. Lipscomb, that those
Indians were on the reservation set apart for them and were well
pleased; but, that the survey of the lands, while in progress, was
not completed.

The Austin City Gazette of November 11, publishes a
nicely worded note, signed by a number of leading citizens

* Army Archives.

inviting Col. John H. Moore and men (who had returned from an Indian expedition and were camped near town) to attend a barbecue which would be given in their honor Monday, November 16; and, also, Col. Moore's reply extending thanks to the committee and citizens for the invitation, but saying that most of his men had been away from their families for a long time and were anxious to get home and he and his command were, therefore, unable to accept the invitation.

Nothing further seems to have been done toward launching into the wilds the "grand expedition" that had been so much discussed.

* * * * *

The work done by Moore and his followers was of such a thorough nature and so far reaching in its effects, that it was doubtless deemed unnecessaray to go to the expense and trouble of other expeditions for awhile.

On Gilleland Creek, in Travis county, July 4, a party of Indians killed and scalped a negro girl, who belonged to Mr. Clipton. She was driving cows home and hollowed at them. Her cries attracted the attention of the Indians, who crept toward her through the tall grass unperceived and shot her without warning.

Usually Indians did not kill negro slaves, but held them for large ransoms, which they seldom, or never, failed to get. In this instance, and in some others, the love of blood was stronger with them than the love of gain. When circumstances were such as to preclude the savages from holding negroes for ransom, the darkies were killed, and generally scalped, like other victims.

## INDIAN TROUBLES ALONG RED RIVER.

Shifting the scene of conflict—the bloody warfare between the red men and whites was being waged all along the frontiers—we will give some incidents that transpired in the extreme northern part of the Republic. The following as related by that early pioneer and historian of that section, the late Judge

J. P. Simpson:

"In the winter and spring of 1839 and '40 the citizens at Fort Inglish, Warren and Preston moved home to the Fort with the determination to defend themselves and property against the forays of the Indians, the effort of the government having proved abortive to give protection to these settlers, on account of its lack of men and resources adequate for the purpose. The president was opposed to a war policy, and favoring pacific and treaty measures, instructed the officers and requested the citizens to use their influence and energy in collecting detached and broken tribes of Indians then scattered over the Republic, in order that they might be treated with, and reservations of land be granted them for settlement. Dr. D. Rowlett, congressman from this district, had collected a small part of a tribe of Cooshattees at his place on Red River, and had the oversight of them until they could be provided for by the government.

"Daniel Dugan, who lived some miles southwest of Warren, was often annoyed by the Indians. His son, Daniel, was killed by them while at work a short distance from the house. His house was attacked at night, one man killed and another wounded. The circumstances and incidents of the killing I will more minutely detail. Three young men—Green, Hoover and Gordon—were occupying one room of the house, the old man Dugan and family the other room, and G. C. Dugan (who died recently in California) and his brother, William, occupied the stable loft to guard their horses. The young men had retired to bed (the family had not retired) when the Indians suddenly forced open the door of the room in which the young men were sleeping, and discharged a number of shots into the bed, killing Green, wounding Hoover, and then rushed into the house. Gordon seized the door-shutter and with force closed the door, throwing the Indians to the outside, where the dogs attacked them, and they commenced shooting the dogs, and the old man Dugan shooting at them as fast as he could, and they at him in the house with his family. During this dangerous, exciting, conflict, George and William were not idle spectators of the surroundings. The moon was shining very brightly and they had discovered an Indian who had set his gun at the door, and during the fight at the house had been working at the lock trying to get the horses out. He was in such a position, however, that those in the loft could not shoot him. After the fight was over at the house two Indians came up to the stable with lariats on their necks, when the Dugans let them have the contents of their guns. One of the Indians fell dead and the other ran a short distance and fell, uttering savage groans in his dying agonies. The Indian at the stable door then ran off, leaving his gun. The Indians then began to blow on their whistles and hoot like owls, as a signal to rally and get together.

"Next morning the dead Indian was found to have on a calico hunting shirt which Dr. Rowlett had given him, and the gun at the door proved to belong to the Cooshattee chief who lived at Dr. Rowlett's. Catherine, the youngest daughter of Daniel Dugan, had solemnly vowed when her brother, Daniel, was killed, scalped, and tomahawked, that she would cut off the head of the first Indian she got a chance at. She accordingly shouldered an ax and marched to the stable, as bold as an experienced and adroit surgeon going to dissect a subject, with a few direct blows severed the head from the body and carried it to the house as a trophy of revenge for the murder of her brother. The headless body was left as food for beasts of prey. I saw the skull about the house years after.

The old lady Dugan was a very smart, industrious economical, domestically inclined woman, much more so than women of today. She spun her thread, wove her cloth and made her own wearing apparel. She found use for the Indian skull as one of the fixtures to her loom as a quill gourd and had it attached accordingly. Catherine married a Methodist preacher, B. W. Taylor, and moved to California."

---

## FATE OF A PIONEER FAMILY—OTHER TRAGEDIES.

The following incidents occurred during 1840, but the exact

dates have not been preserved:

Dr. Hunter and family—consisting of his wife, nearly grown son, three daughters (aged respectively, about ten, twelve and eighteen years), and negro woman—located in the Red River valley at a point about eight miles below Old Warren and several miles from any neighbor. Subsequently his eldest daughter married William Lankford of Warren and settled at another place. Sometime thereafter Dr. Hunter and his son left home. During their absence his ten and twelve year old daughters were attacked at the spring, about a hundred yards from the house, and one of them killed and scalped, and the other taken prisoner by eleven Indians. The Indians crept to the house and rushed into it and killed Mrs. Hunter and the negro woman, and scalped the former, but not the latter. They then looted the premises, and were just disappearing from view, when young Hunter returned. He called to his mother, but received no reply, and running through the open doorway, stumbled over her lifeless and mangled body. The little girl was compelled by the Indians to dress her own mother's scalp. Six months, or a year, later she was sold to friendly Choctaws and, her brother learning of the fact, went to the Nation and ransomed her.

McIntrye and his family located near Shawneetown in what is now Grayson county; but being annoyed by the Indians, moved to what is known as McIntyre's crossing on the Chotaw, in the same county. Moody, who resided in the same region, started to Warren on business and at dusk, when opposite McIntyre's house, was shot and killed by Indians, who scalped him, built a bon-fire and laid his body on it, and danced and yelled around the pyre all night. McIntyre and his two sons, the latter aged respectively twelve and fourteen years, plainly heard the noise, and barricaded the doors of their cabin, expecting to be attacked. Some months later his sons were killed and scalped while hunting.

Two brothers, named Sewell, living at Old Warren, heard a noise in their horse lot at night and one of them went out to investigate. When near the lot, a voice called to him, saying:

"Lay the gap lower." Believing that white thieves were trying to steal the stock, he exclaimed: "I've caught you!"

A moment later he was struck in the breast by an arrow. He ran to the house, exclaiming as he passed his brother: "I am shot," and, staggering on a few feet further, fell dead. The Indian who killed him pursued him closely; but being confronted by the other Sewell, halted and was in the act of discharging an arrow at his new antagonist when he was fired on and killed by the surviving brother.

Moody, the McIntyre boys, and young Sewell were believed to have been killed by Shawnees, but the white people were not able to confirm the suspicion by proof. For their part, the Shawnees disclaimed having committed the murders, and charged them to "wild Indians."

## SAVING OSBORN'S SCALP.

Claiborne and Lee Osborn, James Hamilton and several other young men separated while buffalo hunting—Claiborne Osborn and James Hamilton going in one direction and their companions in another. Indians attacked and pursued Osborn and Hamilton, badly wounding the horse of Osborn. The young men galloped from the spot toward where their comrades could be found; but had gone only a short distance when Osborn's horse fell throwing him heavily to the ground. Hamilton kept on, reached the other hunters, and dashed back to the rescue with them. They arrived barely in time to save Osborn's life. He was lying where he fell. Indians were all around him, beating and stabbing him, and had partly removed his scalp. A fusilade from the party sent the Indians scurrying to the cedar brakes. Osborn's scalp was carefully replaced and, in time, healed. He settled near Webberville, Travis county, where he lived many years and reared a large and respectable family.

Kenny says: "From a fierce raid on Bastrop the trail of retreat led through Burleson county. . . . They (the Indians) were pursued by Gen. Burleson with a party of citizens, and seven Indians killed. Around Austin . . . the predatory incursions continued without cessation, the Wacos and Comanches chiefly dividing the responsibility."

"At Fort Inglish, . . . two boys named Cox were captured. The Indians were chased, but made good their escape, carrying away the captives. On the way, they killed a one-armed man and cut off his remaining arm, which at night they roasted and ate, making signs to the boys that they would soon eat them also. But they did not, and six months afterwards the boys were purchased by traders and sent home."*

* * * * *

The year closed with a large portion of Texas conquered from the savage foes of settlement and civilization, and further redemption of the wilderness assured. It is remarkable that so much should have been accomplished when the public treasury was empty, the Republic unable to borrow money, and the paper currency of Texas was circulated with difficulty at only a small fraction of its nominal value. The only explanation is that both government and people co-operated loyally for the attainment of the object in view, and looked to the future, instead of the present, for reward—a sane prescience and valiant optimism that hastened increase of population, wealth and security as nothing else could have done.

Casting up the account today, it can be truthfully said the price was none too great for that which it obtained for those who paid it, and for those who have come after them.

* Scarff's "Comprehensive History of Texas."

# CHAPTER XIV.

he year 1841 has been treated by Texas historians as one practically free from Indian atrocities and serious depredations—a fact due to their not having access to archives and other sources of information that are now available. While the list of horrors perpetrated by the vanishing race—still strong enough to strike, and with hatred and sanguinary impulses intensified rather than diminished by what it had suffered—was not so long and gruesome as those of some former years, it was still of an extent to harrow the sympathies and make the blood run cold, and requires the year to be marked in red in the annals of the commonwealth.

The struggle for mastery was yet on, and was prosecuted by the Anglo-Americans with a courage and a resolution that came down to them from Senlac, Agincourt and Crecy, and that has ever caused them to reject from the hands of Fortune anything save victory and dominion, when waging contests for supremacy. The reader will therefore find that the incidents of border warfare in Texas in 1841, are not inferior in interest to those that preceded them.

## INTERNAL AFFAIRS—INDIAN HOSTILITIES.

The Fifth Congress passed a joint resolution, approved Jan. 6, 1841, providing "That the sum of $10,000.00 which was appropriated for the purpose of volunteer expeditions against the hostile Indians on the upper Brazos river be, and the same is hereby, transferred for the purpose of raising and subsisting any force that the President may authorize to be raised for said expedition."

An act of Congress, approved January 18, abolished the office of Secretary of the Navy and devolved the duties of that office on the Secretary of War, who was afterwards sometimes addressed by his former title but more often and correctly as Secretary of War and Marine. The act abolished, or consolidated, various other offices; required the President to reduce the number of officers holding commissions in the regular army, and provided that all further recruiting for the army should be discontinued.

The Travis Guards, a uniformed company, were incorporated by an act approved January 23.

January 23, Capt. John T. Price, who had just completed a scout to the west with his spy company, sent a despatch* to the Secretary of War, containing such information as he could gather concerning the intention of Mexico to invade Texas—an event that was then deemed certain to occur during the spring, or summer, but which was prevented by a series of fortuitous circumstances, that befriended Texas, as it had been several times before. He said that it was reported that an army of 10,000 men was being mobilized and that it would be reinforced by each of the Mexican states furnishing 2,000 men.

The Galveston Artillery Company, a uniformed company, was incorporated by an act of Congress, approved Jan. 30.

An act, approved Feb. 1, appropriated $8,000.00 for the support of troops then on the frontier under the command of Col. Wm. G. Cooke.

An act approved February 4, 1841, authorized the settlers on the frontier borders of each of the following counties to organize a company of not less than twenty nor more than fifty-six minute men, rank and file: Fannin, Lamar, Red River, Bowie, Paschal, Panola, Nacogdoches, Houston, Robertson, Milam, Travis, Bexar, Gonzales, Goliad, Victoria, Refugio, San Patricio, Montgomery and Bastrop. The companies were to

* Army Archives.

elect their own officers and hold themselves in readiness to afford a ready and active protection to the frontier settlements. The act provided: "The members of said companies shall at all times be prepared with a good substantial horse, bridle and saddle, with other necessary accoutrements, together with a good gun and one hundred rounds of ammunition; and in addition to this, when called into service, such number of rations as the captain may direct. . . . The captains . . . may, when they deem it prudent, detail from their companies a number of spies, not more than five, to act upon the frontiers of their several counties."

Members of the companies were exempted from the payment of state, county and corporation poll tax and the tax assessed by law upon one saddle horse, and from the performance of any kind of military duty and working on the public roads.

The pay provided for each minute man was one dollar per day for service actually rendered; "provided," says the act, "that the members of the companies shall not receive pay on any one expedition for a longer period than fifteen days; and, on the several expeditions within one year after their organization, shall not receive pay for a longer period than four months in the aggregate, excepting the spies, for every year thereafter . . . ."

Possibly about this time (the date is uncertain) a number of settlers, who had come to Warren, Fannin county, to attend district court, which was to convene the following day, were gathered Sunday night around a stove in a tavern kept by Capt. Sowell and J. S. Scott, and were industriously engaged in stowing toddies and talking. They were suddenly startled by a commotion in the stable and horse lot of the tavern, and rushed out into the darkness and toward the spot—most of them neglecting to take their firearms with them. As they surmised they would, they found that Indians were attempting to steal the stock. Capt. Sowell, who was in front, fired his pistol at the marauders, without effect, and was himself shot and instantly killed, one arrow penetrating his stomach and another entering his back and coming out in front. Scott killed an Indian, and the balance of the redskins took to their heels. The district court organized, but immediately adjourned and the judge, lawyers and litigants started for home, upon a scout informing them he had discovered the trail of a large band of Indians going in the direction of Fort Inglish. Capt. Bird, ____ Simpson and several others waited until night to set forth, and had gone but a short distance when they stopped for Capt. Bird to recover his hat, which had fallen off. While he was looking for it, a number of Indians ran toward the party, yelling and shooting arrows. Simpson fired his shot gun at them and cried in a stentorian voice, as if addressing a company of rangers: "Charge!" The effect on the Indians was magical; they tore into the woods as if Jack Hays, himself, was after them, and the travelers wended their way toward where they were going, possibly without wasting time on the hat or complimenting Simpson on his ready, resourceful wit.

January 9, Judge James Smith and son, of Austin, the latter mounted behind the Judge on a horse, were pursued by Indians near the capital. Father and son were well mounted and might have escaped, but for the fact that, riding under a tree they were knocked off by one of the limbs. Scrambling to their feet, they ran into a thicket; but were pursued by the Indians, who killed and scalped Judge Smith, and took the boy into captivity. On the same day a brother of Judge Smith was chased by Indians, but escaped by the fleetness of his horse. Ten days later Judge Smith's father-in-law, while cutting a bee-tree four miles south of Austin, was killed and scalped by Indians.

In a despatch dated January 10, Capt. Benjamin T. Gilliam, of the 1st Infantry, commandant at San Antonio, says that Capt. Jack Hays and his spy company were on a scout toward the Nueces and Rio Grande, and a report was daily expected from him, and that Mexican banditti, who infested the Mexican border and preyed upon ranches and traders, had committed thefts of horses and cattle.

## OFFICIAL REPORTS OF BORDER DOINGS.

Capt. Geo. M. Dolson of Travis County Minute Men made the following report* to Secretary of War Branch T. Archer, April 2:

"I have the honor to report that the company of minute men, under my command, was organized on the 28th ult. On the 29th I sent Lt. Newcomb and two men to reconnoitre Brushy, who returned the next day and reported a fresh trail of Indians leading towards Austin. A portion of my men were soon mounted, and accompanied by some volunteers, went in immediate pursuit. We were unsuccessful in finding these Indians, but discovered the trail of the party who had stolen Capt. Brown's horse a few nights previous. We followed the trail and succeeded in gaining their vicinity, a few miles above the Pedernales river. Here I ordered a halt for the purpose of refreshing our horses, having traveled about sixty miles in twenty-four hours over a mountainous country. I sent out my spies (mounted on the best horses) who returned, bringing into camp three of the enemy's caballado and reporting fresh signs in the Colorado bottom. At midnight we were in our saddles and again upon their trail, with the hope of discovering their camp and attacking them at dawn; but the darkness of the night prevented. Having halted again for a short time, we continued our route. At daybreak we discovered their horses, and a few minutes afterwards found ourselves upon their camp. The action commenced, on the part of the Indians, by a rapid discharge of rifles. We immediately charged, and drove them from their camp. Twice they rallied, under orders of their chief, who acted with considerable bravery; but nothing could stop the impetuosity of my men, and the Indians broke in every direction, leaving us in possession of their camp. The nature of the ground would not admit the operation of cavalry, but we pursued them a short distance on foot. They were suffered to escape, however, bearing off their wounded, the number of

* Army Archives.

which could not be ascertained, and leaving their chief and seven others dead on the field. We returned from the chase, burned their bows and arrows, and destroyed the camp. We arrived in town last night, bringing the horse that had been stolen from Captain Brown. I am happy to say, none of my men were wounded. I, myself, received in the commencement of the chase, one shot in my breast and one in my thigh. My horse was also shot through the neck. After being shot, I continued the chase on foot until so completely exhausted I could neither proceed further nor command my men. At this instant, Captain Daniels came gallantly to my aid, and called to the men, 'For God's sake,' not to permit the charge to end! At this I was satisfied and desisted from further efforts to proceed. The men under Captain Daniels continued the charge until the Indians were dispersed. The Indians numbered about thirty-five."

## BEN McCULLOCH ROUTS PARTY OF INDIANS.

Early in May, Capt. Ben McCulloch and fifteen companions (Arthur Swift, James H. Callahan, Wilson Randell, Green McCoy, Eli T. Hankins, Archibald Gipson, W. A. Hall, Henry E. McCulloch, James Roberts, Jeremiah Roberts, Thos. R. Nichols, Capt. Wm. Tomlinson, William P. Kincannon, Alsey S. Miller and William Morrison) marching from Gonzales to the principal mountain tributary of the Guadalupe,and thence to where Johnson's Fork of the Llano empties into the latter stream, surprised and attacked an encampment of twenty-two Indians at dawn. Five Indians were killed, and half the remainder wounded. They lost everything except the arms they had in their hands. Some of the same Indians had stolen horses at Gonzales. McCulloch did not pursue them immediately thereafter, as there would have been little probability of overtaking them. He waited for several days, so that they would believe that no pursuit was intended and relax their vigilance. The result attested the wisdom of the plan adopted.

## SERVICES OF CHANDLER'S RANGING
## COMPANY.

Capt. Eli Chandler, of the Robertson County Minute Men, writing to Secretary of War Branch T. Archer, from Franklin, April 16, 1841, says:

"I beg leave to report that the company of minute men under my command was organized on the 29th of March. . . . Upon the evening of the 9th of April I received information that an Indian enemy had killed Mr. Stephen Rogers, Jr., and had driven away eight head of horses from the easterly side of the Navasota River. I immediately collected twenty-five of my men and, by a forced march, was enabled to come up with two of them about 11 o'clock a.m. of the 11th inst., at the distance of two miles, moving the stolen horses. . . . I immediately gave chase at full speed for the distance of seven miles and . . . recovered all of the horses . . . and took one from the enemy. I am sorry to say that, from the jaded condition of our horses and the start which they had, they were able to elude us. While we must regret their escape, it affords me pleasure to say that, from the perseverance manifested on the march and in the chase by every man under my command, I believe that nothing is wanting on the part of this command but a fair opportunity, to sustain that character for chivalry which is always anticipated from Texas citizens."

Further supplementing his report to the Secretary of War, Captain Chandler says: "On the 16th inst. I received information from spies that they had accidentally met Messrs. Hardesty and Porter, who had been despatched by Col. Thos. I. Smith and B. J. Chambers (who were on a surveying expedition) to inform me that they had discovered the appearance of a body of Indians on Pecan Creek, a tributary of the Trinity River, at the distance of about one hundred miles from this place. I forthwith took up the line of march with forty-five men of my command, and was joined on the march by Thos. I. Smith and Mr. Branch (both of Milam county), B. J. Chambers, C. M. Winkler, John Copeland, F. Flint and M. M. Ferguson, as volunteers, making the aggregate force fifty-three.

"On the morning of the 20th, by traveling all of the preceding night, I was able to gain a position in the neighborhood of the . . . Indians, and believing that we had not been discovered, I concealed my men and despatched reconnoitering parties, which resulted in Lieut. Love reporting his having found, down the Creek a few miles, a deserted village, which had been visited within a few days by the enemy. But the lateness of the hour induced me to remain until the dawn of the next morning, at which time we took up the line of march for the deserted village. Having proceeded about five miles, we discovered at the distance of three hundred yards, eight or ten of the enemy, . . . immediately gave chase, and pursued them about three miles in a contrary direction, as we afterwards learned, from their village, but by their superior knowledge of the woods, they evaded us. I then retrograded to hunt the deserted village, which we found, containing twenty-eight lodges, and also a trail, which we pursued. At the distance of one mile we discovered our former foe, on the same trail. I immediately charged with all my force at full speed on the path, which ran on a ridge not more than three hundred or four hundred yards wide, enclosed on each side by two creeks running nearly parallel, and on each side of which was an extended bottom, grown up with underwood so as to be impassable for horsemen, a distance of about five miles, which brought us up with the enemy's new village, without overtaking them; but continuing directly through the camp, thereby alarming men, women and children, who all fled before we could get within gunshot distance, to almost impenetrable thickets, abandoning every vestige of their property. I had dismounted my men, leaving the captured property and our horses under charge of Lieut. Love and a detachment, and commenced scouring the bottom, and succeeded in collecting some property; and had a few shots from the enemy, which were returned with effect. During my absence Lieut. Love received a few shots, which were promptly returned with effect.

"I have only to report Col. F. I. Smith slightly wounded in the hand; three of the enemy killed, some wounded; and nine mules, twenty-three horses, some powder, lead and axes, pelts, etc., taken—all of which we estimate worth three thousand dollars.

"After burning their village and destroying everything that could be useful, which we could not transport, I took up the line of march for this place, and arrived here last night, all well."

\* \* \* \* \*

Yucatan declared its independence May 16, and engaged in war with Mexico, which gave the latter country something, besides invading Texas, to think about. This circumstance was of course fortunate for the people of Texas. Nevertheless, peace did not prevail, as the Indians were constantly plundering and murdering in all parts of the Republic, and more especially along the northern frontier during this year.

## BIRD'S FORT.

As a prelude to what follows, it must be remembered that late as 1841, Clarksville was the most westerly town of any note in the valley of Red River—there were scattered settlements in Lamar and Fannin counties; principally along the river; and a few cabins along the Sulphurs, and between these streams and Red River, high up as Fort Inglish, (near where Bonham now stands); at old Warren (in Fannin county); and the most westerly settlement at Preston, opposite the mouth of the Washita River, known as Coffee's Trading House.

Bands of hostile Indians were constantly depredating on these exposed settlements and murdering the less protected inhabitants—as their massacre of the Ripley family on Ripley's Creek, in Titus county, early in April, 1841\* and various out-

---

\* Early in April Indians attacked the Ripley family at their home on the old Cherokee trace, on Ripley Creek, in Titus county. Mr. Ripley was absent from home at the time. His son (twenty years of age) was shot and killed while plowing in the field; his eldest daughter (about sixteen years old) was shot and killed while running from the house; two younger

rages in the Warren neighborhood and elsewhere, as we shall narrate.

In the winter of 1840-41, Captain John Bird organized and led a company of three months rangers from Bowie and Red River counties, up the Trinity River, for the purpose of locating and establishing a military post, as a means of encouraging settlements in that section. At that time there was a law of the Republic donating lands for this purpose. A site was chosen, and a stockade erected, some two or three miles east of the present town of Birdville, on the Main or West fork of the Trinity, which was named Bird's Fort, but for some cause—the time of their enlistment expiring—the rangers returned home, leaving the post unoccupied. A little later Capt. Robert Sloan led a prospecting party as far out as the fort; but soon returned, one of the party, David Clubb, late of Illinois, and a soldier in the Black Hawk war of 1832, having been killed by Indians at a small lake on Elm fork of the Trinity, a short distance above its mouth, and below the Keenan crossing.

Following these expeditions, in the fall of 1841, the brave and hardy pioneers, Hamp Rattan, Captain Mabel Gilbert, and John Beeman, with their families, and a few single men, located at Bird's Fort. Expecting to find an abundance of game in the country, the settlers carried out a scant supply of provisions, but the Indians had burned off the grass from all that section, and no game of any kind was to be found. So, late in November of this year, a wagon was sent back to Red River for supplies. Being overdue, three of the settlers, Alex W. Webb, (in 1905 living at Mesquite, in Dallas county), Solomon Silkwood, and

daughters escaped by reaching and taking refuge in a thicket. Mrs. Ripley and all of her smaller children save one were beaten to death with clubs while trying to make their way to a cane brake situated two hundred yards from their cabin. The child, not with the mother, was asleep in the house and was burned to death, the Indians plundering and then setting fire to the habitation which was reduced to ashes. This horrible crime led to the organization of a retaliatory expedition, which took some time to organize in that sparsely settled section, and which was led into the Indian country by Gen. Tarrant.

Hamp Rattan, went in search of the wagon party. Reaching a point about one and a half miles south-east of the present town of Carrollton, on the east side of Elm Fork, Christmas day, they halted to cut a bee tree, when they were attacked by a small party of concealed Indians. Rattan was killed; but Webb and Silkwood, after killing one of the Indians, escaped to the fort. One of the single men now went out, and soon met the relief wagon, which reached the scene of the tragedy on the 30th of the month, where they found Rattan's body, still guarded by his faithful dog. The remains were carried to the fort, and in a rude coffin made of an old wagon bed, committed to earth. This worthy pioneer and martyr was a brother of Mrs. A. J. Witt (deceased) of Dallas county, and Mrs. W. J. Throckmorton and Mrs. Wm. Fitzhugh, of Collin county. Two of his brothers—John and Littleton Rattan participated in the Village Creek fight.

At the time of the tragedy snow was six inches deep and the weather intensely cold, and from the exposure on the trip, Silkwood sickened and died. And thus commenced the first permanent settlement on the upper waters of the Trinity.

## GENERAL TARRANT'S EXPEDITION.

General Edward Tarrant was a gallant soldier, and one of the successful leaders of volunteers and rangers in the defense of the northeastern part of Texas against Indians. He was also a brilliant and noted lawyer—long residing in Bowie county, but later removing to Ellis county, where he died. The success of the expedition which he headed against the great Indian encampment on Village Creek in 1841, was reason for attaching his name to the county embracing the theatre of his fearless exploits on that occasion., The honor conferred was well bestowed. The location of this formidable force of depredating Indians was at a point some distance east of Fort Worth, and a few miles west of the town of Arlington, a little south of where the Texas and Pacific railroad crosses Village Creek—within sight of the interurban cars that now speed to and fro every few minutes between Fort Worth and Dallas.

No full and reliable narrative of Tarrant's expedition, the Village Creek fight and tragic death of the celebrated pioneer preacher, lawyer and Indian fighter—John B. Denton—has ever before been published. The official account which follows, was recently discovered among the Army Archives in the State Library at Austin. The document was written by Acting Brigade Inspector Wm. N. Porter, under date, Bowie county, June 5, 1841, reporting to Secretary of War Branch T. Archer, and reads:

"By order of Gen. Edward H. Tarrant, Brigadier General of the Fourth Brigade Texas Militia, I communicate to you the following facts relative to an expedition which he has lately completed against the hostile Indians.

"On the 14th of May, he left Fort Johnson, above Coffee's Station (the then abandoned post, established by Wm. G. Cooke at or near the present city of Denison.—Author) with one company of men commanded by Capt. James Bourland. Owing to late depredations by Indians of a more frequent and daring character, and learning that the village of Indians had lately been discovered on the headwaters of the Trinity River, he determined, with the small number of sixty-nine men, if possible, to find the Indians and attack them. We marched five days in a direction a little south of west, passing through the lower cross-timbers, and crossing the head branches of the middle fork on the Trinity. On the fifth day we entered the upper cross-timbers and changed our direction a little more south. On the 19th we discovered tolerably fresh signs. We had every reason to believe there were Indians in the vicinity. We soon found two villages, which we found to be deserted. The Indians, at some time previous, had cultivated corn at these villages. There were some sixty or seventy lodges in these two villages. They were on the main western branch of the Trinity. They being situated on high branches of the mountains, Gen. Tarrant deemed it imprudent to burn the villages, for fear of giving alarm to the Indians. From such elevated positions the smoke could have been seen for many miles; but they were, in a great measure, destroyed with our axes. We changed our course southeast, following the course, for some distance, of the main western branch of the Trinity; and on the 21st we crossed the high divide, and that night camped on the eastern branch of the Brazos. Finding no Indian signs here, we changed our course east until we again struck the Trinity, intending to scour the western branch to its mouth. On the 24th we came to the ford of the Trinity, where Generals Rusk and Dyer charged the Kickapoo camp in 1838, in sight of the lower cross-timbers. Here we recrossed the Trinity from the eastern side to the western side, and upon the high prairies one mile from the ford, we found very fresh signs of Indians. The spies were sent ahead, and returned and reported the Indian village in three miles. We arrived in three or four hundred yards, and took up a position behind a thicket. The men were ordered to divest themselves of their blankets, packs, and all manner of incumbrances, after which the line was formed and the order given to charge into the village on horseback."

## FAMOUS VILLAGE CREEK FIGHT.

"Are you all ready? . . . Now my brave men, we will never all meet on earth again; there is a great confusion and death ahead. I shall expect every man to fill his place and do his duty" were the all too true words of admonition uttered by the grim and fearless Tarrant as he gave his orders and led his brave men in the desperate charge. In a moment the sound of firearms, with a voice of thunder, rang out over the alarmed and terror-stricken inhabitants of that rude city of the wilderness. The onslaught was fierce and the surprise complete—the Indians falling in death before they could escape from their lodges, or fleeing in wild confusion. "The village was taken in an instant," says the official report, which we now resume:

"Discovering a large trail leading down the creek and some of the Indians having gone in that direction, a few men were left at the last village and the rest at full speed took their course down the creek upon which the village was situated.

"Two miles from the first village we burst suddenly upon

another village. This was taken like the first. There was another village in sight below. Many of the horses having failed, the men ran towards the village on foot; but the Indians, having heard the firing at the second village, had time to take off their guns and ammunition and commenced occasionally to return our fire.

"From this time there was no distinction of villages, but one continuous village for the distance of one mile and a half, only separated by the creek upon which it was situated. We had now become so scattered that Gen. Tarrant deemed it advisable to establish some rallying point to which smaller parties should be expected to rally. We marched back to the second village, and the rear guard with the pack having come up, the General chose this as the position. From this point Capt. John B. Denton (aide to Gen. Tarrant) and Capt. Bourland took each ten men, for the purpose of scouring the woods. The parties went in different directions, but formed a junction one mile and a half below the second village. From this point they intended to return, but discovering a very large trail—much larger than any we had seen, one end of which led over a mountain west, the other east towards the main Trinity, crossing the creek upon which the villages were situated—they were compelled to cross the creek at the lower end of a bend which was formed like a horse-shoe. They turned to cross the creek, perceiving through the timber what appeared to be a village still larger than any they had heretofore seen; but just as the two detachments were on the eve of entering the creek, they were fired on by an enemy that could not be seen. At the first fire Gen. Tarrant's aide, Capt. Denton, was killed and Capt. Stout severely wounded—Capt. Griffin slightly; the clothes of many others were pierced with balls, but fortunately no one else was touched. Situated as they were, it was impossible to maintain their position, being fired at from almost every quarter and unable to see the enemy. In this situation the men did the best they could—dismounting, some of them raising the yell, and making every demonstration as though they intended to charge the creek. The Indian yells and firing soon ceased, and both parties left the ground. It was not the wish of Gen. Tarrant to take any prisoners. The women and children, except one,* we suffered to escape, if they wished, and the men neither asked, gave or received any quarter.

"From the prisoners whom we had taken, we learned that at those villages there were upwards of one thousand warriors, not more than half of whom were then at home. The other half were hunting buffalo, and stealing on the frontier. Here was the depot for the stolen horses from our frontier, and the home of the horrible savages who had murdered our families. They were portions of a good many tribes—principally the Cherokees who were driven from Nacogdoches county, some Creeks and Seminoles, Wacos, Caddos, Kickapoos, Anadarcos, etc. We counted two hundred and twenty-five lodges, all in occupation, besides those that they could see a glimpse of through the trees in the main village. They had about three hundred acres in corn, that we saw; and were abundantly provided with ammunition of every kind. They had good guns and had moulded a great many bullets. Each lodge had two or three little bags of powder and lead, tied up in equal portions; and, at one lodge, a sort of blacksmith shop, where we found a set of blacksmith's tools. We found over a half bushel of moulded bullets, and we also found some sergeant's swords, musket flints, rifle and musket powder, pig lead, and musket balls, which we supposed that they must have taken from the place where the regular army buried a portion of their ammunition. They had all manner of farming utensils of the best quality, except plows. In some of the lodges we found feather beds and bedsteads.

"We felt convinced if the Indians could ascertain the smallness of our numbers, they might, with so great a number, by taking advantage of us at the crossing of the creeks with such immense thickets in their bottoms, which we were compelled to cross, if not defeat, at least cut off a great many of our men; and, if we had remained at the village all night, it would have given the Indians time to have concentrated their forces, ascertained

---

* Gen. Tarrant kept an Indian child that was captured, but returned it to its mother at a council held in the Indian Territory in 1842.

our numbers, and with ease have prevented our crossing a stream of the size of the Trinity. It was deemed advisable, therefore, to take up the line of march and cross the Trinity that night. At 5 o'clock with our poor, dead companion tied across a horse, we left the village, marched twelve miles back on the trail we came, crossed the Trinity, and camped in the open prairie. The next morning, twenty-five miles from the village, we buried our friend,* and in five more days we arrived in the settlements.

"We had one killed; one badly, and one slightly wounded. The Indians had twelve killed, that we counted; and a great many more must have been killed and wounded, from the quantity of blood we saw on their trails and in the thickets where they had run.

"We brought in six head of cattle, thirty-seven horses, three hundred pounds of lead, thirty pounds of powder, twenty brass kettles, twenty-one axes, seventy-three buffalo robes, fifteen guns, thirteen pack saddles, and three swords, besides divers other things not recollected."

## DEATH OF DENTON.

But little can be added to the foregoing. A few words anent the tragic death of the noble Captain Denton. During the terrible engagement in which Denton was killed, the brave old pioneer Indian fighter, Capt. John Yeary, called out at the top of his voice: "Why in the h—l don't you move your men out where we can see the enemy? We'll all be killed here." To which Captain Henry Stout, himself a brave and noted pioneer leader and Indian fighter, said: "Men, do the best you can for yourselves. I am wounded and powerless," and at once an irregular retreat began. The detachment had fallen into an ambuscade.

---

* Accounts differ as to the name of the creek where Denton was first buried. One that it was on a rock ridge in Fossil Creek bottom near where Birdville now stands, and another that it was on a bluff of Oliver Creek in Denton county.

The shot that pierced Denton was so deadly that there was evidently no death struggle. He had balanced himself in his saddle, raised his gun, and closed one eye, intending to deal death upon the enemy when the death shock struck him. When his death was discovered his muscles were gradually relaxing, and his gun, yet in his hand, was inclining to the ground. The men nearest to him took him from his horse and laid him on the ground.

The late venerated pioneer, Rev. Andrew Davis, then a lad, who participated in the Village Creek battle, says: "After tenderly wrapping the body of Denton and securing it on a gentle horse, about 4:30 p.m., we moved out from the village, and up the river to a point near Fort Worth, and there spent the night. Early next morning we crossed the river at a place where the timber was narrow. After crossing the river, we traveled in the direction of Bird's Station, aiming for Bonham—then Fort Inglish—as our objective point. At about 11 a.m. we halted on a prairie on the south side of a creek, with a high bank on the north. On one of those elevations Captain Denton was buried— tools having been brought along from the village for that purpose. His grave was dug a good depth. A thin rock was cut so as to fit in the bottom of the grave, similar rocks being placed at the sides and also at the head and foot. Another rock was placed over the body, and the grave filled up. Thus was buried one of God's noblemen." And so perished one of Texas' brainiest and best men, a fine orator, far above the average in intellect, and, had he lived, would have proved a blessing to his country and assisted materially in its advancement—

"The pioneer was laid to rest,
The red man set him free,
Disturb him not, but let him sleep
Beneath the old oak-tree."*

But the precious bones of the beloved Denton were disturbed, and finally, after three quarters of a century, properly

* Wilbarger's "Indian Depredations in Texas."

honored—having been interred three times. First, by his sorrowing comrades in arms, in that lonely wilderness grave, in
May, 1841; a second time, when the pioneer cattleman of Denton
county, John Chisum, exhumed the remains and gave them
burial in his yard at the Chisum ranch, near Bolivar, in 1860; and
a third time, in 1901, when, through patriotic promptings of
members of the Old Settlers Association of Denton county, all
that remained mortal of the hero were gathered up, and after an
appropriate address by the late Rev. Wm. Allen, extolling the
deeds and illumining the character of the deceased, and amid
solemn and imposing ceremonies, the remains were laid to final
rest beneath a suitably inscribed slab, in the court house yard at
Denton,the capital town of that fair county, each of which, as
well as the principal stream which courses through that county,
and an institution of learning, were named for and will ever
perpetuate the memory of one of the bravest and noblest defenders of the Texas frontier.

## OTHER EXPEDITIONS AGAINST THE INDIANS.

June 13, 1841, Brig. Gen. James Smith, 3rd Brigade, Texas
Militia, wrote from Nacogdoches to President Lamar, saying
that Major Gage and his spy company had attacked a party of
fifteen Indians and pursued the survivors, eight in number, and
ambushed them at the crossing of the Trinity, where they killed
seven of them—only one of the fifteen escaping.

Capt. Eli Chandler, in a report* dated June 19, 1841, gives
an account of an expedition to the northwest boundary of the
cross-timbers, on the divide between the Brazos and Trinity
rivers, from which he had just returned with a command of
forty-one men. Near the point specified, he captured a young
Mexican who conducted him to an Indian village from which
the warriors were absent. On the way to and in, the village, he
took fourteen prisoners. One of these informed him that sixty

---

* Army Archives.

Death of Capt. John B. Denton

Houston's Indian Pow Wow

warriors were to meet at the village to go on a hunt. Thereupon, he despatched an aged woman to tell her people to bring in the American prisoners they had, and the Indian prisoners would be released and a friendly compact entered into. Continuing, he says: "I then proceeded immediately to where I left my baggage, where I arrived about 1 o'clock p.m. The party of warriors above spoken of, to the number of sixty, had arrived early in the day and attacked my baggage guard, who retreated a short distance to a ravine, took position and by their union and valor, succeeded in driving back the enemy with the loss of their chief and one other killed. The whole number of Indians killed were four, and three or four wounded. None of my command received the slightest injury from the enemy. He says that he abandoned further pursuit as his force was small and he had the prisoners to guard, and returned to Franklin. He asks instructions as to what he shall do with the prisoners. He says: "The Mexican prisoner taken is a young man of smart intelligence—speaks the English language quite well—states that he has been living among the Choctaws—was among these Indians trading—says they were principally Ionies, some Shawnees, a few Wacos; that the Wacos and Cherokees live not far distant; that the Tehuacanas, Caddos, Kickapoos, etc., all make corn between the Brazos and Trinity rivers; that many of them live at what is called the Big Bend Village on the Brazos, which he says is about twenty miles above where the Americans were last winter; that all of the different tribes talk of getting together and living at one place; that there is some little talk among them of making peace with the Americans; that they are generally nearly destitute of provisions and have great difficulty in obtaining the same; that they say they obtain their large quantities of lead by finding it buried in the upper country; says he can take us to several encampments. I expect to make another expedition as soon as my horses recruit, if circumstances should indicate the same."*

* From July 15th to 20th between four hundred and five hundred volunteers from the Texas side of the Red River assembled at Fort Inglish for the purpose of another expedition into the Indian country. They organized by

## THE SANTA FE EXPEDITION.

The Santa Fe expedition, recommended by the Secretary of War and sanctioned by President Lamar, left Brushy Creek, near Austin, June 20, 1841, to traverse six hundred miles of wilderness to Santa Fe. It was commanded by Brig. Gen. Hugh McLeod, brother-in-law of President Lamar and consisted of five companies of mounted infantry and an artillery company with one brass six-pounder (a total of two hundred and seventy soldiers), about fifty other persons (traders, teamsters and adventurers), and Wm. G. Cooke, R. F. Brenham, and J. A. Navarro, commissioners instructed to say to the people of Santa Fe that, if they were willing to acknowledge that portion of New Mexico as a part of Texas, the laws of the Republic would be extended over them but if they did not, Texas wished to establish friendly commercial relations with them and would not use force to assert its territorial claims. President Lamar had previously issued a proclamation covering the same ground and declaring the objects of the expedition to be wholly pacific.

Friends of the enterprise had introduced a bill in Congress, authorizing it, but the measure had been rejected by both houses. It was, therefore without statutory warrant, and was undertaken solely upon executive responsibility. The only legal sanction that could be claimed for it was that the act of 1836, defining the boundaries of Texas, included Santa Fe in the limits of the Republic and it was the duty of the President to enforce the sovereign jurisdiction asserted.

It is said that the season selected for the undertaking was too late and as a consequence, there was much suffering for

electing William C. Young, colonel; James Bourland, lieutenant colonel; John Smither, adjutant, and William Lane, David Key, and others, captains. While this was transpiring Indians captured two little boys on the Bois d'Arc fork of river, a few miles distant, and carried them off. The children were recovered about two years later. Gen. Tarrant assumed command of the expedition. It moved southward into what is Wise county, and received news of its coming returned to Fort Inglish and disbanded.

want of grass and water. The wagons were overloaded, the distance to Santa Fe was under-estimated, and the guides were unfamiliar with the route. There seems to have been a fatal combination of circumstances, that foredoomed the expedition to the humiliating disasters and tragic sufferings it encountered. Not knowing what awaited it, it started forth in the gayest spirits and with the most sanguine expectations. "The long train of wagons," says George Wilkins Kendall, "moving heavily forward with the different companies of volunteers, all well mounted and well armed and riding in double file, presented an imposing as well as animating spectacle, causing every heart to beat high with the anticipation of exciting incidents on the boundless prairies."

Finally reaching New Mexico, after much suffering and many adventures, the advance troops of the Santa Fe Expedition under Col. Wm. G. Cooke, were induced, by treacherous representations, to lay down their arms and surrender to Commandant Col. Salazar, in New Mexico, on Sept. 17th, 1841. The remainder of the expedition followed. The prisoners were marched on foot to the interior, (some perishing on the long journey) where many of them were imprisoned in gruesome and foul dungeons in the City of Mexico, and other at Puebla and Perote. News of the disaster to and fate of this expedition was not received in Texas until in January, 1842. Some of the unfortunate men were released at the instance of Gen. Andrew Jackson and other friends in position to intercede for clemency; some died in prison, and the remaining survivors, 119 in number, were eventually all released by order of Gen. Santa Anna, June 13, 1843.

## BATTLE IN CANON DE UVALDE.

In June, 1841, Capt. Jack Hays having slightly augmented his company, pursued and defeated a depredating party of Comanches near Uvalde Canyon, the particulars of which are given thus in his official report:

San Antonio, July 1, 1841

To the Hon. Branch T. Archer, Secretary of War:

I have the honor to inform you that I have this morning returned from an expedition in pursuit of a party of Indians that had been committing depredations, and driving off stock from the vicinity of this place. On the 24th of this month I set out with a company of thirty men, and took the trail which led in the direction of the Canyon de Uvalde. When within two miles of the entrance of the canyon, we came upon a party of Indians, on their way from the main camp of the vicinity of this town. I immediately attacked them and succeeded in killing eight, and taking the two other prisoners,* capturing all their horses and property. I would have continued on to their main camp, but as my horses were much jaded, and I found the camp more distant than I expected, I concluded to return, and after recruiting proceeded to the encampment, the situation of which I have ascertained. But one of my command was wounded—Mr. Miller—and he not severely. The company consisted of sixteen Americans. In addition I was aided by Captain Flores, with about twenty Mexicans.

I have the honor to be your obedient servant,
JOHN C. HAYS
Captain Commanding.

---

* To take a Comanche prisoner was an affair of great difficulty. One reason was the fact that the Indian rule of warfare was opposed to letting a captive live longer than certain ceremonies could be performed. In some instances they seem to make an exhibit of the captured persons to the tribe or nation. After this was accomplished a cruel and lingering torture was inflicted. It is reasonable to suppose that the Comanches believed that the whites inflicted similar outrages and similar death upon the Indian prisoners.

## BORDER BANDITTI.

John T. Price wrote to Secretary of War and Marine Branch T. Archer, from Victoria, July 2, as follows:

"In accordance with a requisition made by the Sheriff of this county and Refugio, in company with some forty citizens, went to the Nueces for the purpose of arresting the marauders who have for some time past infested our frontier.

"Our party was composed of citizens of this county, Refugio and San Patricio. We reached the Nueces on the 22nd, ult., and there learned that a short time previous a Mexican had been to Kinney's Ranch and stated that a party of 300 soldiers were within thirty-five miles of that place, under the command of Col. Verial. He stated that the troops were in search of robbers and had succeeded in surprising a party of ten and had killed them all but one. The bodies of these men were found by our party. It appears that they (the robbers) had a short time before killed a party of traders and robbed them of several hundred dollars, a lot of blankets, etc. This party of Americans was led by a Mr. Yearby who formerly resided at Austin.

"We learned also from some Mexicans recently from Camargo that Owensby, with about fifteen men, had been surrounded by two or three hundred Mexicans, and that eight or nine of his men were killed and himself and five others taken prisoners. Verial with his command had returned to the Rio Grande before our arrival at the Nueces.

"It appears from the statement made by the traders who have visited our country of late, that it is the settled purpose of the Mexican authorities not only to assert, but maintain, the control of the territory between the Nueces and Rio Grande. . . ."

Capt. Sanchez (aide de camp to Gen. Ampudia), in command of fifteen Mexican cavalrymen, made a descent upon Flower Bluff, fifteen miles south-east of Kinney's and Aubrey's ranch, and captured Phillip Dimitt, J. C. Boyd, Stephen W. Farrow and Henry Graham.

He also took $6,000.00 worth of goods that had been purchased as stock for the mercantile establishment of Dimitt,

Gurley and Farrow. Boyd and Graham were employees of Gurley and Farrow. Gurley was absent from the Bluff at the time the raid was made. Sanchez did not disturb the store of Kinney and Aubrey, which led Gurley and others to entertain and give expression to opinions that were perhaps unjust. Gurley writing* to Secretary Archer from Gonzales, said that indignation meetings had been held at Victoria, Lamar, Gonzales and other towns, and the people were willing and eager to turn out en masse, make good the claims of Texas to the territory between the Nueces and Rio Grande, and inflict retaliation on Mexico for injuries suffered; that they waited only for the Texas government to authorize them to act.

Dimitt and his companions were taken to Matamoras and thence to Monterey where they were delivered to Arista. By his order they were manacled and marched to Saltillo. On the way their irons were removed by Capt. Chaffind who commanded their guard.

At Saltillo, they made an attempt to escape. Some of them got off a considerable distance. Capt. Chaffind sent them word that he would forgive them if they returned, and if they did not, he would have Dimitt shot. This message was uttered in the presence of Dimitt, who as soon as he saw that he was unobserved, took a large dose of morphine which caused his death. Yoakum says: "Thus fell a noble spirit by whom the first Lone Star banner was unfurled on the heights of La Bahia."

## CAPTAIN ERATH'S FIGHT.

Capt. George B. Erath, of the Milam County Minute Men, writing from Fort Bryant August 12, 1841, to the Secretary of War, says: "Agreeable to appointment made with Capt. Chandler, from Milam county, I met the Robertson County Company on the 26th of July, 1841, at the Ionie village on the Brazos, and were also joined by Maj. Lewis, Mr. Archer, Mr. Landers, and

* Army Archives.

several other gentlemen from Austin. Captain Chandler took command by consent of parties and we proceeded slowly up the Brazos, having to contend and tarry with sickness daily. We passed several evacuated towns of the enemy in the cross-timbers and our spies used every exertion to ferret out the grand village, but without success. On the 3rd, of August, being encamped in the upper edge of the cross-timbers and anxiously waiting the return of our spies to commence retrograde movements, our provisions being exhausted, a few Indians made their appearance about camp. I was detached, with twenty men, in pursuit; and in search of the trail, divided my party, leaving some men with Capt. Love of Robertson county on the left. My men, in the meantime discovered the trail, and I pushed hard on the same, when I was fired upon by a party of Kickapoos, or Cherokees, from behind a cliff of rocks which secured the enemy completely, being only on one side possible to ascend it with the utmost difficulty; which passage was defended bravely by the rifles of the enemy. Their first fire killed one of my men, Capt. A. J. Smith of Milam county, and several balls grazed others without injury. I formed in a little grove of timber and returned the fire, which was kept up for half an hour, during which time it is thought that we killed two Indians and, perhaps, wounded others. At that time Capt. Love arrived, and another re-enforcement came up from camp. A charge was then made and the bluff carried. The Indians left the ground carrying their dead. The mountainous situation of the country made pursuit impracticable; and after burying our dead man, we commenced our return through the cross-timbers. The 7th of August I separated my company from Capt. Chandler's and returned to the settlements by way of the Bosque, finding no sign of the enemy on our return. We still feel convinced that a strong village exists on the Brazos, but that only a well fitted campaign can capture it.

The toils and sufferings of the company were greater than usual, and the perseverance and vigilance of the men highly commendable. . . ."

The general election of the Republic occurred Sept. 6, 1841, and resulted in the choice of Gen. Sam Houston as President by a vote of nearly two to one over his opponent, David G. Burnet, and of Gen. Edward Burleson as Vice-President by a large majority over Memucan Hunt.

Col. Martin Francisco Peraza, as envoy of Yucatan, arrived in Austin September 11, to solicit for his country naval aid from Texas. This was granted after the Secretary of State received from John D. Morris and C. Van Ness, commissioners who had been sent to Gen. Arista, a communication stating the result of their mission and that no agreement had been entered into that rendered improper the granting of such aid.*

## DEATH OF MAJOR HEARD.

In August of this year a company of eight "minutemen," consisting of John Kerner, Charles Sevier, Gilbert H. Love, John Hardister, Thomas Sypert, William McGraw, and Thomas Dromgoole, led by Maj. Heard, left Old Franklin for a scout up the country. They left on a rainy day afternoon and followed the trail leading towards Parker's Fort. Early next day, when about fourteen miles from Franklin, while riding in single file and passing a couple of deep ravines, near their junction, about eighteen Indians rose from under the bank of the one parallel to the trail, and only thirty or forty yards distant, and fired on them, completely surprising the party. Major Heard, riding in front, fell dead from his horse, pierced by three balls. Some of the men retreated a short distance and halted, others dismounted near by, and Love stood by the dead body to prevent its being scalped, but was soon compelled to join the others, all of whom rallied together. Love lost his mule, but succeeded in mounting the dead man's horse, and after some skirmishing the seven men returned to Franklin, when a party went out and carried in for burial the dead body which had been scalped, the head and hands cut off,

---

* Yoakum is mistaken in asserting that the negotiation with Peraza was effected while Arista's "peace envoy" was in Texas and that this circumstance and the Santa Fe expedition were responsible for the continuance of border warfare, murders, robberies, etc.

and otherwise mutilated.*

The Indians were pursued for several days by a party composed of John Kerner, William M. Love, Gilbert H. Love, William McGraw and a number of others, but they failed to overtake them.

*     *     *     *     *

John Wahrenberger, employed as a gardener by Col. Louis T. Cook, was attacked at night in the fall of 1841 by Indians while he was carrying a sack of meal from the mill near the edge of town, to the home of his employer in Austin. He ran for his life, but held on to his burden, which was a fortunate circumstance, as some of the arrows shot at him by the pursuing Indians struck and stuck in the sack of meal, only one hitting him, making a slight wound in the arm. He fell breathless in the doorway of Col. Cook's house. Cook fired on the Indians, bringing one of them to the ground. This halted them. As soon as they could rally they picked up their wounded companion and ran for cover. The marauders were pursued the next day, but were not overtaken.

In the fall of 1841 Captain Jack Hays and his rangers were attacked by, but defeated with great slaughter, a large force of Comanches at the "Enchanted Rock," in Gillespie county. During the action, Capt. Hays became separated from his men, but took position on the summit of a mass of broken, lava-like rocks, that sloped steeply down in every direction.

The savages swarmed up the escarpment, in mad endeavor to kill him and take his scalp. He shot them faster than they could ascend. The fortunes of the day went equally ill with them in other parts of the field, and at last they were forced into rout and retreated, uttering howls of defeat.

*     *     *     *

The sixth Congress convened at Austin, Nov. 1, 1841. President Houston and Vice-President Burleson were inaugurated

---

* Heard's Prairie in Robertson county perpetuates the name of this worthy pioneer.

December 13.

President Houston's assertions that Lamar's Indian policy had resulted in failure and that millions of dollars had been wasted in useless expenditures, were due to misapprehension of facts. However, the pacific policy pursued by President Houston during his first administration (as the first constitutional president of the Republic) did not secure peace for the frontier, and left at its close the greater part of Texas in the possession of hostile, bloodthirsty and exultant savages.

The Cherokees entrenched in the east, and the Comanches, lords of the west, afforded the Mexican government opportunity and means to plot and wreak vengeance on the people of Texas, and retarded the settlement and development of the country, which Lamar removed. He expelled the Cherokees, broke the power of the Comanches, rendered impossible serious co-operation of the Indians with Mexico in any plan of invasion and attempted conquest, and prevented Indian depredations and murders ever recurring on so large a scale and over such a wide extent of territory as in former years. Ill-timed and profitless as the Santa Fe expedition appeared to be at the time it occurred, it made Texas' claim to its "northwestern territory" sufficiently good for the state to obtain for its relinquishment in 1850, $10,000,000 from the United States government. The financial cost of the expedition was less than $80,000. The greatest cost was the loss of so many noble lives. It is pleasing to reflect, however, that the men who fell perished not in vain. The large increase in the public debt, deplored in the message did not in the end amount to much. The debt was scaled to a fraction of its nominal total and was discharged by other millions of money paid to Texas, after annexation, by the United States, and not by taxes wrung from the people. The gains obtained were enormous, and would have been fully compensatory if they had represented returns for actual dollars contributed in part by the Texans of that day, and in part by their successors.

Perhaps, after all, the aggressive Indian policy of Lamar was of imperative necessity at the period of his administration. There were at least extenuating circumstances and conditions, and much of public sentiment brought to bear upon him. But the genius and policies of Houston met emergencies that could have been moulded to advantage by no other means and manner. Each was a good and great man, and each labored bravely and conscientiously for what he believed to be for the good of his countrymen.

The patriotic Texan of the present day—unbiased by the jealousies, animosities and politics of the past and viewing the men and measures of old in the clear light of accomplished results—finds much to applaud, and little to censure in the administration of Lamar, and can say truly those measures for which he was most criticised, brought the largest benefits to Texas and will longest preserve his fame and keep aglow the gratitude of posterity.

By the failure of Gen. Hamilton to negotiate a $5,000,000 loan for Texas in Europe, Lamar was saved from a great folly that he would probably have committed, viz: the invasion of Mexico with a Texas army. Diplomacy, resulting in later years in annexation, accomplished without cost and bloodshed, what any Texas army that could have been marshalled and supported with such a loan, would have failed to attain. The loan is said to have been defeated by the influence of Saligny, the French minister to Texas. One of his servants killed a hog belonging to Bullock, a hotel keeper at Austin. The boniface thrashed the hostler and afterwards insulted and threatened Saligny, who demanded of, and failed to secure from the Texas government, the redress to which he considered himself entitled.

His brother-in-law, M. Human, the French minister of finance, was instrumental in having the banking firm, Lafitte & Co., of Paris, abruptly drop the loan after they had led Gen. Hamilton to believe they would place it. The difficulty with Saligny was adjusted after Gen. Houston succeeded to the presidency, and the French minister returned to his post. Saligny always stoutly denied that he took any action that contributed to the defeat of the loan. Whether he did, or did not, is immaterial. The fact remains that failure to obtain the money was a genuine blessing, though disguised as a calamity at the time.

# CHAPTER XV.

lancing over the history of the last years of the Texas Republic, one finds many stirring events and tragic episodes transpiring—as the ill-starred Santa Fe expedition during the latter half of 1841; the dual Mexican invasion of Texas and capture of San Antonio, first by the forces under Vasquez, and second, those led by General Woll, in the spring and summer of 1842, leading up to the battle of Salado and the horrible Dawson massacre, and the sad sequence, the Mier expedition, the break at Salado, "lottery of death," and castle Perote; the "Archive War," resulting from President Houston's attempt to remove the records from the exposed and recently (1839) selected seat of government at Austin, in December 1842; the celebrated Snively expedition and its deplorable, shameful, failure; the bloody and fearful vendetta or feud known to history as the "War of the Regulators and Moderators," and which raged with fearful violence in the eastern part of the Republic for nearly three years, quelled finally per force of government arms, in 1844; and other momentous happenings. 'Twas indeed a swift moving period of fiery history making. But of these, and such matters, it is not our purpose to narrate in this connection. Other incidents and equally thrilling affairs now engage our attention.

At the general election, Sept. 6, 1841, Gen. Sam Houston was chosen by a large majority for a second term as President of the Republic, with Gen. Ed. Burleson, as Vice President. Both were tried soldiers and patriots, and able statesmen—a most fortunate circumstance for Texas at that critical period. The

Republic was then laboring in a sea of difficulties that many believed no one, save "Old Sam" Houston, could safely guide it over. All had confidence in his great and directing mind, and his triumphant election and vigorous handling of the reins of government was joyously hailed with general satisfaction throughout the country.

## PEACE OR WAR.

It is not our wish to discuss the political issues of that day and time, nor to voice opinion regarding the opposing policies advocated relative to dealing with and treating the various Indian tribes yet, formidable and hostile, residing in the Republic. Houston's predecessor, President Lamar, believed that vigorous war should be waged until all the tribes, both native and migrated, should be exterminated or subdued. His favorite slogan, as so tersely expressed by acting President David G. Burnet, being "Let the sword do its work." And, in accordance with this idea Lamar had encouraged expeditions and sent forces against the wild tribes and all other Indians, inflicting chastisement at every opportunity, and hence, when Houston again came into office he found the Indians exceedingly hostile and vengeful—"the whole frontier lit up with the flames of fierce and savage warfare."

Houston's policy for dealing with the savages was exactly the reverse of Lamar's. He uniformly and ever favored a peace policy, the forming of peace-treaties and the disbursement of presents, talks, etc., to conciliate and pacify the wild men. "On this policy (says John Henry Brown) the country was divided in opinion, and the question was often discussed with more or less bitterness. Nothing could be more natural, respecting a policy affecting so deeply the property and lives of the frontier people, who were so greatly exposed to the raids of the hostiles, and had little or no faith in their fidelity to treaty stipulations; while the President, realizing the sparsity of population and feebleness in resources of the government and the country, hoped to bring about a general cessation of hostilities, establish a line of demarkation between the whites and Indians, and by establishing along the same a line of trading houses, to promote friendly traffic, with occasional presents by the government, to control the wild men and preserve the lives of the people. It was a policy in keeping with his high character as a wise and faithful guardian of the lives of the people. The lack of confidence by many in the fidelity of the tribes was no reason why the effort, so fraught with good, should not be made."

## HOUSTON'S INDIAN TALKS.

Houston's letters and reported talks to the red men go to show he understood their character, their sentiments and sensibilities, and the cast of their minds perfectly, as well as the thoughts and modes of expression best calculated to affect them favorably, and there can be no doubt but that President Houston wielded an influence and did much to reconcile and keep the Indians in subjection, and thus enabled the settlers to push forward and gain a more substantial hold. When Houston would treat with the hostiles and dissuade them from the warpath he wrote: "The red brothers all know that my words to them have never been forgotten by me. They have never been swallowed up by darkness, nor has the light of the sun consumed them. Truth cannot perish, but the words of a liar are as nothing. I wish you to come, and we will again shake hands and counsel together. Bring other chiefs with you. Talk to all the red men to make peace. War cannot make them happy. It has lasted too long. Let it now be ended and cease forever. Tell all my red brothers to listen to my communications, and to walk by the words of my council. If they hear me and keep my words, their homes shall be happy; their fires shall burn brightly and the pipe of peace shall be handed around the hearth of their wigwams. The tomahawk shall no more be raised in war, nor shall the dog howl for the master who has been slain in battle; joy shall take the place of sorrow; and the laughter of your children shall be heard in place of the cries of your women."

These "talks" or letters make interesting reading even at

this far time, and they clearly illustrate the policy Houston was wont to pursue, besides giving a glimpse of affairs and conditions along the border, as well as the embittered feelings then existing between the whites and Indians. Mark the simple, yet beautiful, and even lofty, style, so suited to the untutored minds of the red men. The Indians loved and confided in Houston, and in return, Houston never betrayed a trust, nor forgot the welfare of, his forest friends.

An incident transpired that shocked him greatly, and that raised up bitter and revengeful enemies for the whites, viz: the killing of the celebrated Lipan chieftain, Flaco. The Lipans had always been friends of the white people, and had acted as scouts and guides side by side with them. Flaco had charged often with Hays and other frontier leaders, had displayed signal wisdom, good feeling and gallantry on many occasions, and was worthy of the highest esteem in which he was generally held. He was killed, it was claimed, by a party of white men who mistook his identity, and acted with inexcusable haste. The Lipans denounced the act as murder, and joined the wild prairie tribes. Houston sought in vain to console and placate them by the following letter, written to Flaco's father:

Executive Department, Washington, March 28, 1843.

To the Memory of Gen. Flaco, Chief of Lipans.

My Brother: My heart is sad. A dark cloud rests upon your nation. Grief has sounded in your camp. The voice of Flaco is silent. His words are not heard in council. The chief is no more. His life has fled to the "Great Spirit." His eyes are closed. His heart no longer leaps at the sight of the buffalo. The voices of your camp are no longer heard to cry: "Flaco has returned from the chase!" Your chiefs look down upon the earth and groan in trouble. Your warriors weep—the loud voices of grief are heard from your women and children. The songs of the birds are silent. The ears of your people hear no pleasant sounds. Sorrow whispers in the winds. The noise of the tempest passes; it is not heard.

Your hearts are heavy. The name of Flaco brought joy to all hearts. Joy was on every face. Your people were happy. Flaco is no longer seen in the fight. His voice is no longer heard in the battle. The enemy no longer make a path for his glory. His valor is no longer a guard for your people. The right arm of your nation is broken. Flaco was a friend to the white brothers. They will not forget him. They will remember the red warrior. His father will not be forgotten. We will be kind to the Lipans. Grass shall not grow in the path between us. Let your wise men give the council of peace. Let your young men walk in the white path. The gray-headed men of your nation will teach wisdom. I will hold my red brother by the hand.

Thy brother,
Sam Houston.

---

## HOUSTON'S INDIAN POW WOW.

A contemporary writer* and eye-witness, thus graphically describes one of the President's Indian pow wows, which occurred at the capital. The scenes and incidents described will never be re-enacted—the picture is of a scene forever past:

"It was in the early summer of the year 1844, before the close of President Houston's second term, that an Indian council was held at Washington, about three quarters of a mile from the village center. Upon invitation some fifty or more Indian braves with their women and children, aggregating a hundred or more, came in a body. A grove was selected, in which they were directed to camp. Their tents were erected of buffalo skins. They brought in honey, bear oil, and meats of wild animals. The president caused them to be furnished with corn for bread and hominy, and beef, as needed. They were presented with blankets and other useful articles, including trinkets. Their ponies were pastured on the rich grass. The range was open.

"Exhibitions of skill with bow and arrow, lance and toma-

---

* Veteran Frank Brown, yet (1912) living.

hawk, were given. Games were indulged in. Indians and whites freely mingled. The red men were in the village nearly every day parading the streets and visiting the whites at their places of business and dwellings. They were often invited to the tables of the white folks, where they sat down and ate heartily. Their table manners were extremely awkward. It was amusing to see an Indian with a piece of bread in hand, at the same time holding a fork in the same hand. In conveying the bread to his mouth he was likely to stick the prongs in his eyes. After meals all hands sat in the shade and smoked the pipe. It was customary, as an act of friendship and courtesy, for the same pipe to be used by both whites and red men. It required a stomach for the average white man to conform. The pipe was filled with a preparation of mixed tobacco and sumach leaves, called kil-likinick.

"At night the whites were in the habit of going to the Indian camp to see their amusements. These consisted of games and dances after the Indian fashion. Their dancing is difficult to describe. The men and women did not dance together as we do. The men would form a circle and dance to the right in a forward manner, after a rude fashion. After the men were through they left the ring, when the women took their places. Instead of dancing in a forward way, as did the men, they advanced to the right sideways, all in a circle. There was little or no grace in the movements of either. The music consisted of a drum, made from a dried deer skin, tightly stretched over a stout hoop, and a seasoned Spanish gourd with the dry seed rattling in it when shaken.

"A day was set for the council. In the forenoon President Houston, with his cabinet officers, went to the camp. They were neatly dressed as became the occasion. President Houston sometimes affected a rather gaudy style—he frequently wore a vest made from spotted leopard skin. The red chiefs and their leading men were painted in gorgeous colors, their heads adorned with large feathers, the leggings with beads and painted designs. A council fire was lighted in the center of a space cleared for the purpose. The president and his cabinet officers occupied one side of the council ground, sitting in a sort of half circle. The Indians occupied the opposite side, also sitting in a half circle, facing the whites. All sat on buffalo robes spread on the ground. Spectators consisting of white men, women and children, with the red men not of the council, their women and children, surrounded the councilmen. In a short time after the conference met a large pipe, with a long stem, duly ornamented and filled with killikinick, was lighted. President Houston took the pipe, drew two or three whiffs in a deliberate manner, and then handed it to the first chief on the left of the half circle of red men. This chief placed the stem in his mouth, slowly drew two whiffs, and then handed it to his nearest neighbor on the right. In this manner the entire circle of councilmen, Indians and whites, partook of the pipe.

"After the smoke was finished, the president arose, and through an interpreter made a talk to the red chiefs. But few Indians could understand English; nearly all of them spoke Spanish. The president, from his long association with Indians and intimate knowledge of their views and prejudices, knew how to address them. Nearly every time a sentence was translated the chiefs would utter a grunt of approval. At the conclusion of President Houston's address the chiefs were invited to talk. Some of them did so. The ceremonies lasted quite a while. At the conclusion the council formally adjourned with good feeling on both sides.

"The Indians remained some three or four weeks. They finally broke camp, packed their effects on horses, mounted their ponies and departed on a west course. In a day or two they were beyond the white settlements."

## HOUSTON'S INDIAN TREATY.

In September 1843, the President, through his fearless commissioners, Captains Eldridge, Torry and Bee, effected a peace treaty with the Wacos, Anadarkos, Towash, Caddos, Keechies, Wichitas, Tehuacanas, Ionies, Beedies, Delawares, Biloxi, and other small tribes, including a band of thirty

Cherokees, who had assembled at a designated point on the Trinity, now in Wise county. Keechi-ko-so-qua head chief of the Tehuacanas, was the leader and most influential Indian in the council. In council a boundary line was discussed and finally agreed upon between the whites and the Indians, along which trading houses were to be established—one at the mouth of the clear fork of the Trinity (Fort Worth), one at Comanche Peak (Hood county) on the Brazos and one at Fort San Saba. The treaty had the effect it is said, to allay hostilities for a time, though, of course, the boundary was not always respected by either whites or Indians.

Thus, during his term of office, Houston was diligent and determined in his efforts to conciliate in some degree at least, the incensed savages, and dissuade them as much as possible from such constant and vengeful hostilities. No opportunity in this direction was overlooked. The President was constantly sending out "talks" and presents by faithful commissioners and agents, who visited the Indians in their own wild haunts, at great peril, as special representatives; and always inviting the chiefs and head men to visit and council with The Great White Father—the President—at his home, the capital.

At the close of his term of office, Houston was warranted in saying, among other things, portending a better condition of affairs and brighter hopes for the future welfare of the struggling Republic: "Our Indians affairs are in as good condition as the most sanguine could reasonably have anticipated. . . . It is not denied that there are among the Indians, as among our own people, individuals who will disregard all law and commit excesses of the most flagrant character; but it is unjust to attribute to a tribe or a body of men disposed to obey the laws, what is properly chargeable to a few renegades and desperadoes. Other governments of far greater resources for imposing restraints upon the wild men of the forests and prairies, have not been exempt from the infraction of treaties, and occasional commission of acts of rapine and blood. We must, therefore, expect to suffer in a greater or less degree from the same causes. But even this, in the opinion of the Executive, does not furnish overruling testimony against the policy which he has constantly recommended, and which he has had the happiness to see so fully and satisfactorily tested."

Though a marked difference is perceptible, and a decrease of hostilities is observable, especially during the latter half of Houston's second term, yet many crimes and depredations were committed in various sections, and especially along the advancing and exposed line of frontier; atrocities, captivities, and fierce conflicts—enough indeed in volume to far exceed the limits here ascribed. But, perhaps, one can tire his readers with telling too much, however thrilling and absorbing the subject. A few other notable incidents and engagements, without further preface, must suffice.

## DEATH OF CHIEF "BIG FOOT."

The following thrilling incident well illustrates the trials and perils of the pioneer settlers and the manner and mode of border warfare as carried on in Texas at that period of time.

Captain Shapley P. Ross, father of the late Gen. L. S. Ross, was one of the early, staunch, pioneers of Texas, having emigrated from Bentonport, Ohio, and settled near the present town of Cameron, Milam county—then a howling wilderness—in 1839. Captain Ross was of powerful frame, with cool courage and a sagacity equal to the Indian with whom he was so often thrown in contact; in fact Ross was endowed with all the qualities necessary to the makeup of the hardy pioneer and successful border trooper, and hence he soon became a recognized leader of the whites against the Comanches and other hostile tribes of Indians who then ruled that region. Captain Ross led his neighbors in many expeditions against the wily red foes and encountered many thrilling adventures and narrow escapes. One incident has, more than any other, made his name famous in the border annals of Texas. This was the celebrated hand-to-hand fight between Captain Ross and the powerful Comanche chief, "Big Foot," which occurred in 1842, and in which combat the famous Indian warrior lost his life.

1. Capt. Shapley P. Ross, 2. Capt. Henry S. Brown,
3. Capt. Henry Stout and 4. Capt. Sam Highsmith

1. John Neely Bryan, Father of Dallas, 2. Capt. Geo. B. Erath,
3. Capt. Randall Jones and 4. Capt. Robt. M. Coleman

The details of this celebrated encounter are here given substantially as told by Captain Ross himself.

Captain Ross had just returned home from a business trip to the lower settlements, bringing with him a fine mare he had purchased, the Indians having stolen all his other horses. A short time after his return the bold and alert frontiersman heard in the woods nearby what an unsophisticated person would have thought the whinneying of a colt and the hooting of owls. But the quick ear of Ross soon detected the cheat, and he knew the house was watched and surrounded by savages. He kept indoors till the next day, when word was conveyed to a neighbor named Monroe, whose horse had been carried off the night previous by the Indians. The object of the Comanches in imitating the whinneying of a colt was to draw the settler from his cabin and murder him. The ruse did not work that time.

The marauding thieves having hastily fled with their booty, it was determined to raise as good a force as possible and follow the Indians. The party included six, one of whom was a young man, Shapley Woolfork, a nephew of Captain Ross. On examining the trail, the settlers readily recognized the tracks of the notorious Comanche chief, "Big Foot," of whom the settlers far and near stood in mortal dread, so cruel were his outrages. The little pursuing company dashed forward some thirty miles in a drenching rainstorm, which wet the powder in their flintlock rifles and rendered them useless. Two of the party became discouraged and returned, but Captain Ross and three determined companions continued the pursuit.

## THE HAND-TO-HAND STRUGGLE.

Suddenly, at a point known as "The Knobs" near the present town of Temple, in Bell county, the Indians were discovered, having halted to skin a buffalo they had just shot. The surprise was apparent, but the Indians had no chance of escape, and dropping their knives, seized their guns and bows and prepared for the contest—a most desperate one. The savages repeatedly snapped their guns but failed to fire, their powder also being wet. Both parties now clubbed their guns, and in close contact the battle royal raged, many daring acts of individual heroism transpiring. It was a deadly match, a struggle for life between fearless red and white warriors, and for a time the issue was indeed doubtful. Finally, one of the settlers, Bryant, killed an Indian with the butt of his rifle. Toward the close of the fight, Captain Ross saw Big Foot mounted on a fine animal, Monroe's mare he had stolen, and riding toward him. He drew both his holsters, but discovered to his chagrin that the powder was wet. He threw one of them at Big Foot's head, but struck him on the shoulder. He was about dealing the chief a terrific blow with the butt of his rifle when an Indian rode up close behind and was in the act of cleaving Ross' head, when Woolfolk came to his uncle's rescue and quickly dealt a blow that tumbled the savage from his pony, at the same time pulling Woolfolk off his horse. A personal combat between the two was prevented by the Indian mounting behind Big Foot. The two Indians dashed off and attempted to escape, but they were again hotly pursued by Ross and his nephew. The race was an exciting one. On went Big Foot and his companion, whom the mare bore along swift as the wind. Suddenly they came to a ravine bluff. They saw it too late to stop the animal in her flight, and headlong over the bluff went the mare and her two riders. They were soon floundering in the mire and water. Quickly the pursuers dashed up—Woolfolk in the lead, himself dashing down the declivity, alighting between the two savages. Ross managed to halt on the brink. He sprang from his mare and jumped down and into the melee, his first intention being to separate the two Indians and prevent them from "double teaming" on his nephew. The four combatants were now on the ground and on an equal footing, and now it was that the desperate death struggle commenced. Big Foot and Captain Ross regarded each other for an instant. Both knew it was death for one or the other. Fire flashed from their eyes. Desperation was depicted on their countenances. They drew their knives—bright, keen butcher blades, which a hunter always carried. Both wore moccasins, while the Comanche chief was bedecked in full war paint, his long plaited hair hanging far down his back—he was indeed ferocious looking. Captain Ross wore a slouch hat and buckskin hunting shirt, with an old fashioned powder horn slung around his waist. With a wild, guttural shout the chief advanced, knife in hand, and made a determined lunge at his powerful white antagonist. The Indian's foot slipped on the wet sod and he missed Ross. Before he could rise, Ross seized Big Foot by the hair with his left hand, while with his right he brandished and drove his knife to the heart of the Indian chief. The contest was over; the spirit of the renowned Chief Big Foot winged its way to the "happy hunting grounds." Both combatants sank to the ground—Big Foot in death, Ross unnerved and exhausted. While this was transpiring, Woolfolk was engaging the other Indian in a similar struggle, and finally succeeded in dispatching him. After scalping their victims the settlers returned to their homes with the trophies, and the stolen horses recovered.

Captain Ross lived to a ripe age, dying at Waco, a few years ago. He experienced many of the trials and vicissitudes incident to frontier life, and participated in numerous Indian fights, but this was his most desperate encounter, and when narrating the incident the old veteran always grew serious. It was a life and death struggle, and his call was so close he never jested over the matter.

---

## FATE OF THE GILLELAND FAMILY—CAPTURE AND RESCUE OF MRS. FISHER.

The narrative which follows is one of the most instructive, yet pathetic, in all our Texas history, not only because it is the story of two helpless children, made orphans by Comanches, the most cruel and bloodthirsty of all the Indian tribes, and who were dragging them to a captivity worse than the fate their parents had just suffered at their hands, but, because the story in its simple, unvarnished recital throws upon the great white, peaceful canvas of today, a faithful picture of the hardships and dangers of our early pioneers in their efforts to establish homes and civilization in Western Texas. Be it remembered, too, that this tragedy was enacted six years after peace had been won at San Jacinto.

We quote from a letter written by A. B. Hannum, First Lieutenant Matagorda Riflemen:

"In 1841-42 the Mexican Government sent several marauding expeditions into Texas, and in the latter year San Antonio was twice captured and plundered. In the spring of 1842 we were in force on the San Antonio River to repel a Mexican invasion, when news came to us that the Indians had killed a Mr. Gilleland and his wife at or near the Mexican village, Don Carlos Ranch. After the massacre they evidently moved up the river, holding two little white children prisoners.

"Gen. Albert Sidney Johnston, then in command of the military, and in camp near the scene of the tragedy, called for ten men, well mounted, to reconnoiter. With General Johnston we proceeded about one mile below the town, where I found and pointed out to him an Indian trail leading into the river bottom. Here, after dismounting and making coffee, Gen. Johnston returned to the command, leaving me in charge of half a dozen men and fifteen scouts under Captain Price, who had joined us. We soon discovered the trail of the Indians and were in hot pursuit. There were Dr. A. T. Axsom, distinguished afterwards as President of the Board of Health of New Orleans; Colonel Kerr, purser of the Texas navy; Dallam, author of the Digest of Texas Statutes, still an authority, also author of the novel, 'The Lone Star.'

"Two miles away in camp were our noble ex-President, M. B. Lamar, and the hero of Shiloh, Albert Sidney Johnston, and not far from the site of Fannin's massacre.

"The Comanches scattered and our yelling men followed, making it impossible for them to escape. After clearing the timber, they formed in line to receive us, while a tall old chief ran up and down the line playing the flute. They had evidently counted us and intended to give battle.

"Firing commenced when a gay Indian on a finely caparisoned horse presented too fair a picture to be resisted, and I fired at him; he dropped from the horse, one he had captured the day before, and all took to the woods. We fastened our horses to the trees and pursued, thinking to give them fight in regular Indian fashion, but they never rallied, and left guns, feathers, shields and horses behind. We rescued the prisoners, a little boy, lanced in the side, and a pretty little girl with long, golden curls and eyes so soft, so mystic; she was one of the politest little things on earth. The little boy, bleeding at every gasp, was given water. Dr. Axsom lay pale on the ground. 'What is the matter, Axsom?' 'Oh, that child's wound makes me sick.' The case of the healing of the wound of that little boy, William M. Gilleland, was published in the New Orleans Medical Journal by Dr. Axsom.

"The little girl was, when I saw her in 1886, one of the handsomest of the very handsome women for which Texas is justly distinguished, and she, Mrs. Rebecca J. Fisher, a veritable queen of society.

"The Gilleland children were taken just as the sun was setting, and were rescued the next morning, the Indians traveling all the time until overtaken by the riflemen.

"General Johnston was in command, and carried Rebecca the little girl, from the Carlos Ranch to the home of a Presbyterian minister, Dr. Blain, in Victoria. The boy was left behind under Dr. Axsom's nursing and my directions."

## STORY OF THE HEROINE.

Mrs. Fisher, who here tells her terrible experience, is at present (1912) living in Austin. Her story further illustrates the dangers of frontier life in early Texas:

"My parents, Johnstone and Mary Barbour Gilleland, were living in Pennsylvania, surrounded with everything to make life pleasant, when they became so enthusiastic over the encouraging reports from Texas that they concluded to join the excited throng and wend their way to this, the supposed 'Eldorado of the West.' They hastily and at great sacrifice, sold their home near Philadelphia, and set sail for Galveston with their three children. Not being used to the hardships and privations of frontier life, they were ill prepared for the trials which awaited them. I know not the date of their arrival. They moved to Refugio county, near Don Carlos Ranch, which proved to be their last earthly habitation.

"My father belonged to Captain Tomlinson's company for some months, and when not in active warfare was engaged in protecting his own and other families, removing them from place to place for safety. They frequently had to flee through blinding storms, cold and hungry, to escape Indians and Mexicans. The whole country was in a state of excitement. Families were in constant danger and had to be ready at any moment to flee for their lives.

"The day my parents were murdered was one of those days which youth and old age so much enjoy. It was in strange contrast to the tragedy at its close. We were only a few rods from the house. Suddenly the warwhoop of the Comanche burst upon our ears, sending terror to all hearts. My father, in trying to reach the house for weapons, was shot down, and near him my mother, clinging to her children and praying for God to spare them, was also murdered. As she pressed us to her heart we were baptized in her precious blood. We were torn from her dying embrace and hurried off into captivity, the chief's wife dragging me to her horse and clinging to me with a tenacious grip. She was at first savage and vicious looking, but for some cause her wicked nature soon relaxed, and folding me in her arms, she gently smoothed back my hair, indicating that she was very proud of her suffering victim. A white man, with all the cruel instincts of the savage, was with them. Several times they threatened to cut off our hands and feet if we did not stop crying. Then the woman, in savage tones and gestures would scold, and they would cease their cruel threats. We were captured just as the sun was setting and were rescued the next morning.

"During the few hours we were prisoners the Indians never stopped. Slowly and stealthily they pushed their way through the settlement to avoid detection, and just as they halted for the first time the soldiers suddenly came upon them and firing commenced. As the battle raged the Indians were forced to take flight. Thereupon, they pierced my little brother through the body, and striking me with some sharp instrument on the side of the head, they left us for dead, but we soon recovered sufficiently to find ourselves alone in the dark, dense forest, wounded and covered with blood.

"Having been taught to ask God for all things, we prayed to our Heavenly Father to take care of us and direct us out of that lonely place. I lifted my wounded brother, so faint and so weak, and we soon came to the edge of a large prairie, when as far away as our swimming eyes could see, we discovered a company of horsemen. Supposing them to be Indians, frightened beyond expression, and trembling under my heavy burden, I rushed back with him into the woods, and hid behind some thick bushes. But those brave men, on the alert, dashing from place to place, at last discovered us. Soon we heard the clatter of horses' hoofs and the voices of our rescuers calling us by name, assuring us that they were our friends who had come to take care of us. Lifting the almost unconscious little sufferer, I carried him out to them as best I could. With all the tenderness of women, their eyes suffused with tears, those good men raised us to their saddles and hurried off to camp, where we received every attention and kindness that men could bestow.

"I was seven years of age when my parents were murdered. Sixty odd years have passed since then, and yet my heart grows faint as the awful time passes in review. It is indelibly stamped upon memory's page and photographed so deeply upon my heart that time with all its changes can never erase it."

## LAST RAID INTO ANDERSON COUNTY.

In the year 1843, a party of Indians, about ten in number, made their last hostile raid in the territory embracing what is now Anderson county. "We called it Burnet county at that time," says pioneer Capt. Wm. R. Russell of Harper, Texas, who supplies these facts:

"In the neighborhood where my father and family lived, near Mound Prairie, they stole some horses and killed and butchered a very fat ox, belonging to David Roberts. Taking the greater part of the flesh of the ox, they left in a westward direction. My father, Col. Lewis M. Russell, headed a party of citizens and followed them. They crossed the Trinity River, and on the bank of the river on the west side, the Indians stopped and pulled off the shoes from the horses and cut notches in the front of the horses' feet, so they they would make a track resembling the track of a buffalo. The Indians moved on westward about two miles, and stopped to barbecue their beef. The scouts sighted the Indians at the head of a ravine that led into the river, the ravine being completely enveloped with a thick jungle of brush, briers and vines. The scouts charged on them, but the Indians made good their escape down the ravine. The scouts captured all their horses and returned home without firing again."

---

## CAPTURE OF THE SIMPSON CHILDREN.

A widow named Simpson lived at Austin. Among other children she had a girl, Emma, aged about fourteen years, and a boy, Thomas, about twelve years of age. During the summer of 1844, about 4 o'clock one afternoon, these children went to drive up the cows. They were on the dry branch, near where Maj. C. L. West's residence now stands, when their mother heard them scream. She required no explanation of the cause; she knew at once that the Indians had captured her darlings. Sorrowing, and almost heart-broken, she rushed to the more thickly settled part of the town to implore citizens to turn out and endeavor to recover her children. A party of men were soon in the saddle and on the trail.

They discovered that the savages were on foot—four in number—and were moving in the timber, parallel to the river and up it. They found on the trail shreds of the girl's dress, yet it was difficult to follow the footsteps of the fleeing red men.

From a hill they descried the Indians just before they entered the ravine below Mount Bonnell. The whites moved at a run, but they failed to overtake the barbarians. A piece of an undergarment was certain evidence that the captors had passed over Mount Barker. The rocky surface of the ground precluded the possibility of fast trailing, and almost the possibility of trailing at all. Every conceivable effort was made to track the Indians, and all proved unavailing. They were loath to return to Austin to inform the grief-stricken mother her loved ones were indeed the prisoners of savages, and would be subject to all the brutal cruelties and outrages of a captivity a thousand times more terrible than the pangs of death. The scene which ensued when the dread news reached Mrs. Simpson's ears can not be pictured with pen or pencil. No science, nor art, nor device known to man could compass such an undertaking. The wail of agony and despair rent the air, and tears of sympathy were wrung from the frontiersmen who never quailed when danger came in its most fearful form.

In about one year Thomas Simpson was restored to his mother. He had been purchased from the Indians by a trader at Taos, New Mexico. From him many particulars of the capture were obtained. He said his sister fought the Indians all the time. They carried her by force, dragging her frequently, tore her clothing and handled her roughly. Thomas was led by two Indians. He offered no resistance, knowing he would be killed if he did.

When the Indians discovered they were being followed, they doubled, coming back rather in the direction of Austin. They made a short halt not far from Hon. John Hancock's place. Thomas begged his sister not to resist, and told her such a course would cause her to be put to death. She was eventually separated from him. When the Indians who had her in charge rejoined their companions, young Simpson saw his sister's scalp dangling from a warrior's belt. No one will know the details of the bloody deed. But a knowledge of Indian customs justifies the belief that the sacrifice of an innocent life involved incidents of a more revolting character than mere murder. In the course of time the bones of the unfortunate girl were found near the place where Mr. George Davis erected his residence, and to that extent corroborated the account of Thomas Simpson.

It is no difficult matter to conceive what were the impressions produced upon parents then living in Austin by this event. It is easy to imagine how vivid the conviction must have been that their sons and daughters might become the victims of similar misfortunes, sufferings and outrages. Let the reader extend the idea, and include the whole frontier of Texas in a scope extending, as it then did, from Red River to the Rio Grande, a sinuous line upon the outer tiers of settlements, and including a large extent of the Gulf coast. Let him remember that the country was then so sparsely populated it was quite all frontier, and open to incursions of the merciless tribes who made war upon women and children, and flourished the tomahawk and the scalping knife in the bedrooms and the boudoirs, as well as in the forests, and upon the bosom of the prairie. When he shall have done this, he can form an approximate conception of the privations and perils endured by the pioneers who reclaimed Texas from the dominion of the Indian, and made it the abode of civilized men.

## BRUTAL MURDER OF CAPT. KEMPER AND PERILOUS ESCAPE OF HIS FAMILY.

The reader has already learned in the opening chapters of this work, much of the troubles of the early settlers with the ferocious tribe of Caranchua Indians, and of their final expulsion and fate. The last notable hostile act of this tribe was the murder of Capt. John Frederick Kemper, at his ranch home, "Kemper's Bluff," on the Guadalupe River, in Victoria county. This hardy pioneer was a native of Kentucky, but came from Tennessee to Texas in 1836, having been previously united in marriage to Miss Eliza Miller, daughter of Col. Miller, who brought volunteers to the Texas army three separate times—the first as early as the year 1835. Capt. Kemper was in command of an artillery company in Colonel Miller's regiment. The command was made prisoners of war at Copano, immediately after Fannin's disastrous battle of the Calito; were separated and spared from the inhuman massacre perpetrated a few days afterwards.

Captain Kemper settled at Kemper's Bluff in 1845. At the time of his death the family consisted of himself, wife and two children, Amanda Jane, aged three years, and James, aged five months. Mrs. Miller was also present, on a visit with her daughter.

The killing of Capt. Kemper by the Caranchuas occurred in November, 1845. About 3 o'clock in the afternoon the milch cows were seen running to the pen, pursued by a party of Indians. Captain Kemper, gun in hand, stepped outside the house and motioned them to desist; their only reply was a volley of arrows, one of which took effect, striking the captain in the shoulder, back of the collar bone and passing out beneath the shoulder blade. He re-entered the house, Mrs. Miller pulling the arrow out of the wound, and expired in a few minutes. The Indians came about the house, not venturing, however, in front of the only door. Mrs. Kemper fired a gun at them once through a crack between the logs, but was ignorant as to the effect of the discharge. About dark the red devils procured a quantity of dry moss, which they placed under the floor and fired. Mrs. Kemper raised a plank and Mrs. Miller extinguished the flames by pouring on them a pail of water. They then left the house, and with the timber for a guide, proceeded to the residence of Mr. Alonzo Bass, on the Calito, about twelve miles distant, arriving at 3 o'clock in the morning. Their mournful flight was through a dark, rainy night—and later accompanied by a fierce norther. The party that went down the next day to inter the remains of Capt. Kemper, found the house robbed of all articles esteemed of value by the savages. Feather beds were emptied of their contents and the crockery was all broken. Upon their departure, the fiends laid a brand of fire upon the breast of their victim, the significance of which is left to the elucidation of those more conversant with the lore of aborigines.

The venerable Colonel Miller died at Victoria, Feb. 16, 1862. Mrs. Kemper resided but a short time at Kemper's Bluff after her husband's death. Amanda J. was married to Mr. David F. Williams in Victoria, Nov. 4, 1868.

## THE LATER COLONIES AND FRONTIER EXPANSION.

Elsewhere we have briefly noticed the early colony grants to Austin, Edwards, DeWitt, Robertson, and others, which were in force and building during the period of Mexican domination over American Texas—1822 to 1836. The promotion and carrying out of these contracts by the enterprising empresarios, of course, resulted in the more rapid settlement of the country and the expansion of its frontiers.

After the revolution and the establishment of independence, quite a tide of emigration flowed into the new and famed Lone Star Republic, and many daring and adventurous spirits drifted in, and fearlessly abode at San Antonio, Corpus Christi, and at other points along the exposed frontier—along and up the Colorado and the Brazos, and even to Red River on the fearfully exposed northern boundary. But during the first half of the Republic's ten years existence no regular colony contracts of any consequence were made. On Feb. 4, 1841, however, an act was passed authorizing the President to enter into contracts for the colonization of wild lands in Northwest and Southwest Texas—the act being amended, with more liberal and encouraging conditions, on Jan. 1, 1843.

Under this law, as originally enacted, President Lamar, on Aug. 30, 1841, entered into the contract for what became known as the famous Peter's Colony, in North Texas. The east line of this grant ran from the mouth of Big Mineral Creek, in Grayson county, due south, passing about ten miles east of Dallas, to a point in the eastern part of Ellis county, and thence west and north to Red River, embracing a large district of the best lands in North Texas. "Beginning in 1842," says John Henry Brown, "it was rapidly settled, chiefly by farmers from Missouri, Illinois, Indiana, Kentucky, Tennessee, and other states. It has developed in the fifty years, (Brown wrote twenty years ago. The increase in population and strides of progress during this period has been even greater than the preceding half century), despite bloody Indian wars, the Civil War and the calamities following, into the wealthiest and most populous portion of the State, in which are comprehended the whole or large parts of the counties of Grayson, Collin, Dallas, Cooke, Montague, Wise, Parker and several others on the west."

The inducement offered to settlers in this colony was a headright of 640 acres to the heads of families, and 320 acres to each single man—the company receiving its pay in liberal premium lands lying further west. In the sequel to this volume—"Texas Frontier History"—the trials endured and the dangers encountered and combatted by these brave settlers in defense of their homes, as well as the similar troubles of colonists in other of the later settlements, along the expanding frontier, will be fully noted.

The Mercer Colony, attemped about this time—the grant covering the territory now embraced in Kaufman and some adjoining counties—was not at first successful. But the enterprise at least served to augment the Peters settlements, where most of Mercer's colonists re-settled.

About the time that the Peters Colony was gotten under headway, another important, and finally prosperous, settlement, known as the Castro Colony, was commenced in the southwestern part of the Republic. Henri de Castro was a wealthy, highly enlightened and noble Frenchman. On January 15, 1842, he contracted with President Houston for settling a colony of his countrymen and others in the fertile prairies west of the Medina River. At great expense—more than $150,000—for ship transportation (at different times and in all, 37 ships were chartered) and conveyance overland, Castro brought over and settled during the period of his eight years contract, over 5,000 immigrants, "farmers, orchardists, and vine-growers, chiefly from the Rhenish provinces." These people he sustained and fed at his own expense till they could prepare homes and lands and raise food crops, and get a foothold in the new country, whither they had so confidently followed their bene- factor and noble leader; and whose prototype is found only in his predecessor, the great empresario, Austin. Space prevents a narration of the troubles of these colonists during the first years—harassed, as they were, by both Indians and Mexicans— and but for the constant vigilance of Capt. Jack Hays and his brave rangers, who so faithfully patrolled that exposed section, they must have failed and perished.

Speaking of Hays and his rangers during this period, the noble old Franco-Texan empresario, Henry Castro, says:

"I take this occasion to do justice to Captain Jack Hays and his noble company. They were equal to any emergency, but such a company can, in my opinion, only be compared to the old Musketeers of Louis XIV, who represented the chivalrous gen- tleman soldiers of France. Hays and his men represented the true and chivalrous, disinterested American gentleman soldier, who at all times was ready to shed the last drop of his blood for his country and the protection of the feeble."

At every opportunity the Indians harassed these exposed colonists, and from the time they set foot on land and began their journey overland, and mostly afoot, to their wild prairie homes, they were beset with dangers. "In the rear of one of their first emigrating parties, the Indians forty miles below San Antonio, attacked and burned a wagon. The driver, an American, rifle in hand, reached a thicket, and killed several of the Indians; but they killed a boy of nineteen—a Frenchman—and cutting off his head, nailed it to a tree. In the burnt wagon was a trunk contain- ing a considerable amount of gold and silver. In the ashes the silver was found melted, the gold only blackened."*

The founding and sustaining of the Castro Colony in that remote and exposed section was indeed a bold step. John Henry Brown says: "He confronted dangers unknown to the first

---

* Brown's History of Texas.

American colonists in 1822, for besides hostile savages, now accustomed to the use of firearms, it challenged inroads from the whole Rio Grande Mexican frontier, which in 1822, furnished friends and not enemies to foreign settlements in Texas."

An interesting volume could be written descriptive of the efforts of Henry Castro to settle his colony, then exposed to the attacks of bandit and guerilla Mexicans, but a little to its west, and to all the hostile Indians north and west of his proposed settlement. It was an achievement entitling the name of Castro to be enrolled among the most prominent pioneers of civilization in modern times. Yet the youth of today, joyously and peacefully galloping over the beautiful hills and valleys he rescued from savagery, are largely ignorant of his great services.

\* \* \* \* \*

The contract entered into by President Houston with Fisher and Miller, for what became known as the German colony, and which grant covered the beautiful mountain sections drained by the Pedernales, Llano, San Saba and the lower Conchos, after passing to the management of "The German Immigration Company," also proved successful—though perhaps fraught with more dangers and tribulations than that of any other of the later colony enterprises.

A large number of industrious settlers were introduced between 1844 and 1848, who followed the pursuits of stock raising and farming, and eventually triumphed over the hostile savages who domiciled, as it were, in their very midst, infesting every valley and mountain. But the fierce conflicts of these brave German pioneers hardly come within the period of time allotted to this volume.

Thus was the spirit of emigration again set in motion, and continued, with increasing volume and energy.

## THE REPUBLIC OF TEXAS IS NO MORE.

And now we have arrived at that period in Texas history

which marks the close of the Lone Star Republic, and with it we shall conclude the present compendium of border annals, having closely followed the doings of the brave pioneers from the day of their first advent under Austin; during the uncertain colonial period and on down through the dark years of the Republic, constantly struggling for an existence, and fighting the common foes, both Indians and Mexicans, till they finally triumphed, and won a great state to American civilization, commerce and education. Of the further affairs of Texas as a State and of her continued struggle with the red men for mastery and frontier expansion the reader will to be told in a second volume, under the title—"Texas Frontier History."

Of the fortunes of the Lone Star Republic, it may be said that for nearly ten years it proudly claimed an existence, and struggled forward in financial straits and under all sorts of most adverse circumstances, as one of the independent nations of the world. Nothing but the wise and careful councilings of her statesmen, chief among whom was the great Sam Houston, and the determined valor of patriotic and fearless defenders in the mighty contest all along her extended and exposed borders, saved and upheld the young nation—a feat that astonished mankind, and is well reckoned as one of the anomalies of the worlds' history. A vast empire reclaimed from a wilderness of savagery, and wrested from a grasping and populous nation; and then held against both Mexican and Indian claimants. All this, too, by a mere handful of fearless pioneers—that bold little body of buckskin-clad and poorly fed border troopers and dashing rangers, in their constant strife and bold, wonderful exploits—the like of which the world has never before or since witnessed.

The history of every state in the American Union is tinged with the life's blood of their early settlers and pioneers in their struggles for possession over and against the red men. In no land or country was this strife waged with more bitterness and cruelty, and bloodthirsty stubbornness than in our own Texas; beginning, as it did, in the opening chapter of its pioneer history, and carried on with relentless and determined fury, as it was,

"O Lord, Mary Ann's a Widow"

"Gone to Burnham's"

The Lurking Foe

"Take it D—n You"

for more than half a century—ending only in recent times.

Referring to internal affairs and the condition of Texas with regard to her Indian foes at the time of annexation, and her ability to cope with this foe, Garrison ("Texas," p. 271-2) says: "It was possible for the United States to protect the State from invasion, but Texas had an enemy that was practically within her gates, with whom it was much more difficult to deal. This was the Indian. The tribes inside the limits of the State on the north made frequent raids into the country south of Red River and were very troublesome. Of course, the most annoying Indians, now as of old, were the Comanches, along the western frontier, who liked especially to kill and scalp Mexicans, but were willing on occasion to accept a Texas victim. The interior was protected with tolerable effectiveness from their ravages by the advance line of settlements, yet at no little cost to the settlers themselves. They were the brave hand with which the deadly blows of savagery must be received and warded off. The State employed its ranger force to good advantage, but it was difficult to prevent or anticipate an Indian raid, and the line of exposure was several hundred miles in length."

The circumstances invited the application of the system of colonizing the Indians on reservations, and in 1855, the State having set apart the necessary lands, most of the Texas tribes were induced to locate on reservations under the protection and supervision of agents—one on the upper Brazos and one on its tributary known as Salt Fork.

In regard to affairs and conditions of the Republic during the administration of President Anson Jones—Dec. 9th, 1844, to Feb. 19th, 1846—Historian Wooten says: "During that period there was but one Congress, the Ninth, which met in regular session the first Monday in December, 1844, and adjourned February 3, 1845, and again convened in special session on June 16, which continued until June 24. Aside from the usual legislation necessary to perfect the laws and run the government, there was no incident of special importance in the acts of the Ninth Congress. The country was at peace, both at home and abroad; the population was rapidly increasing, there was the prospect of early annexation to the kindred states of the north, and the finances were so improved that the Republic's paper was at par, while there was a cash balance in the treasury sufficient to operate the government for two years without a dollar of additional receipts."

The destiny of the giant Republic of the Lone Star was foreordained, as it were, however, and its people earnestly sought union with the land of freedom—preferring the flower of statehood to the pompous-sounding title of republic. The bill introduced for the annexation of Texas to the United States, having received the approval of the House of Representatives, February 25, and a favorable majority vote having obtained on March 1, 1845, the measure was signed—being one of the very last official acts of President John Tyler—and Feb. 19, 1846, Texas became a State.

The dream of the Austins had come to pass; Sam Houston had realized his far-planned hopes and won immortal fame; the matchless pioneers had triumphed; a vast domain had been established in the far and wild southwest; its position well defined and ably maintained, till voluntarily surrendered and added to the galaxy of states—to continue in growth, progress and grandeur, forever most resplendent. The deed was one of great moment, and it thrills, as one reflects—stands in vivid imagination with the vast throng assembled on that memorable occasion, listening to the silvery ringing and swelling oratory of Anson Jones, the out-going and last President of the Republic of Texas, as he delivered his valedictory, concluding with the significant but solemn utterance: "The final act in the great drama is now performed. The Republic of Texas is no more."

# THE END

# INDEX

Bowles (Cherokee Chief), 272, 274-75, 277, 278, 285-86, 302
Bowles, John (Cherokee Chief), 285-86, 302
Boyd, J.C., 341-42
Bradburn, Juan Davis, 50, 58, 69, 71-72
Branch, Mr., 325
Brazoria, Tex., 48, 69-70, 72
Breedings, Mr., 195
Brenham, R.F., 338
Bridges, Mrs. William B., 206
Brookshire, Nathaniel, 262
Brotherton, Robert, 6
Brown, Capt., 323-24
Brown, Dr., 280, 301
Brown, Frank, 149, 352n, 352-54
Brown, Geren, 236
Brown, Henry S., 38, 40-41, 42-46, 172, 206, photo 356
Brown, John "Waco", 42-46
Brown, John Henry, 17, 18, 19, 23, 24, 38, 40, 44-46, 47-48, 50-51, 80-81, 83n, 85n, 87, 93, 98, 105, 106, 108n, 109-12, 115, 126-27, 143-44, 145, 147, 147n, 167, 172, 214, 237, 254, 297n, 349, 369, 370-71
Brown County, Tex., 45
Bryan, John Neely, photo 357
Bryant, Mr., 358
Bryant, Benjamin, 256, 258n, 259
Buchanan, David, 60, 61-62
Buckner, Aylett C., 19, 19n, 21n, 22
Buffalo Hump (Comanche Chief), 260, 262
Bugg, William, 268

Bulloch, J., 232n
Bullock, Mr., 347
Bullock, James W., 70
Burleson, Edward, 114, 115n, 171n, 236, 268, 273, 274, 277-80, 284-86, 294, 299-304, 317, 344, 345, 348
Burleson, Rufus C., 296n
Burleson County, Tex., 44, 71, 127, 149, 177, 180, 317
Burnam (Burnham), Jesse, 10, 15, 16n, 24, 25
Burnet, David G., 68n, 77, 250, 277, 278, 344, 349
Burnet County, Tex., 363
Burton, J.W., 277
Burton, Isaac W., 282
Burton, Sam, 205
Bustamente, Anastasia, 49, 69-70, 88
Button, Mr., 226, 227, 230, 231, 232n
Byrd, Mrs., 12

Caddo Indians, 61, 89, 113n, 130-31, 135, 149, 188, 199, 205, 211, 249, 268, 333, 337, 354
Cage, Capt., 242-44
Caheen, Capt., 117
Cain, Mr., 178-79
Caldwell, John, 235
Caldwell, Matthew, 110, 111n, 273, 286, 292-93, 299-304
Caldwell, Tex., 180
Calhoun County, Tex., 19
Callahan, James H., 324
Callahan County, Tex., 211
Cameron, Tex., 146, 149, 181, 199, 356
Camp Carter, Tex., 278

Camp Colorado, Tex., 218
Camp Hudson, Tex., 217
Camp Wood, Tex., 218
Campbell, Mr., 242
Campbell, David W., 256, 257
Campbell, J., 282
Campbell, James, 244
Campos (Tonkawa Chief), 223
Canalizo, Gen., 272, 296, 301
Canoma (Caddo Chief), 86-87, 102-3, 112-15
Capt. Jim Kerr (Tonkawa Chief), 263
Caranchua Indians, 3, 3n, 4, 6-7, 14, 15, 16-20, 21, 33, 366-68
Carita (Tonkawa Chief), 7, 14
Carras (Carracas), Capt., 244
Carrasco (early settler), 13
Carrollton, Tex., 329
Carson, Mr., 292
Carter, Capt., 278, 279
Carter, Mr., 159
Casey, Mr., 292
Casiano, Jose, 78
Castenado (Castaneda), Francisco, 105n
Castleman, Benjamin, 116
Castleman, John, 106-9, 110, 111
Castelman, Michael, 205
Castro, Henri de, 369-71
Castro (Lipan Chief), 265, 308-11
Castro Colony, 369-71
Catlin, George, 94, 95-97
Cavanaugh (early settlers), 19
Cavitt, Andrew, 204
Cavitt, Volney, 204, 206
Chaffind, Capt., 342
Chambers, B.J., 325
Chambers, Thomas Jefferson, 50, 149
Chambers, Tolbert, 84
Chandler, Eli, 257, 325-27, 336-

37, 342-43
Chaplin (Fredonian), 28
Chapman, George W., 122-24
Chapman, Mrs. George W. (nee Taylor/Frazior), 122-24
Chapman, W.S., 124
Charles (Black servant), 60
Chenault, Mr., 241
Cherokee County, Tex., 213
Cherokee Indians, 29, 50, 51-57, 135, 213-14, 221, 246-47, 270-82, 285-86, 302, 343, 346, 355
Chickasaw Indians, 39
Chiconie (Comanche Chief), 185-86
Childers, Frank, 198-99, 201
Childers, Robert, 145, 182, 198
Childress, Frank, 146
Childress, Gouldsby, 121-22, 123-24, 146-47
Childress, Hugh M., 171
Childress, Robert, 146
Chisum, John, 336
Choctaw Indians, 316, 337
Choctaw Tom (Caddo Chief), 115
Chrisman, Horatio, 5, 11, 12, 17n, 22
Christian, Mr. & Mrs., 80-84
Clare (colonist), 5
Clark, Daniel, 198
Clark, Dave, 232n
Clark, David, 199, 200-1
Clark, John C., 6
Clark, John V., 15
Clarksville, Tex., 140, 327
Clay, Nestor, 39
Clayton, Joseph, 42
Clendenin, Capt., 286, 295
Clifton, Margaret, 83-85
Clipton, Mr., 313
Clubb, David, 328
Cobb, David, 257-58

206, 207

Ham, Caiaphas (Cephas) K., 58-60, 62, 64-65

Hamilton, Gen., 347

Hamilton, James, 317

Hancock, John, 365

Hanie, Mr., 80-82

Hankins, Eli T., 324

Hanna, David, 110

Hannum, A.B., 360-61

Hard, J., 232n

Hardeman (family), 236

Hardeman, "Old Gotch", 299-304

Hardesty, Mr., 325

Hardister, John, 344

Hardy (Negro guide), 98-99

Hargis, William H., 244

Harper, Tex., 363

Harrell, Mr., 172, 178

Harris, Mr., 138-39, 179-80

Harris, Mrs., 138-42, 161

Harris, Dilue, 48

Harrison County, Tex., 229n, 277

Hart, Mr., 236

Harvey (family), 175-76

Harvey, John, photo 199, 237-38

Hays, John C. "Jack", 101, 242n, 242-43, 305-6, 322, 339-40, 345, 351, 370

Hays County, Tex., 110, 241

Hazlitt (frontiersman), 35-37

Heard, Maj., 344

Hearne, Tex., 148

Heath, Mr., 206

Helm, Mary Sherwood Wightman, 5n

Hemphill, John, 291

Henderson, James Pinckney, 183

Henderson, William F., 225, 227, 230, 231, 232n, 233, photo 199

Henderson County, Tex., 165

Henson (Hanson), David, 258, 263-64

Hibbins, John, 166, 168, 172

Higgenbottom, Mr., 292

Highsmith (family), 236

Highsmith, Sam, photo 356

Hill (New Mexico merchant), 140

Hill, Capt., 149, 196

Hill County, Tex., 230

Hinchey (Negro), 255-56

Hinds, Gerron, 23, 25

Hockley, George W., 184, 223

Hoggett, Mr., 178-79

Holland, Mr., 233

Hood, Judge, 244, 244n, 292

Hood, John B., 216-18

Hood County, Tex., 355

Hoover, Mr., 314

Hopson, Jack, 146, 147, 181

Horn, John, 138-39

Horn, John (son), 138, 141-42

Horn, Mrs. John, 138-42, 161

Horn, Joseph, 138, 141-42

Hornsby, Malcolm, 179

Hornsby, Reuben, 80, 82, 83-85, 169, 170, 172, 178-80, 197, 214, 215, 284

Hornsby, Reuben, Jr., 179

Hornsby, William, 85, 179

Horton, Albert C., 282

Houston, A., 232n

Houston, Sam, 69, 101, 132, 133, 134, 135, 160, 183, 184, 184n, 186, 187-88, 198, 219-20, 224-25, 245, 246-47, 250, 266, 343, 345-47, 348-49, 350-56, 369,

Sparks, Sam, 127
Sparks, W.C., 126-27
Spaulding (trader), 193
Spears, Robert, 48
Spencer (killed 1824), 17
Spikes (surveyor's fight), 232
Springfield Settlement, Tex., 233
Standifer, Mr., 80-82
Steele (Scotsman), 209-10
Stevens, Mr., 195
Stevens, John, 57
Stevens, Thomas, 57
Stiffen, Mr., 218
Stiffier, Mr., 207
Stiles, Richard, 98-99
Stinnett, Claiborne, 166, 172-73
Stoal (trader), 162
Stout, Henry, 99, 332, 334, photo 356
Strickland, 23, 24
Strother, Mr., 80-84
Stroud, Ethan, 256
Stubblefield, Thomas G., 312
Sturgis, Maj., 280
Sublette, Lt., 164
Sweet Home, Tex., 168
Swift, Arthur, 324
Sylvester, Jas. A., photo 24
Sypert, Thomas, 344

Taos, N. Mex., 365
Tarrant, Edward, 328n, 329-34, 338n
Tarrant County, Tex., 164-65
Taylor, Mr., 145
Taylor, B.W., 315
Taylor, Joseph, 118-25
Taylor, Stephen Frazier, 118
Tehuacana (Tawakoni) Indians, 8, 21-22, 33, 37, 39, 40, 44, 50,

53-57, 61, 93, 112, 113n, 116-17, 135, 136, 144, 224, 337, 354
Temple, Tex., 124, 182, 357
Teran, Gen., 72
Tenoxtitlan, Tex., 114, 126, 148
Texas Rangers, 186-87, 196-97, 251, 251n, 259-63, 308, 370
Thompson, Judge, 292
Thompson, Alex S., photo 24, 71-73, 148-49
Thompson, Edward A., 292
Thompson, Empson, 198
Thompson, John S., 280
Thompson, "Mac," 71
Thompson, Thomas, 34, 35, 37
Thompson, W.D., 71
Thrall, Homer S., 88, 93, 100, 104-5, 243, 243n
Throckmorton, Mrs. W.J., 329-34
Thurmond, Alfred, 174
Timson, Jeremiah, 88
Tinnin's, 159
Tipp, Capt., 279
Titus County, Tex., 327
Todd, Capt., 279, 280
Tolbert, James, 176
Tomlinson, Capt., 362
Tomlinson, James, 33
Tomlinson, William, 324
Tonkawa Indians, 6-7, 10, 13-14, 19, 86, 87n, 101, 113n, 122, 135, 174, 188, 189, 223, 253, 258, 263-64, 284, 285, 300
Topasannah (Prairie Flower), 164-65
Torry (Indian Commissioner), 354
Towash Indians, 112, 224, 354
Towers, Dr., 280
Townsend, John T., 99-103
Townsend, Stephen, 100